Ballistic Imaging

Committee to Assess the Feasibility, Accuracy, and Technical Capability of a National Ballistics Database

Daniel L. Cork, John E. Rolph, Eugene S. Meieran, and Carol V. Petrie, *Editors*

Committee on Law and Justice
Committee on National Statistics

Division of Behavioral and Social Sciences and Education

National Materials Advisory Board

Division on Engineering and Physical Sciences

NATIONAL RESEARCH COUNCIL
OF THE NATIONAL ACADEMIES

THE NATIONAL ACADEMIES PRESS
Washington, D.C.
www.nap.edu

THE NATIONAL ACADEMIES PRESS 500 Fifth Street, N.W. Washington, DC 20001

NOTICE: The project that is the subject of this report was approved by the Governing Board of the National Research Council, whose members are drawn from the councils of the National Academy of Sciences, the National Academy of Engineering, and the Institute of Medicine. The members of the committee responsible for the report were chosen for their special competences and with regard for appropriate balance.

The project that is the subject of this report was supported by contract 2003-IJ-CX-1013 between the National Academy of Sciences and the National Institute of Justice. The work of the Committee on National Statistics is provided by a consortium of federal agencies through a grant from the National Science Foundation (Number SBR-0112521). Any opinions, findings, conclusions, or recommendations expressed in this publication are those of the author(s) and do not necessarily reflect the views of the organizations or agencies that provided support for the project.

Library of Congress Cataloging-in-Publication Data

National Research Council (U.S.). Committee to Assess the Feasibility, Accuracy, and Technical Capability of a National Ballistics Database.
Ballistic imaging / Committee to Assess the Feasibility, Accuracy, and Technical Capability of a National Ballistics Database ; Daniel L. Cork ... [et al.].
p. cm.
Includes bibliographical references and index.
ISBN 978-0-309-11724-1 (pbk. : alk. paper) — ISBN 978-0-309-11725-8 (pdf : alk. paper) 1. Forensic ballistics—Atlases—Data processing—Government policy—United States. 2. Bullets—Identification—Databases. 3. Images, Photographic—Databases. 4. Electronic records—United States—Management—Data processing. I. Cork, Daniel L. II. Title.
HV8077.N38 2008
363.25'62—dc22
2008015181

Additional copies of this report are available from the National Academies Press, 500 Fifth Street, N.W., Lockbox 285, Washington, DC 20055; (800) 624-6242 or (202) 334-3313 (in the Washington metropolitan area); Internet, http://www.nap.edu.

Printed in the United States of America

Second printing with corrections.

Cover illustration and design by Van Nguyen.

Suggested citation: National Research Council. (2008). *Ballistic Imaging*. Committee to Assess the Feasibility, Accuracy, and Technical Capability of a National Ballistics Database. Daniel L. Cork, John E. Rolph, Eugene S. Meieran, and Carol V. Petrie, eds. Committee on Law and Justice and Committee on National Statistics, Division of Behavioral and Social Sciences and Education; National Materials Advisory Board, Division on Engineering and Physical Sciences. Washington, DC: The National Academies Press.

THE NATIONAL ACADEMIES

Advisers to the Nation on Science, Engineering, and Medicine

The **National Academy of Sciences** is a private, nonprofit, self-perpetuating society of distinguished scholars engaged in scientific and engineering research, dedicated to the furtherance of science and technology and to their use for the general welfare. Upon the authority of the charter granted to it by the Congress in 1863, the Academy has a mandate that requires it to advise the federal government on scientific and technical matters. Dr. Ralph J. Cicerone is president of the National Academy of Sciences.

The **National Academy of Engineering** was established in 1964, under the charter of the National Academy of Sciences, as a parallel organization of outstanding engineers. It is autonomous in its administration and in the selection of its members, sharing with the National Academy of Sciences the responsibility for advising the federal government. The National Academy of Engineering also sponsors engineering programs aimed at meeting national needs, encourages education and research, and recognizes the superior achievements of engineers. Dr. Charles M. Vest is president of the National Academy of Engineering.

The **Institute of Medicine** was established in 1970 by the National Academy of Sciences to secure the services of eminent members of appropriate professions in the examination of policy matters pertaining to the health of the public. The Institute acts under the responsibility given to the National Academy of Sciences by its congressional charter to be an adviser to the federal government and, upon its own initiative, to identify issues of medical care, research, and education. Dr. Harvey V. Fineberg is president of the Institute of Medicine.

The **National Research Council** was organized by the National Academy of Sciences in 1916 to associate the broad community of science and technology with the Academy's purposes of furthering knowledge and advising the federal government. Functioning in accordance with general policies determined by the Academy, the Council has become the principal operating agency of both the National Academy of Sciences and the National Academy of Engineering in providing services to the government, the public, and the scientific and engineering communities. The Council is administered jointly by both Academies and the Institute of Medicine. Dr. Ralph J. Cicerone and Dr. Charles M. Vest are chair and vice chair, respectively, of the National Research Council.

www.national-academies.org

COMMITTEE TO ASSESS THE FEASIBILITY, ACCURACY, AND TECHNICAL CAPABILITY OF A NATIONAL BALLISTICS DATABASE

JOHN E. ROLPH *(Chair)*, Marshall School of Business, University of Southern California
EUGENE S. MEIERAN *(Vice Chair)*, Fellow, Intel Corporation, Santa Clara, California
ALFRED BLUMSTEIN, H. John Heinz III School of Public Policy and Management, Carnegie Mellon University
ALICIA CARRIQUIRY, Department of Statistics, Iowa State University
SCOTT CHUMBLEY, Department of Materials Science and Engineering, Iowa State University
PHILIP J. COOK, Sanford Institute of Public Policy, Duke University
MARC DE GRAEF, Department of Materials Science and Engineering, Carnegie Mellon University
DAVID L. DONOHO, Department of Statistics, Stanford University
WILLIAM F. EDDY, Department of Statistics, Carnegie Mellon University
GEORGE (RUSTY) GRAY, Materials Science Division, Los Alamos National Laboratories
ERIC GRIMSON, Department of Electrical Engineering and Computer Science and Department of Medical Engineering, Massachusetts Institute of Technology
DANIEL HUTTENLOCHER, Department of Computing, Information Science, and Business, Cornell University
MICHAEL M. MEYER, Google, Inc., Seattle, Washington
VIJAY NAIR, Department of Statistics and Department of Industrial and Operations Engineering, University of Michigan
ANGELO NINIVAGGI, Plexus Corp., Neenah, Wisconsin
DAVID W. PISENTI, Consultant, Fredericksburg, Virginia
DARYL PREGIBON, Google, Inc., New York, New York
HERMAN M. REININGA, Rockwell Collins, Cedar Rapids, Iowa
JAMES K. (CHIPS) STEWART, CNA Corporation, Alexandria, Virginia
MICHAEL STONEBRAKER, Department of Computer Science, Massachusetts Institute of Technology
HARRY WECHSLER,* Department of Computer Science, George Mason University
JULIA WEERTMAN, Department of Materials Science and Engineering, Northwestern University (emeritus)

CAROL V. PETRIE, *Study Director*
DANIEL L. CORK, *Senior Program Officer*
GARY FISCHMAN,** *Director, National Materials Advisory Board*
MICHAEL SIRI, *Senior Program Assistant*
ANTHONY A. BRAGA, *Consultant*
LAWDEN YATES, *Consultant*

*Served until May 2004.

**Served as liaison member to the committee from the National Materials Advisory Board until becoming that board's staff director in March 2005.

COMMITTEE ON LAW AND JUSTICE
2007

COMMITTEE ON NATIONAL STATISTICS
2008

Preface

The Committee to Assess the Feasibility, Accuracy, and Technical Capability of a National Ballistics Database is pleased to submit this final report and wishes to thank the many people who have contributed to our work over the committee's lifetime.

This project was sponsored by the National Institute of Justice (NIJ), Office of Justice Programs, U.S. Department of Justice. We are grateful for the support of NIJ staff and their participation in our meetings. We are particularly indebted to Christopher Miles, the program manager for this project, and to John Morgan, deputy director, NIJ Office of Science and Technology, for their assistance and their patience as our committee worked through this complex project.

Through a separate contract initiated by NIJ, the National Institute of Standards and Technology (NIST) was engaged to conduct experiments in support of the committee's work. As described in Chapters 7 and 8 of this report, NIST's work for the panel focused on the potential of one possible major enhancement to current ballistic imaging technology: a change from two-dimensional photography to three-dimensional surface measurements. Just as this committee required extensive collaboration between disparate units within the National Academies and representation from a breadth of disciplines, so too did the NIST experimental work for the committee draw together staff from several NIST units, and we have benefited greatly from this collaboration. Susan Ballou, Office of Law Enforcement Standards, provided excellent oversight of the NIST team, and Theodore Vorburger, Surface Metrology Division, was unstinting in his zeal for this work. NIST subcontracted and partnered in this work with Benjamin Bachrach of

Intelligent Automation, Inc., whose insights from past and current three-dimensional analysis of bullet and cartridge evidence gave shape to many of the committee's discussions. As the work developed, James Filliben of NIST's statistical unit oversaw the final experiment design and analysis plan, and he provided outstanding assistance. We are grateful to all the current and former NIST staff who worked on this project, including Dewey Foreman, John Libert, Brian Renegar, Mike Riley, John Song, James Yen, and Alan Zhang.

Throughout the panel's deliberations, we benefited from the counsel of two consultants, Anthony Braga and Lawden Yates. Braga, a senior research associate and lecturer at the Kennedy School of Government at Harvard University, provided empirical analysis and extended and elaborated on previous work on the use of ballistic imaging in the Boston area. His paper on the latter topic appears as Appendix A.

When the committee was being formed, it was decided not to include an active firearms examiner. Instead, the committee had the counsel of Lawden Yates, a former firearms and toolmark examiner and laboratory director, who also served as general counsel to the Alabama Department of Forensic Sciences and as assistant district attorney for Blount and Saint Clair Counties, Alabama. He provided invaluable information and advice to the committee on a range of technical matters.

Though motivated by questions concerning a new data collection system, this project also required a comprehensive review and assessment of the current National Integrated Ballistic Information Network (NIBIN) Program of the Bureau of Alcohol, Tobacco, Firearms, and Explosives (ATF). The ATF responded to our requests with exceptional openness and enthusiasm. In particular, we are grateful for the assistance of Benjamin Wilson, firearms project manager at ATF's Office of Laboratory Services. The committee's analyses, described in Chapter 8, required image acquisition and analysis by staff at ATF's Ammendale, Maryland, laboratory; we appreciate the effort of firearms examiner Martin Ols and the other ATF examiners who contributed to this work. We also appreciate the initial guidance to our work provided by Robert Thompson and by Patricia Galupo, former director of the NIBIN program. ATF afforded the committee and staff the opportunity to participate in a meeting of its NIBIN Users' Congress, which proved most valuable.

In March 2005, a nondisclosure agreement was negotiated between Forensic Technology WAI Inc. (FTI) and the National Academies to facilitate a site visit to FTI's headquarters in Montréal by selected members of the committee. FTI is the creator and manufacturer of the equipment and software (IBIS) used by the nation's forensic laboratories to create and maintain a database of ballistic images consisting of evidence collected from crime scenes or confiscated during arrests. The nondisclosure agreement covered information about this system that FTI and the National Academies Office of Legal Counsel agreed are proprietary within the meaning of Exemption 4 of the U.S. Freedom of Information Act, 5 U.S.C. Section 552(b)(4). The meeting, which took place at FTI's offices in Montreal on March 22, provided a detailed understanding of the features and capabilities of the imaging technology developed by FTI. Only information that was not designated as proprietary information is included, referenced, or quoted in this final report. The committee is grateful to FTI for its cooperation and for the high degree of professionalism and scientific competence it demonstrated at this meeting.

We are particularly grateful for a thoughtful and candid discussion with FTI technical staff; both Michael McLean, project manager for the Integrated Ballistics Identification System (IBIS), and Pete Gagliardi, vice president of marketing and strategic planning, took special interest in the committee's work and provided much useful information. Along with McLean, Alain Beauchamp gave a useful presentation at a committee meeting and responded to other committee requests for information. We appreciate the contributions of other past and present FTI staff, including Robert Walsh, chairman and president; René Bélanger, vice president and general manager; John O'Neil, firearms examiner consultant; Michael Clamen; Cybele Daley; Tim Heaney; Serge Labrecque; and Danny Roberge.

Gerald Zeosky, inspector and director of the New York State Police Forensic Investigation Center (FIC), and John Hicks, director of forensic services for the New York State Division of Criminal Justice Services, were invited to a committee meeting to describe their state's Combined Ballistic Information System (CoBIS), a state-level reference ballistic image database. Following that presentation, both men then invited the committee and staff to the FIC in Albany to perform experimental runs on the CoBIS database. During that visit (and a follow-up visit by committee staff), FIC staff gave freely of their time and talent; for this, we are particularly grateful to Rebecca Barretta, James Campbell, Mike D'Allaird, Craig Grazier, and Mark Heller.

Similarly, a presentation to the committee by deputy chief Denis McCarthy of the New York City Police Department (NYPD) led to an invitation to visit and perform limited analyses using the NYPD's ballistic image database, which uses the same technology as the NIBIN program but is not directly linked. At that visit to the NYPD crime laboratory in Jamaica, Queens, Lt. James Kenny, commanding officer of the firearms analysis section, and detective Anthony Pellicio, firearms examiner and microscopist were extremely helpful.

Over the course of the study, every committee member visited at least one NIBIN installation at a state or local law enforcement agency, and various members also visited the ATF national laboratories in Ammendale,

Maryland, and Walnut Creek, California. We thank all involved for their time and talent. Subgroups of the committee also visited firearms and ammunition manufacturers and developers of microstamping technologies. We are grateful to all those who helped make the visits smooth and informative, including from Federal Cartridge Company, Gary Svendsen, Mike Larsen, Mike Hollen, Ken Croteau, and Rick Vickerman; from Hi-Point Firearms, Tom Deeb; and from Beretta Firearms, Jeffrey Reh, general counsel. Todd Lizotte of Hitachi Via Electronics attended a committee meeting and generously spent time discussing the microstamping of firing pins and other firearms parts at his facility in Londonderry, New Hampshire. Ammunition Coding Systems, a Seattle-based firm acting as a proponent of a methodology for microstamping ammunition that was then under active consideration by the California legislature, convened a very helpful session with the firm's staff and related contractors in Seattle for a group of committee members. We thank Steven Mace, Russell Ford, John Knickerbocker, David Howell, Patrick Grace, and Paul Curry for their guidance in that meeting. We also appreciate the participation of Randy Rossi, California Department of Justice, in the Seattle subcommittee discussion.

Ann Davis, Virginia Division of Forensic Sciences, was president of the Association of Firearm and Tool Mark Examiners (AFTE) when our committee began operations. She offered comments at our first meeting and assembled a liaison committee to interact with the committee as needed; for these contributions, we are grateful. Lucien Haag (Forensic Science Services, Inc., Carefree, Arizona) attended and participated in a panel discussion at a committee meeting in Chandler, Arizona, and subsequently discussed trials that he had performed on microstamped firing pins for a committee meeting in Washington; we thank him for the information he shared with us.

We appreciate the time taken by other experts to present issues to our committee, including Kenneth Green of the Sporting Arms and Ammunition Manufacturers' Institute, Inc., and Marianne Hinkle, former assistant U.S. attorney for the district of Massachusetts. At the committee's meeting in Chandler, Arizona—hosted by committee vice chair Eugene Meieran at Intel Corporation—we made use of the fact that several NIBIN sites are located in the Phoenix metropolitan area. Representatives of the various NIBIN-hosting law enforcement agencies participated in a very useful panel discussion: they included Judie Welch, Eric Brown, and Randy Leister of the Phoenix Police Department Crime Laboratory; Patrick Chavez of the City of Mesa Crime Laboratory; Steve Valdez of the City of Scottsdale Crime Laboratory; Dustin Engel of the Maricopa County Sheriff's Office; and Vince Figarelli and Lisa Peloza of the Arizona Department of Public Safety.

Emily Ann Meyer provided initial literature collection for the committee during her service as a research associate with the National Materials

Advisory Board (NMAB). Michael Siri, senior program assistant with the Committee on National Statistics (CNSTAT) deftly provided logistical support to the committee in the later phases of its work; he was preceded as program assistant and coordinator for the committee's activities by Ralph Patterson during his tenure with the Committee on Law and Justice. Special thanks are due to Barbara Boyd for pinch-hitting as program assistant for one of our committee meetings during a gap in staffing and for generally providing back-up assistance when needed. Toni Marechaux, former director of the NMAB, contributed to the formation of the committee and its early work, and we have also benefited from the counsel of Constance Citro, CNSTAT director, and Jane Ross, director of the Center for Economic, Governance, and International Studies of the Division of Behavioral and Social Sciences and Education.

We were extremely fortunate to have two experienced and extremely capable individuals as staff: Carol Petrie and Daniel Cork. Carol was particularly helpful in the process of forming the committee, managing the panel's consultations with its sponsor and other external parties, organizing meetings, and stewarding this report through the Academies' review process. Dan managed much of the panel's analytic work and had primary responsibility for drafting the report. Together they organized the work of the committee and guided its evaluation of the NIBIN program and its consideration of a national reference ballistic image database. To say we have benefited enormously from their talents and knowledge and are very grateful to have had the opportunity to work with them is a considerable understatement. Regardless of the committee's expertise and commitment, this report would have significantly less value than we believe it does have, but for Carol's and Dan's contributions.

This report has been reviewed in draft form by individuals chosen for their diverse perspectives and technical expertise, in accordance with procedures approved by the Report Review Committee of the National Research Council (NRC). The purpose of this independent review is to provide candid and critical comments that will assist the institution in making the published report as sound as possible and to ensure that the report meets institutional standards for objectivity, evidence, and responsiveness to the study charge. The review comments and draft manuscript remain confidential to protect the integrity of the deliberative process.

We thank the following individuals for their participation in the review of this report: William A. Ellingson, Nuclear Engineering Division, Argonne National Laboratory; David L. Faigman, Hastings College of Law, University of California, San Francisco; Stephen E. Fienberg, Department of Statistics, Carnegie Mellon University; Barry A.J. Fisher, Los Angeles County Sheriff's Department Crime Laboratory, Los Angeles, California; David C. Hoaglin, Abt Associates Inc., Cambridge, Massachusetts; Paul

F. Johnson, Emeritus Professor of Ceramic Engineering, Alfred University, Alfred, New York; Alan F. Karr, Director's Office, National Institute of Statistical Sciences, Research Triangle Park, North Carolina; Diane Lambert, Google, Inc., New York, New York; Lyle H. Schwartz, Consultant, Chevy Chase, Maryland; Pete Striupaitis, Northeastern Illinois Regional Crime Laboratory, Vernon Hills, Illinois; Charles F. Wellford, Department of Criminology, University of Maryland; and James Q. Wilson, School of Public Policy, Pepperdine University.

Although the reviewers listed above provided many constructive comments and suggestions, they were not asked to endorse the conclusions or recommendations nor did they see the final draft of the report before its release. The review of the report was overseen by John C. Bailar, III, Professor Emeritus, Department of Health Studies, The University of Chicago, and Hyla S. Napadensky, Office of President, Napadensky Energetics, Inc., Grand Marais, Minnesota. Appointed by the NRC, they were responsible for making certain that an independent examination of the report was carried out in accordance with institutional procedures and that all review comments were carefully considered. Responsibility for the final content of this report rests entirely with the authoring panel and the institution.

John E. Rolph, *Chair*
Eugene S. Meieran, *Vice Chair*
Committee to Assess the Feasibility, Accuracy, and
Technical Capability of a National Ballistics Database

Contents

Tables, Figures, and Boxes

TABLES

FIGURES

BOXES

Executive Summary

Since the late 1980s computerized imaging technology has been used to assist forensic firearms examiners in finding potential links between images of ballistics evidence gathered from crime scene investigations, namely, cartridge cases and bullets from fired guns. To support this effort, the Bureau of Alcohol, Tobacco, Firearms, and Explosives (ATF) in 1997 formed the National Integrated Ballistic Information Network (NIBIN). Law enforcement agencies participating in NIBIN contribute to a database of images of bullet and cartridge case evidence recovered from (or test-fired from weapons linked to) crime scenes. This system facilitates rapid comparison with archived evidence and with evidence gathered at other crime sites; when matches look promising, the physical evidence can be retrieved for direct examination and confirmation by an examiner. NIBIN was designed as a tool for search, not for verification, which is always done by an examiner.

The rapid development of computerized ballistic imaging technology has led to speculation about its future potential. A particularly interesting proposal is to create a national reference ballistic image database (RBID) that would house images from firings of all newly manufactured or imported firearms. Proponents of this proposal argue that such a database could provide a quick investigative lead from evidence recovered at a crime scene to the underlying firearm's original point of sale. State RBIDs already exist in Maryland and New York, and wide attention was drawn to the issue when California studied the feasibility of creating its own RBID.

In 2004 the National Institute of Justice (NIJ) of the U.S. Department of Justice requested that the National Academies appoint a committee of experts to address the issues raised by the computerized ballistic imaging technology. The Committee to Assess the Feasibility, Accuracy, and Technical Capability of a National Ballistics Database was asked to "assess the feasibility, accuracy and reliability, and technical capability of developing and using a national ballistics database as an aid to criminal investigations." To accomplish this, the panel's charge is to:

> (1) Assess the technical feasibility, through analysis of the uniqueness of ballistic images, the ability of imaging systems to capture unique characteristics and to parameterize them, the algorithmic and computational challenges of an imaging database, the reproducibility of ballistic impressions and the ability of imaging systems to extract reproducible information from ballistic impressions.
>
> (2) Assess the statistical probabilities that ballistics evidence presented would lead to a match with images captured in a database, whether and how the base rate can be estimated for those crimes that present bullet or casing evidence that do in fact come from a gun that produced a database entry, and the probabilities and consequences of false positives and false negatives.
>
> (3) Assess the operational utility of ballistics evidence in criminal investigations—that is the extent to which it is used or can be used to identify crime guns and suspects and to solve specific crimes.
>
> (4) Assess the sources of error in ballistics database matching (from examination, digitization, computer matching, chain of custody and documentation of tests, and expert confirmation), how they may be quantified, and how these errors interact.

The charge continues:

> The committee's work will provide scientific and technical knowledge to inform the government's deliberations on three policy options with regard to ballistics databases:
>
> (1) Maintain the National Integrated Ballistic Information Network (NIBIN) on ballistics recovered from crime scenes. It is operated by the Bureau of Alcohol, Tobacco, and Firearms.
>
> (2) Enhance the NIBIN system so that it can be used to match crime scene evidence with the gun used.
>
> (3) Establish a national ballistics database of images from bullets fired from all, or nearly all, newly manufactured or imported guns for the purpose of matching ballistics from a crime scene to a gun and information on its initial owner.

Addressing the issues raised by the tasks of the charge permitted the committee to provide guidance to NIJ on the three federal policy options. Specifically, for option 2, enhancing the NIBIN system, we address how to increase its effectiveness as a search tool, including changes to the basic imaging standard used by the system, and improving procedures for working with the existing hardware and software. For option 3, establishing a national RBID, the committee considers it a counterpart to NIBIN, containing images of ballistic samples from all newly manufactured and imported weapons. The committee also considered the feasibility of alternative technologies that could achieve the same goal as a national RBID. These alternative technologies include microstamping to imprint a known, unique marker on firearms parts or ammunition: analysis of such marks would complement or perhaps replace the need to examine the currently used toolmarks.

Underlying the specific tasks with which the committee was charged is the question of whether firearms-related toolmarks are unique: that is, whether a particular set of toolmarks can be shown to come from one weapon to the exclusion of all others. Very early in its work the committee found that this question cannot now be definitively answered.

Finding: The validity of the fundamental assumptions of uniqueness and reproducibility of firearms-related toolmarks has not yet been fully demonstrated.

Notwithstanding this finding, we accept a minimal baseline standard regarding ballistics evidence. Although they are subject to numerous sources of variability, firearms-related toolmarks are not completely random and volatile; one can find similar marks on bullets and cartridge cases from the same gun.

A significant amount of research would be needed to scientifically determine the degree to which firearms-related toolmarks are unique or even to quantitatively characterize the probability of uniqueness. Assessing uniqueness at, say, a submicroscopic level, though probably technically possible, would be extremely difficult and time consuming compared with less definitive but more practical and generally available methods at the macroscopic level. It is an issue of policy and of economics as to whether doing so would be worthwhile. The committee did not and could not undertake such research, nor does it offer any conclusions about undertaking such research. Although it appears to the committee that the needs for research are extensive, specifying the nature of that research was not part of the committee's charge. We also note that the committee does not provide an overall assessment of firearms identification as a discipline nor does it advise on the admissibility of firearms-related toolmark evidence in legal proceedings: these topics are not within its charge.

The committee's charge is to determine the extent to which the toolmarks left on bullets and cartridge casings after firing a weapon can be captured by imaging technology. It is also to assess whether a ballistic image database—particularly a national RBID containing images of exhibits fired from all newly manufactured and imported guns—would be feasible and operationally useful, by which we mean capable of generating leads for follow-up and further investigation. Whether or not toolmarks are unique to a given weapon does not preclude the committee from addressing this charge. Indeed, in many situations a sufficient level of toolmark reproducibility can be picked up by imaging or other measurement systems to be useful for narrowing a search down to a set of possible weapons, as is currently done. The final determination of a "match" is made by a human examiner.

FEASIBILITY OF A NATIONAL REFERENCE BALLISTIC IMAGE DATABASE

Independent of the reliability and effectiveness of the technology used in making comparisons of images in a national RBID, there would be significant limitations in the usefulness of such a database. Most importantly, there is a huge existing supply of weapons and ammunition that would not be entered into the database. In addition, revolvers do not eject cartridge cases at crime scenes as do other handguns. Consequently, even under the best of circumstances, when random variability is kept to a minimum, the database itself would be incomplete. Finally, to implement a national RBID, national protocols would have to be created for the test firing of new and imported guns; ensuring that test-fired cartridge cases or bullets are correctly packaged with their corresponding firearm and maintaining a chain of custody for the exhibits after they are imaged would create a formidable logistical challenge.

In our detailed assessment, three additional points regarding the implementation of a national RBID have particular salience.

First, the current technology in use for automated toolmark comparison, based on two-dimensional greyscale images, is useful for gross categorization and sorting of large quantities of evidence. However, it is less reliable for distinguishing extremely fine individual marks that would be necessary to make successful matches in RBIDs in which large numbers of exhibits on file would share gross class and subclass characteristics.

Second, basic probability calculations under reasonable assumptions suggest that the process of identifying a subset of possible matches that contains the true match with a specified level of certainty depends critically on as-yet underived measures of similarity between and within gun types. This process is very likely to return too large a subset of candidates to be practically useful for investigative purposes.

Third, the large influence of ammunition type and variability introduces a significant source of error in identification. A standard, protocol type of ammunition could be specified in an RBID (as it is in NIBIN), but it is likely not to correspond with the ammunition actually used in a crime; the choice of protocol ammunition, or a requirement to use multiple ammunition types, would have significant financial implications for both ammunition and firearm manufacturers, as well as on the information systems involved.

Conclusion: A national reference ballistic image database of all new and imported guns is not advisable at this time.

MAINTAIN OR ENHANCE NIBIN

By facilitating access by state and local law enforcement agencies to ballistic imaging technology, the NIBIN program provides a valuable service in helping to solve gun-related crimes. However, agencies differ in the degree to which they use the NIBIN resources and, consequently, they differ markedly in the benefits they derive in establishing links between crimes and investigative leads. The committee's principal task includes offering guidance on either maintaining NIBIN as it currently operates or enhancing it in various ways to improve its effectiveness. The former is not really a viable option: there are always opportunities for improvement in any program, particularly one as broad as NIBIN.

Conclusion: NIBIN can and should be made more effective through operational and technological improvements.

To this end, the committee offers 15 specific recommendations to improve NIBIN's performance and effectiveness. Seven of the recommendations are oriented principally at the operation of the NIBIN program itself and the practices of NIBIN partner agencies, and they address:

- priority for NIBIN entry of cartridge casings collected from crime scenes;
- ballistic imaging as a part of the criminal investigation process for state and local agencies;
- cross-jurisdictional tally of hits using the NIBIN system;
- streamlining of the ballistic image acquisition process and reporting requirements;
- development of "best practices" in using NIBIN;
- a protocol for the entry of more than one exhibit from the same crime scene or test firing; and
- allocation of NIBIN system technology.

We also offer eight specific recommendations for enhancing the current technical platform for the NIBIN program, the Integrated Ballistics Identification System (IBIS), and the hardware and software system developed by Forensic Technology WAI, Inc. These eight recommendations address:

- research on the distributions of comparison scores;
- an "audit trail" in the NIBIN system's hardware and software systems;
- ammunition brand information in NIBIN;
- the capacity for national or cross-regional searches against the NIBIN database;
- NIBIN's database partition structure;
- enhancements to the NIBIN interface;
- side-light imagery of breech face impressions; and
- the 20 percent threshold used in the IBIS.

In support of this study, the National Institute of Standards and Technology (NIST) was separately contracted by NIJ to perform experimental work at the committee's request. This experimental work considered the value of one major technical enhancement to the current NIBIN system: a change in imaging standard from two-dimensional, greyscale photography to three-dimensional surface measurement using noncontact microscopy. NIST's work included analysis of an extract of cartridges from one of the major existing studies of ballistic imaging performance as well as a new dataset of test-fired cartridges designed by the committee. The work highlights the promise of three-dimensional surface measurement, which performs comparably with—and, for some cartridge markings, often better than—the current two-dimensional methodology. However, there are major substantive challenges—among them the reduction of data collection time and the refinement of image comparison algorithms that make use of three-dimensional information but are still compatible with existing two-dimensional imagery—that need to be addressed before full consideration can be given to adopting the new standard.

ALTERNATIVE TECHNOLOGIES

The goal of a national reference ballistic image database is to provide an investigative link from ballistics evidence to the point of sale of the weapon or ammunition used in a crime. The same goal could be achieved through an entirely different approach, microstamping, which is to place a known, unique, and unalterable identifier on gun parts, cartridge cases, or bullets at the time of manufacture. These uniquely microstamped products could then be associated with their purchaser when sold. Microstamping, if feasible and practical, would have the advantage of imposing uniqueness as a characteristic of ballistics evidence, substituting known and fixed markings for microscopically fine, individualizing characteristics that result from random processes in manufacture and weapon firing.

A distinct advantage of microstamping is that the marks could be examined at a crime scene using equipment no more sophisticated than a magnifying glass, vastly simplifying and speeding up the process of developing investigative leads. The state of California recently passed a law, to take effect in 2010, which requires microstamping on internal parts of new semiautomatic pistols. However, the committee believes that for such a technology to be implemented successfully, in-depth investigations on several topics are needed. These topics include the reliability and durability of the marks in a variety of firing conditions, their susceptibility to tampering and countermeasures, whether it would be best to place them on guns or ammunition or both, and the cost implications and feasibility of adding a microstamping process to established manufacturing processes.

PROCESS FOR IMPROVING COMPUTER-ASSISTED FIREARMS IDENTIFICATION

The current technology used in automated examination of images of ballistics evidence is produced and maintained by a single vendor. As a result, it does not benefit from the improvements that could be gained through competition and vetting among the broader research community, and its potential for advancement and innovation is limited. The committee suggests that improvements in matching ballistics evidence be made through government procurement efforts that demonstrate best practices.

Two recent examples of government-mandated large-scale imaging system developments based on initially, nonmature technologies include systems for fingerprint identification and for facial recognition. Both systems required the creation of dedicated pattern recognition algorithms, similar to the requirements of NIBIN. Instead of relying on a single system produced by a single vendor, both systems were organized as competitions between vendors with the goal of advancing the technology as quickly as possible. Both competitions required that well-vetted datasets from several sources be made available to researchers so that the correct features could be identified for extraction. Finally, the results of both competitions were subjected to independently administered evaluations, using well-defined and published evaluation methodologies that allowed for a direct quantitative assessment of the relative strengths and weaknesses of different approaches.

This approach to procurement—removing strict dependence on a sole-source provider and ensuring government ownership of and access to result data—should be applied for all work related to the improvement in ballistics evidence analysis, including large-scale two-dimensional image search engines, three-dimensional topographical techniques, and micro-stamping processes.

PART I

Context for Ballistic Imaging Analysis

1

Introduction

For decades, direct comparison of bullet and cartridge case evidence has been used to link crime incidents to other crime investigations to link specific pieces of evidence to each other and to particular weapons. Since the late 1980s, emerging technology has allowed such links to be drawn between computerized images of bullets and cartridge case evidence. The development of this technology has led to speculation about its potential to generate critical investigative leads to possibly related incidents both at the local level and across broad geographic areas. A specific question that has been raised concerns the utility of a national reference ballistic image database (RBID), which would include images from test-fired rounds of most (if not all) new and imported firearms. In concept, a national RBID would permit bullet or cartridge case evidence recovered at crime scenes to be easily and rapidly linked to a firearm's point of sale—information that is currently available only if the gun itself is recovered at the crime scene and is put through a full tracing process (see Chapter 9).

The concept of a national RBID differs from existing systems in two important ways. First, a national database of ballistic image evidence already exists, but it is not a *reference* database because it does not collect test firings from new weapons. In 1997, the Bureau of Alcohol, Tobacco, Firearms, and Explosives (ATF) formed the National Integrated Ballistic Information Network (NIBIN); as of 2005, NIBIN connects 230 law enforcement agencies, which contribute to a database of images of bullet and cartridge case evidence recovered from (or test-fired from weapons linked to) crime scenes. The NIBIN program equips agencies with Integrated Ballistics Identification System (IBIS) equipment, developed and manufactured by its contractor, Forensic Technology WAI, Inc. (FTI), of Montréal, Canada (see Box 4-1 in Chapter 4 for an important note on the use of the term "IBIS"). The IBIS platform acquires greyscale photographs of bullet or cartridge case evidence, scoring and ranking pairs of exhibits by deriving a mathematical signature from images. The scope of NIBIN is limited by legislative language, prohibiting it from including noncrime gun evidence in the database.

Second, RBIDs do currently exist but not at the *national* level. Two states—Maryland and New York—established RBID systems for new handguns sold in those states in 2000 and 2001, respectively. Both states use the same IBIS platform for acquiring images, but are barred from directly networking their RBID data with crime-scene-based NIBIN data. State legislation directed the California Department of Justice to study the feasibility of establishing an RBID in that state; its assessment in 2001 was that such a database was not feasible, but suggested that further study be conducted at the national level. In the wake of the October 2002 sniper shootings in the Washington, D.C., area, legislative proposals to create RBIDs were advanced or discussed in Connecticut, New Jersey, and Massachusetts (Butterfield, 2002), as well as Missouri (George, 2004a).[1]

As of 2002, a national-level RBID was said to be under discussion in Belgium, and "a similar debate is going on in a number of member states of the European community" (De Kinder, 2002a:198). Recent U.S. Congresses have seen bills introduced that would create a national RBID, though none of the bills have advanced past referral to the appropriate committees.[2] In

[1]Both chambers of the New Jersey state legislature have, at different times, passed bills requiring some form of ballistic imaging, but not the same bill. In May 2000, the Senate passed S. 2048 on a 37–0 vote; the bill prohibited sales of handguns unless a "ballistics identifier" was obtained from the gun and put in a "qualified database." A "ballistics identifier" was defined as "a digitized or electronic image of a bullet and shell casing . . . clearly showing the distinctive firing pin, ejection, extraction and land marks for that particular handgun." In November 2002, the Assembly passed A. 438 on a 48–18–10 vote; initial bill text made submissions to an image database voluntary by handgun owners, but the passed bill had been amended to make submission of identifiers mandatory for all sold handguns. The bill was not acted upon by the Senate. In the 2004–2005 session, proposed bills would have required firearms repair shops to obtain ballistics identifiers for handguns or rifles before returning them to their owners; as of September 2006, no similar bills had been introduced in either chamber. In Massachusetts, a Boston police official lauded the idea as a "great law enforcement tool," pointing to a case that had been solved using NIBIN (linking the same .22 caliber Ruger pistol to shootings of seven people in four cities," as one where an earlier investigative lead to the gun's purchaser would have been useful (Butterfield, 2002).

[2]See, e.g., in the 108th Congress, the Technological Resource to Assist Criminal Enforcement (TRACE) Act (S. 469/H.R. 776) and the So No Innocent Person Ever Repeats (SNIPER) the Sniper Tragedy Act of 2003 (S. 1983), the latter of which incorporated the former in its entirety, as well as the Bullet Tracing Act to Reduce Gun Violence Act (H.R. 24). In the 107th Congress, see the Ballistics, Law Assistance, and Safety Technology (BLAST) Act (H.R. 5663)

part, the bills did not progress because they have been caught up in the nation's ongoing gun control policy debate: Proponents see such laws as essential to reducing gun violence; opponents see them as a first step toward a national gun registry and a perceived violation of their Second Amendment right to bear arms.

In both the 107th and 108th Congresses, bills were introduced in each chamber to require that the National Academies conduct a study of the state of ballistic imaging technology.[3] Independent of that legislation, but with a similar charge, the National Institute of Justice (NIJ) of the U.S. Department of Justice requested that the National Academies execute such a study.

1–A COMMITTEE CHARGE

In 2004, as requested by NIJ, the National Academies appointed the Committee to Assess the Feasibility, Accuracy, and Technical Capability of a National Ballistics Database. The committee was asked to:

> assess the feasibility, accuracy and reliability, and technical capability of developing and using a national ballistics database as an aid to criminal investigations. To accomplish this, the [committee] will
>
> (1) Assess the technical feasibility, through analysis of the uniqueness of ballistic images, the ability of imaging systems to capture unique characteristics and to parameterize them, the algorithmic and computational challenges of an imaging database, the reproducibility of ballistic impressions and the ability of imaging systems to extract reproducible information from ballistic impressions.
>
> (2) Assess the statistical probabilities that ballistics evidence presented would lead to a match with images captured in a database, whether and how the base rate can be estimated for those crimes that present bullet or casing evidence that do in fact come from a gun that produced a database entry, and the probabilities and consequences of false positives and false negatives.
>
> (3) Assess the operational utility of ballistics evidence in criminal investigations—that is the extent to which it is used or can be used to identify crime guns and suspects and to solve specific crimes.
>
> (4) Assess the sources of error in ballistics database matching (from examination, digitization, computer matching, chain of custody and documentation of tests, and expert confirmation), how they may be quantified, and how these errors interact.

---

and the Bullet Tracing Act to Reduce Gun Violence Act (H.R. 422). Earlier versions of the Bullet Tracing and BLAST Acts were also introduced in the 106th Congress.

[3]See H.R. 3491 and S. 2581 in the 107th Congress and H.R. 2436 and S. 980 in the 108th Congress. These bills also failed to advance beyond referral to subcommittees.

The charge continues:

> The committee's work will provide scientific and technical knowledge to inform the government's deliberations on three policy options with regard to ballistics databases:
>
> (1) Maintain the National Integrated Ballistic Information Network (NIBIN) on ballistics recovered from crime scenes. It is operated by the Bureau of Alcohol, Tobacco, and Firearms.[4]
> (2) Enhance the NIBIN system so that it can be used to match crime scene evidence with the gun used.
> (3) Establish a national ballistics database of images from bullets fired from all, or nearly all, newly manufactured or imported guns for the purpose of matching ballistics from a crime scene to a gun and information on its initial owner.

We note that the committee was specifically tasked by NIJ to consider these policy options on the basis of the scientific evidence of system performance and not to include or exclude options based solely on their cost. That is, assessing the cost-effectiveness of ballistic imaging and related techniques is not a dimension of our charge.

The wording of the charge raises a few questions. In several instances—as in the formal name of the committee—the term "ballistics" is used in an imprecise manner; see Box 1-1. The charge also provides no specific direction on how the existing NIBIN system might be "enhanced" in its second policy option. The third policy option is also somewhat imprecise in representing basic assumptions about the nature and intent of a national RBID; see Box 1-2 (see also Section 9–B in Chapter 9).

At the outset, it suffices to say that reasonable proposals for a national RBID would most likely focus exclusively on images of cartridge casings (not bullets, as described in the charge) due to the longer time necessary to recover and process test-fired bullets, and—at least at the outset—would likely be further restricted to samples from handguns and small arms. The charge also suggests that the intent of a national RBID is to provide "information on [a gun's] initial owner." That is certainly the goal of criminal investigations that would make use of an RBID, but the RBID search itself would be intended to provide an investigative lead to a point of sale, one step removed from information on the initial owner. As with the current gun tracing system, additional investigative work based on the point of sale would be needed to determine a gun's initial ownership; as discussed in Chapter 9, the content of a national RBID does not necessarily involve entering purchaser-specific data.

---

[4]In January 2003, the agency was renamed the Bureau of Alcohol, Tobacco, Firearms, and Explosives, though it commonly retains the acronym ATF.

BOX 1-1
"Ballistics" Terminology

Ballistics, literally, is the study of the dynamics of projectiles in flight. It is not equivalent to "firearms identification," though in common usage, as in the title of this committee, the word has been interpreted that way. Calvin Goddard—considered the father of modern firearms identification—was chagrined at his own role in initiating this use of language. He titled his landmark 1925 paper on the use of the comparison microscope "Forensic Ballistics," a name selected "after long and prayerful consideration, and in an effort to employ terms that would be concise and at the same time meaningful;" it was, however, "a title that has plagued me ever since" (Goddard, 1999:233):

> Forensic was good enough, since it means that which has to do with public disputation, and was what I meant to say. "Ballistics" was bad, very bad, since ballistics strictly used applies solely to projectiles in motion, and the forces that influence that motion. Thus far, I never made an attempt to identify a projectile in motion, and if I ever have to, it will be too soon, so far as I am concerned. However, the man in the street found ballistics [an] interesting word, and seized upon it avidly, at the same time discarding the "forensic" which, when used jointly with ballistics, partly takes the curse off the latter.

Likewise, Hatcher (1935:20) rued the way "the word 'ballistics' has in the past several years become associated in the public mind with the science of Firearms Identification. . . . I realize fully that usage makes language, and that the recent rather extensive mis-use of the word Ballistics in this way may be a valid excuse for continuing the practice; but still it seems to me that the use of the word to describe the Science of Firearms Identification is somewhat undesirable in any case, as being loose English."

Forensic scientists distinguish between four types of "ballistics" (Rinker, 2004):

- *Internal ballistics* refer to the forces—pressure, ignition, and so forth—that operate on the bullet while still inside the firearm.
- *External ballistics*, closest to the literal definition of ballistics, describes the flight of a bullet between the firearm muzzle and its impact at target.
- *Terminal ballistics* describe the mechanics of impact on both the projectile and the target.
- *Forensic ballistics*, in Goddard's sense, is the analysis of bullet and cartridge case evidence and the use of that evidence to link specimens to each other and to particular weapons.

"Ballistics" is convenient shorthand but in this report—save for the committee's formal name—we try to refrain from the use of the word on its own. Our use of the adjective "ballistic" (as in "ballistic imaging" and "ballistics evidence")—like any instances of "ballistics" that may still appear in the text—is properly interpreted as referring to "forensic ballistics."

BOX 1-2
Content of a Reference Ballistic Image Database

A major part of our committee's charge is to assess the feasibility of a reference ballistic image database. However, many of the parameters governing the content of such a database are not specified by the charge—for instance, whether cartridge casings or bullets (or both) should be entered into the database, whether one bullet or casing is sufficient or whether multiple exhibits are needed, whether all firearm types should be covered. The bills introduced at the federal level have been worded to be as inclusive as possible. In the 108th Congress, the BLAST Act, SNIPER Act, and TRACE Act (H.R. 5663, S. 1983, and H.R. 776, respectively) bore identical language on the nature of the envisioned database. "A licensed manufacturer or licensed importer" would be required to

(A) test fire firearms manufactured or imported by such licensees as specified by the Attorney General by regulation;
(B) prepare ballistic images of the fired bullet and cartridge casings from the test fire;
(C) make the records available to the Attorney General for entry in a computerized database; and
(D) store the fired bullet and cartridge casings in such a manner and for such a period as specified by the Attorney General by regulation.

The database envisioned by these bills would require both bullets and casings to be entered; it would also put the responsibility for image acquisition and exhibit archival on the manufacturers or importers. The question of whether image data would be collected for long guns as well as handguns was not directly answered.

The existing state reference ballistic image databases in Maryland and New York both made key limiting assumptions, restricting their content to cartridge

In structuring our work, we have taken the three policy options as a guide; addressing them necessarily involves addressing the issues suggested in the preceding four substantive points of the charge. Cast in language more consistent with usage in the field, we have interpreted our principal task as providing information on three different federal policy options:

1. *Maintain the NIBIN* as it presently exists—that is, retaining the restriction that only crime-gun-related evidence be included in the database.

2. *Enhance the current NIBIN system* in order to increase its effectiveness without expanding its scope to include new or manufactured firearms; such improvements could include changes to the basic imaging standard used by the system (e.g., three-dimensional surface measurement rather

casings from handguns only. The enabling law in Maryland created a centrally located "Statewide Shell Casing Data Base," later called MD-IBIS, and a "Statewide Shell Casing Repository," both to be administered by the Maryland State Police Crime Laboratory. The shell casings in question were to be "provided by dealers from all handguns sold in the state" and transmitted to the Crime Laboratory (Maryland Code 29.05.02.02). In later years, a bill to expand MD-IBIS coverage to long guns was introduced in the legislature but was not enacted. Similarly, the New York Combined Ballistic Identification System (CoBIS) database was established as the "pistol and revolver ballistic identification databank" (New York General Business Laws, Article 26, Section 396-ff):

> Any manufacturer that ships, transports or delivers a pistol or revolver to any person in this state shall . . . include in the container with such pistol or revolver a separate sealed container that encloses: (a) a shell casing of a bullet or projectile discharged from such pistol or revolver; and (b) any additional information that identifies such pistol or revolver and shell casing.

The language of the previous federal bills notwithstanding, we generally assume throughout this report that a national reference ballistic image database would be similar to the Maryland and New York models albeit at the larger, national scale. At the minimum, we assume that operational constraints would limit the national reference database to cartridge casings, owing to the time-consuming process of discharging weapons in a water tank or other trap so that expended bullets can be recovered in "pristine" condition. Whether rifles and long guns would be included in such a database is an open question; again, the Maryland example leads us to assume that initial coverage would be focused on handguns (as the major class of guns used in crime).

than two-dimensional photography), improvements to database handling, improved procedures for working with the existing hardware and software, and so forth.

3. *Establish a national reference ballistic image database*, as a counterpart to (and possibly linked to) NIBIN, containing images of ballistic samples from all newly manufactured or imported guns, in order to generate investigative leads to the original point of sale of a firearm.

1–A.1 Experimental Study by National Institute of Standards and Technology

In support of the committee's work, NIJ separately contracted with the Office of Law Enforcement Standards of the National Institute of Standards and Technology (NIST) for experimental work with the direction and advice of the committee, on the feasibility and accuracy of identification using a national ballistic image database. In particular, the NIST work considers the relative advantages of three-dimensional metrology techniques as compared to the current two-dimensional imaging used in NIBIN. NIST's experimentation in support of this study builds on NIST's ongoing work, under other contracts, on the development of standard bullets and cartridge casings for the calibration of ballistic imaging systems. The NIST work is summarized in Chapter 8, and the full NIST report has been published separately (Vorburger et al., 2007).

1–A.2 Limitations: What the Committee Study Does *Not* Do

In the balance of this chapter, we provide additional basic context for the committee's work and give an overview of the structure of the report. However, we believe that it is first important to be clear on certain limitations of our work and our charge. Our task is to assess various policy options related to ballistic imaging; it is possible for this basic charge to be misconstrued or overinterpreted in at least three major ways.

First, and most significantly, *this study is neither a verdict on the uniqueness of firearms-related toolmarks generally nor an assessment of the validity of firearms identification as a discipline*. Our charge is to focus on "the uniqueness of ballistic images"—that is, on the uniqueness and reproducibility of the markings (toolmarks) left on cartridge cases and bullets as they are recorded or measured by various technologies (e.g., photography or surface metrology).

The uniqueness of firearms-related toolmarks generally is a much broader question—and a very important one—but it is not one that our committee was constituted to address. At a minimum, assessing the general validity and uniqueness of toolmark evidence would require a much wider range of gun and ammunition selections and firing conditions than was supported in our experimentation through NIST (see Chapter 9). It would also require precise quantification of the myriad sources of variability inherent in the firing of a gun (see Chapter 2). In short, it would be a major undertaking, requiring a sustained program of research over many years, and it is impossible to definitively answer the question of the uniqueness of ballistic toolmarks as a by-product of a more targeted study of the uniqueness of ballistic images.

Although a definitive statement on firearms toolmark uniqueness is not within our purview, some discussion of issues related to uniqueness—particularly the sources of variability in generating such toolmarks—are essential to our work. Chapters 2 and 3 of this report are largely dedicated to these matters, covering the sources of variability inherent in firing a gun and the uniqueness and reproducibility of firearms-related toolmarks as judged by firearms examiners using the comparison microscope. From these reviews, some readers may attempt to infer a stance by this committee, for or against the validity of firearms identification generally. From this perspective, some may argue that our narrow focus on the uniqueness of ballistic images amounts to missing the proverbial elephant standing in the room: that is, we should extend any conclusions on the strength or weakness of ballistic *image* evidence to infer the strength or weakness of ballistic toolmark evidence more globally. We reiterate that no such broader conclusion is intended by this report, which was not developed to support more sweeping statements. Rather, the examination in Chapters 2 and 3 is intended to identify major sources of variability, as well as particularly challenging (or easy) contexts for linking pieces of ballistics evidence, in order to best construct our experimental work with NIST and understand the results of ballistic image database comparisons.

Other readers may see a definitive statement on the uniqueness and reproducibility of toolmarks as a first and necessary building block to any further work: without such a statement—if firing processes and resulting toolmarks are completely random—then the basic utility of a ballistic image database (of any sort or scope) to try to suggest connections between pieces of evidence comes into question. We appreciate this argument but conclude that it is possible to speak meaningfully about ballistic image database performance without first fully accepting or concluding the fundamental uniqueness of toolmarks. In this regard, the analogy of fingerprints may be useful: to date, there exists no definitive proof that no two people can have identical fingerprints. Instead, the credence of fingerprint evidence rests mainly on the assertion that—across all the years in which fingerprints have been manually compared—no two people sharing the same individual prints has yet been found. The emergence of computerized image databases for fingerprints has served not only to facilitate links between pieces of evidence, but also to allow for further probing of basic assumptions. Searches across large databases of fingerprint images begin to add quantitative weight to the claim of fundamental uniqueness, and reconciliations between manual examinations and computer algorithms generate useful debates over how many specific points of similarity must be found before a match can be determined. In time, ballistic image databases may similarly be an important resource for evaluating the basic assumptions of firearms identification; however, development and study of image databases need not wait until those basic assumptions are definitively examined.

Second, *our work is not intended to speak to the question of whether firearms identification by a human firearms examiner can be replaced by mechanical routines*. A point that we return to throughout in the report is the distinction between systems designed for *search* and those designed for *verification*; the two are very different, although commonly confused. NIBIN was designed as a search tool and not for verification, and as we argue, ballistic image databases are most appropriately seen as tools for search. For ballistics evidence, verification is formally made by experienced firearms examiners, who provide sworn expert testimony on evidence matches in court: hence, only direct physical examination of exhibits—and the judgment of a human firearms examiner—can certify a "hit," or a "true" match. Our focus is on the question of whether ballistic imaging technologies perform reliably as a search tool to assist human examiners—spanning large volumes of image data and returning high-likelihood candidate matches for an examiner to consider—and not on whether computer technology can replace human examiners.

Third, *the proposal for this study explicitly precluded the committee from assessing the admissibility of forensic firearms evidence in court*, either generally or in specific regard to testimony on ballistic imaging comparisons. We note, however, that high-subjectivity branches of forensic science are now confronting growing skepticism with regard to discernible uniqueness as a result of a number of legal and scientific studies. The standard for scientific evidence created by the U.S. Supreme Court's decision in *Daubert v. Merrell Dow Pharmaceuticals* (509 U.S. 579, 1993) places high probative weight on quantifiable evidence that can be tested empirically and for which known or potential error rates may be calculated, such as identification using deoxyribonucleic acid (DNA) markers (Saks and Kohler, 2005; National Research Council, 1996). The legal context in which ballistic image evidence may be presented is too important to steer clear of entirely, and we briefly review some of the relevant legal issues and cases in Chapter 3. However, we do not in any way offer a determination of whether ballistics evidence should or should not be admissible in court proceedings.

1–A.3 Microstamping

Over the course of the committee's deliberations, debates over the feasibility of alternatives to imaging technologies that would achieve the same basic goal as a national RBID—providing an investigative lead to a point of sale—have grown in prominence. Of particular interest is the use of microstamping to directly imprint firearm parts or ammunition so that known, unique markers are imparted on bullets or cartridge casings and a connection can be made to a gun (and its point of sale) without recovery of the gun itself. The technology is also sometimes referred to as "ballistic ID tagging" or "virtual serial numbering." Just as the issue of creating RBIDs grew in prominence when it came under serious consideration in the state of California, so, too, has legislative attention in the nation's largest state fueled debate over microstamping. Versions of bills requiring some form of microstamping passed in one chamber of the California legislature (but not both) during the 2005–2006 session. However, in September 2007, AB 1471—a bill requiring microstamping on parts of new semiautomatic handguns sold in the state after January 2010—was passed by the legislature and was signed into law by the governor in October.

Microstamping has grown sufficiently in stature that no bill before the 109th or (as of August 2007) 110th U.S. Congresses called for a national RBID; instead, one repeatedly introduced bill on ballistic imaging has been changed in focus to require the use of microstamping.[5] Though the feasibility of a national RBID remains the committee's primary focus, we also consider the feasibility of alternative technologies to achieve the same goal.

1–A.4 Committee Activities

In carrying out its charge, the committee held six meetings beginning in February 2004, the first four of which included public sessions. Given the committee's size and the multiple subject areas contained in its charge, the committee conducted much of its work in small working groups, including one set up to provide specific guidance to the NIST experimentation portion of the study. Committee members and staff visited local NIBIN installations at law enforcement agencies and the headquarters of Forensic Technology WAI, Inc., makers of the computer platform on which NIBIN presently operates. Committee subgroups were also permitted to perform limited experimentation using New York State's CoBIS RBID and the ballistic image database maintained by the New York City Police Department, which is not actively linked to NIBIN but uses the same technology. To get a sense of sources of variability in bullet and cartridge markings, committee subgroups visited three firearms and ammunition manufacturers: Beretta USA, Hi-Point Firearms, and Federal Cartridge. Finally, committee subgroups examining alternative technologies visited developers of microstamping or tagging technologies for both firearms parts and ammunition.

1–B CONTEXT: THE GUN CRIME PROBLEM

The primary motivation for considering the implementation of a national RBID—and for the analysis and matching of ballistics evidence,

---

[5]See H.R. 5073, the Technological Resource to Assist Criminal Enforcement (TRACE) Act, in the 109th Congress. Introduced in April 2006, it was referred to the House Judiciary Committee but no further action was taken prior to adjournment. The same legislation was introduced in the House in the 110th Congress as H.R. 1874 on April 17, 2007, following the mass shooting at Virginia Polytechnic Institute and State University.

in general—is to reduce gun-related crime.[6] Ballistics evidence matching is intended to assist police investigations of crimes involving firearms, thereby increasing the chance of arrest, conviction, and punishment of criminals. The desired result is the incarceration of gun-using criminals and the deterrence of gun crime: if a higher percentage of such criminals are incarcerated, it may deter other criminals from using guns, and incapacitate those who get caught from committing further crimes (see, e.g., Nagin, 1998).

Although gun crime constitutes a small percentage of violent crimes, guns are used in two-thirds of homicides. Criminal assaults with guns are more lethal in comparison with those involving other common weapons, and the misuse of guns by criminals creates a sense of insecurity, of "no safe place" for residents of a neighborhood where gunfire is common. The social costs of gun violence in the United States include both the direct damage of injury and death to victims and the indirect damage to the larger population whose quality of life is reduced by the threat of gun violence (Cook and Ludwig, 2000). In general, property values, business location decisions, commuting routes, and other lifestyle choices are influenced by the public's perception of the threat of gun violence. The Washington, D.C., sniper attacks of 2002 are an extreme example that directly affected an entire metropolitan area; for some inner-city neighborhoods, gunfire is a routine occurrence that places the public in fear and distorts day to day living (Cook and Ludwig, 2002). The total annual social cost of gun crime is estimated to be $80 billion (Ludwig and Cook, 2001). Thus, tools, such as ballistic imaging technology, that can assist police in solving gun-related crime have a clear benefit for the population at large, particularly if they have some deterrent effect on gun violence.

The Federal Bureau of Investigation's Uniform Crime Reports (UCR) program provides yearly data on the number of firearm crimes known to the police. The UCR figures are based on counts of the number of murders, robberies, and aggravated assaults committed with firearms. In 2003, there were 282,641 reported total firearms crimes comprised of 137,657 (48.7 percent) robberies with firearms, 135,346 (47.9 percent) aggravated assaults with firearms, and 9,638 murders with firearms (3.4 percent).[7] As shown in Figure 1-1, the yearly number of crimes committed with firearms in the United States fluctuated between 300,000 and 400,000 between 1973 and 1988, increased over the next 5 years to a peak of 581,697 in 1993,

[6]The nature of gun-related crime and the adequacy of existing data related to it are comprehensively reviewed in National Research Council (2005).

[7]Separate estimates for 2003 by the National Center for Injury Prevention and Control of the Centers for Disease Control and Prevention indicate approximately 47,000 nonfatal gunshot injuries for which the intent of the injury was violence-related. The data are generated from the center's National Electronic Injury Surveillance System; see http://www.cdc.gov/ncipc/wisqars [accessed February 2008].

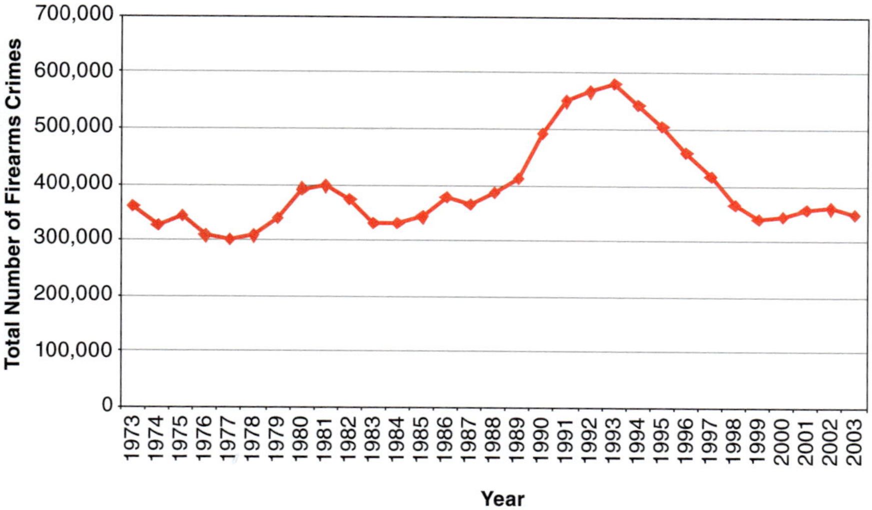

FIGURE 1-1 Crimes committed with firearms, 1973–2003.
SOURCE: Federal Bureau of Investigation, *Crime in the United States* (annually; see http://www.ojp.usdoj.gov/bjs/ [accessed February 2008]).

decreased dramatically over the course of the 1990s, and remained stable through 2003. Firearms crime rates per 100,000 U.S. residents followed the same trajectory; see Figure 1-2.

UCR data on the yearly number of homicides committed with firearms between 1973 and 2003 follow the same trajectory as the total number of firearms crimes per year; see Figure 1-3. However, the peaks and valleys were more pronounced in the gun homicide trend data. Gun homicides peaked in 3 years: 1974, 1980, and 1993. After 1993, there was a steep decrease to 1999. Gun homicide rates follow a similar trajectory; however, when population size is considered, the 1974 and 1993 peaks are the same (6.6 gun homicides per 100,000). The steep increase in gun homicides beginning in the 1980s and peaking in 1993 was largely driven by minority youth in urban settings (Cook and Laub, 2002; Blumstein, 1995). The youth gun violence epidemic was further concentrated among highly active criminal offenders who tended to be involved in street gang or illegal drug activity (Braga, 2003; Kennedy et al., 1996). In most cities, gun violence problems remain concentrated among a small number of criminally active youth who are involved in gangs or criminal groups (Braga et al., 2002).

Cities vary widely in the amount of gun crime they experience and

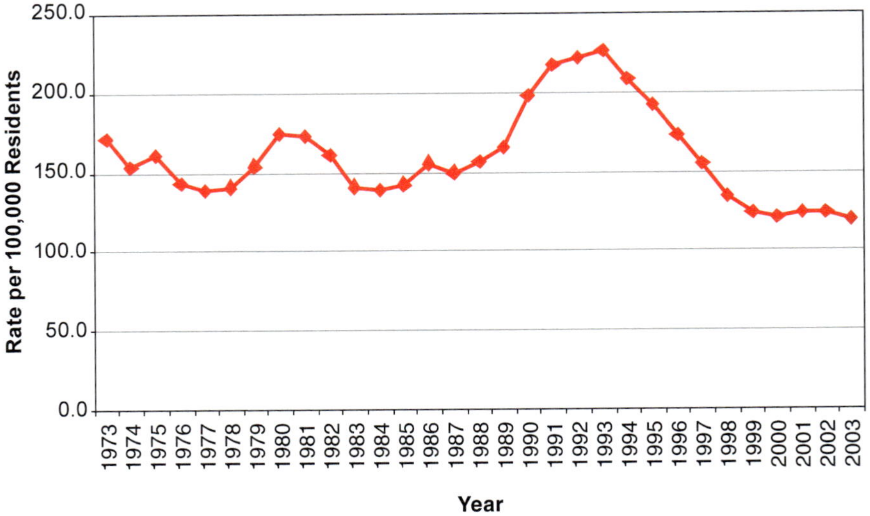

FIGURE 1-2 Firearms crime rates, 1973–2003.
SOURCE: Federal Bureau of Investigation, *Crime in the United States* (annually; see http://www.ojp.usdoj.gov/bjs/ [accessed February 2008]).

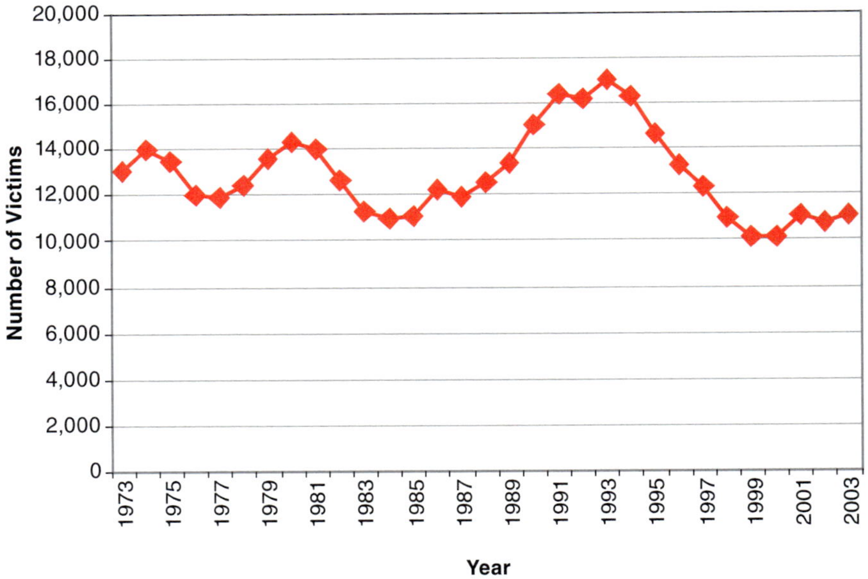

FIGURE 1-3 Homicides committed with firearms, 1973–2003.
SOURCE: Federal Bureau of Investigation, *Crime in the United States* (annually; see http://www.ojp.usdoj.gov/bjs/ [accessed February 2008]).

the numbers of crime guns local police departments recover. Table 1-1 presents gun homicide counts and rates, as well as the number of crime guns recovered, for 32 cities that participated in ATF's Youth Crime Gun Interdiction Initiative (YCGII) in 2000 and were judged by ATF to be submitting all recovered firearms for tracing (U.S. Bureau of Alcohol, Tobacco,

TABLE 1-1 Gun Homicides and Crime Gun Recoveries in 32 Cities in 2000

City	Gun Homicides	Homicide Rate per 100,000	Gun Recoveries
Atlanta, GA	108	25.9	1,141
Baltimore, MD	202	31.0	4,295
Baton Rouge, LA	33	14.5	1,068
Boston, MA	26	4.4	896
Camden, NJ	17	21.3	165
Charlotte, NC	57	9.1	2,041
Chicago, IL	415	14.3	8,570
Cincinnati, OH	7	2.1	877
Dallas, TX	177	14.9	3,005
Gary, IN	56	54.5	792
Houston, TX	165	8.4	3,909
Indianapolis, IN	67	8.4	3,592
Los Angeles, CA	430	11.6	3,877
Louisville, KY	33	12.9	1,637
Memphis, TN	110	16.9	3,244
Milwaukee, WI	90	15.1	2,283
Minneapolis, MN	38	9.9	949
Nashville, TN	56	10.5	2,297
New Orleans, LA	175	36.1	1,965
New York, NY	434	5.4	6,284
Newark, NJ	40	14.6	584
Oklahoma City, OK	24	4.7	856
Philadelphia, PA	259	17.1	3,041
Phoenix, AZ	110	8.3	4,778
Piedmont Triad, NC[a]	38	7.7	699
Portland, OR	14	2.6	857
Richmond, VA	53	26.8	1,109
Salinas, CA	16	10.6	327
San Antonio, TX	45	3.9	1,294
San Jose, CA	8	0.9	1,476
St. Louis, MO	90	25.8	2,612
Tucson, AZ	49	10.1	2,135

[a]Greensboro, High Point, and Winston-Salem, NC.

SOURCES: Gun homicide data from FBI Supplementary Homicide Reports, 2000; see http://www.icpsr.umich.edu [accessed February 2008]. Gun recovery data from U.S. Bureau of Alcohol, Tobacco, and Firearms, 2002.

and Firearms, 2002; see Box 9-1). Not surprisingly, large cities—New York, Los Angeles, and Chicago—report the largest numbers of gun homicides. However, there are smaller cities that experience dramatically higher rates of gun violence relative to the large cities. Gary, Indiana, had the highest rate of gun homicides per 100,000 residents with 54.5, followed by New Orleans with 36.1 percent, and Baltimore with 31.0 percent. Because of the variability in gun crime rates by locality, different localities may have different baseline needs for ballistic imaging technology (and, potentially, different levels of benefit from its refinement).

1–C BALLISTIC IMAGING, FIREARMS IDENTIFICATION, AND "BALLISTIC FINGERPRINTING"

Analysis of ballistics evidence may provide a link between two shooting incidents if it is determined that the same weapon was fired in both. That information may be helpful to investigators since it suggests that the incidents involved the same shooter, or involved two shooters who were linked by the transfer of the gun in question. Alternatively, the ballistics evidence match can provide a link between a shooting incident and a particular gun, perhaps one that has separately been found and placed in police custody; this information may be helpful to the investigation if the identity of the owner or possessor of that gun is known or could be determined through further investigation.

It is important to clarify several terms and the distinctions among them. First, *ballistic imaging* is not identical to *firearms identification*. Traditional firearms identification techniques, relying on the direct viewing of specimens under a comparison microscope by a trained firearms examiner, have been used in investigations for decades. As discussed in Section 1–A.2, the identification and confirmation of fired bullets or cartridge cases as having been fired from a specific firearm is the responsibility of human examiners. Ballistic imaging is a means of searching across a large number of exhibits—in greater numbers and across broader expanses of geography than a human examiner could possibly achieve—to suggest possible matching candidates. Ballistic imaging would more accurately be described as a form of *computer-assisted firearms identification*.

The unique innovation that ballistic imaging technology has added to the field is the "cold hit"—the generation of possible links between specimens and cases arising only through querying a database. A cold hit can be particularly valuable for furthering the investigation of shooting crimes that lack an obvious suspect or even any clear leads. Research on police clearance of homicide cases (Wellford and Cronin, 1999, 2000) suggests that the availability of witnesses (who can identify the offender or victim and who may be able to suggest the whereabouts of the offender) and swift action by the first officers on the scene are major contributors to success in closing a case. By comparison, crimes for which eyewitness testimony is not available (or where witnesses may be unwilling to come forward), such as is common in drug-related homicides, are harder to solve. In cases for which witnesses and early data on possible suspects are lacking, a cold hit on ballistics evidence generated through a routine database search could provide an important investigative lead.

Generally, ballistic imaging offers the opportunity for more rapid searching across a high volume of candidates than is possible using conventional techniques. In traditional firearms identification, a firearms examiner's cognitive task in examining specimens under a comparison microscope is to form a mental pattern of identifying marks and features on bullet and cartridge case evidence and to match that pattern against those from other exhibits. Accordingly, searching through large amounts of ballistic evidence and verifying a match can be a very labor-intensive and time-consuming task. Making connections between different cases relies on the visual memory of the firearms examiner or—if all exhibits are not viewed and remembered by the same person—recognition of features from photographs in open case files or posts on bulletin boards. Ballistic imaging technology allows images of bullets or casings to be cataloged, indexed, scored, and ranked. A firearms examiner can visually compare high-ranked pairs of images on the screen, much as a radiologist might read a digital mammogram or other X-ray, and the physical evidence items for promising matches can then be requested as appropriate for confirmation.

The general ballistic imaging methodology we describe in this study has been popularly referred to as *ballistic fingerprinting*, a term that carries both positive and negative connotations and that is misleading in a very important sense. Most commonly used in relation to a national reference ballistic image database, with the idea of logging a newly sold gun's "fingerprint" before or as a condition of sale, "ballistic fingerprinting" naturally suggests a connection to the more widely known practice of recording human fingerprints. What is fundamentally misleading about equating "ballistic imaging" and "ballistic fingerprinting" is the point of reference—a human fingerprint is an attribute of that human, and a determined match between a latent fingerprint found at a crime scene and a fingerprint in police files suggests a direct connection between a crime and a suspect. However, the markings imparted to fired bullets and casings are attributes of a firearm, not the person who fires it.[8]

---

[8]Though "ballistic fingerprinting" has become a popular term in recent years, references to ballistic toolmarks as mechanical fingerprints date back to the formative days of firearms identification. Hatcher (1935:265, 275), one of the seminal texts in the field, notes that "these [toolmarks] are what might very aptly be described as the 'finger prints of the firing pin and

Absent other evidence, firearms identification and ballistic imaging do not automatically generate a mapping from ballistics evidence to a possible perpetrator. We return to this point in Section 3–A, but it is important to note here that fingerprint (and DNA) evidence refer to attributes of a particular person, but they do not necessarily point to that person as the criminal *offender*. That is, the presence of this evidence can place a person at the location of a crime, but not necessarily demonstrate that they were there at the time of the crime or that they committed the act in question. The intent of a national RBID is to provide a relatively quick connection between recovered ballistics evidence and a point of sale. However, additional work from a national RBID "hit" would still be necessary to derive a person's name from the point of sale and that this person—the original purchaser of the firearm—is not necessarily the person who used the gun in crime.

1–D OVERVIEW OF REPORT

Part I of this report describes the context for ballistic image analysis. Chapter 2 describes the toolmarks imparted on bullets and cartridge casings as a result of firing, reviewing the sources of variability inherent in the manufacture of firearms and in the process of firing a gun. Chapter 3 describes the nature of ballistics evidence in more detail, focusing on traditional firearms identification techniques and the studies that have been performed on the uniqueness and reproducibility of firearms-related toolmarks as discerned using conventional microscopy.

Part II deals with the current state of ballistic imaging and the existing national image database, NIBIN. Chapter 4 discusses the technology used for acquiring images and scoring and ranking them, focusing on the IBIS platform used by the NIBIN program. Chapter 5 describes the evolution of the NIBIN program and its structure and summarizes what is known about the NIBIN system's performance. Drawing from both these chapters, Chapter 6 outlines operational and technical enhancements that could improve NIBIN.

Part III addresses the basic titular charge to the committee, describing evidence on variability in ballistics evidence and the implications for a national reference ballistic image database. Chapter 7 introduces a major technical enhancement that the committee chose to explore as an option

breech block on the primer.'" If all the gross, class marks are the same between two bullets, "this does not, however, prove in any way that [a suspect bullet] came from that particular gun as there are hundreds or even thousands of guns of each type manufactured. . . . Fortunately, however, each and every barrel has its own 'finger prints' which it leaves on a bullet, and identification by these marks is just as certain as identification of a criminal by his finger prints."

for either the current NIBIN program or a wide-scale national reference database. That enhancement is the replacement of two-dimensional photography with three-dimensional topography, and we briefly describe that technology along with historical alternatives to photography in firearms analysis. Chapter 8 reviews the experimental efforts conducted by NIST in support of the committee's work, as well as limited experimental work using the New York State CoBIS database. Chapter 9 builds from the new experimental evidence and from studies (described in Chapter 4 and elsewhere) in articulating the arguments associated with creating a national reference database.

Part IV, on future directions, begins in Chapter 10 by discussing alternative technologies to achieve the same goal as a national reference ballistic image database. In particular, we review proposals to microstamp firearms parts or individual pieces of ammunition with unique etched identification codes. Chapter 11 closes the report with general guidance on the process of developing systems for image search, retrieval, processing, and scoring, suggesting "best practices" for development of any such program (whether advancing current two-dimensional photography techniques or changing to three-dimensional topography).

Appendix A offers additional detail on the use of ballistic imaging technology in Boston, one locale where the current NIBIN system appears to be well used and well supported.

2

Firearms and Ammunition: Physics, Manufacturing, and Sources of Variability

A firearm is a dynamic system for delivering maximum destructive energy to a target, in the form of a high-velocity bullet, with minimum delivery of energy to the shooter. To that end, the firing of a firearm and the subsequent generation of ballistic toolmarks are the end results of processes that are simultaneously characterized by high uniformity and great variability. Modern firearms and ammunition manufacture relies heavily on the uniformity and interchangeability of component parts, yet each step in the production cycle presents an opportunity for microscopically fine differences from part to part. Likewise, the firing of a gun depends on the rapid and repeated performance of numerous mechanical steps that is designed to produce combustion, done in a controlled manner yet still not creating exactly identical conditions in repeated firings.

In this chapter, we summarize the basic parts of firearms and ammunition (Section 2–A) and describe the physical processes that take place when a trigger is pulled and a gun is fired (2–B). These sections are not intended to be comprehensive examinations of the history and features of firearms and ammunition nor a complete catalogue of firearms products in current use. Rather, they provide context for the principal focus of this chapter: describing the types of toolmarks left on ballistics evidence by firing (2–C), particularly those that are typically imaged and input into ballistic image databases.[1] We close in Section 2–D with brief descriptions of concepts in the manufacture of both firearms and ammunition. A general understanding of manufacturing is essential not only for an appreciation

[1]More detailed information and images are available at http://www.firearmsid.com.

of the sources of variability in ballistic toolmarks, but also in assessing the feasibility of implementing technologies like wide-scale ballistic imaging or microstamping.

2–A ANATOMY OF FIREARMS AND AMMUNITION

2–A.1 Firearms

Firearms come in a wide array of designs and specific makes, and each represents a complex assemblage of numerous constituent parts. In this section we focus on the parts most central to the basic firing assembly since the interest is in toolmark creation. Due to their widespread use in crime, we also discuss some terminology in the specific context of handguns, as in differentiating between revolvers and pistols.

Barrels

Gun barrels are manufactured from solid pieces of steel whose composition is carefully selected for its chemical and metallurgical properties. A first step of the process, drilling, results in a comparatively rough hole of uniform diameter extending from one end of the barrel to the other. Next the barrel is bored with a reamer, designed to produce as smooth a surface as possible on the inside of the barrel. The interior surface or bore bears numerous scars and scratches from this drilling process; it is these random imperfections—more so than subsequent steps—that are said to account for individual characteristics on fired bullets (Heard, 1997:124–125).

Barrels are further subjected to a rifling process, creating a pattern of grooves on the inside the barrel. This rifling is essential to the firing accuracy of the weapon; as it is forced out of the barrel by gas pressure, the bullet impacts with the barrel rifling and is given a rotation—somewhat akin to the spin on a thrown football—that gives the bullet a more direct flight. Some weapons, typically shotguns, have no rifling ("smoothbore"). Most handguns and rifles have a spiral pattern of rifling to improve their accuracy. The rifling may be created by forcing a carbide button through the reamed barrel; it is the normal wear on this button, as many riflings are performed, that is said to impart individual microscopic variability in markings in the barrel (along with residual scars or imperfections from the original drilling). Additional steps in the process to finish a barrel include heat treating (to impart hardness) and cleaning.

Across manufacturers, barrels can vary in two fundamental features, each of which are basic class characteristics (see Section 3–B.1). The first is the *direction* in which the grooves in the barrel twist, whether left- or right-handed. Most U.S. makers use a right twist, although Colt revolvers are known for their left twist (Rinker, 2004:128). The second is the number of *grooves* that are cut into the barrel—normally at a depth of 0.004–0.006 inch—to create the rifling, and, correspondingly, the number of raised *lands* between those grooves. Historically, "no standard was established and makers used, normally, six, seven, or eight grooves"; this remains the usual range, although firearms have been fielded with as few as 2 and as many as 24 grooves (Rinker, 2004:130, 131).

Barrels also vary in the degree of twist in the rifling, which affects how much rotation is put on bullets as they pass through the barrel and exit. Rinker (2004:127) observes that "few people agree on what is the proper twist. Some people want an over stabilized bullet from a fast twist. They claim best accuracy at all ranges. Other shooters believe a fast twist builds pressure and heat and they want a slow twist for minimum stability, and they have claims to back their theory."

Some firearms differ from conventional rifling with square-edged grooves, using *polygonal* rifling instead. "Polygonal rifling has no sharp edges," and instead the raised lands in the barrel have a smooth, "rounded profile which can be difficult to discern when looking down the barrel. This type of rifling is almost exclusively manufactured using the hammer or swage process" (Heard, 1997:123).

Chamber, Breech Face, and Firing Pin

The rear section (away from the muzzle) of the barrel bore is known as the chamber; it is designed and sized to fit a specific caliber of cartridge (see Section 2–A.2). The part of the firearm against which a cartridge sits when it is placed in the chamber is the breech, and the whole assembly may be referred to as the breechblock or breech bolt.

The specific surface of the breech that makes contact with the base of the cartridge is the breech face; Figure 2-1 depicts the breech faces of two firearms. The exact steps used to form the breech assembly can vary by manufacturer, and the breech face may vary in terms of the amount of filing or polishing done on it and whether any paint or other materials is applied to it. Basic filing can create gross striation marks in linear arrangements; in others, a rotary milling operation may be applied to the breech face surface, creating a pattern of concentric circles (American Institute of Applied Science, 1982:77). These steps are crucial to the theory of firearms identification as it is random imperfections created in these machining and filing processes that is said to make the surface (and the negative impressions of said surface, left on fired cartridge casings) unique.

A hole drilled through the breech assembly holds the firing pin, a very hard steel rod that can be forced to protrude from the breech to strike the primer of a cartridge seated in the chamber. While most firing pins have a

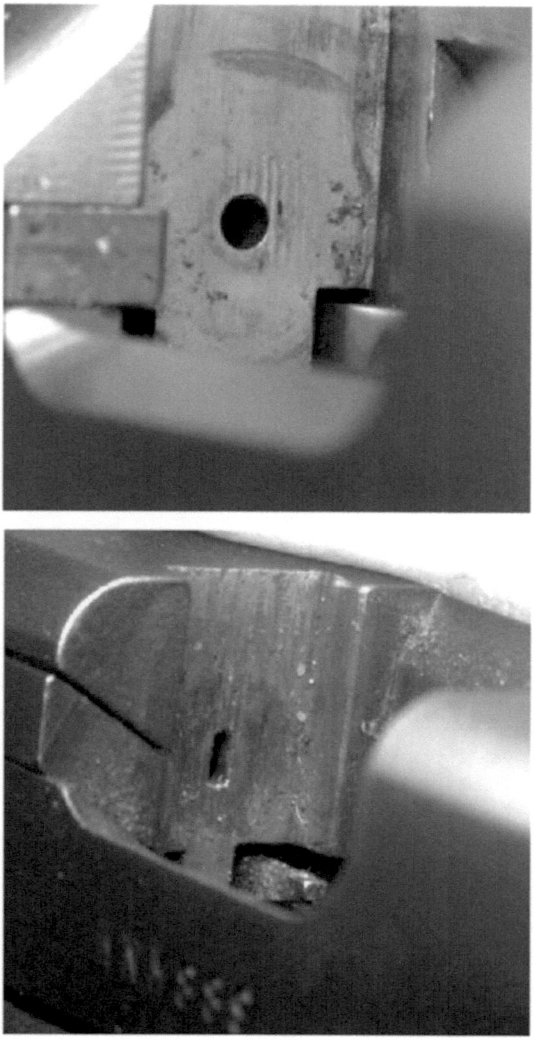

FIGURE 2-1 Breech faces with firing pin holes: Two firearms.
NOTES: The top image is the breech face of a Smith & Wesson firearm; the bottom image is the breech face of a Glock firearm. The shape of the firing pin hole for the Glock firearm indicates its characteristic rectangular firing pin.
SOURCE: Excerpted from Tulleners (2001:Fig. 3-3).

small rounded end or nose, some have more distinctive shapes; in particular, Glock firearms are known for a rectangular firing pin. Firing pins are generally made on a standard screw machine. Like the breech face, the tip of the firing pin is subject to machining and filing steps that impart microscopic imperfections.

Revolvers and Pistols

Handguns may be divided into two basic types—revolvers and pistols—by the manner in which ammunition is loaded and cycled through the firearm.

In a revolver, "the supply of ammunition is held in a cylinder at the rear of the barrel with each round having its own chamber," and a ratchet mechanism is then used to cycle the cylinder to the next position (Heard, 1997:18). Revolvers may be further subdivided by the manner in which this cycling is performed. In *single-action* revolvers, the shooter manually cocks the hammer, pulling it back and setting the ratchet action in motion. A trigger pull then causes the hammer to drop and commence the firing process. More complex—and more common—*double-action* revolvers save a step: "A long continuous pull on the trigger cocks the hammer, rotates the cylinder, then drops the hammer all in one operation" (Heard, 1997:18).

By comparison, pistols are self-loading, making use of ammunition "contained in a removable spring-loaded magazine housed within the grip frame." Pistols have a single chamber, and individual rounds of ammunition are cycled into the chamber by mechanical means; pulling back the slide rearward until the breech face is behind the top round in the magazine, and then releasing it, forces the round forward and into the chamber for firing. After firing, the spent cartridge case is ejected "through a port in the side, or occasionally top, of the slide. At the end of its rearward motion, the spring-loaded slide moves forward[,] stripping a fresh round off the top of the magazine and feeding it into the rear of the barrel" (Heard, 1997:19).

Pistols are often referred to as *semiautomatic* pistols (or semiautomatics); they are semiautomatic in that they are self-loading but require separate, distinct trigger pulls to fire different rounds. "Automatic" is used to describe "a weapon in which the action will continue to operate until the force is removed from the trigger or the magazine is empty." Though a few fully automatic pistols have been marketed, they are rare "due to the near impossibility of controlling such a weapon [for accurate shots]. . . . Each shot causes the barrel to rise during recoil and before the firer has time to reacquire the target within the sights, the next round has fired"; consequently, "even at close range it is unusual for more than two shots to hit a man-sized target" (Heard, 1997:17, 18).

For the objective of the recovery of ballistics evidence and imaging thereof, the distinction between revolvers and pistols is vital: while pistols forcibly eject spent rounds, revolvers do not. Hence, casings may only be recovered at a crime scene involving a revolver if they are specifically emptied by a shooter (e.g., for reloading).

Extractor and Ejector

Both revolvers and pistols make use of an extractor, typically a small arm that fits over the rim of the cartridge. As the name implies, the extractor serves to pull a spent cartridge from the chamber so that a new cartridge can take its place. In a revolver, the extractor—which can remove all cartridges simultaneously by depressing the ejection rod (or extractor rod)—also has ratchet notches that advance the cylinder to the next chamber. In a semiautomatic pistol, however, the extractor removes the cartridge so that it makes contact with the ejector, typically a fixed protuberance that strikes the rim of the cartridge. Because these steps are performed very quickly, and with some speed and force, both the extractor and ejector mechanisms can leave marks on expended cartridge casings.

2–A.2 Ammunition

Modern ammunition takes the form of integrated, self-contained *cartridges*, integrating three key elements in one unit:

- a *bullet*, the actual projectile that is expelled from the firearm's barrel;
- *propellant*, which generates the force and pressure needed to put the bullet in motion and into flight; and
- a *primer*, which in modern usage is a volatile and pressure-sensitive chemical mixture that is responsible for igniting the propellant.

Historically, with firearms of the 18th century, shooters had to assemble these components manually in order to reload, inserting black gunpowder, wadding, and a spherical lead ball into the gun's barrel. With the intent of making reloading faster, early cartridges featured premeasured and prepackaged charges of powder, in small bags, but they still required an external source to provide a thermal "flash" to ignite the powder and fire the projectile. The innovation of the breechloader, by which the ammunition is loaded at the rear of the gun's barrel, made modern integrated ammunition possible. Modern ammunition links these three components together, placing them inside an outer *case*.

Ammunition is commonly identified based on the diameter of its bullet, for proper fitting with firearms barrels. The original designation of ammunition size was by caliber: The unit of measurement was hundredths of an inch (e.g., .38 caliber corresponding to a bullet with diameter 0.38 inches). However, such caliber labels are only approximations, for example, a .38 caliber is actually 0.357 inches in diameter and a .40 caliber is actually 0.429 inches in diameter. Ammunition (and corresponding gun barrels) are also now identified using the metric system, such as 9mm or 10mm.[2]

Ammunition cartridges are primarily divided into two categories—rimfire and centerfire—depending on where the primer is located (and, correspondingly, where the gun's firing pin strikes the cartridge during firing). We explain the distinction in the next section.

Primer

The use of a chemical primer to ignite the propellant dates back to the development of the percussion cap in the early 1800s, when it was discovered that striking a cap containing fulminate of mercury created a flame that could then move into the main charge of powder. Today, the exact chemical composition of primer mixtures can vary and remains proprietary. "Lead styphnate is the main ingredient," generally, although individual primers may also include some of the following: "[trinitrotoluene (TNT)], lead or copper sulphocyanide, lead peroxide, sulfur, tetryl, barium peroxide, and barium nitrate" (Rinker, 2004:19). Ground glass may also be added as a "sensitizer," to create friction when impacted by the firing pin (Matty, 1987:10). A primer mixture is a high explosive; working with it and placing the primer in the case are extremely sensitive parts of the ammunition manufacture process.

Rimfire cartridges were first developed in the 1800s, and rimfire ammunition remains in heavy usage in .22 caliber cartridges. As the name implies, "the primer composition is spun into the rim of the cartridge case," putting it in immediate contact with the powder propellant (Rinker, 2004:19–20). By comparison, *centerfire* ammunition has a cylindrical cap seated in the cartridge head that contains the primer mixture. The cap consists of a cup-

[2]Care is needed with the use of the word "caliber." Here, "caliber" is shorthand for the *nominal caliber* of the ammunition, which refers specifically to the diameter of the bullet. However, *specific caliber* of ammunition "refers to a name given to a cartridge representing the entire design of the cartridge as intended by the manufacturer, [including not only] the diameter of the bullet but the entire shape and size of the cartridge" (Moran, 2000:235). That is, a nominal-caliber ammunition group may include a wide variety of specific varieties that can vary significantly in their length, case design, powder charge, and so forth. Both "nominal caliber" and "specific caliber" are used to describe and label firearms as well, referring to the "group of firearms which share the same bore diameter" and the "name given to a firearm representing the specifically designed cartridge which will fit into the firearm," respectively (Moran, 2000:235).

and-anvil combination and a pellet of primer mixture. During firing, the firing pin "compresses the primer composition between the cup and anvil," causing a flame that passes through a hole or vent to ignite the propellant charge (Rinker, 2004:19). Practically, the development of the centerfire system "was the great milestone in weapon and ammunition development;" with it, "only the primer cup needed to be soft enough to be crushed by the firing pin," freeing the main body of the cartridge case to be harder, providing "a gas seal for much higher pressures than could be obtained with rimfire ammunition" (Heard, 1997:11). Centerfire cartridges also developed, in part, due to the desire to reuse "the most expensive part of the cartridge, the case"; the centerfire configuration permits new primer assemblies to be inserted into expended casings (Matty, 1987:8).

Given its purpose, the primer assembly must meet specific criteria. The primer mixture "must always have a uniform flash that is hot enough without being too violent. In other words, it must always consistently produce the proper amount of heat" (Rinker, 2004:20). Likewise, the material holding the primer—either the cartridge brass of the rim in a rimfire cartridge or the cup in a centerfire primer—must withstand the impact of the firing pin, the detonation of the primer, and the expansion of gas from the ignited propellant without rupturing. Centerfire primer cups are typically brass or nickel.

Propellant

Though it derives from centuries of development, a critical part of ammunition is subject to popular misunderstandings and mislabelings. It is commonly referred to as *powder*, tracing from ancient formulations of black powder and more modern incarnations of smokeless gunpowder. As Hatcher (1935:96) observes, powder "originally meant, and still does mean, fine dust; but at the present time we find substances called powder which do not in any manner resemble dust and which are not even finely divided." *Propellant* is a more generic and more apt term for the substance used in modern ammunition. The individual particles of propellant may still be referred to as grains, even though they may not have a gritty or granular texture; however, the common use of *grains* to describe the exact quantity or charge of propellant in a cartridge has nothing to do with texture (a grain is a measured weight equal to 0.0648 grams).

Fundamentally, a propellant is not devised to *explode* violently: It is designed to *burn*, and burn rapidly. As Rinker (2004:21) summarizes, "all gunpowder produces the force to move a projectile as the result of 3 things. (1) When it burns, it produces a huge quantity of gas. (2) As it burns, it produces a huge amount of heat. (3) After ignition, it creates its own oxygen and needs no outside air. All three are required. At first, the need for heat may not be as obvious as the other two, but hot gas expands and requires more space then cold gas," heightening the buildup of pressure in the gun's chamber.

Modern propellants are a form of nitrocellulose, first discovered in 1846 when cotton, nitric acid, and sulfuric acid were mixed. One pound of nitrocellulose-based powder contains 1.2–1.5 million foot pounds of stored chemical energy, in comparison with about 600,000 foot pounds of stored energy in one pound of the traditional saltpeter, charcoal, and sulfur combination of black powder (Rinker, 2004:23). "If ignited in an unconfined space," nitrocellulose propellant will burn gently; if, however, combustion occurs in a confined space—as in a cartridge—"the heat and pressure built up will accelerate the rate of combustion exponentially" (Heard, 1997:76). The charge of propellant utilized in cartridges is carefully tuned to the caliber, bullet weight, barrel length, and desired performance of the ammunition. Chemical "moderating" agents or other additives (e.g., graphite or barium nitrate) are often used to control the burn rate of the propellant, and the mixes used in final propellants are "very tightly-controlled trade secrets" (Heard, 1997:59).

Cartridge Cases

Cartridge cases have traditionally been manufactured from brass, an alloy of copper and zinc, although other materials have been used; in particular, steel casings (coated with copper or a lacquer) were developed during World War II due to brass shortages, and steel cases remain in use in some countries because of their lower cost. Cartridge brass is almost universally of the same composition: a 70-to-30 or 75-to-25 alloy (in percentage of weight) of copper and zinc, respectively. This combination was developed, along with methods for working with it, as a result of the physical demands put on the case during the firing of a gun. As described below, a cartridge case expands during firing, pressing against the chamber walls to create a seal and containing the high-pressure gases created in firing. To accomplish this *in situ* deformation, the hardness of the cartridge brass must be precise so that the case retains its original shape and can be readily extracted from the breech. Too hard a starting brass and the case may crack during firing; too soft and it will expand and deform too much and be difficult to extract. Although there are a number of manufacturing processes currently used to produce cartridges, the salient features of the general manufacturing process are similar. Within the same case, thickness must also vary in particular ways, tailored to suit various tasks: maximum hardness in the rim (of a centerfire cartridge) in which the primer cap is seated, medium hardness with good elasticity in the central walls of the case, and softest at the neck or mouth end where the bullet is seated.

One modern manufacturing process for producing a centerfire case starts with brass rod or wire, in coils. A machine called a cold header, similar to the one used to make common nails, feeds in the rod or wire, cuts off a piece large enough to make one case, and transfers it to a cavity in the machine, where it is struck by a punch. This process forms the irregularly shaped cylindrical piece into a precise sort of button shape. The button is annealed (heated and then cooled) to reduce its hardness, and is then fed into a two-stage transfer press that transforms the cartridge blank into a low, wide cup. The half-formed cup is next pushed through a die or series of dies that draw the blank to its final shape and dimensions. Additional annealing, cleaning, and forming steps are done sequentially until the blank is in the final shape of the cartridge case.

Bullets

The last major component of the cartridge is the bullet or projectile. Bullets in modern ammunition can consist of a variety of metals. There are bullets made entirely of aluminum, steel, and sometimes brass; nonmetallic substances like rubber and wood have also been used to make bullets. However, to provide the needed weight for improved accuracy and performance, bullets most often contain some amount of lead.

Bullets are designed for two basic purposes—penetration on impact with a target and perforation and expansion to increase damage—and the exact composition and construction of bullets are tailored to those purposes. An all-lead bullet is very soft and therefore expands rapidly on striking a target. Indeed, "pure lead is not used for lead bullets" precisely because "it is too soft [and] damages too easily in handling and loading"; antimony is most commonly added to lead as a hardening agent, though tin has also been used (Frost, 1990:27). Better penetration power at greater distances and accuracy can be attained by covering a lead core with a full jacket or partial jacket composed of a copper alloy. High-velocity, fully jacketed bullets are designed to penetrate deeply, while lower velocity jacketed bullets may tumble within the target and cause additional damage due to expansion. Mushrooming or expanding bullets, such as hollowpoints, are designed to transfer a maximum amount of energy to the target and to penetrate but not exit. The composition and design of bullets—along with what materials they do or do not strike—are important to forensic ballistics analysis as they affect what condition a recovered bullet will be in and hence how difficult it is to match to other evidence.

A lubricant is applied to bullets before they are seated in cartridge casings; it acts to cut down on metal fouling of the bore, the deposition of particles or residues from the bullet (Frost, 1991:31). In centerfire cartridges, where "grease grooves" are created in the case by knurling, the lubricant is usually a wax or heavy grease type; due to its placement, it must be a substance that will neither contaminate the powder nor react with lead or copper plating.

2–B THE FIRING OF A WEAPON: INTERNAL BALLISTICS

The general concept of "ballistics" can be divided into separate stages; see Box 1-1. External ballistics (the flight path and behavior of the bullet between its exit from the barrel and its arrival at its target) and terminal ballistics (behavior of the bullet on striking a target) are both critical to complete firearms investigations.

Our primary focus is on internal ballistics—the actions that occur between the pulling of the trigger and the bullet's exit from the barrel of a firearm. Internal ballistics is "a series of actions or operations that every firearm must go through, whether .22 caliber revolver or a .50 caliber machine gun," all of which occur in a time span on the order of 0.003 seconds (Rinker, 2004:1, 2). The trigger pull starts the mechanical process of allowing the firing pin to strike the primer of the chambered cartridge. The pressure from the firing pin creates a dent in the primer surface of the cartridge; more significantly, it causes a small explosion, the heat from which passes through the hole in the primer cap and into the main body of the cartridge. There, the charge of powder burns rapidly in a confined space, converting from a solid to a gas and exerting great pressure against all surfaces. "When the pressure has built up to a sufficient level, known as *short shot*, the bullet will start to move because the pressure is greater than the holding force of the case neck." As the powder burn continues, "the pressure increases and the neck and body walls of the case expand to meet and grasp the inside chamber walls," creating a seal and increasing the pressure acting on the bullet's base, propelling it forward (Rinker, 2004:1). The bullet, being slightly larger than the barrel diameter, is forced to seat into the rifling (the lands and grooves) on the bore of the barrel, picking up rotation as it passes down the length of the barrel.

While this sequence of events drives the bullet through the barrel and out of the firearm, forces are also at work on the head of the cartridge. Hatcher (1935:270, 272) describes the processes for a centerfire cartridge:

> When a primer is struck by the firing pin, the very brusque and powerful mixture that it contains explodes with violence, [causing the flame that ignites the powder charge]. But the explosion of the primer mixture also reacts in a backward direction onto the primer cup itself, and blows it part way out of the primer pocket, unless the primer is strongly crimped in place, as is done with some kinds of rifle ammunition. Then when the main charge ignites, the powder pressure inside the case forces the case

> back sharply against the breech face or recoil plate, and this action seats the primer again. . . .
>
> When the material of the primer is very soft, or the breech pressure is very high, or more particularly if the soft primer has a very strong mixture in it and the vent hole is small, the metal forming the surface of the primer cup often is forced back more or less into the firing pin hole in the breech block, thus leaving a raised rim all around the firing pin impression.

The firing pin is often not fully retracted, and so it may impact the casing multiple times (Krivosta, 2006:42). Likewise, the firing pin may scrape or drag somewhat against the edge of the surface.

Also emitted from the barrel as a result of firing is gunshot residue, a mixture of partially burned and unburned particles of propellant, leftover primer mixture, and particles of metal and lubricant from the release of the bullet and its passage through the barrel. Some residue may also remain in the barrel and possibly on other internal surfaces of the gun; with time, and in the absence of cleaning, these residues can build up and alter the surface to which the bullet and cartridge case are exposed during firing.

2–C BASIC TOOLMARKS ON BALLISTICS EVIDENCE

2–C.1 Cartridge Case Markings

Breech Face Marks

Gas pressure created during the firing process exerts pressure in all directions, including forcing the head of the cartridge against the breech face. Hence, the surface area of the cartridge head may pick up negative impressions of any linear striations or other features left on the breech face when it is filed and machined. Some of these marks may register on the relatively hard cartridge brass that forms the outer ring (head stamp area) of the cartridge case, but most of the features show up in the softer surface of the primer cap. Hence, what is known as the breech face mark is the pattern of linear striations and other textural features on the surface of the primer, surrounding the indentation of the firing pin impression. Figure 2-2 illustrates the breech face marks and firing pin impression for two different firearms, one Glock and one Smith & Wesson.

Hatcher (1935:265–266) provided an early description of the breech face mark and recognized the mark's importance as a potentially identifiable feature:

> In both [semi]automatic pistols and revolvers there are certain fine tool marks or scratches left on the breech face or the metal against which the

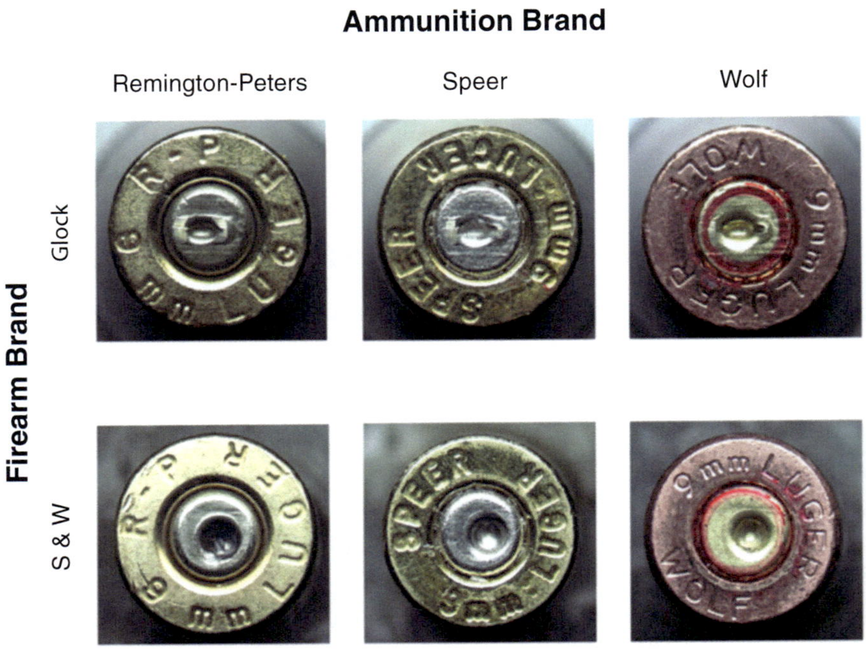

FIGURE 2-2 Breech face markings and firing pin impressions for three ammunition types and two firearm brands.
NOTE: S & W = Smith & Wesson.
SOURCE: Adapted from Tulleners (2001:Fig. 3-4).

> cartridge presses when it is being fired. These marks are quite pronounced on metal surfaces that have been finished by a file as is commonly done on the breech face of the average [semi]automatic pistol or revolver. Examined under a microscope this surface appears to consist of a number of ridges or scratches, and when the cartridge is fired, the primer, being of copper or brass, which is much softer than the steel of the breech face, will take the impression of these fine ridges.

In gross appearance, features in the breech face impression may fall into some general categories depending on the specific filing or polishing steps used by the manufacturer. Straight filing creates linear features; other breech face impressions may feature cross-hatching or circular patterns. For example, Kennington (1995) documents the class of 9mm pistols for which the rotary cutting tool used in milling the breech face not only leaves distinctive arched markings that are impressed on the primer surface, but may also be evident elsewhere on the cartridge head. Kennington suggests that the rifling characteristics from bullet evidence at a crime scene can be combined with evidence of arched markings on cartridge casings to rapidly identify the pistol make in question.[3]

Because breech face impressions are created by the pressure of firing, Tulleners (2001:3-2) notes that their detail "is dependent on cartridge chamber pressure and the type of breech face manufacture/condition. [Chamber pressure varies within caliber and depends on such factors as the bullet size and weight and the powder charge contained in the cartridge.] Lower pressure cartridges are not expected to consistently produce decent breech face impressions." He adds that cartridge chamber pressure, bullet weight, and primer hardness "can vary to such an extent that an examiner will not be able to identify test 1 to test 2 when different ammunition is used in the same gun;" hence, "one of the cardinal rules in firearm examination is to test fire the gun with similar ammunition as the evidence ammunition if at all possible" (Tulleners, 2001:3-3).

Firing Pin Impressions

The firing pin impression on the surface of the primer provides important information on the general class of the firearm that discharged a casing. The shape of the "pit" marking the firing pin's strike indicates the shape of the firing pin in the firearm (e.g., round, elliptical, rectangular). The firing pin impression will also bear the marks created by filing or smoothing the tip of the firing pin. "The point of the firing pin will have small ridges, and no two . . . firing pin points will be exactly alike," conjectured Hatcher (1935:266). However, Burrard (1962:113) notes that "great caution is necessary" in distinguishing individual markings from grosser features of firing pin marks, which "often take the form of a number of small concentric rings." Yet individual imperfections on the tip of the firing pin can be telltale: "Another by no means rare feature of a [firing pin] is the presence of a small 'pimple' on the extreme end," and so the presence of a corresponding mark on one cartridge and the absence on another "would be proof positive that the [second] cartridge could *not* have been fired" from the same weapon as the first.

For some guns and some firings, the firing pin impression may not be a clearly defined indentation on an otherwise flat surface. Instead, primer "flowback" may occur: a larger crater is created as the primer material

[3]However, he cautions that "the arch-producing machine process . . . may not be the final breechface treatment at the factory. The breechface can still be broached, filed, sandblasted, tumbled and/or plated," and residue buildup as a result of firing can obscure the arch markings.

around the pit is forced outward by gas pressure, partially flowing into the aperture in the breech from which the firing pin emerges. Though "flow-back" is commonly attributed to firearms in which excessive pressure can build during firing, Kreiser (1995) suggests other explanations that also correspond to characteristics of the particular make of firearm. Among these is the diameter of the firing pin aperture: the wider the aperture, the more primer surface is unsupported (not positioned directly against another object) during firing and hence more likely to crater outward.

In some firings, the firing pin may scrape against the surface of the primer as it is withdrawn. In these cases, the firing pin impression is not purely a mirror of the shape of the firing pin (e.g., circular) but has a drag mark trailing away from the main impression. Because drag marks may be repeated—that is, they may be a function of the behavior of the firing pin in a particular gun—they become important landmarks for traditional firearms identification and ballistic imaging alike, providing a benchmark to orient casings consistently. It is also important to note that the mechanics of firing is such that there is variability in the exact position where the firing pin impacts the cartridge across different firings; the pin may wobble slightly and strike at slightly different points and angles.[4]

In rimfire weapons, the firing pin strikes the brass of the outer rim of the cartridge head. As Hatcher (1935:68) observed, "[rimfire ammunition] takes a good impression showing the shape of the firing pin, but it does not often take a clear impression of the fine file marks and other irregular scratches on the breech block, which form the 'finger-prints' of the gun." Accordingly, he noted that "when an empty rim fire cartridge is found at the scene of a shooting, it is often easy to say what type of arm was used; but it is seldom possible to identify a rimfire cartridge to a definite individual gun by the impression of the file marks it left on the head, as is so often done in the case of a center-fire cartridge."

Ejector Marks

The ejector arms in automatic or semiautomatic firearms can vary in shape (e.g., rectangular, round, or triangular) and size; the footprint of the ejector determines the size and shape of the mark left by the ejector on the rim of the spent casing. Ejector marks can vary from tiny divots to

[4]Fadal (1995) provides an unusual but vivid example of the difference that placement and angle of the firing pin strike can have on the resulting marks. The Hi-Standard Model DM-101 is a .22 caliber derringer handgun that is double-barreled; however, the same rectangular firing pin is used to initiate the firing in each of the two barrels. The difference in the way the same pin hits the (rimfire) casings in the two barrels—one using the top part of the pin and the other the lower—is sufficiently large that an examiner cannot match firings from one barrel to firings from the second barrel on the firing pin marks alone.

more substantial indents on the cartridge head near the rim. Analysis of ejector marks can be made more difficult by the fact that the rim of the cartridge head is also where ammunition makers put their headstamp (brand identifier) and information on the size and caliber of the cartridge. These heavy-set alphanumeric characters are inscribed on the cartridge brass and—depending on where the ejector happens to hit—parts of the stamp may bleed into the ejector mark.

In addition to the shape of the ejector mark and any individual scrapes or textures therein, ejector marks also serve the same important purpose as a firing pin drag mark: They provide a point of reference for proper orientation of cartridge cases relative to each other in comparison.

Other Markings

During the firing process, gas pressure works on all surfaces, forcing the material of the cartridge against the chamber of the weapon; particularly in semiautomatic weapons, other firearms parts are used to circulate ammunition through the weapon and eject spent casings. These actions and parts can lead to a host of marks on the cartridge case that—though not imaged using current techniques—are sometimes used by examiners studying matches between pieces of evidence.

Chamber marks are parallel striated marks along the outer walls of the cartridge case, impressions from the scraping used to bore or ream the chamber (along with the rest of the barrel) from a solid piece of alloy. The extractor in a pistol that helps move a spent cartridge out of the chamber is typically a small arm that fits over the rim of the casing, holding it as the breech assembly slides backward. Accordingly, the extractor can leave marks where it makes contact, either on the edge of the rim of the cartridge head or on the neck separating the head from the main body. The slide that moves back and forth in semiautomatic pistols, allowing ejected casings to move away from the weapon, may leave a scuff mark on the edge of the cartridge head and a rough drag mark along the cartridge wall. As individual cartridges move from a magazine into chamber, a mark on the outer wall of the case may be caused by the magazine lip.

2–C.2 Bullet Markings

Hatcher's (1935:255) seminal text on firearms identification referred to "the fine ridges and grooves on the surface of the bullet, parallel to the rifling marks," as "the most important individual characteristics which are used" in the field. These marks on the bullet—known as striations or striae—"are caused by its passage over surface irregularities and rough spots on the interior of the gun barrel that got there principally during the machining operations of reaming the bore and rifling the grooves. Any such machining operation will leave the bore at least slightly rough, and each rough spot will leave a mark on the bullet during its passage through the bore."

The rifling carved into the barrel takes the form of grooves separated by raised areas, known as lands. These lands and grooves create corresponding engraved areas—dubbed land engraved areas and groove engraved areas (and commonly abbreviated as LEAs and GEAs)—on the bullet surface, separated by shoulders. The land engraved areas, being the part of the bullets that scrape against the raised lands on the barrel, are the principal areas of interest for observing striations.

The pattern of land and groove engraved areas on recovered bullets can be used to determine basic information about the rifling characteristics of the gun that fired them, in order to identify a class of guns from which it came. Specifically, the number of lands is an important class characteristic, as is the direction of twist evident from a side view of the bullet. Bullets (and corresponding rifling characteristics) are commonly labeled by these two pieces of information—e.g., 5R for five lands and a right-hand twist. A recovered bullet can also be measured to suggest the caliber of the ammunition and weapon. However, this is not always possible—nor is a full analysis of striation marks—due to the condition of some bullets recovered from crime scenes (and victims).

Bullets fired through weapons using polygonal rifling create special difficulties. Compared to conventional, square-edged rifling, polygonal rifling has key advantages: it reduces metal fouling, and it increases bullet velocity by reducing friction as the bullet passes through the barrel (Heard, 1997:123). However, the smoothness and subtlety of polygonal rifling can make it difficult to discern even gross features on recovered bullets—the shoulders defining lands and grooves—much less fine individual detail. Heard (1997:131) concludes that "generally speaking it is possible, although extremely difficult, to match bullets from polygonally rifled barrels."

2–D THE MANUFACTURING OF FIREARMS AND AMMUNITION

The underlying theory of firearms identification depends critically on manufacturing processes, positing that the tools used to form component parts wear with use so that each part may share the same gross features yet differ in microscopic (and, presumably, uniquely individual) ways. Manufacturing processes are also essential to consider in assessing the costs and benefits of wide-scale ballistic imaging or alternatives such as microstamping. Introducing stages to the process of producing firearms or ammunition—for example, systematic test-firing to produce exhibit cases, imaging of exhibits in large batches, or laser-etching a unique mark on the base of a bullet—can have major impacts on the cost of production and, perhaps, the feasibility of compliance with proposed changes.

We have already touched on some aspects of manufacturing in describing the anatomy of firearms and ammunition earlier in this chapter, and aspects of manufacture will arise in Chapter 3 as well (particularly in discussing challenging issues for firearms identification, generally). This section introduces basic issues but is not a comprehensive discussion.

2–D.1 Firearms

The manufacturing of most guns is highly automated and generally efficient, and as many as 5 million new firearms (domestic and foreign) enter the U.S. market each year. Befitting its historical development, dating to Samuel Colt's popularization of interchangeable parts and production line assemblies, the modern firearms industry remains one that is characterized by solid process control. That is, the process of mass-producing firearms is one that can be well partitioned: constituent parts of a new firearm can be drawn from large bins of fairly standardized parts and automatically fitted together with low yield loss, resulting in weapons of reasonably identical properties in terms of size, weight, and performance.

Yet individual manufacturers differ on the exact steps used in machining and assembling firearms, and choices on the amount of filing or polishing to do on firing pins or whether to apply paint to the breech face can have an impact on the resulting toolmarks. In addition, some manufacturing techniques affect the type and quality of marks created in firing. Champod et al. (2003:307) argue that "machining marks made by grinding, filing and some other machining methods are random and hence we expect no repeatability between tools." In comparison, "machining marks made by stamping, some cutting processes such as broaching, and some forging processes may be repeatable."

Various manufacturing techniques used by Lorcin Engineering drew interest in the 1990s, as firearms produced by the firm became more widely used in crimes;[5] they serve as useful illustrative examples. Thompson (1996:95) found two Lorcin L9MM semiautomatic pistols, bought at the same time, that produced sufficiently similar breech face markings that a match could be made to either weapon on that mark alone; they could, however, be distinguished by sidewall and extractor marks. Similarly, Matty

[5]In 2000, the Lorcin L380 semiautomatic pistol was the most traced firearm after recovery from juvenile possessors, and a Lorcin .25 caliber pistol ranked seventh. The L380 was also traced with high frequency after recovery from older offenders, ranked second among firearms recovered from 18–24-year-olds, and ranked third among firearms recovered from adults aged 25 and older (U.S. Bureau of Alcohol, Tobacco, and Firearms, 2002:15–16).

(1999:134) reports on a case where a search on a DRUGFIRE database—an initial competitor to the current Integrated Ballistics Identification System (IBIS) for ballistic imaging (described in Chapter 4)—suggested enough similarity to cause the physical evidence (both test-fired cartridge casings and the recovered Lorcin L9MM that produced them) to be retrieved from storage. On more detailed examination, "the breech face signatures were similar, but there was insufficient detail for an identification"; however, chamber and extractor marks failed to coincide at all.

"The heavy black 'paint' that adhered to the breech face" was originally believed to be a cause of this phenomenon (Thompson, 1996:95).[6] Ultimately, though, it was attributed to the fact that the breech faces for that model being formed by stamping, with no further grinding. In earlier Lorcin models, "the breechface area would become battered during firing as [a relatively soft alloy slide] hit the rim of a cartridge in the magazine as it fed the cartridge into the chamber"; this caused the breech face markings to be unstable and to change from firing to firing (Matty, 1999:135). Lorcin revised its process—in newer models, "a solid stamped steel insert is placed into a non-ferrous alloy slide"—but this stamped steel insert is prone to have marks that "can carry over from one steel insert to another" (Tulleners, 2001:3-4). (This phenomenon is an example of subclass carry-over, discussed in fuller detail in Section 3–B.1.)

More generally, Collins (1997:498) observed that "the bullets and casings of the [Lorcin] L380 [.380 caliber semiautomatic] pistol are easy to characterize. The bullets exhibit slippage[7] and/or extremely shallow land impressions that often make even shoulder location difficult to determine," and even "breech face marks are either non-existent or change from shot to shot." Collins' specific inquiry into the manufacturing pistol was based on attempting (unsuccessfully) to replicate crescent shaped marks observed in some firings, imprinted directly below the firing pin impression and believed to be caused by peening of the breech face surface under repeated firings.

Another example of manufacturing processes that can directly affect the marks left by firearms and the ability to match them is the button rifling technique used by some manufacturers, notably Hi-Point (Roberge and Beauchamp, 2006:166):

[6]A thick coat of black paint was also judged to be the probable cause of highly similar breech face marks produced by two different 45 ACP Haskell semiautomatic pistols; individual characteristics would emerge on the breech face marks for each gun with repeated firings, as the paint chipped and wore off (Tulleners, 2001:3-4).

[7]"Slippage" means that a bullet does not fully grip the rifling on the barrel interior; hence, it can wobble and shift, rather than following the clear path of the rifling (and having marks carved into the side of the bullet as it passes through).

> This process creates the grooves in the barrel by compressing rather than removing the excess material resulting in a relatively shallow barrel groove. Another distinct characteristic of the Hi-Point barrels is the metal tailings left along the shoulder of the groove. The combination of button rifling and metal tailings creates a relatively smooth barrel with very coarse shoulders. With each shot fired, all or part of the metal tailings break off changing the coarse stria on the fired bullet. The shallow rifling also allows a great deal of slippage to occur. Furthermore, the crowning[8] of these barrels can add additional subclass characteristics.

All newly manufactured firearms are required to bear a unique serial number, and this number may be stamped or etched on various parts of the firearm frame and assembly. However, guns with consecutive serial numbers are generally not consecutively manufactured in full. Production of firearms is typically an assembly line process, drawing various preconstructed parts from large bins for assembly into a finished weapon. Hence, two firearms that bear consecutive serial numbers may have rolled off the line in sequence, but their frames, barrels, firing pins, and so forth need not have been manufactured right after each other. There are some exceptions to this rule; for instance, Lardizabal (1995) found that consecutive serial numbers in a set of Hechler & Koch 9mm USP semiautomatic pistols meant that the slide for these weapons had in fact been consecutively manufactured.[9]

2–D.2 Ammunition

Like firearms, ammunition cartridges are the result of numerous tooling and machining operations, and individual manufacturers vary in the specific techniques they use. It is standard practice for manufacturers to apply a head stamp, engraved on the rim of the cartridge head, to identify the manufacturers and perhaps the specific make of the ammunition; they may also use colored paints or other indicia to differentiate between specific makes and calibers. Ammunition manufacturers also vary in some post-processing steps, such as the application of a lacquer sealant to the primer surface. "Primer sealants are routinely applied to centerfire cartridges to increase the power and reliability of the ammunition," "placed at the junction between the primer and the primer cup [to] create a water and airtight

[8]"Crowning" is a finishing step on the muzzle or discharge end of a barrel, rounding or grinding the mouth so that it is flush or recessed slightly and thus providing no obstacle to the bullet's exit.

[9]Lardizabal (1995:50) found that firings from a set of these pistols with similar serial numbers could not be distinguished from each other by any mark, and this "persistence of detail" continued through 250 firings. A pattern of striations was observed on the breech face itself, above the firing pin hole; this mark appeared to have been created after a chemical finishing process.

seal [and prevent] oil and other foreign matter from entering the cartridge." The sealant also makes the cartridge resistant to moisture. However, while "most ammunition manufacturers limit the application of the sealant to the junction of the primer and primer cup," some (primarily European) manufacturers "apply the sealant so that it extends across the entire surface of the primer." The Czech-made Sellier and Bellot ammunition, in particular, is known for a red lacquer sealant over the entire primer (Hayes et al., 2004:139). The lacquer can act as a cushion, "absorb[ing] and dissipat[ing] a greater amount of energy" when involved in a collision (compared with metals), and consequently "reduc[ing] the amount of energy that reaches the metal surface of the primer" (Hayes et al., 2004:142).

The specific techniques of a manufacturer can combine with more ornamental and postprocessing steps to leave distinctive marks on the cartridge. Box 2-1 reviews these nonfiring manufacturing marks—features that are present on the cartridge before firing and traces of which may endure after firing. In comparing exhibits, firearms examiners must compensate for the presence of these nonfiring marks, lest they lead to a false identification or exclusion. While many of these nonfiring marks are deliberate design choices, others arise inadvertently due to other steps in manufacture. Yborra and McClary (2004) report finding distinct striated markings near the edge of the primer surface on a batch of 115 grain Remington 9mm Luger ammunition. The marks appeared to be due to manufacturing and not firing: when a pair of casings was rotated so that identifying marks in the firing pin impression were in the same orientation, the extractor marks on the cartridges also lined up but the newly found striated marks on the primer surface were 90 degrees out of alignment. Remington managers indicated that they had never previously experienced such a phenomenon but suggested that a possible cause might be the way the primer is seated in the cartridge. Two separate punches drive the primer to its final position about 0.002 to 0.005 inches below the level of the cartridge head; "a misalignment or damage to one of these punches MAY have caused the observed [marks], and being machine-based, would be consistent" (Yborra and McClary, 2004:309). But no such defect could be found; nor could similar marks be detected on other boxes of ammunition from the same lot. The punches used in primer seating were also suspected of causing parallel markings near the edge of the primer on some Winchester 9mm ammunition (Flater, 2002:315); it was also suggested that the die used to flatten the surface of the primer cup could also have impressed such a mark.

BOX 2-1
Nonfiring Manufacturing Marks

Nonfiring manufacturing marks on ammunition are features created by individual firms' manufacturing processes. They are not defects, in that they do not diminish the ammunition's performance or otherwise detract from the ammunition's quality. However, they may be mistaken for textures or striations created by the firing of a gun or that may complicate the determination of a pattern match between exhibits. Amassing knowledge of these marks—and developing the skill to adjust for their presence—is an important part of the experience of a firearms examiner.

Cataloging these nonfiring manufacturing marks, Tam (2001) suggests a rough typology based on their impact on the determination of a match between evidence: (1) marks that are not expected to cause a problem for identification (or exclusion); (2) marks that may cause problems but can be compensated for with some effort; and (3) marks that are problematic for comparison and difficult to analyze.

In the first class, there are marks that would easily be overwritten by firing-related marks, as in extremely fine pre-existing parallel marks on the primer surface. Other marks—being relatively simple and known in advance—are not problematic because the examiner can mentally compensate for their presence (e.g., a V-shaped or other stamped mark on the primer surface used to indicate certain brands). Other marks that may fall into this category are those that are on areas of the cartridge not typically considered for ballistic imaging or routine analysis, such as unique marks on the rim of the cartridge.

For the second class, manufacturing marks that may cause problems, Tam (2001) suggests that these features can be overcome by simple procedures. Marks in this class include thick striation-like parallel marks across the primer surface; these may obscure texture patterns in the breech face impression and may extend into the firing pin impression. Russian-made Wolf ammunition is well known for these marks, which have also been observed in other ammunition types. An IBIS image (using side light) of a fired round of Wolf ammunition is shown below; most of the visible horizontal parallel marks on the primer surface existed prior to firing.

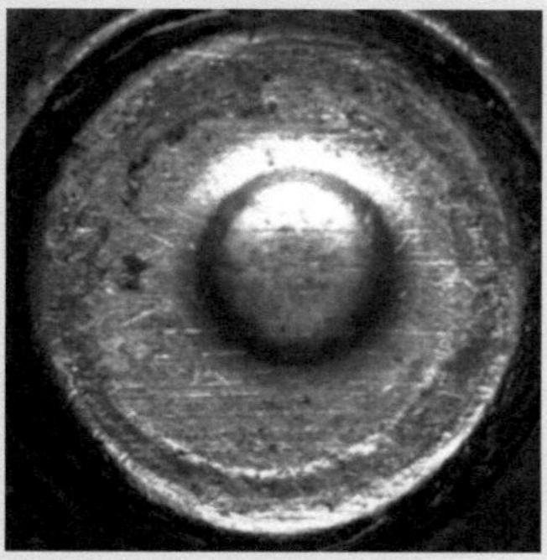

Side light IBIS image of fixed casing using Wolf ammunition; heavy horizontal lines are preexisting manufacturing marks.

continued

BOX 2-1 Continued

Reitz (1975:103) observed "matchable striations on unfired primers of [exhibits from particular lots of] Winchester, .38 special cartridges." These marks were attributed to a particular punch used during the primer seating process, which had not been produced to the same smoothness as is typically the norm. "These markings remained prevalent even after firing, which could be perilous to comparison examinations by unwary examiners." Similarly, Robinson (1996:164) observed Russian-made ammunition with primers that, before firing, "had parallel marks like one might find as a result of breechface impressions." Finding that "the marks continue around the curve of the primer into the sides which were not visible," he concluded that "the only way that marks could have gotten there was by the rollers in the brass mill where the sheets of brass were made."

The third class of marks, those that are problematic for comparison, include ammunition types with existing distinct parallel and cross marks on the primer surface, making it difficult to discern which textural features were created by firing. Murray (2004:314) reports on toolmarks on the primer surface of Fiocchi .25 Auto ammunition whose cause is unknown; the manufacturer suggested that they might be attributed to a rare, imperfect configuration of the feeder during the process in which the primer is seated in the empty shell. The marks were problematic because they were not consistently prominent across the whole primer surface. When, as in the Wolf ammunition toolmarks, the markings span the whole primer, an examiner can compensate for them because they can be traced from the face of the primer into the pit of the firing pin impression. Maruoka (1994a; see also Maruoka and Ball, 1995) had previously noted parallel marks on the primer surface of some Fiocchi ammunition, but those marks did span the entire surface. But these inconsistent marks offer no such traceability, so that "differentiating these marks from breech face marks would be very difficult, if not impossible" (Murray, 2004:314). Some ammunition may also bear random marks on the rim of the cartridge that could be mistaken for ejector marks.

3

Firearms Identification and the Use of Ballistics Evidence

This chapter provides a key context for the next part of the report by examining the nature of ballistics evidence itself and the ways it has been analyzed and used over the past century. Since the primary focus in this study is the ability of computer-based systems to discern unique characteristics in ballistics evidence on the basis of images of different sorts, it is useful to first consider how uniqueness and reproducibility of characteristic marks have been discerned through the particular media of the comparison microscope and the human eye.

We briefly describe the general nature of toolmarks as evidence (Section 3–A) and then outline the basic history and theory of firearms identification (3–B). Section 3–C summarizes the literature on the uniqueness, reproducibility, and permanence of marks as detected by traditional methodology. The circumstances of firing a weapon, the manufacture of firearms and ammunition, and measures taken (or not taken) by firearms users can all pose various complications to the identification and linking of ballistics evidence; we review some of these issues in Section 3–D. Section 3–E offers key commentary on the scope of the committee's work in the context of the material in this chapter. The final section (3–F) briefly describes the general role of imaging and photography in firearms identification, as a prelude to the next section of the report.

3–A TOOLMARKS AS EVIDENCE

Various branches of forensic science—dealing with the analysis of evidence as diverse as handwriting samples and soil or mineral samples—are increasingly compared with one of their sister branches: the analysis of deoxyribonucleic acid (DNA) markers and identification based on those markers. As we note in Section 1–C, the term "ballistic fingerprinting" has also come into common (albeit somewhat inaccurate) usage to describe some features of firearms identification, suggesting a comparison with fingerprint evidence.

Firearms toolmark evidence differs from DNA and fingerprint evidence due to their basic point of reference: the former links to a particular firearm while the latter two link to a particular person. Links between pieces of ballistics evidence can point to a common gun from which exhibits were fired, but not necessarily to the same person pulling the trigger. A potential match suggested by a national reference ballistic image database could suggest a link from a piece of crime scene evidence to an original firearm point of sale, but that link is at least doubly indirect: the link is only to the location of the transaction and not immediately to the firearm's purchaser, and subsequent identification of the purchaser does not necessarily mean that the purchaser still possesses the gun (or fired the shot in a crime). However, it is important to consider that—alone, absent any other evidence or knowledge of circumstances—even person-specific fingerprint and DNA evidence is necessarily one step removed and indirect. It is possible for fingerprint or DNA evidence to be present and retrievable at crime scenes without its source person having been the crime's perpetrator. Forensic evidence can be used—in combination with other investigative findings—to develop a theory of what transpired at the scene and who may have committed the crime, but the link to any specific person from the ballistics evidence alone is necessarily indirect.

Toolmark evidence and DNA evidence are markedly different in another crucial respect, which is the subjectivity inherent in the analysis. Firearms identification ultimately comes down to a subjective assessment—specifically, a subjective probability statement (although practitioners often render these as absolute statements). Firearms examiners observe concrete, objective phenomena, but—as Thornton and Peterson (2002:24–25) observe, "there is an incredible amount of difficulty attached to the development of a statistical basis for evidence evaluation" in forensic science fields like firearms examination:

> Behind every opinion rendered by a forensic scientist there is a statistical basis. We may not know what that basis is, and we may have no feasible means of developing an understanding of that basis, but it is futile to deny that one exists. . . . The most common and coherent theory of forensic identification is that where there is a high degree of variation among attributes (of toolmark striations, writing, friction ridges on skin, and so on), then where a "match" is observed the probability that the match is

> coincidental rather than reflecting a shared source will be very small. . . . Forensic individualization sciences that lack actual data, which is most of them, have no choice but to either intuitively estimate those underlying probabilities and calculate the coincidental match probability from those subjective probabilities, or simply to assume the conclusion of a miniscule probability of a coincidental match (and in fact they do the latter).

In the specific context of firearms and toolmark examination, derivation of an objective, statistical basis for rendering decisions is hampered by the fundamentally random nature of parts of the firing process. The exact same conditions—of ammunition, of wear and cleanliness of firearms parts, of burning of propellant particles and the resulting gas pressure, and so forth—do not necessarily apply for every shot from the same gun. Ultimately, as firearms identification is currently practiced, an examiner's assessment of the quality and quantity of resulting toolmarks and the decision of what does or does not constitute a match comes down to a subjective determination based on intuition and experience. By comparison, DNA analysis is practically unique among forensic science specialties as having a strong objective basis for determination and as being amenable to formal probability statements.

Thornton and Peterson (2002:Fig. 1) rank various forensic science subfields on a continuum of relative subjectivity. On the low end of that scale is DNA analysis, along with serology (blood type determination) and drug and narcotic identification. They identify firearms and toolmark identification as having relatively high subjectivity, on par with fiber identification. They identify blood spatter interpretation, voiceprint analysis, and bitemarks as a group of forensic science specialties just slightly more subjective than toolmark identification, and handwriting and hair identification as a cluster slightly more subjective yet.

3–B TRADITIONAL FIREARMS IDENTIFICATION

Smith (2004:130) succinctly summarized the basic task of a firearms examiner in making an identification between pieces of evidence:

> Before a microscopic comparison begins, a foundation is built by measuring and comparing available class characteristics, such as General Rifling Characteristics (GRCs). These objective criteria are used to narrow the pool of candidates for determining a common source. Once an available foundation has been established, a common source often can be determined by evaluating individual microscopic marks of value using pattern recognition.

In traditional firearms identification—part science and part art form, still carried out today using the same basic tools that gave rise to the field in the 1930s—the firearms examiner faces the formidable cognitive task of forming a mental pattern of identifying marks and features on bullet and cartridge case evidence. That pattern must then be matched to those from other exhibits.[1]

3–B.1 Individualization and Identification: Class, Subclass, and Individual Characteristics

The label "firearms identification" is another instance in which language can be a bit elusive. Although "the terms 'identification' and 'identity' are used constantly by practitioners" of criminalistics, or the forensic analysis of evidence, Kirk (1963:236) argued that the usage is an "unfortunate failure of nomenclature." Rather than identification (as that term is commonly understood), Kirk argues that "criminalistics is the science of individualization:"

> The criminalist does not attempt identification except as a prelude to his real function—that of individualizing. The real aim of all forensic science is to establish individuality, or to approach it as closely as the present state of the science allows. . . . What was actually done was not the identification of the fingerprint, but rather the individualization of a person as the one who left the fingerprint. . . . [Likewise,] if the firearms examiner said that the bullet was a Colt 45 A.C.P. but could not individualize the gun that fired it, his value would be relatively slight.

Thornton and Peterson (2002:8, 9) further differentiate between the two terms: "Individualization is the process of placing an object in a unit category which consists of a single unit. Individualization implies uniqueness; identification, strictly speaking, does not require it." They also note the frequent use in forensic science of "identification" when "individualization" is meant, but recognized that "it is a constraint imposed by our language"; relying on the term "individualize" would likely lead to public confusion. "It should be appreciated, however, that the process of identification means one thing to the forensic scientist, and another thing to the botanist or the zoologist." (See also Champod [2000:1077] on "individualization" versus "identification.")

The phrasing of "individualization" as the act of associating an object

[1]Further information on current practice in firearms identification and images connected with that work are available through resources at the Association of Firearm and Tool Mark Examiners (http://www.afte.org) and the Scientific Working Group for Firearms and Toolmarks (http://www.swggun.org). Additional information and images—and tools for simulating the use of the comparison microscope for comparing bullet and cartridge evidence—are accessible at http://www.firearmsid.com.

with a category that contains only one unit is a useful one in addressing the basic approach of firearms examination. Firearms examiners typically give testimony to the effect that *this particular gun*, and not any other gun in the world, was used to fire particular shots. Yet even in the profession's earliest days, Hatcher (1935:266) anticipated a common reply to this type of argument:

> The firearms witness may expect to be asked how he can be sure of his findings, in view of the fact that he can have examined only a few of the countless thousands of guns that exist. But how does [an eyewitness to the crime] that identified the prisoner know that some other person may not look exactly like him? He will say that he has seen enough people in his life to know that the rule is that all people look different, and that the chances are overwhelmingly against finding two people who look so much alike that they cannot be told apart.
>
> In precisely the same way, the firearms expert, who admittedly cannot have actually examined more than the tiniest fraction of a percent of all the guns in the world, can still have had enough experience to be well aware of what differences do occur, and to know that the chance of finding two bullets from different guns that are exactly alike in every detail of their surface markings is infinitesimally small. The same thing applies with equal force to the finger-print method of identification.

Subsequently, he posited this idea more succinctly: "It may be quite common for two or more prominent individual marks on bullets from two entirely different guns to match exactly, but the chance that there will be a correspondence of a great many of the individual characteristic marks on two bullets that came from different guns is so remote as to amount to a practical impossibility" (Hatcher, 1935:288).

The basic approach to identification in forensic science developed into the concept of *class characteristics* and *individual characteristics*. Thornton and Peterson (2002:5–6) define these concepts:

> Class characteristics are general characteristics that separate a group of objects from a universe of diverse objects. In a comparison process, class characteristics serve the very useful purpose of screening a large number of items by eliminating from consideration those items that do not share the characteristics common to all the members of that group. Class characteristics do not, and cannot, establish uniqueness. Individual characteristics, on the other hand, are those exceptional characteristics that may establish the uniqueness of an object. It should be recognized that an individual characteristic, taken in isolation, might not in itself be unique. The uniqueness of an object may be established by an ensemble of individual characteristics. A scratch on the surface of a bullet, for example, is not a unique event; it is the arrangement of the scratches on the bullet that mark it as unique.

In the context of examining bullet and cartridge case evidence, such parameters as caliber and the number of lands and grooves are class characteristics that can be used to screen or filter out possible comparisons that could not possibly have been fired from the same gun. Other class characteristics include firing pin shape (for instance, the distinctive rectangular firing pin impressions left by Glock firearms[2]) or pronounced "drag marks" that can be caused by firing pins as the cartridge case goes through the ejection process. Individual characteristics—the fine striations on a bullet's surface or peculiar microscopic textures in the firing pin impression, for instance—allow for the set of possible guns from which an exhibit could have been fired to be narrowed.

However, a binary split between class and individual characteristics proved too limited to describe the full range of phenomena observed by experienced examiners. In 1985, the Association of Firearm and Tool Mark Examiners (AFTE) convened a committee to develop a consensus document on a theory of toolmark identification and a range of basic conclusions that could be reached from comparison of toolmark evidence. The result, produced in 1989 and unanimously approved by the organization's membership, is reproduced in Box 3-1. Importantly, the 1989 standard also added a new term to the firearms identification lexicon: *subclass characteristics*, defined as follows (Moran, 2002:228):

> Discernable surface features of an object, which are more restrictive than "class characteristics" in that they are
>
> - Produced incidental to manufacture
> - Significant in that they relate to a small group source (a subset of the class to which they belong)
> - Can arise from a source which changes over time
>
> Caution should be exercised in distinguishing subclass characteristics from individual characteristics.

As a middle ground between class and individual characteristics, subclass characteristics covered marks or features that—arising from specific manufacturing techniques, or flaws in said techniques—could induce similar marks on pieces of evidence even though they originated from different

[2]Rectangular firing pin marks were a telltale sign of Glock pistols "prior to the introduction of Smith & Wesson's Sigma Series, Model SW40F, semi-automatic pistol," the design of which is very similar to Glock standards. Nichols (1995:133, 134), in documenting the similarity between this firearm's marks and the known Glock characteristics, notes that the two highly similar gun types can be distinguished by ejector and extractor marks, as well as a characteristic "dimple on the [casing] head above the firing pin drag" on Glock rounds.

BOX 3-1
Association of Firearm and Tool Mark Examiners (AFTE) Theory of Identification and Range of Conclusions

Theory of Identification as It Relates to Toolmarks

A. The theory of identification as it pertains to the comparison of toolmarks enables opinions of common origin to be made when the unique surface contours of two toolmarks are in "sufficient agreement."

B. This "sufficient agreement" is related to the significant duplication of random toolmarks as evidenced by the correspondence of a pattern or combination of patterns of surface contours. Significance is determined by the comparative examination of two or more sets of surface contour patterns comprised of individual peaks, ridges, and furrows. Specifically, the relative height or depth, width, curvature, and spatial relationship of the individual peaks, ridges, and furrows within one set of surface contours are defined as compared to the corresponding features in the second set of surface contours. Agreement is significant when it exceeds the best agreement demonstrated between toolmarks known to have been produced by different tools and is consistent with the agreement demonstrated by toolmarks known to have been produced by the same tool. The statement that "sufficient agreement" exists between two toolmarks means that the agreement is of a quantity and quality that the likelihood another tool could have made the mark is so remote as to be considered a practical impossibility.

C. Currently, the interpretation of individualization/identification is subjective in nature, founded on scientific principles and based on the examiner's training and experience.

Range of Conclusions Possible When Comparing Toolmarks

The examiner is encouraged to report the objective observations that support the findings of toolmark examinations. The examiner should be conservative when reporting the significance of these observations.

The following represents a spectrum of statements:

A. IDENTIFICATION: Agreement of a combination of individual characteristics and all discernible class characteristics where the extent of agreement exceeds that which can occur in the comparison of toolmarks made by different tools and is consistent with the agreement demonstrated by toolmarks known to have been produced by the same tool.

B. INCONCLUSIVE:

a. Some agreement of individual characteristics and all discernible class characteristics, but insufficient for an identification.

continued

BOX 3-1 Continued

b. Agreement of all discernible class characteristics without agreement or disagreement of individual characteristics due to an absence, insufficiency, or lack of reproducibility.
c. Agreement of all discernible class characteristics and disagreement of individual characteristics, but insufficient for an elimination.

C. ELIMINATION: Significant disagreement of discernible class characteristics and/or individual characteristics.

D. UNSUITABLE: Unsuitable for comparison.

SOURCES: Excerpted from AFTE Criteria for Identification Committee (1992) and Grzybowski et al. (2003).

sources. Two examples of carryover of subclass characteristics are described in Box 3-2.

The AFTE theory of identification is rooted in the recognition that "the interpretation of individualization/identification is subjective in nature." However, it melds that recognition with more objective, quasi-quantitative benchmarks—"sufficient agreement," "significance," "likelihood . . . so remote," and agreement in both "quantity and quality"—but no specific empirical definition is given for these terms. Importantly, the AFTE theory does set up two cognitive thresholds that must be crossed in order to arrive at the conclusion that two exhibits share the same source, to the exclusion of all others. In describing the comparison of fingerprints, Stoney (1991; quoted in Moran, 2002:233) wrote of the basic cognitive process:

> When more and more corresponding features are found between two patterns, scientists and lay person alike become subjectively certain that the patterns could not possibly be duplicated by chance. What has happened here is somewhat analogous to a leap of faith.[3] It is a jump, an "extrapolation," based on the observation of highly variable traits among a few characteristics, and then considering the case of many characteristics. Duplication is inconceivable to the rational mind and we conclude that there is absolute identity.

[3]The "leap of faith" involved in extrapolating to all possible sources in the world was echoed, in specific reference to firearms identification by Rowe (1991). Understandably, some firearms examiners have objected to some overtones of the "leap of faith" phrasing; for instance, Miller and McLean (1998:17–18) "respond [to the phrasing] by stating that the published data which does exist, certainly presents enough statistical data to indicate more substance to the identification theory than a 'leap of faith.'"

BOX 3-2
Examples of Subclass Carryover

- Lomoro (1974:18) described test firings from F.I.E. Titanic revolvers, in a particular serial number range (but later shown to include some of a different make from the others). These firings produced seemingly similar striation patterns on fired bullets that could be naively matched to each other even though they had been fired from different weapons. "This pronounced stria [pattern] was only present on the lands of the bullets and very little if any matching stria was found on the grooves of the bullets. Examination of the bore revealed that either a worn or a very poor rifling tool was used during manufacturing," causing the similarity be imparted within a batch of separate barrels.
- Matty and Johnson (1984) observed that the particular tooling used on some Smith & Wesson firing pins results in a pattern of concentric rings that is repeatable in consecutively tooled pins. This pattern appears in the firing pin impression, meaning that examiners need to downweight the ring patterns and focus on other individual features to make correct matches on the firing pin impression.

He continues that this "leap" occurs—in fingerprinting, as in other branches of forensic science, "without any statistical foundation."

In a sense, the AFTE theory of identification requires two extrapolations: first, that marks are sufficiently consistent with true matches (produced by the same tool) to have come from the same source, and, second, that the quality and similarity of corresponding features exceed the best known apparent agreement between true nonmatches (produced by different tools). It follows that both of these extrapolations—but particularly the latter—require considerable experience in comparing exhibits and training in recognizing significant features.[4]

3–B.2 Historical Evolution

Some of the major advances in the field of traditional firearms identification are described in Box 3-3. Calvin H. Goddard, a founder of the Bureau of Forensic Ballistics in the New York City Police Department, is typically credited as the "father" of forensic ballistics in the United States;

[4]Biasotti and Murdock (2002:219–220) advocated the addition of the known nonmatch criterion, beginning with their conclusion in 1984 that "existing research was insufficient to validate the quantitative objective criteria necessary to conclude that a working surface is unique." The known nonmatch criterion "added a quantitative dimension" to the mix.

BOX 3-3
Highlights in the History of Traditional Firearms Identification

- **1900:** The *Buffalo Medical Journal* published "The Missile and the Weapon" by Albert L. Hall, commenting on his observations that firearms of different mark impart different striated marks and impressions on fired bullets.
- **1907:** Cartridge case evidence was examined as part of the investigation of the 1906 Brownsville, Texas, riots in which black soldiers allegedly fired upon a white crowd in retaliation against racial slurs. Thirty-nine cartridges were recovered; all but six were matched to four rifles, based on examination of enlarged photographs of firing pin impressions. [Examiners concluded that no identifications could be made on the basis of recovered bullet evidence.]
- **1915:** Charlie Stielow, an illiterate farmer in New York state, was convicted and sentenced to death for killing his employer and the employer's housekeeper, the latter of whom was found dead on the doorstep of Stielow's nearby home. Stielow's conviction was due in part to testimony by an examiner who claimed to find nine abnormal scratches on the recovered bullets that corresponded to particular defects in the alleged murder weapon. However, a more careful subsequent analysis of the evidence by Charles Waite concluded that Stielow's revolver could not have been the murder weapon; Stielow was pardoned and released from prison.
- **1925:** Philip Gravelle was credited with the development of the comparison microscope for side-by-side comparison of ballistics evidence in Calvin Goddard's article "Forensic Ballistics" in *Army Ordinance*. Goddard used the technique in the article, and the comparison microscope technique grew in popularity after the *Saturday Evening Post*'s two-part "Finger-printing Bullets" article in 1926 profiled New York City's Bureau of Forensic Ballistics, which Goddard, Gravelle, and Waite helped found.
- **1929:** On February 14, six members of George "Bugs" Moran's North Side gang (and one acquaintance) were brutally killed in a Chicago warehouse by six men impersonating police officers, believed to be operatives of rival Al Capone's South Side gang, in what quickly became known as the "St. Valentine's Day Massacre." As part of the investigation, Goddard prepared a detailed examination of recovered bullet and cartridge case evidence, connecting them to two Thompson submachine guns and a 12-gauge shotgun. Goddard—considered the father of modern firearms examination—subsequently left New York City to establish the Scientific Crime Detection Laboratory of Chicago, affiliated with Northwestern University.
- **1934–1935:** First editions of two seminal texts on firearms examination were published: Gerald Burrard's *The Identification of Firearms and Forensic Ballistics* and Julian Hatcher's *Textbook of Firearms Investigation, Identification and Evidence.*
- **1958:** John Davis' *An Introduction to Tool Marks, Firearms and the Striagraph* argued for the use of the striagraph, an early tool for direct measurement of the surface contours of ballistics evidence. Though the striagraph never advanced beyond the research stage, it was a precursor to the use of imaging and profilometry techniques for firearms identification.

BOX 3-3 Continued

- **1962:** J. Howard Matthews, a retired chemistry professor from the University of Wisconsin who became interested in forensic science after being called in to assist on a bombing case, published the two-volume *Firearms Identification*.
- **1969:** At a 35-member conference hosted by the Crime Laboratory of the Chicago Police Department, firearms identification practitioners form the Association of Firearm and Tool Mark Examiners (AFTE). The new association's newsletter developed into the *AFTE Journal* in 1973 and continues as a quarterly, peer-reviewed publication; the international association continues to hold an annual Training Seminar.

SOURCES: Information from Hamby and Thorpe (1999), Hatcher (1935), and Goddard (1999).

the text by Hatcher (1935) is generally considered the text on which the modern field of firearms and toolmark examination is based (Nichols, 2003).

The modern field of firearms identification owes much to the development of the comparison bridge, a system of mirrors or prisms that permits the views from two separate microscopic lenses to appear side by side in the same field of view. The device equipped with this optical bridge, called the comparison microscope, was not designed for analysis of bullet or cartridge case evidence, nor was it first used in such forensic applications (see, e.g., Thornton, 1978; Goddard, 1980). Even early advocates of forensic firearms analysis cautioned against making too much of the technology at hand, noting that the comparison microscope, on its own, has limitations. Foreshadowing some contemporary claims about the capability of ballistic imaging systems, Burrard (1962:131–132) lamented:

> The most fantastic claims have been put forward for, and the most ridiculous descriptions of, [the comparison microscope] which are enough to suggest that it has magical properties, and that it automatically, and wholly of its own accord, rings a bell or utters some similar warning, when the two cartridge cases under examination exhibit the same [individual markings]. Unhappily there is no foundation for this comforting belief. In the hands of a trained microscopist the comparison microscope can be of great value in determining the identity of fired bullets; but for cartridge cases I have come to the conclusion that a high-class single instrument is preferable. . . . And even for fired bullets the comparison microscope offers

> difficulties in illumination which are never encountered when using a single instrument, for the illumination of opaque objects such as the surfaces of fired cartridge cases and bullets is a far more difficult problem than the illumination of transparencies, fibres or spermatozoa.

Nevertheless, the application of the comparison microscope to firearms evidence analysis led the field of firearms identification to flourish and reinforced the analysis of ballistics evidence as a critical part of criminal investigations.

In recent years, as the increased workload of state and local law enforcement forensic laboratories has created a shortage of firearms examiners, placing increased attention on the training and recruitment of examiners. Noting that "there is no college degree a firearms examiner can pursue to reach true proficiency in firearms identification," and that the core of training activities consists of "extended on-the-job training," the Bureau of Alcohol, Tobacco, and Firearms (ATF) established a National Firearm Examiner Academy in 1998. The original plan for the academy was for a "16-week intensive program . . . to train candidates to become apprentice firearms examiners" and a pairing of apprentice examiners with participating law enforcement agencies (Ethridge, 1998:703, 704).

3–B.3 Pattern Matching and "Line Counting"

Traditional firearms examination is, fundamentally, one whose central task is pattern matching.[5] Moran (2002:227) summarizes the approach:

> Toolmark examiners (and examiners in other comparative evidence disciplines) in the United States approach the interpretation of evidence by employing a combination of their cognitive ability to recognize agreement between patterns that in their "minds eye" constitutes an identification or "match" between a questioned pattern or toolmark and toolmark patterns produced from known tools. . . . This traditional "pattern match" approach (for a lack of a better term) relies on art (the cognitive ability to recognize agreement of pattern) and science (supporting the uniqueness of tool surfaces as a means to establishing an identification between a questioned toolmark and the tool that produced it).

Hayes et al. (2004:139–140) add: "In traditional pattern recognition methodology, the details used to determine a match include the height,

[5]Technically, "pattern matching" in forensic science may further be differentiated into two categories, pattern fit and pattern transfer. Pattern fit is akin to a jigsaw puzzle, determining whether pieces or fragments of some object were once part of a whole object. Firearms toolmarks follow the pattern transfer form, in which patterns are created by the interaction of more than one object (Biasotti and Murdock, 2002:208).

weight, depth, spatial relationship and consecutiveness of the class and individual characteristics. When viewed as a whole, these components become significant."

Pattern matching—aided by the dual, side-by-side inspection made possible by the comparison microscope—has been the historical norm since the field of firearms identification emerged into prominence in the 1930s. As the AFTE theory of identification indicates (Box 3-1), the standard of identification is "currently . . . subjective in nature." In the late 1950s, two important developments were made in order to provide the field with a more objective and quantitative basis. The first, mentioned in Box 3-2, was the development by Davis (1958) of an instrument he called a "striagraph" to quantitatively measure the microscopic markings left by firearms on bullets and cartridge cases. The striagraph made traces of the contours of a bullet's surface using a stylus to record depth. Though the instrument was never developed commercially, it marked the first attempt to develop an explicit "signature" from pieces of evidence for comparison with each other, foreshadowing the signatures that are the basis of today's ballistic imaging systems.

A more significant development was a study by Biasotti (1959) that formed the foundation for what is now known as the consecutive matching striations (CMS) approach to identification. Nichols (2003:299) relates that this approach has developed and emerged to the point that a "fray appears to have developed within the discipline," pitting "the old school tradition of 'pattern matching' versus the new school of 'line counters.'"

Biasotti's (1959:34) work was motivated by what he described as "an almost complete lack of factual and statistical data pertaining to the problem of establishing identity in the field of firearms identification." Accordingly, he sought to "conduct a direct statistical count of the elements which actually form the basis of the identity; e.g., the individual characteristics;" he did so using a set of test firings from .38 Special Smith & Wesson revolvers. For each pair of bullets, Biasotti (1959:37–44) conducted a complete inventory of all striations; from this inventory, he noted that same-gun bullets yielded a greater number of corresponding marks than different-gun bullets, but he cautioned that a simple percentage of matching lines is an inappropriate measure of similarity:

> The average percent match for bullets fired from the same gun ranged from 36 to 38% for lead bullets and from 21 to 24% for metal-cased bullets. For bullets fired from different guns . . . 15 to 20% matching lines per land or groove mark was frequently found. Relatively speaking, this data indicates that even under such ideal conditions [as the experimental test firings] the average percent match for bullets from the same gun is low and the percent match for bullets from different guns is high, which

> should illustrate the limited value of percent matching lines without regard to consecutiveness. As frequently happens in actual practice, when there is a preponderance of non-matching lines and only a few land and groove marks available for comparison, the total number of matching lines is often no higher or even less than the number which could occur. [These results, along with those of Burd and Kirk (1942) on toolmarks generally] should dispel the erroneous conception of the "perfect match" which is actually only a theoretical possibility and a practical impossibility.

What Biasotti (1959:44) found compelling, though, was evidence of runs or series of consecutive matching striations:

> It should be obvious that consecutiveness; viz., the compounding of a number of individual characteristics, is the very basis of all identities. When individual characteristics are grouped or related by the criteria of consecutiveness, which is a simplified means of expressing a correspondence of contour, the chance occurrence of even a very small number of consecutive matching lines (e.g., more than 3 or 4) is for all practical purposes impossible except as the result of a common agent, e.g., same gun.

Based on subsequent research, Biasotti and Murdock (2002:224–225) formalized a set of "conservative quantitative criteria for identification:"[6]

> (1) In three-dimensional toolmarks when at least two different groups of at least three consecutive matching striae appear in the same relative position, or one group of six consecutive matching striae are in agreement in an evidence toolmark compared to a test toolmark.
>
> (2) In two-dimensional toolmarks when at least two groups of at least five consecutive matching striae appear in the same relative position, or one group of eight consecutive matching striae are in agreement in an evidence toolmark compared to a test toolmark.
>
> For these criteria to apply, however, the possibility of subclass characteristics must be ruled out.

These criteria differentiate between three-dimensional marks, which Biasotti and Murdock (2002:208) characterize as contour or impression, and two-dimensional marks, described as surface or imprint. That is, two-dimensional marks are "striae lacking depth and therefore appearing two-dimensional" (Biasotti and Murdock, 2002:224), giving rise to the "line

[6]The Biasotti and Murdock criteria were first published in 1997; no changes were made in 2002, though it was noted that in the intervening years "no known non-matching (two- or three-dimensional) toolmarks were found in [any follow-up] studies which exhibited agreement" of the conservative criteria (Biasotti and Murdock, 2002:225).

counting" appellation that has been applied to CMS methods. Recently, as surface metrology techniques have been applied to studying bullets—particularly the development of a three-dimensional-analysis system for bullets by the manufacturer of the Integrated Ballistics Identification System (IBIS) currently in use—this distinction has come under some question (see, e.g., Thompson, 2006). Striated toolmarks necessarily have depth, however slight; the availability of detailed measures of surface contours invites the question of significance levels in determining whether corresponding striations match. (We revisit the two-dimensional and three-dimensional distinction in Chapter 7.)

3–B.4 Legal Context of Firearms Examination

In order to testify to their findings at trial, firearms experts are subjected to qualifying questions in the *voir dire* process. If they are favorably ruled on by the trial court judge, the expert must testify to matches (or nonmatches) of ballistics evidence based on what is ultimately a subjective assessment. Molnar (1970:39) described the pressures that come with that task:

> [Serious criminal] cases very often never get off the ground until the firearms examiner has made a finding, which incidentally has to be correct, at which time the police file charges and the wheels of justice begin to grind. There is no second or reanalysis to be made, no excuses, no bad or spoiled reagents. The examiner's area of conclusions is more often either black or white, hardly ever the grey area enjoyed by other criminalists. Others may come along to say that he was wrong, or that they can't arrive at the same conclusion, but the firearms examiner has to be RIGHT and has to say so FIRST.

Consequently, firearms examiners may often express their findings in bold absolutes—matches made to the same gun, to the exclusion of all other firearms in the world—yet they tend to be conservative in reaching their opinions. If a firearms examiner is impeached through the *voir dire* process, his or her ability to testify in other cases can be severely affected; being associated with an error or misidentification can tarnish reputations. Thornton and Peterson (2002:21) argue that this belief—which they note "is not entirely without justification"—makes forensic science, in general, resistant to proficiency testing of examiners; "the potential exists that in court, counsel for the opposing side will in a self-serving fashion misconstrue, pervert and abuse a missed proficiency test." The AFTE range of conclusions (Box 3-1) envisions four possible outcomes when an examiner is asked to compare pieces of evidence. Regardless of which of these options the examiner deems fit after careful consideration, it is in keeping with the nature and weight of their testimony—and the adversarial nature of courtroom questioning—that their findings are expressed as unequivocal and unyielding.

An examiner's conviction in the findings about the interrelationship of evidence, and the basic admissibility of that evidence in court, depends critically on the careful maintenance of the "chain of evidence." This begins at the crime scene itself, where the site must be preserved until an evidence technician can collect it in a safe and timely manner, maintaining its integrity. Collected evidence must not be allowed to be contaminated, lest its credibility be undermined; physical custody must be maintained and monitored throughout the laboratory examination, and processing steps should not be destructive or injurious to the physical evidence. Any break or delay in the sequence of events, or any miscommunication, may lead investigations to stall, crimes to remain unsolved, and prosecutions to lose key support.

Like other branches of forensic science, firearms and toolmark identification has had to grapple with the question of how well the field fits emerging standards for scientific evidence in legal proceedings. In 1923, *Frye v. United States* (293 F. 1013, DC Cir) observed that:

> Just when a scientific principle or discovery crosses the line between the experimental and demonstrable stages is difficult to define. Somewhere in this twilight zone the evidential force of the principle must be recognized, and while courts will go a long way in admitting expert testimony deduced from a well-recognized scientific principle or discovery, the thing from which the deduction is made must be sufficiently established to have gained general acceptance in the particular field in which it belongs.

The ruling established a "general acceptance in the field" standard that became the basis for subsequent decisions.

In 1993, the U.S. Supreme Court's ruling in *Daubert v. Merrell Dow Pharmaceuticals* (509 U.S. 579) concluded that the legislatively enacted Federal Rules of Evidence superseded the *Frye* "general acceptance" standard. Justice Harry Blackmun's majority opinion tasked judges with a gatekeeper role, "assess[ing] whether the reasoning or methodology underlying the testimony is scientifically valid [and] whether that reasoning or methodology properly can be applied to the facts in issue." More concisely, the task is the assessment of reliability and relevance. Though the opinion expressly noted that "we do not presume to set out a definitive checklist or test," it also identified five criteria for reliability that have since become known as the *Daubert* standard: (1) "whether the theory or technique has been subjected to peer review and publication," (2) "whether it can be (and has been) tested" or falsified, (3) the techniques "known or potential rate of error," (4) "the existence and maintenance of standards controlling the technique's operation," and (5) the *Frye* criterion of "general acceptance" by the scientific community. Due to its grounding in the Federal Rules of Evidence, the *Daubert* standard is not binding on individual states, about half of which continue to use the *Frye* test.

Branches of forensic science like toolmark evaluation are increasingly concerned with how their fields fit either standard, cognizant that the precedent of a single ruling of inadmissibility could jeopardize future proceedings. That question has grown ever greater with the Florida Supreme Court's December 2001 ruling in *Ramirez v. State of Florida* (No. SC92975). In that ruling, the court reversed the 1983 murder conviction (and death sentence) of Joseph Ramirez by excluding testimony on the toolmarks left by the knife on human cartilage. The ruling summarized the critical issue under review:

> Ramirez asserts that the trial court erred in allowing the State's experts to testify that the knife found in Ramirez's car was the murder weapon to the exclusion of every other knife in the world. He contends that [the toolmark examiner's] identification method is novel and untested and the State has failed to present sufficient proof of its reliability.

Moran and Murdock (2002:215) note that the court "reviewed testimony of five AFTE members who provided traditional justification for the identification of striated toolmarks throughout these proceedings based only on qualitative criteria established through 'training and experience.' The court found that these explanations did not satisfy Florida's rigorous [*Frye*] standards for *reliability*."[7] The court's ruling concluded that "the record does not show that [the examiner's] methodology—and particularly his claim of infallibility—has ever been formally tested or otherwise verified, [nor has it] ever been subjected to meaningful peer review or publication." They concluded further that that the examiner's claim of a match lacked documentation or substantiation and that "the error rate for [the examiner's] method has [never] been quantified."

For reviews in the firearms examiner literature on the applicability of *Daubert* criteria in the field, see Grzybowski and Murdock (1998) and Rosenberry (2003), among others. More recently, Schwartz (2005) extends what was originally an *amicus curiae* brief into a fuller argument as to why firearms and toolmark evidence should be ruled inadmissible in legal proceedings, to which Nichols (2005) offers a response.

---

[7]Florida is one of the states in which the courts have elected to continue applying the *Frye* "general acceptance" criterion rather than the *Daubert* standard. However, as the quotations from the ruling suggest, the *Ramirez* court considered elements of the *Daubert* criteria.

3–C UNIQUENESS, REPRODUCIBILITY, AND PERMANENCE OF MARKINGS IN TRADITIONAL FIREARMS IDENTIFICATION

In recent years, several review articles have summarized the findings of individual studies on the basic principles of firearms and toolmarks—the uniqueness, reproducibility, and permanence of individual characteristics, as seen by trained examiners using comparison microscopy. Most of these studies are limited in scale and have been conducted by firearms examiners (and examiners in training) in state and local law enforcement laboratories as adjuncts to their regular casework. The review articles attempt to piece together major themes from decades of such studies, most having been published in the *AFTE Journal* but also in other forensic science publications. Nichols (1997, 2004) contributes a two-part narrative with the goal of characterizing the state of the field. Bonfanti and De Kinder (1999a, 1999b) review a broad array of experimental studies—on the influence of manufacturing techniques (e.g., consecutive tooling) and the endurance of marks over repeated firings, respectively—distilling the studies as entries in extensive summary tables. We draw from these review papers in this section and excerpt additional detail from individual studies, as appropriate.

3–C.1 Uniqueness of Markings

A fundamental assumption in firearms identification is that individual firearms vary microscopically in ways that leave unique markings on bullet and cartridge case evidence. Accordingly, the "gold standard" for demonstrating the uniqueness of toolmarks in ballistics evidence would be sets of firearms that are consecutively manufactured—that is, more than one gun where every constituent part is subjected to identical tooling and machining operations (e.g., minimizing the wear on cutting tools between different pieces). This is difficult to achieve in practice given the assembly-line nature of firearms manufacturing, where individual parts may be made in advance (and not necessarily at the same facility) and are drawn from bins prior to assembly. Due to the time and manufacturer cooperation needed to ensure consecutive manufacture, those studies that have been done—as summarized by Bonfanti and De Kinder (1999a)—deal with small numbers, typically less than 15.[8] It is also typically the case that only one part (or

---

[8]One entry in the tables in Bonfanti and De Kinder (1999a) stands out: amidst studies with small numbers of firearms with some level of consecutively manufactured parts, Grooß (1995) is reported as having examined 3,704 Walther P5 pistols. The entry is misleading in its placement in the tables—Grooß makes no claim of consecutive manufacturing or serial numbering—but the study is still interesting as a case study of a wide-scale search of evidence using conventional microscopy rather than being assisted by imaging methodology; see footnote 17 in this chapter.

very few) of the guns in these studies are consecutively manufactured—e.g., consecutively reamed barrels or machined breech faces.

Several of the studies documented by Bonfanti and De Kinder (1999a) deal with firearms that have sequential serial numbers. That is, the weapons effectively came off of the assembly line consecutively. Lutz (1970:24) reiterated that "mere serial number sequence has no significance [in assessing the similarity of firearms], because firearm manufacturers usually have assembly line procedures that join the various weapons parts, without regard to actual manufacturing sequence." Still, depending on the manufacturer and where in the process serial numbering occurs, guns that have similar serial numbers may have at least some components that were manufactured in close temporal proximity; hence, it remains popular as a weak proxy for consecutive manufacture.[9]

Bonfanti and De Kinder (1999b:Table 1) profile 27 separate studies of bullets from firearms with some indication of consecutive manufacture (or close serial numbering); these studies spanned a variety of calibers and barrel rifling techniques.[10] From their review, they conclude that "for all types of rifling no problem occurs concerning the identification of the individual firearm if certain criteria are followed." Some firearms cannot be identified correctly solely by examination of the bullets (e.g., Churchman, 1981; Lomoro, 1974; Matty, 1985), but Bonfanti and De Kinder (1999b:5) explain some of these results through their suggested criteria: "correspondence between fine striation lines in (the central part) of the land impressions must be sought," as striations on the edges of the land engraved areas or in the groove engraved areas "may display subclass characteristics" that could be confused with individual features. For instance, Lomoro's (1974:18) test firings from different but close serial-numbered F.I.E. Titanic revolvers were very similar in groove markings but more readily distinguishable by markings in the land areas. Among more recent efforts, Brundage's (1998) set of 10 consecutively rifled Ruger barrels is prominent because it was conducted as a blind study—that is, a test set of firings from the barrels, without indication of the circumstances of the underlying barrel manufacture, was given to various firearms examiners for comparison. More recently, a set of bullets fired through consecutively manufactured Hi-Point

[9]This concept arises in discussing experimental results in Chapter 8. In addition to being a weak proxy for consecutive manufacture, sequential serial numbers may also suggest large batch purchases of firearms, such as the deployment of new duty firearms among police officers. In our analyses of the New York CoBIS reference ballistic image database, we encounter runs of consecutively serial-numbered firearms with similar IBIS comparison scores.

[10]This count excludes the Grooß (1995) study (see footnote 8 in this chapter) and the Biasotti (1959) study profiled in Section 3–B.3, neither of which made explicit claims of consecutiveness. They are included in the Bonfanti and De Kinder (1999b:Table 1) table but have no entry in the "Particularity" column.

barrels (described in Beauchamp and Roberge, 2005), has become a similar proficiency test of sorts.

For markings on cartridge cases, Bonfanti and De Kinder (1999b: Table 3) summarize 13 studies with some indication of consecutive manufacture.[11] The conclusion that they derive from these studies is more nuanced than for bullets: "Depending on the firearm that was used, different results were used [and] in a number of cases a correct identification was difficult to perform." Among these problematic cases were the studies of Matty and Johnson (1984), Uchiyama (1986), and Lardizabal (1995), which we describe elsewhere in this chapter and in Chapter 2. Bonfanti and De Kinder found it hard to classify these problematic cases by manufacturing technique, but offered as "a probable solution to this problem" a common theme that recurred in several of the studies. Specifically, individual examiners noted remarkable similarities on some of the marks but found that they could make identifications using the full range of markings on the cartridge cases, not just the firing pin impression or breech face mark. Hence, Bonfanti and De Kinder (1999b:5) suggested making use of all applicable marks, including ejector and extractor marks, since "it is less likely that all these parts are manufactured consecutively and that they all bear subclass characteristics."

3–C.2 Reproducibility and Permanence of Markings

To be useful for identification, the characteristic marks left by firearms must not only be unique but reproducible—that is, the unique characteristics must be capable of being deposited over the multiple firings so that they can be found on recovered evidence and successfully compared with those on other items. This requirement is not the same as saying that every individual mark must be registered with equal clarity on every firing; as described in Chapter 2, the firing process depends on combustion processes and gas pressures that are inherently variable, and so will influence the exact conditions under which marks are imparted from shot to shot. But it is crucial to the theory of firearms identification that the unique marks of a firearm have a certain endurance (if not permanence) and do not change from shot to shot or change as the gun is subjected to increasing levels of wear.

Bonfanti and De Kinder (1999a) summarize 10 studies from the firearms identification literature that addressed the effect of wear or repeated use of a firearm on the markings it left on evidence; most of the studies con-

[11]Again, this excludes Grooß (1995), which is listed in the Bonfanti and De Kinder table, as well as a few other studies in which the firearms parts in question are described as being randomly selected from production runs.

centrated on the effect on the striations left on bullets, while four included consideration of the markings left on cartridge cases. The numbers of shots fired in these studies range from 20 to 5,000.

From the 10 studies, Bonfanti and De Kinder (1999a:319, 321) conclude that the major cartridge case markings are relatively less vulnerable to change: "no substantial change in characteristics left by the breech face of the weapon can be discerned" over repeated firings; firing pin impressions and extractor marks are subject to "slight variations," while "in one study the ejector marks were seen to vary more strongly." Bullets, by comparison, showed more dramatic effects due to wear; this is not greatly surprising given that a firearm's barrel is subject to the most fouling (deposition of firing residue) and the most metal-against-metal scraping (as the bullet travels out of the barrel) of the firearm's internal surfaces. "Changes consist of disappearing fine and coarse striation lines," with the fine striations being more variable over time than the coarser. The composition and design of the bullet makes a great difference; simple lead bullets may be unmatchable to a first shot after 50 firings while the identifying stria left on jacketed bullets have been observed to endure for 500 or 5,000 shots.

Most of these studies either compare the first to the last firings in sequence or focus on a sample of the firings: for instance, the Ogihara et al. (1989) study retained 69 bullet and cartridge case sets from the total of 5,000 firings, and their major conclusions concern the comparison between firings 1 and 5,000.[12] Likewise, Hamby (1974) retained bullets from firings 1, 101, 201, 301, 401, and 501 from a M16A1 rifle; these were compared with each other in sequence (e.g., 1 to 101 and 101 to 201), as well as comparing shot 1 to shot 501.[13]

More recently, Vinci et al. (2005) examined a set of exhibits consisting of every 100th round in a sequence of 2,500 firings of 230 grain FMJ Giulio Fiocchi Lecco ammunition through a .45 caliber HP (ADLER customized) semiautomatic Springfield Armory pistol. Batches of 100 firings were performed at separate times; "the pistol was disassembled, cleaned and oiled after each 100 round firing session in respect of findings previously reported that accumulated residue on the weapon can affect the [breech face] marks on cartridges" (Vinci et al., 2005:369, citing findings from Molnar, 1977; see Section 3–D.1). Vinci et al. (2005:371) concluded that "there was a slight observable modification in the quality of the marks" over the long firing, but that "the gun could still be identified" even in the late-stage

[12]Ogihara et al. (1989) retained every 10th shot from firings 1–100, every 50th shot from firings 150–1,000, and every 100th shot from firings 1,100–5,000.

[13]Hamby (1974) chose the particular rifle because it was known to generate high pressures during firing, "which should hasten the barrel wearing process." The specific gun had already been fired "approximately 40,000 times." The barrel was not cleaned at any point during the test firings.

exhibits. However, the breech face marks were "not useful for matching any of the 2500 cartridges to the weapon" because the presence and clarity of these marks were inconsistent. Firing pin impressions proved more useful although, "after round 70, the nose of the firing pin was beginning to lose its imperfections resulting in a small flattened circular area at the bottom of the marks. Although firing pin drag marks were not consistently produced throughout the 2500 round firing sequence, the last 200 rounds did contain sufficient stria to match the cartridges to the weapon." Meanwhile, the value of ejector marks to making identifications "was enhanced" over repeated firing; the size and depth of the ejector mark increased "after firing 600 rounds."

In comparison with these longevity studies, Uchiyama et al. (1988) completed a rarer study of actual shot-to-shot variability for a string of 100 firings. Specifically, they collected bullets and cartridge casings from each of the 100 test firings, divided between four different combinations of gun brand and caliber. Each mark—land areas on the bullets and breech face and firing pin marks on the cartridges—was examined separately by examiners to assess the quantity of unique, individualizing lines or features. Each mark was then assigned an identifiability score of 1, 2, or 3; 1 indicated few or no identifiable features and 3 indicated sufficient features to support an identification based on that mark alone. Each bullet and casing was then assigned a score corresponding to the maximum identifiability score of its constituent marks. The analysis stopped short of true shot-to-shot comparison of features, although this was done for some sequences of well-marked (identifiability score 3) bullets.

For centerfire cartridges, they observed an approximately 10–50–40 percent division across identifiability grades 1, 2, and 3, respectively. Breech face marks generally showed higher identifiability scores than firing pin marks, which Uchiyama et al. (1988:378) attribute to the greater surface area of the breech face marks; however, for firings from a .38 Special Smith & Wesson (for which "the surface of the breech face is rather smooth and the firing pin is large and has irregular markings"), firing pin marks outperformed breech face. Identifiability scores dropped markedly for rimfire cartridges, with only about 5 percent having score 3 and 35 percent score 1; none of the breech face markings for rimfire casings was judged to have identifiability level 3. For bullets, identifiability level 3 ranged from 20 to 60 percent across the different gun/caliber combinations, and Uchiyama et al. (1988) judged that none of the test-fired bullets fell into identifiability level 1.

Blackwell and Framan (1980:16) cite discussions with an examiner at the Los Angeles Police Department in suggesting a "reproducibility spectrum," a continuum of manufacturing standards and firearms user practices that can affect the reproducibility of individual marks. At one extreme are police officers, for whom a firearm is such a vital part of their equipment that they "[develop] pride and interest in maintaining it in superior working condition." However, this "constant attention to cleaning and polishing" serves to "completely obliterate many, if not all, of the original identifying imperfections in the bore." "Many officers mount their pistols in a drill press and actually wire-brush the bore to the point that individual features originally in the bore are removed, and new ones created." Military small arms represent the other end of the spectrum:

> These firearms, because of the nature of mass production, frequently retain their identifying characteristics for the life of the firearm. During manufacture, the bores are not carefully polished or lead lapped and the small blemishes that cause striations are retained virtually unchanged. Subsequent perfunctory or even diligent cleaning frequently does not obliterate them.

"The firearms that most frequently find their way into the firearms identification laboratory" fall in between these two extremes.

From the available studies of the reproducibility and endurance of firearms toolmarks, it is difficult to conclude that any of the markings are inherently more reliable than others. De Kinder (2002a:200) argued that "the breech face of the firearm seems to provide the most stable trace on the components of the fired round" and hence suggested that it might be the primary mark collected in a large-scale reference ballistic image database (RBID). However, he also observed that "important similarities were seen between marks left by the breech faces of subsequently manufactured firearms"—that is, the breech face may be prone to subclass carry-over effects—and so an RBID would likely have to include other marks like the firing pin. Likewise, Tulleners (2001:3-2) wrote that, "for automated imaging, the only areas used are the firing pin impressions, breech face marks, and ejector marks" because "these are the marks that are typically repeatable." However, "in most cases the firing pin may not leave sufficient detail for analysis and most examiners rely on the breech face marks" to make identifications (Tulleners, 2001:3-2).

3–D CHALLENGING SITUATIONS IN FIREARMS IDENTIFICATION

Over the course of years of analysis, forensic firearms examiners encounter numerous situations that complicate identification. These may be deliberate measures taken by the shooter—countermeasures to identification—but they may also be mechanical problems in firing. Smith (1971) cataloged 24 such situations, which he dubbed "jokers" in the field of firearms identification. He suggested that the top 10 such complications, "in the approximate order of frequency of occurrence," are:

- automatic pistol bullets fired from revolvers;
- pistol bullets fired from rifles by using adapters;
- pistol bullets fired from rifles after being handloaded into rifle cartridge cases;
- revolver-type bullets fired from automatic pistols;
- replacement of barrel of an automatic pistol with another;
- replacement of firing pin in automatic pistol;
- refiling of breech face of automatic pistol or revolver;
- refiling firing pin of automatic pistol or revolver;
- replacing revolver barrel (which is more difficult than with more modular semiautomatics); and
- relining a pistol or rifle barrel with a new rifled liner.

Other complications include "firing a bullet of one caliber through an arm chambered for a larger caliber" ("such a bullet will show sketchy and erratic rifling marks which will be of little help in establishing identification") and "firing a pistol or revolver cartridge through a smooth bored barrel" ("the bullet will obviously show no rifling marks").

In this section, we briefly review what has been discussed in the firearms identification literature about some of these challenging situations. It is not an exhaustive list but covers particular topics that are more germane to RBIDs containing images from new firearms.

3–D.1 Condition of Evidence: Damage, Corrosion, and Cleanliness

In forensic laboratories, firearms can be discharged into water tanks (or other nondestructive trap mechanisms) so that bullets may be recovered with no damage other than those left by the firing process; similarly, cartridge casings may be quickly and safely retrieved following controlled test firings. A basic, fundamental challenge of firearms identification is that crime scenes are not necessarily such controlled settings. The task of pattern matching between pieces of bullet or cartridge case evidence—considering which microscopically fine markings may be unique to the source firearm, filtering out other marks, and evaluating various possible alignments of the exhibits (including, for bullets, all possible rotations of the exhibit pairs)—is already a difficult one. But it can be made more difficult by the nonpristine nature of crime scene evidence. Bullets can strike wood, asphalt, human tissue and bone, or other substances and, consequently, can be seriously warped, deformed, or fragmented; they can be lodged such that even their recovery for analysis can cause damage. Likewise, cartridge casings expelled onto the ground may be crushed underfoot or exposed to the elements. The possible differences between pristine exhibits and crime-scene samples are a continuing challenge for conventional firearms identification and ballistic imaging techniques, particularly in the context of an RBID for which the basic point is the comparison of crime scene evidence with a pristine sample from a gun in brand-new condition. Because the basic theory underlying firearms identification is that fine microscopic imperfections on the surface of internal parts of a firearm impart those marks on bullets and cartridge cases fired in them, it also follows that abrasion and erosion of the firearm's internal parts can change the unique marks left on ballistics evidence. Gun users vary in the degree of care and maintenance they give to their firearms, from meticulous cleaning to neglect. Hence, guns generally—and the subset of guns used in crime—are subject to different levels of residue and dirt build-up and to different levels of corrosion. Corrosion "is the rusting or the eating away of the metal by some chemical action. This condition is usually due to firing ammunition loaded with corrosive primers and to improper care of a gun between the times it is used" (American Institute of Applied Science, 1982:81).

Fouling and barrel cleanliness are prominent concerns in the analysis of bullet striations, given the tendency for residue and metal scrapings to build up in the barrel. It might be expected to be a relatively minor concern for the markings on cartridge cases, but Molnar (1977:21) advised examiners that this is not necessarily the case. "An examination of the breech face is in order" in cases where "you are having trouble with a firearm that is not reproducing breech face marks on the primer or cartridge cases on your tests," he wrote. "On many occasions the fouling of previous shots have built up to such an extent that the accumulated crud obliterates the breech face mark configurations to such an extent that their impressions on the primers are affected and sometimes precluded. On small caliber guns with low chamber pressures, even a few unburned powder granules adhering to the breech face can cause amazing differences in registrations, even altering some characteristics." Tulleners (2001:3-2) makes a similar observation, noting that "dirt or lead build up on the breech face can reduce the detail of breech face impressions."

Hess and Moran (2006:112) observed that, "periodically, firearms examiners and [IBIS] technicians receive requests to examine firearms that have been oxidized (rusted) and/or corroded due to a variety of factors." This corrosion can be so pronounced as to make it difficult to operate and test fire the weapon. Moreover, "any test firing conducted while the firearm is in this condition risks permanent alteration of the weapon's signature on these working surfaces for purposes of IBIS entry and future comparison," and test-fired evidence from a corroded weapon may not match evidence already on file in databases. They conclude that, "given the backlog that most agencies are facing in this time of budget restraints, increasing caseloads, and understaffing in firearms units across the country, the probability that firearms received in corroded condition will not be test fired at all is likely," missing possible hits. Corrosion is also problematic because some means of dealing with it—including scrubbing with metal or other brushes—may also damage the weapon for the purposes of generating matchable marks.

Corrosion is a concern not only for the internal parts of firearms, but also for recovered ballistics evidence. Though it is certainly ideal to process and collect evidence from crime scenes rapidly, such is not always possible. Bullet and cartridge case evidence may be exposed to the elements for days, weeks, or months until they are found and recovered, and bullet evidence may be irretrievable from shooting victims because rapid extraction could be harmful to their health. See Larrison (2006) for a study of the rate of degradation of bullets and cartridges—monitored every 6 months over 2 years—in four different and demanding environmental conditions: soil, water, open air, and an animal carcass.

3–D.2 Countermeasures

Smith's (1971) listing of "jokers," which introduced this section, includes some deliberate countermeasures that might be taken by criminals—perhaps after firing a lethal shot—to try to mislead investigators. Aside from Smith's rough ordering of situations by frequency and the rough impressions formed by examiners over their years of experience, there are no firm and systematic data on the frequency with which criminals deliberately alter firearms parts (or attempt to obliterate serial numbers) in order to avoid detection.

Some countermeasures, like crude filing of the barrel, are relatively easy to perform (if not always effective).[14] As Smith (1971) articulates in fleshing out his list of problematic situations, some countermeasures are particularly rare because they are inherently more difficult to perform. The barrel of a revolver, for instance, is a more integrated part of the firearm assembly than the more modular barrel of a semiautomatic, so swapping out a revolver barrel requires special tools and considerable knowledge.

With expert knowledge, the range of countermeasures that might be taken is immense. For instance, Schecter et al. (1996:97) concluded that it was possible to replace the entire breech block of a SIG Sauer P226 9mm Luger pistol, so that "only the ejector will remain to give possible individual marks on the cartridge case base area from the 'original' weapon." However, the registration of "good ejector and chamber marks on weapons

[14]Of course, it is possible for quick measures to be very effective at changing toolmarks. At the committee's December 2004 meeting, firearms examiner Lucien Haag shared an evocative presentation entitled "'New' Bores and Breechfaces in 60 Seconds," which suggests two quick ways in which a knowledgeable user could rapidly alter the striations left by the barrel or the breech face markings left on cartridge casings.

of this quality can be poor to non-existent," and this technique would not be immediately obvious on inspection of the weapon. But the issue is how often people who use guns in crime would go to such lengths, akin to the proverbial question of why more criminals do not wear gloves while committing crimes (given the ease of leaving fingerprints).

Smith (1971:18) argued that replacing pistol barrels "may happen not infrequently;" he personally reported having seen two such cases in criminal cases.[15] He, however, "never personally encountered [a case of replacing a firing pin in an automatic pistol], and it is obvious that such replacement of other parts, (extractor and ejector), refiling of breech face exists, still the possibility of the replacement of this part alone must be kept in mind" (Smith, 1971:19). Refiling the breech face is problematic, but "much refiling would leave the breech surface bright & fresh in appearance"; for full concealment, "it would be much simpler to discard the arm entirely and replace it with another, rather than go to the effort" to make it appear that an arm with a refiled breech face had not been altered (Smith, 1971:19).

It should be noted that while some countermeasures may successfully alter the "signature" markings left on ballistics evidence, they also serve to create new sets of markings—and, in some instances, prominent signs of the alteration—that can be used to match to evidence from later cases. Konior (2006) describes a case in which three cartridge casings and a pistol were recovered in investigating a homicide. The evidence casings did not appear to match test firings from the firearm; the latter all showed much greater levels of flowback around the firing pin impression. Subsequent analysis determined that an attempt had been made to alter the firearm by drilling the entire length of the pistol's barrel; however, the person attempting the modification apparently inserted the drill bit into the firing pin aperture, widening the hole but also damaging the tip of the firing pin. The flowback and a new distinctive mark in the firing pin impression could be attributed to this attempted modification.

3–D.3 "Settle-In" Effect

From the standpoint of establishing an RBID, a phenomenon of extreme interest is what might be called a "settle-in" or "breaking-in" effect: the notion that it takes several firings for a firearm's unique, characteristic markings to stabilize. When the settle-in effect has been documented, it

---

[15] In this context, Smith (1971:18) notes that the interchangeability of barrels was made vivid "in the famous Sacco-Vanzetti case." Specifically, "the barrel of the fatal arm was, following a demonstration before the court by an expert for the defense, found present in one of the two other arms of the same type which had been introduced as exhibits, all three having been disassembled and reassembled in the course of the demonstration."

has been almost exclusively in the context of the striations left on bullets and not on markings left on cartridge cases. This—in addition to the time-intensive process of firing into a water tank or other nondestructive trap and retrieving individual bullets—is a major reason that the restriction of RBIDs to cartridge case entries is sensible.

Murdock (1981:90) analyzed 10 test-fired bullets from each of three new and consecutively rifled barrels. He found that, "in general, the comparison between the first, second, and third firing from any one barrel failed to result in an identification. Some good agreement was present, however. The third, fourth, and fifth test firings from any one barrel could, however, generally be identified as having been fired through the same barrel." From this, "it became obvious that each barrel needed to have a few bullets fired through it before it began marking in a reproducible, identifiable manner." Similar work by Hall (1983:43) using a set of consecutively reamed polygonal barrels noted "rapid change during the first few shots," so that firings 1 and 2 from the same barrel looked much different compared to each other than did firings 19 and 20. Hall found a "lack of identifications where bullets from any of the first five shots were compared to any others." Matty (1985:65) noted similar behavior but was not as precise in suggesting the number of firings after which individual characteristics were discernible; instead, he observed that "it was not possible to make a conclusive match between test bullets #1 and #2 [from the same barrel, but] bullets #9 and #10 . . . were very similar in appearance."

From these and other works, Bonfanti and De Kinder (1999a:5) concluded that "about five to nine shots" are needed "so that [barrels] transfer a signature to a bullet." They note that the studies of consecutively manufactured barrels that they summarize in their review meet this standard. However, at least one of those studies—work by Lutz (1970:25) using two new and consecutively manufactured .38 Special Smith & Wesson barrels—began with the barrels in a completely unfired state and downplays any settle-in effect. Indeed, Lutz described the completely unfired nature of the barrels as the key advantage of the study, as it "offer[s] the ultimate as far as similarities between two successive barrels. It is certain that the similar markings visible now would become less prominent after being subjected to normal firing, cleaning, and wear." Even though all the test firings Lutz examined were among the first 12 uses of the barrel, "sufficient matching individual striae were noted on the bullets to enable the examiners to easily identify the barrel of origin for each of the bullets. Similarities in class characteristics were noted; however, microscopic comparison of the bullets revealed that each barrel had caused different markings to such an extent that each land and groove impression on each of the bullets had a great number of individual identifying striae."

Though a prominent settle-in effect for the breech face or firing pin—

the prominent markings on cartridge cases—has not been documented, there may be structural or design features that may cause a similar effect. The Thompson (1996) investigation of highly similar marks resulting from different Lorcin L9 9mm pistols (see Section 2–D.1) included some firings from guns right off the manufacturing line, with no previous proof firing. It was noted that the "breech face impression . . . can change considerably shot-to-shot [in early firings] due to the paint wearing/chipping off."

3–E COMMENTARY

As detailed in Chapter 1, it is not the function of this committee to assess the general validity of firearms identification and toolmark examination nor their admissibility in court proceedings. The discussion in this chapter on the nature of toolmark evidence and the context in which it is applied, as well as an overview of existing research among firearms examiners on the uniqueness and reproducibility of toolmarks, is presented to frame the discussion in the rest of this report. For instance, understanding situations that may pose particular challenges for associating two images of evidence requires some knowledge of situations that are generally known to be complex in the field; likewise, recommendations for the setup and maintenance of any ballistic imaging system that would do harm to the maintenance of clear chain of custody—so important in the legal context of toolmark evidence—would be ill-advised. However, as we also note in Chapter 1, we understand that some readers may try to infer a position—a leaning, one way or the other—based on the preceding analysis.

Accordingly, we believe it important to make the committee's finding clear and unambiguous:

> **Finding: The validity of the fundamental assumptions of uniqueness and reproducibility of firearms-related toolmarks has not yet been fully demonstrated.**

There is one baseline level of credibility, however, that must be demonstrated lest any discussion of ballistic imaging be rendered moot—namely, that there is at least some "signal" that may be detected. In other words, the creation of toolmarks must not be so random and volatile that there is no reason to believe that any similar and matchable marks exist on two exhibits fired from the same gun. The existing research, and the field's general acceptance in legal proceedings for several decades, is more than adequate testimony to that baseline level. Beyond that level, we neither endorse nor oppose the fundamental assumptions. Our review in this chapter is not—and is not meant to be—a full weighing of evidence for or against the assumptions, but it is ample enough to suggest that they are not fully settled, mechanically or empirically.

Another point follows directly: *Additional general research on the uniqueness and reproducibility of firearms-related toolmarks would have to be done if the basic premises of firearms identification are to be put on a more solid scientific footing.* A designed program of experiments covering a full range of sources of variability is important to test the fundamental assumptions, as well as to better document phenomena like "settle-in" effects. In such a program, it could be useful to study the level of agreement of marks generated by the whole system of parts that make up a firearm, rather than treating each mark type in isolation. For example, in a large number of test firings, how comparable is the quality of breech face marking with firing pin impressions, and how do those compare with the clarity of striations etched on bullets? Fully assessing the assumptions underlying firearms identification would require careful attention to statistical experimental design issues, as well as intensive work on the underlying physics, engineering, and metallurgy of firearms, but is essential to the long-term viability of this type of forensic evidence.

A third point is important in reading this report—stopping short of commenting on whether firearms toolmark evidence should be admissible: *Conclusions drawn in firearms identification should not be made to imply the presence of a firm statistical basis when none has been demonstrated.* Specifically, as described in Section 3–B.4, examiners tend to cast their assessments in bold absolutes, commonly asserting that a match can be made "to the exclusion of all other firearms in the world." Such comments cloak an inherently subjective assessment of a match with an extreme probability statement that has no firm grounding and unrealistically implies an error rate of zero. Thornton and Peterson (2002:24–25) note the basic flaw in this reasoning:

> Since the basis of all forensic identification is probability theory, examiners can never really assert a conclusion of an "identification to the exclusion of all others in the world," but at best can only assert a very small (objective or subjective) probability of a coincidental match. . . . It is ironic that those areas of forensic science that have real underlying data offer more modest statements of individualization, while those limited to subjective or impressionistic data make the strongest statements, sometimes of absolute certainty.

As described in Box 3-4, recent court decisions in which admissibility of firearms toolmark evidence was in question have generally accepted that the field has validity but have refused to accept "exclusion of all other firearms" arguments. The committee agrees with the basic point: statements

BOX 3-4
Recent Court Decisions: "To the Exclusion of All Other Guns"

As part of a larger trial on racketeering, assault, and gun charges, Judge Nancy Gertner of the U.S. District Court for Massachusetts rejected a motion to exclude ballistics evidence but strictly limited the scope of the testimony (*United States v. Green*, 405 F.Supp. 2d 104; 2005 U.S. Dist. LEXIS 34273). Fourteen .380 caliber shell casings were recovered from two sites in September 2000, six of them at the site of a shooting; about a year later, a loaded .38 caliber pistol was found in the front yard of a residence. As part of the trial, prosecutors wanted to introduce testimony from a Boston Police Department sergeant that all of the casings came from the same gun, namely, the recovered pistol. At a preliminary hearing, the sergeant indicated that he could make this determination "to the exclusion of every other firearm in the world."

Gertner's opinion noted that the "exclusion of every other firearm in the world" claim was "needless to say, extraordinary, particularly given [the sergeant's] data and methods": the examiner "took no notes, recorded no measurements, made no photographs, and drew no diagrams." After reviewing toolmark issues in some detail, the court concluded:

> [The examiner in question] is a seasoned observer of firearms and toolmarks; he may be able to identify marks that a lay observer would not. But while I will allow [him] to testify as to his observations, I will not allow him to conclude that the match he found by dint of the specific methodology he used permits "the exclusion of all other guns" as the source of the shell casings.

Separate rulings in *United States v. Monteiro*—also from the U.S. District Court for the District of Massachusetts, and coming before and after the *Green* ruling—adopted similar stances on testimony "to the exclusion of all other firearms." Defendants in *Monteiro* challenged the specific examiner (a Massachusetts State Police sergeant) as not being qualified in firearms identification; challenged firearms identification as unreliable under *Daubert*; and asserted that—even if firearms identification were reliable—that the examiner did not apply the techniques properly. The defense also challenged the validity of any identification because the examiner replaced—"among other parts"—"the firing pin, recoil spring, barrel, and trigger lever (but, significantly, not the breech face)" of the gun in order to get it back into firing condition.

Prior to *Green*, Judge Patti Saris ruled on a motion to exclude ballistics evidence (2005 U.S. Dist. LEXIS 39062), allowing testimony in part but giving the government "two weeks to ensure that its proffered firearms testimony comported with the established standards in the field." As in *Green*, no notes or photographs were made on the identification: Saris ruled that "until the basis for the identification is described in such a way that the procedure performed by [the sergeant] is reproducible and verifiable, it is inadmissible under Rule 702." Saris further

continued

BOX 3-4 Continued

directed that the identification be subjected to independent review and verification in order to be admissible.

Judge Saris' subsequent ruling on the general challenge to firearms identification (407 F.Supp.2d 351, 2006) concluded that "the underlying scientific principle behind firearm identification—that firearms transfer unique toolmarks to spent cartridge cases—is valid under *Daubert*. However, the process of deciding that a cartridge case was fired by a particular gun is based primarily on a visual inspection of patterns of toolmarks, and is largely a subjective determination based on experience and expertise." The court ruled that the government must demonstrate basic standards for the qualification of the examiner. However, like Judge Gertner, Saris precluded—in any event—any testimony of a match to the exclusion of all other guns in the world. Saris noted that "examiners testified to the effect that they could be 100 percent sure of a match," a statement that could not be sustained. An examiner may "testify to a reasonable degree of ballistic certainty," but "an expert may not assert any degree of statistical certainty, 100 percent or otherwise, as to a match."

Most recently, in *United States v. Diaz* (2007 U.S. Dist LEXIS 13152), Judge William Alsup of the U.S. District Court for the Northern District of California accepted that:

> the theory of firearm identification . . . is reliable under *Daubert*. While there is some subjectivity involved, it is the subjective judgment of trained professionals with a keen practiced eye for discerning the extent of matching patterns. . . . The record, however, does not support the conclusion that identifications can be made to the exclusion of all other firearms in the world. Thus, the examiners who testify in this case may only testify that a match has been made to a 'reasonable degree of certainty in the ballistics field.

In defense of firearms identification, Alsup remarked:

> It is important to note that—at least according to this record—there has never been a single documented decision in the United States where an incorrect firearms identification was used to convict a defendant. This is not to say that examiners do not make mistakes. The record demonstrates that examiners make mistakes even on proficiency tests. But, in view of the thousands of criminal defendants who have had an incentive to challenge firearms examiners' conclusions, it is significant that defendants cite no false-positive identification used against a criminal defendant in any American jurisdiction.

on toolmark matches (including legal testimony) should be supported by the work that was done in the laboratory, by the notes and documentation made by examiners, and by proficiency testing or established error rates for individual examiners in the field and in that particular laboratory, but should not overreach to make extreme probability statements.

3–F ROLE OF IMAGING IN FIREARMS IDENTIFICATION

In the next several chapters, we explore the current state of ballistic imaging technology. As context for this discussion, we note that imaging and photography have a long and somewhat controversial history in traditional firearms identification.

Moran (2003) summarizes some of the historical debate over the use of comparison photographs, culling relevant quotations from source materials. Some of the pioneers of the field of firearms identification—Goddard, Burrard, and Hatcher—considered photography to be valuable, if not essential, Burrard going so far as to comment that "any evidence unsupported by photographs cannot be regarded as being anything more than an expression of opinion. Photographs are, accordingly, essential; and such as are deemed necessary must be taken through the microscope" (Moran, 2003:175). However, Hatcher sounded a note of concern: "There is a difference in the ability of the various experts to use the microscope and camera, so that in the hands of a very skilled operator they may show the correspondence or lack of correspondence very clearly, while in the hands of a poor or mediocre operator, they may show the same thing faintly, or may even fail to show them at all" (Moran, 2003:176). However, with the passage of time, the practice of using photographs to document identifications fell out of favor, so much so that a 1957 revision of Hatcher's 1935 text now stipulated that "photo micrographs are now rarely used," for a variety of reasons (Moran, 2003:177):

- Courts tended to accept examiners' testimony on identifications without the "visual proof," obviating the need to prepare the photographs.
- Preparation of the photographs took time, time that laboratories were unwilling to commit due to increased caseloads.
- Static views of an evidence match were deemed unsatisfactory, relative to the full range of panning and rotation possible during direct manipulation of the evidence.
- "These pictures were not understood by juries," and "a good deal of knowledge and experience are necessary to evaluate them."
- "Some men after years of working in Firearms Identification refuse to make a positive identification from pictures alone."

- Photographs depict striations and features that do not match as well as those that do, which could create doubt among jurors.

In subsequent decades, the use of photographs as part of documentation remained a matter of personal and agency tastes, with some favoring it and others opposing it: for example, Heard (1997:113) stated that "the use of comparison photomicrographs in a court of law to illustrate stria comparisons should be discouraged" (although he suggested that a video might be more informative). Ultimately, in 2005, the AFTE membership approved a "standardization of comparison documentation" stipulating that "photography is the preferred method of documentation" but noting that other forms of documentation (including "narrative descriptions") "may serve to satisfy the requirements of this standard." This standard, revised as of June 13, 2005, was promulgated in a 2006 issue of the *AFTE Journal* (Vol. 38, No. 1).

Prior to the use of automated ballistic imaging, law enforcement agencies such as the Los Angeles Police Department (LAPD) relied on cruder means—and a certain amount of luck—to make connections with evidence in their open case files. Quite literally, making those connections depended on reference to Polaroid photomicrographs, posted on a bulletin board or shared with colleagues, in order to jog memories and generate possibilities. As of 1994, the process used by the LAPD was to post Polaroid images on two walls in "a hallway that we pass through constantly. On one side are the 'unknowns,' like cartridge cases collected as evidence at a homicide scene. On the other side are 'knowns.' When we recovered a gun from a suspect or a crime scene, we test-fire it in the lab—that makes it a known. . . . When we get a new known, we compare it to all the unknowns. When we get a new unknown, we compare it to all the knowns and all the unknowns," and the pictures are added to the hallway for future reference (Maruoka, 1994b:214).[16] The next chapter begins to describe efforts to go beyond Polaroids in the hallway: to use computer imaging to make it possible to more readily draw connections with exhibits in other open cases.[17]

---

[16]The Maruoka article is, in fact, a reprint in the *AFTE Journal* of a profile written for the Polaroid Corporation's *Instant Evidence* newsletter for law enforcement officials, circulated in 1993. As such, it touts the specific Polaroid equipment and film used for the standard imaging.

[17]As an example of the way a large-scale search of exhibits is conducted using conventional methods, without imaging assistance, Grooß (1995:29, 30) describes a series of three murders in West Germany in 1984–1985. Cartridge cases from the second and third crimes were easily matched by examiners but the cases from the first crime bore only limited similarity in markings to the others. Still, the headstamp information on the casings from all three crimes, and the bullet evidence, strongly suggested that a member of the police might be the killer. So strong was this suspicion to investigators that all 7,862 Walther P5 duty pistols then in use by the police forces throughout the state of Baden-Württemberg were test fired and the cartridges

compared with the crime scene exhibits. "As the comparison work in this specific case [was done] using conventional microscopes," it "was very complicated and time-consuming"; up to 3 firearms examiners at a time worked continuously on the comparisons. Ultimately, test-fired casings from the 3,704th pistol in sequence matched the casings from the second and third murders; this led investigators to an officer in Stuttgart who was ultimately found dead in southern Italy, having also murdered his wife and sons. Grooß concluded that the experience was strong testament to "the individuality of marks on fired bullets and cartridge cases": that the German examiners were able to observe "marks . . . which left no doubt that they were identical to those observed on the evidence ammunition," against a backdrop of "approximately 4000 pistols of the same manufacturer, same model, approximately the same age and same degree of wear." Apparently, the comparisons with test-fired exhibits were halted with the positive result on the 3,704th pistol, even though the linkage to the casings from the first murder was unclear.

Even when the officer's pistol was recovered and test fired with a variety of ammunition brands, no casing could be generated that matched the evidence from the first murder. It was originally suspected that the pistol "got a new blue finish" (a refurbishing process that may affect the marks left by the gun) at a time between the first and second murder, which might explain the differences. However, "a more careful examination showed that the pistol had been blued in the period between the second and third murder" (why this did not impede the ability to match the second and third crimes is left unspecified). It was also speculated that the officer might have deliberately planted a different casing at the first crime scene to mislead detectives.

PART II

Current Ballistic Imaging and Databases

4

Current Ballistic Imaging Technology

"It has been common practice for firearms examiners to maintain an 'open-case file' of physical evidence from unsolved crimes, sorted by caliber," Thompson et al. (2002:8) note of the traditional approach to generating investigative leads through firearms identification. "When faced with a crime on which little evidence was available, the examiner would then go to the storage area for evidence from unsolved cases and choose some potentially similar cases for examination of the originals." This process can be extremely time consuming—not only the direct examination of evidence, but also the steps of retrieval, filing, and reporting. "Because of the time required for the manual comparison of evidence, the effectiveness of this method can be severely limited by the staffing and workload of an agency's examiners (which determines how much time examiners have to search the open-case file)."

In this chapter, we briefly review the background of imaging technology in firearms identification (Section 4–A), the basic structure of Integrated Ballistics Identification System (IBIS) equipment (4–B), and the manner in which the IBIS equipment is used to acquire images (4–C). Section 4–D discusses what is publicly known about IBIS procedures for scoring, ranking, and analysis, crucial to assessing the technical capability of this technical platform to "scale up" to meet the demands of a much larger database. Section 4–E reviews the major studies that have been conducted to date on IBIS performance, particularly with large-scale databases or datasets consisting of test fires from new weapons. Section 4–F presents basic assessments of the current technology (specific recommendations related to IBIS usage are in Chapter 6). An appendix to the chapter, Section 4–G, summarizes and elaborates on technical evaluation tests performed on IBIS by the state of California. Because it is important to consider IBIS and the National Integrated Ballistic Information Network (NIBIN) together, a summary and our conclusions on the evidence in this chapter are in Chapter 6, together with those from Chapter 5.

4–A BACKGROUND

Contemporary ballistic imaging technology is the latest step in a gradual move over several decades to use technology to make it easier to maintain and search open case files of ballistics evidence, including cases distant in time. During the 1970s, calls were made to develop automated index systems to assist examiners in search, as well as to explore new directions for the imaging of ballistics evidence. Biasotti (1970:12) made an early call for a computer-based open case file that would permit examiners to describe observed class characteristics "for all rifled weapons [and] unidentified bullets and cartridge cases" in a central repository. However, in this early vision, imaging was not considered; instead, characteristics were to be expressed using an alphanumeric string (e.g., FW105-100-1357-20-0102-001-001), coding such factors as the measured caliber and land widths of bullet evidence. When new evidence arrived, a query on the database could then determine whether cases with similar class characteristics or *modi operandi* were on file. On the technical side, other researchers suggested the utility of more high-powered microscopy techniques for the comparison of ballistics evidence, including several papers arguing for the use of scanning electron microscopy (Gardner, 1979; Goebel et al., 1980; Grove et al., 1972).[1] Grove et al. (1972:20) considered scanning electron microscopy "ideally suited for firing pin impression examination because of its ability to reveal topographical features at the base of the impression." The researchers examined "series of up to 50 rounds" from "numerous .32 caliber semi-automatic pistols," analyzing the first, second, tenth, "and in some instances the fiftieth firing pin impression." "In all the firing pin impressions examined, a match could be made using a criteria of 4 or more points of identification" whereas "no points of identification" could be found for firings from different guns; moreover, they concluded that "the first and fiftieth impressions can be matched."

[1] As summarized by Grove et al. (1972:20), scanning electron microscopy "consists basically of a finely focused beam of electrons which sweeps over the sample surface. This primary electron beam causes the formation of low energy electrons (secondary electrons) due to interaction with the sample surface. These secondary electrons are then collected and displayed on a cathode ray oscilloscope producing an image that gives extremely good topographical information with great depth of field."

In the 1960s, the Los Angeles Police Department (LAPD) developed a "Balliscan" camera designed specifically to photograph the exterior surface of a bullet, using a rotated slit to expose the film as a drum turned the bullet at the same speed.[2] Blackwell and Framan (1980) suggested an Automated Firearms Identification System for the analysis of bullet evidence, based on the consecutive matching striations methodology of Biasotti (1959) and utilizing scanned versions of Balliscan images as the image data. Though they sketched a schematic diagram for such a system and did some preliminary analysis of bullets used in the Biasotti (1959) study, no apparent further action on developing the system was taken.

In 1989 the Federal Bureau of Investigation (FBI) announced a program called DRUGFIRE, which used a system for acquiring images from cartridge evidence. A few years later, the Bureau of Alcohol, Tobacco, Firearms, and Explosives (ATF) adopted the BULLETPROOF system for imaging bullet evidence, marketed by what is now Forensic Technology WAI, Inc. (FTI), of Montréal, Canada, as the basis for its CEASEFIRE network. As described in more detail in Chapter 5, the two databases operated in parallel for several years until CEASEFIRE evolved into the NIBIN program, using as its platform the IBIS formed by combining BULLETPROOF with a BRASSCATCHER apparatus for imaging cartridge casings.

IBIS was made the technical base for the new NIBIN database, and the major ballistic image databases in operation today (including NIBIN and the state reference ballistic image databases in Maryland and New York) use IBIS. IBIS is also in use by law enforcement agencies in several foreign countries; through IBIS, FTI is essentially the only provider of ballistic imaging technology. At root, the IBIS platform combines a microscope with a camera that acquires two-dimensional greyscale images of bullet and cartridge case evidence; features of the traditional comparison microscope can then be emulated using the images, and the images can be compared with each other to assess similarity. Box 4-1 makes an important note about current usage of the term "IBIS."

4–B IBIS EQUIPMENT

Formally, IBIS represents the integration of two separate systems. The BULLETPROOF microscope and comparison apparatus for acquiring images from bullets was developed first, beginning in 1991. It was aug-

[2]A subsidiary of McDonnell-Douglas, Corp., later produced the Balliscan camera based on the LAPD design (Blackwell and Framan, 1980). Balliscan images became prominent in later years because images made following the assassination of Robert F. Kennedy were reexamined by firearms examiners in the mid-1970s, in support of the work of the U.S. House Select Committee on Assassinations.

BOX 4-1
"IBIS" Terminology

As of January 2007, Forensic Technology WAI, Inc. (FTI), repositioned its line of products to emphasize its existing BulletTRAX-3D platform and developing BrassTRAX-3D platform for the acquisition of three-dimensional measurements from bullets and cartridge cases, respectively. Both of these are said to constitute the "IBIS-TRAX 3D" line, and as such has begun referring to these as IBIS (e.g., they formally refer to the product as "IBIS BulletTRAX-3D"). The IBIS described in this chapter—based on two-dimensional photography—has now been designated the "IBIS Heritage Series" on the firm's Web site (http://www.fti-ibis.com), and FTI suggests that the two-dimensional product is no longer actively marketed.

Though the name has now been linked with the new three-dimensional products, we use the term "IBIS" throughout this report to refer exclusively to the two-dimensional photography system, dating from the combination of the separate BRASSCATCHER and BULLETPROOF components and running through version 3.4 of the IBIS software. We do so because of the context of our study, which includes offering advice on the existing National Integrated Ballistic Information Network (NIBIN) and suggesting enhancements to it: the entire infrastructure of NIBIN is built on the two-dimensional photography IBIS. What is now dubbed the "IBIS Heritage Line" is in fact the *current* platform deployed to NIBIN partners; accordingly, it is the appropriate benchmark of comparison for our study.

Likewise, the experimental research conducted by the National Institute of Standards and Technology (NIST) in support of the committee's work—described in Chapter 8—compared the current IBIS two-dimensional to a prototype three-dimensional acquisition system. This is because we consider three-dimensional topographic measurement as a possible enhancement within the current NIBIN system, so that it is appropriate to get a sense of how well the three-dimensional measurements and scores compare with the IBIS two-dimensional currently used in NIBIN.

mented in 1995 by BRASSCATCHER, which adapted the apparatus to work with cartridge case evidence (McLean, 1999).

Most of the IBIS installations under the NIBIN program take the form of Remote Data Acquisition Stations (RDASs). One component of an RDAS is the Data Acquisition Station (DAS), a microscope with two built-in cameras mounted to it (one for bullets and one for cartridge cases). The RDAS also includes a computer so that demographic data[3] associated

[3]These auxiliary data might more accurately be described as *metadata*, but we retain "demographic data" as common usage in the field.

with a case (e.g., gun caliber, date of crime, and firing pin shape) can be entered by an operator; the microscope cameras display their output on the computer monitor, so that the operator can determine how the image will be acquired, as described below. In an RDAS, the computer also serves as a Signature Analysis Station (SAS), where the results of comparisons with other images can be reviewed. However, the key component that an RDAS lacks is the "correlation server" that processes results from acquired images and compares them against other cases in a database. An RDAS alone must transmit its images to a correlation server for processing and await the results from the server. Standalone systems that include a correlation server along with the base RDAS equipment are referred to as hubs.

As discussed in Chapter 5, the NIBIN program also makes use of three other related FTI products in addition to the base IBIS RDAS. As it is currently structured, all comparisons of images are routed through correlation servers (separate from an IBIS hub) located in ATF's three national laboratories. To ease the task of reviewing results from image comparisons, FTI also markets Matchpoint systems—essentially, the computer hardware and software of a SAS, except that they are not built into the same physical cabinet as the DAS in an RDAS. Finally, several NIBIN sites make use of Rapid Brass Identification (RBI) units, portable suitcase-size microscope setups that allow technicians to acquire breech face and firing pin images in the field, including at crime scenes. RBI units are meant only for acquisition of images (and transmittal, through an RDAS, to a correlation server), and not the result of image comparisons.

4–C DATA ACQUISITION

The obvious first step in working with IBIS (and NIBIN, using the IBIS platform) is to have bullet or cartridge case evidence to enter into the system. This evidence may be bullets or casings recovered at crime scenes, or it may be test firings from weapons obtained by the police in the course of investigations. In the first case, casings and (particularly) bullets present challenges because they may be damaged and may require cleaning prior to examination and entry.[4] In the case of test firings, the ammunition used in the firings—typically done into a water tank, to facilitate capture of the undamaged bullet—is a critical choice. To the greatest extent possible,

[4]Rector (2002) considers the effect of one cleaning process on IBIS performance for matching bullet evidence. An ultrasonic bath—in which high-frequency sound waves produce vapor bubbles in a liquid—can be used to dislodge some foreign materials that can prove stubborn to conventional means, including soil and drywall. However, Rector (2002) observed that immersion in an ultrasonic cleaner for longer periods of time (up to 30 minutes) generally reduced IBIS scores and that the surface etching done by the cleaner was directly visible on lead bullets.

examiners prefer to match the test fire ammunition to the ammunition used in crimes involving a suspected gun; in order of suitability, from most to least, De Kinder (2002b:9) characterizes the typical preference hierarchy for test firing:

- ammunition from the same lot as the recovered bullets and casings;
- ammunition of the same brand and make as the recovered bullets and casings;
- ammunition from the same manufacturer as the recovered bullets and cartridge cases, having the same primer or bullet jacket composition but not necessarily being exactly the same type; and
- ammunition having the same primer or bullet jacket composition, but not necessarily being from the same manufacturer.

Often, however, no such information is possible—and in the context of creating an reference ballistic image database (RBID), it can never be known what type or lot of ammunition will be used with a new firearm. To address ambiguous cases, ATF recommends certain "protocol ammunition" for particular calibers to its NIBIN agencies in the hopes of "[giving] the best chance overall for [test-fire] items to find matching evidence bullets and casings in a database." The protocol ammunition is chosen to be "intermediate in recording toolmarks and impression hardness," having bullet metal and primer surfaces that are neither too hard nor too soft for registration of marks (Thompson et al., 2002:15).

4–C.1 Mounting of Evidence and Demographic Data Entry

To begin an IBIS entry, operators open a "case," which can contain one or more constituent "exhibits," bullets or cartridge casings. A case can also include information about a firearm, if it has been recovered. Links suggested by IBIS in comparing exhibits are made between exhibits and not cases as a whole. Although the case identification number is displayed in a column when comparison results are returned for analysis, the system does not make it readily apparent where individual exhibits from a particular case fall in the list of rankings reported by IBIS.

IBIS training materials emphasize the importance of correct entry of auxiliary, context data about evidence and exhibits, the "demographic data." For cartridge case markings, the training guide indicates that "automatic correlation requests use *all* of the following demographic information"—occurrence date, caliber, firing pin shape, and event type—"to select the test candidates from the database," and all these pieces of information are described as "crucial for the correlation process" (Forensic Technology WAI, Inc., 2002a:2-10, 3-2). IBIS defines six basic event types, four for exhibits related to crime and two for test firings. The crime-related event codes are homicide (HOM), assaults with a deadly weapon (ADW), other crime (OTH), and unknown (UNK). The distinction between the two test fire events is whether the firearm is retained by police (and hence is out of circulation on the street) or whether it is returned to the owner after firing; these are coded as TF and TFR, respectively. (The basic manner in which the demographic data are used as filters is described in Section 4–D.1.) Bullet exhibits are linked to operator-entered information on certain general rifling characteristics that can be derived from the bullet and can narrow down the database search. These include caliber, twist (the orientation of the land and groove impressions, left or right, when looking from the base of the bullet), and the number of lands and grooves on the bullet. The composition and type (e.g., jacketed or hollow point) of the bullet may also be recorded.

Although accurate demographic data entry is essential to the IBIS comparison process, the physical positioning of bullet or cartridge evidence under the microscope (and camera) is crucial to the acquisition of quality, comparable images. Indeed, Tontarski and Thompson (1998:644) observe that "the greatest initial concern using this technology was whether or not different examiners could enter projectile and cartridge casing images in a sufficiently consistent way for the database to be able to locate a match." Though they go on to assert that "the equipment's image capturing system and its robust algorithm have all but eliminated operator variability as a concern," proper positioning of exhibits is still emphasized in IBIS training, and some studies (e.g., Chan, 2000) suggest that substantial misalignment can still cause problems in comparison. In its documentation, FTI suggests standardized protocols for orienting evidence that have also been adopted as standards by the NIBIN program. For instance, a cartridge bearing roughly horizontal breech face marks across the primer surface is supposed to be oriented so that the marks are as flat (not at an angle) as possible, rotated so that the ejector mark on the cartridge rim is in the southern hemisphere of the image. If the cartridge shows evidence of a firing pin drag mark, where the pin has scraped against the surface, the cartridge is supposed to be rotated so that the drag mark is at or around the 3 o'clock position.

4–C.2 Specification of Regions of Interest

IBIS allows technicians to designate regions of interest on an image. Because these regions are circular for the markings left on cartridge casings, the regions of interest are also known as ring limits. For a breech face impression, the region of interest is indicated based on two circles. The computer derives an automatic, "default" placement of the rings, but they can be adjusted directly by the operator. The outer (blue) circle is to be set to the edge of the primer surface of the stamp and the inner (red) circle marks off the firing pin impact region; the image used in comparing breech face marks is based on the doughnut-shaped area between the two circles. Though marks on the cartridge case area may be irregularly shaped—the pit of the firing pin impression and areas where the primer metal has been pushed back out of the firing pin impression—the region of interest rings are strictly circular. Hence, the IBIS operator must make some judgment about exact placement of the circle, assessing the potential for "washout" areas (reflected light off of the jagged edge of the pit of the firing pin impression) to show up in the final image. Operators may also adjust procedures to accommodate specific firing pin types; for example, Glock firearms have a distinctive rectangular firing pin, and therefore technicians place the inner circle so that it circumscribes the four corners of the impression. Figure 4-1(a) shows an IBIS breech face image with the two circular delimiters superimposed.

Once the regions of interest are set for acquiring a breech face, the image is taken using the IBIS standard ring lighting, intended to provide uniform illumination, and the system automatically suggests a lighting intensity "to provide optimum lighting for acquisition." However, the IBIS training materials note (Forensic Technology WAI, Inc., 2002a:2-18):

> In numerous cases the suggested lighting may not appear optimal (for example, with smooth surfaces or uncommon metal primer compositions). In these cases, you will need to manually adjust the light setting with the light scroll bar in order to minimize washout. Eliminating the washed out (white halo) area surrounding the firing pin impression improves correlation accuracy as this area is sometimes a common feature between cartridge cases. This will increase score results on marks of lesser value. Always keep in mind that your goal is to find the lighting intensity that will provide the best contrast with the least washout.

After acquiring the breech face image using the center light, the user has the option of taking a second picture using alternate lighting, a side light located at the 6 o'clock position relative to the mounted cartridge, while holding the cartridge fixed in the same orientation. Figure 4-1(b) illustrates a side light image of a cartridge breech face impression, side by side with the standard center light image, Figure 4-1(a). The side light image is better for seeing some impression of three-dimensional detail, though it necessarily also casts shadows on other parts of the image. If the side light image is acquired, it is filed with the case and remains available for viewing later on (including the "Multiviewer" interface for viewing multiple exhibits simultaneously, as when reviewing comparison scores). However, the side light

a

b

c

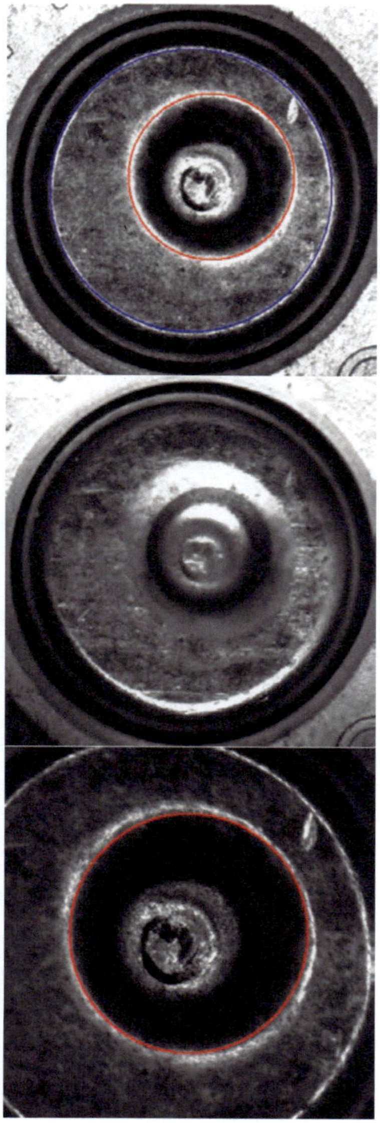

FIGURE 4-1 IBIS breech face images.
NOTES: The three images are (a) breech face image using the standard ring, center light; (b) breech face image using the side light; and (c) firing pin image using the standard ring, center light, acquired from the same cartridge casing. Although they are difficult to see in this reproduction, circular region-of-interest delimiters are indicated on images (a) and (c). The area between the outer circle and inner circle (a) defines the breech face impression, and the area inside the single circle (c) defines the firing pin impression.

image is strictly used for an alternative view by the current IBIS; it is not used in the derivation of a mathematical signature from the image or used in the system's automated comparison with other images.

For the firing pin impression (for exhibits from centerfire guns), the region of interest is defined by a single circle that the computer attempts to automatically place just inside the top edge of the impression; see Figure 4-1(c) for an example. The intent of imaging the firing pin impression is to focus on the footprint or base of the impression; hence, the region of interest is meant to exclude any drag marks, washout lighting, or primer flowback areas. As with the breech face impression, the user may manually adjust the level lighting, but the ring light is the only light source option for the firing pin. The IBIS operators' manual describes "optimal lighting" for the firing pin impression as "eliminat[ing] as many clusters of washed out pixels in the firing pin region as possible, without the region being too dark" (Forensic Technology WAI, Inc., 2002a:2-27).

The ejector mark and the firing pin impression from a rimfire gun (where the firing pin strikes the headstamp area on the rim of the cartridge) differ from the other marks in that the region of interest is free form and the computer does not suggest a default region. Looking at the zoomed image on the computer screen, operators click with the mouse to draw an outline around the mark; they are directed to try to remain about 1 cm from the edge of the impression, as it appears onscreen. In both these cases, the manufacturer's headstamp may interfere with the toolmark; operators try to eliminate as much of the headstamp as possible from their trace of the mark. Two separate images are made of an ejector mark after the region of interest is defined, one using a side light from 3 o'clock and the other from 6 o'clock. Rimfire impressions that are rectangular (noncircular) in shape are also imaged twice, with the 3 and 6 o'clock side lights, while circular rimfire impressions use the ring light. The added difficulty of acquiring images of ejector marks (free-hand specification of regions of interest and the capture of two images), may explain why many law enforcement agencies do not routinely acquire ejector marks for inclusion in NIBIN.

Bullets require more complicated and time-consuming image acquisition. As described in Chapter 2, the raised areas on the interior of a firearm barrel (lands) leave corresponding marks on bullets, dubbed land engraved areas (LEAs); the LEAs are separated by groove engraved areas (GEAs), and the transition points between the LEAs and GEAs are called shoulders. Though GEAs can pick up striation marks as the bullet moves down the barrel, most of the marks are registered in the LEAs, where contact is greatest. Consequently, IBIS images focus on the LEAs. For each LEA on the perimeter of the bullet, the IBIS operator positions two "anchor lines" based on the image on their computer screen; though the shoulders are useful for helping technicians recognize LEAs, they are not intended to be included in the image, and so the anchor lines are meant to be placed just inside the shoulder boundaries. The image section between the anchor lines is used for comparison with other images. The IBIS software attempts to automatically place the anchor lines, but they are typically adjusted by the operator and reoriented so as to be parallel with detectable striation marks in the center of the LEA. The process of placing these lines must be repeated for each of the LEAs.

Since the surface of a bullet can be complicated to focus, two focusing options are available using IBIS. The first is digital optical focusing for which both central and ring lighting are available. Central lighting is most often used in image acquisition; however, ring lighting is available to increase the definition of shoulders, and therefore help verify their position. The other option for focusing an image is by aid of lasers. IBIS has two lasers that intercept a bullet at 45 degree angles. These lasers are not only useful for focusing exhibits, but also for positioning the bullet properly relative to the optical axis, and for finding the "shoulder edges" of bullets.

Bullets are prone to be damaged or deformed, and image acquisition processes must adapt to these possibilities. IBIS operators typically acquire images of LEAs along a band near (but not immediately at) the base of the bullet. However, if the base of a bullet is too damaged to acquire, technicians can attempt to identify representative marks at the nose of the bullet. Alternatively, if there are cannelures (a circumferential groove) on the bullet, the last cannelure can be considered the base of the bullet. Bullet fragments can also be analyzed; however, each bullet fragment is treated as a separate whole bullet specimen.

4–C.3 Reduction to Mathematical Signature and Processing

At the end of the acquisition process, a signature is generated on the basis of the final acquired images. Two versions of a signature for a particular exhibit are derived, which the IBIS users' guide describes as "big and small signatures. Big signatures contain a high level of detail, but take up a great deal of memory space and take a longer time to process. Smaller signatures are less detailed but more efficient to use" (Forensic Technology WAI, Inc., 2001:129). These signatures are sent—along with the images, for later on-screen viewing—to a correlation server for processing. As discussed in Chapter 5, in the NIBIN system this means transmittal to one of the three national labs of ATF; the signature, image, and related information is archived at these regional sites to populate the central NIBIN database.

It is the processed signatures, and not the images themselves, that are further processed, compared against other entries in the database, and scored based on their similarity. The exact manner by which signatures are extracted and compared with others is considered proprietary information by FTI, the maker of the IBIS platform. The description in Section 4–D of the steps of the scoring and comparison processes derives from published articles and other public documents. A subgroup of committee members discussed the signature generation process with FTI technical staff in March 2005 under a nondisclosure agreement that precludes disclosing in this report any information provided to the committee by FTI that it has designated as proprietary. However, our assessment and recommendations in Section 4–F and Chapter 6 specific to the IBIS platform are informed by the discussions with FTI.

4–C.4 Image and Signature Size

An important consideration in discussing the maintenance of a large database of images and querying of that database from multiple remote locations is the size of the image files. The images collected by IBIS are 256-level greyscale graphics. According to FTI specifications reported by Tulleners (2001:4-3), the raw JPEG-type images of a breech face or a firing pin impression take up 230.4 KB of space. For transmission and archiving, the images are "compressed to a proprietary image [format]," and that compression is approximately 10:1 (e.g., the compressed images take up 21–23 KB). Images are also associated with 1 KB of "textual data" from the demographic data entry.

Although the information dates to early incarnations of the IBIS platform, Tontarski and Thompson (1998:643–644) report that "approximately 1800 [raw graphic file] cartridge casing images can be stored on a [1.2 Gb] DAS optical disk, and approximately 10,000 compressed images and 'signatures' can be stored on a [1.2 Gb] SAS optical disk." This information suggests that the combination of a compressed image and signature took up roughly 120 KB in early IBIS. It is not clear whether this estimate corresponds strictly to a single image and its signature or to the complete set of information associated with an evidence cartridge casing: a breech face image and signature, a firing pin image and signature, a side-light breech face image (optional), and an ejector mark image and signature.

Bullet images and signatures are substantially larger due to the acquisition of multiple images (for each LEA). Tontarski and Thompson (1998:643–644) indicated that "a bullet with 6 LEAs requires about 2.1 Mb of storage space. Approximately 500 to 600 bullets [(raw images)] can be stored on each DAS optical disk. . . . The compressed image is stored on the SAS optical disk (currently up to 6000 JPEG images) and the 'signature' is stored on the SAS 1 Gb hard disk (up to 50,000 projectile 'signatures' and associated case data)."

4–D SCORING, RANKING, AND ANALYSIS

The heart of the IBIS operations is the process of comparing the signature associated with a reference exhibit with hundreds or thousands of other signatures in a database in order to assess their similarity. FTI refers to this process as "correlation"; as we discuss further in Section 4–F, we believe that the use of the term is problematic because of the well-known statistical definition of the word. Here, and elsewhere in the report, references to source materials may refer to correlation and related constructs (e.g., "correlation servers," the computer hardware that performs the processing). However, we refer to the process as a scoring process, or, more generically, as the comparison process.

4–D.1 Filtering

An important first step in processing IBIS data is filtering: screening the database based on the information entered by IBIS operators at the time of image acquisition in order to reduce the search space. This filtering—or, equivalently, conditioning on prior information—makes use of what FTI terms the demographic data associated with a case or a specific piece of evidence. Most of these filters are automatic or system defined, but some can be set in nondefault ways during manual correlation requests.

One major filter is the specification of the databases against which particular exhibits are to be searched; particularly in the context of NIBIN, this is equivalent to *geographic selection.* As described in more detail in Chapter 6, NIBIN is structured so that exhibits from a particular agency are, by default, only searched against those agencies that are located in the same "partition" in the NIBIN database; searches against other agencies or wider geographic agencies must be manually requested.

Another critical filter is the *caliber* of the weapon or, more appropriately, the "caliber family." FTI defines a caliber family as the set of calibers "that could be fired by the same gun. For example, .38 auto ammunition can be fired with a 9mm Makarov pistol. This reflects the interchangeability of bullets and cartridge cases in firearms" (Forensic Technology WAI, Inc., 2002a:3-2), but also the reality that nonstandard ammunition can be successfully fired from a particular weapon. Separate caliber family listings are maintained for cartridge cases and bullets, and the lists have been periodically updated based on input from firearms examiners.

The event type and occurrence date entered as demographic data further narrow the search window. For instance, a reference exhibit coded with any of the crime event codes—HOM, ADW, UNK, and OTH—are compared with exhibits from all other event types, except for TF exhibits entered after the reference exhibit's occurrence date because the gun is assumed to be out of circulation. Similarly, a TF exhibit used as the reference is compared with crime-event exhibits bearing dates before the test-fire date, but test fires are not compared against each other.[5]

The IBIS platform distributed in the NIBIN platform defines four choices for firing pin shape; these must be manually entered as demographic data and are not derived from the image. IBIS installations in some countries list 12 firing pin choices. Kennington (1992) suggests that an exhaustive listing of firing pin shapes could include around 22 choices.

The number of exhibits left after the filtering is reported as the "sample size" on IBIS score comparison printouts (see Figure 4-2 and Section 4–D.3).

4–D.2 Steps in Scoring and Ranking

For cartridge case evidence, the IBIS "correlation" scoring process is actually better thought of as a multiple step routine, in which the goal is to rank sample exhibits based on the degree of similarity in their derived signature to a reference exhibit. First-pass scores are generated separately for each of the basic markings (breech face, firing pin, and ejector mark), using the compressed, small signature associated with an exhibit (see Section 4–C.3). This is described as the "crude" correlation (Beauchamp and Roberge, 2005:6) or "coarse" correlation step (George, 2004a, 2004b). The coarse comparison scores are ranked from highest to lowest, separately for each type of mark.

After the ranks are derived, a threshold is imposed: only the exhibits falling in the top 20 percent in the ranked lists for any of the three markings is retained for further processing. For example, in a filtered dataset of cartridge casings of size 100, only between 20 and 60 exhibits form the new, effective sample for further analysis (20 if the same exhibits appear in the top 20 percent of all three lists, 60 if each of the three ranked lists have completely different exhibits in their top 20 percent of entries).[6] The 20 percent threshold was doubtless chosen and fixed for computational efficiency, though a more stringent 10 percent threshold was apparently used in early IBIS (Thompson et al., 1996:196; Thompson, 1998:98; Tontarski and Thompson, 1998:644). Adjusting the threshold level is not impossible but requires intervention from FTI; the study of IBIS performance by George

[5]"To accommodate clerical delays," Forensic Technology WAI, Inc. (2002a:3-2) notes that a 30-day buffer is added before and after the occurrence date for test fires.

[6]Presumably, if the reference exhibit does not have an ejector mark image—as is seemingly common practice for some NIBIN installations—the threshold is based only on the breech face and firing pin images. The alternative would let 20 percent of the sorted list of ejector mark scores (all zeroes, and presumably sorted by default on some other datum such as entry date or exhibit number) into the second correlation step.

IBIS Correlation Results

Reference Case Information

Case ID: *C-OB05-05369
Site Name: NY Crime1
Law Agency: New York State Police
Event: (Unknown)
Comment:

Reference Exhibit Information

Exhibit Number: 1
Event: (Unknown)
Caliber: 9LG*
Acq. Person: [redacted]
Comment:

Sample Size 12353

Tests ordered by ***Breech Face***

Rank	Case Id	Exhibit Number	Site Name	Breech Face	Firing Pin	EM or RF
1	*C-OB05-05369	1	NY Regist3	344	282	0
2	*C-OB04-28766	1	NY Regist3	99	71	0
3	*C-OB04-15862	1	NY Regist3	94	71	0
4	*C-OB04-28500	1	NY Regist3	93	74	0
5	*C-OB04-25809	1	NY Regist3	89	65	0
6	*C-OB04-15815	1	NY Regist4	85	65	0
7	*C-OB04-15744	1	NY Regist2	85	56	0
8	*C-OB04-15738	1	NY Regist3	85	65	0
9	*C-OB04-27965	1	NY Regist4	84	46	0
10	*C-OB04-24774	1	NY Regist1	84	37	0

Tests ordered by ***Firing Pin***

Rank	Case Id	Exhibit Number	Site Name	Breech Face	Firing Pin	EM or RF
1	*C-OB05-05369	1	NY Regist3	344	282	0
2	*C-OB04-14649	1	NY Regist3	16	100	0
3	*C-OB04-25537	1	NY Regist3	52	94	0
4	*C-OB04-16018	1	NY Regist3	49	93	0
5	*C-OB04-15086	1	NY Regist3	43	93	0
6	*C-OB04-20756	1	NY Regist3	23	92	0
7	*C-OB04-15854	1	NY Regist3	25	91	0
8	*C-OB04-16458	1	NY Regist3	28	90	0
9	*C-OB04-15988	1	NY Regist3	39	90	0
10	*C-OB04-15887	1	NY Regist3	53	90	0

Tests ordered by ***EM or RF***

Rank	Case Id	Exhibit Number	Site Name	Breech Face	Firing Pin	EM or RF
1	*C-OB05-05369	1	NY Regist3	344	282	0
2	*C-OB04-28766	1	NY Regist3	99	71	0
3	*C-OB04-28716	1	NY Regist3	56	48	0
4	*C-OB04-28710	1	NY Regist4	8	73	0
5	*C-OB04-28700	1	NY Regist3	54	17	0
6	*C-OB04-28631	1	NY Regist3	9	73	0
7	*C-OB04-28628	1	NY Regist3	10	75	0
8	*C-OB04-28616	1	NY Regist4	23	76	0
9	*C-OB04-28577	1	NY Regist3	22	75	0
10	*C-OB04-28500	1	NY Regist3	93	74	0

03/30/2005 ***For official use only*** ***Sensitive but unclassified*** Pages 1/1

FIGURE 4-2 Sample "cover sheet": Top 10 ranking report from an IBIS comparison. NOTE: Page is from the committee's experimental work at the New York State Police Forensic Investigation Center. This particular sheet is from a comparison of a casing retrieved from files and reacquired into the system to find the image already in the database, hence the large top-ranked scores. The operator's name has been obscured.

(2004a, 2004b) described in Section 4–E.3 is one of the few instances for which the 20 percent threshold was completely waived (and all exhibits were subject to the more detailed comparison step).

The exhibits that remain after the coarse comparison step are then subjected to a more fine comparison based on the full, big signature (described above). As with the coarse comparison, scores are computed independently for each mark. The set of scores for the final, thresholded set of exhibits are then transmitted back to the requesting unit (along with the compressed images, for visual comparison).

The process for comparing signatures from bullet evidence does not involve a coarse comparison or threshold step, but is more complex than the cartridge comparison routine due to the nature of the exhibits. Exhibits are filtered based on general demographic characteristics, particularly the number of LEAs on the bullet. The complexity arises because each of the LEAs on the reference bullet must be compared with all the LEAs on a comparison bullet, and all possible rotations of the two bullets must be considered to try to see for which rotation the two bullets are most likely to be "in phase" (in correct alignment). In a hypothetical comparison of two bullets with three LEAs each, IBIS computes three "phase scores," one for each of the possible rotations of the bullets relative to each other; the phase score is the sum of the individual LEA-to-LEA scores for a particular rotation. Based on the phase scores, IBIS computes three summary scores of similarity:

- Max Phase, the largest of the individual phase scores;
- Peak Phase, the largest LEA-to-LEA score registered for the rotation that yielded the Max Phase score; and
- Max LEA, the largest LEA-to-LEA score registered for any rotation of the bullets.

4–D.3 Interpreting IBIS Output

The results of IBIS comparison requests, whether automatic or manually requested, appear in tabular form on the screen of the SAS (or the standalone Matchpoint unit). Columns are clickable so that the user can review the top-ranked results by any of the marks. For cartridge cases, the initial screen divides the view between the tabular records and side-by-side images of the exhibits from whatever row (pair of exhibits) is selected. In the side-by-side comparison, the IBIS station essentially emulates the function of a comparison microscope; images can be shifted relative to each other and relative to a center line, directly corresponding to the microscope view, so that striations and patterns can be matched between exhibits.

Users have the option of switching to a "Multiviewer" screen, permitting visual comparison between the reference exhibit and several candidates simultaneously. The Multiviewer screen also permits more than one image per case, so that—even if the results are ranked by breech face score—users may see both the center light and side light breech face image as well as the firing pin image.

Full IBIS DAS installations also include a printer. Users can print results for a single pair (including large displays of both images, along with the relevant demographic data). The basic summary report from a correlation request on cartridge case evidence consists of three tables, listing the top 10 ranked results for each of the breech face, firing pin, and ejector mark/rimfire marks. An example of a cover sheet is shown in Figure 4-2. In this case, only breech face and firing pin marks were acquired, yet the report template still includes a "ranking" by ejector mark or rimfire firing pin (those scores are reported as 0). If desired, users can print a lengthy tabular report, sorted by one of the score columns, listing the scores for all of the exhibits in the filtered and thresholded exhibit set.

The basic questions inherent in working with IBIS comparison scores is what meaning to put on a particular score and how deep in a list of sorted results an analyst should look for possible matches. Aside from the basic guidance that "the higher each score is, the more similar the test and reference exhibits are" (Forensic Technology WAI, Inc., 2001:131), IBIS training materials warn against interpreting the system's scores. "The scores themselves have no intrinsic value; they are only used to establish a ranking between pairs" of exhibits, and "no absolute good or bad scores can be given for evidence images" due to the inherent variability in toolmark and image evidence (Forensic Technology WAI, Inc., 2001:128, 139). Users are advised to consider gaps in the distribution of scores—large differences between consecutively ranked pairs—for some idea of where to look for possible matches.

However, with no stated justification, the training materials also suggest a "guideline" for analysis that has become a widespread standard among NIBIN partner agencies and other IBIS users (Forensic Technology WAI, Inc., 2002a:3-13):

> Whether you notice a gap [in score distribution] or not, compare at least the top 10 positions for the breech face, firing pin and ejector mark scores. Most times, matches are found within these top 10 positions, depending on the acquisition parameters, and quality and quantity of repeatable marks.

Thompson et al. (2002:21) later cited "FTI figures" demonstrating that "a match is found within the top 10 ranked items approximately 97% of the time," though no further source was given.

The training manual provides hypothetical examples of score examples. In one (Forensic Technology WAI, Inc., 2002a:3-14), breech face scores decline fairly monotonically from a maximum of 99 to 40 in the 18th-ranked position, where the score drops to 27. In this case, users are advised to "check top 10 only." In a second example, the most sizable gap in scores is a drop of 19 points between the seventh- and eighth-ranked positions. The manual suggests that "the highest probability of a match is in the top seven positions but, once again, you should compare the top 10 positions for each region of interest" (Forensic Technology WAI, Inc., 2002a:3-13).

The focus on the top 10 "is not an immutable characteristics of IBIS" but rather "a protocol developed from experience in using the system [that is] open to change as the system changes," note Thompson et al. (2002:21). Indeed, in earlier work with the BULLETPROOF part of what became IBIS, Miller and McLean (1998:22) used the top five as their cutoff, citing their determination from "actual case work using the computer" that "the best possibility of a matching land impression should be found in the top five choices." The IBIS users' guide indicates that, "in general, the top five to ten scores in any correlation list are potential matches," though "your laboratory administrator will decide how many exhibits in each list will be compared." However, the "top 10" mentality is reinforced by the physical form of IBIS printouts—in the basic "cover sheet" results, only the top 10 scores for each region of interest are listed—but the choice of 10 as the guideline appears to be arbitrary. Reviewing the top 10 results has become a NIBIN program standard, though individual practice varies across police departments; for instance, the New York City Police Department (not affiliated with NIBIN) has made viewing the top 24 pairs its standard for cartridge case comparisons.

If examination of the images on screen suggests particularly promising potential "hits," a request for the physical evidence can be initiated, so a firearms examiner can compare the exhibits using the comparison microscope. We discuss the recording of "hits" in the NIBIN program further in Chapter 5.

4–E UNIQUENESS, REPRODUCIBILITY, AND PERMANENCE OF FIREARMS MARKS AS REGISTERED BY IBIS

As the IBIS technology has matured, its performance has been tested by several firearms examiners and other researchers. Most of the relevant studies are intended to address specific performance issues suggested by the creation of a large-scale RBID, containing many exhibits with common class and possibly subclass characteristics; others have scrutinized specific parts of the IBIS comparison process, such as the 20 percent threshold step.

In this section, we briefly review the major studies of IBIS performance that have been performed to date.

4–E.1 California Feasibility Study

In 2000, Assembly Bill 1717 was enacted into law, directing the California Department of Justice to undertake a study to evaluate the feasibility and utility of current ballistic imaging systems to handle a California RBID. The "technical evaluation" called for by the law was conducted and reported by Tulleners (2001) and was circulated to stakeholders in late 2001 for review and comment. The report drew extensive comments, including lengthy comments by ATF (Thompson et al., 2002) and FTI (2002b). Based on the stakeholder comments, the Department of Justice requested an external independent review, which was secured from De Kinder (2002b). Attorney General Lockyer (2003) issued the department's report to the legislature in January 2003, packaging together the technical evaluation, external review, and the comments from ATF and FTI. He concluded (Lockyer, 2003:7) that "it is apparent that existing research is too limited and that further study of current and emerging technologies is needed before creating an RBID in California"; this further research should include alternatives such as microstamping and "would be most comprehensive if conducted at the federal level." The report expressed optimism on the "potential to develop ballistic imaging into a powerful crime-solving tool," and suggested that "a national RBID could be an extremely valuable tool for law enforcement in generating leads and solving crimes" (Lockyer, 2003:9).

In conducting the technical evaluation, Tulleners (2001) devised a set of eight "performance tests" or experiments; not all of the tests could be performed due to available resources, but the tests spanned a number of conceptual concerns regarding large-scale RBID performance. As the core data resource for the experiments, the California study made use of a natural opportunity to capture exhibits from a large number of test firings of similar, bought-as-new firearms: proof test firings from a batch of 792 new .40 caliber Smith & Wesson Model 4006 semiautomatic pistols received by the California Highway Patrol (CHP). Tulleners (2001) acknowledged this resource as both a strength and a limitation of the study, a limitation because—projecting from gun sales data—.40 caliber arms would be a small part of a California RBID relative to 9mm arms (which could be as much as 45 percent of the database).

IBIS entry and comparison of exhibits for the California tests was done by FTI at its Montréal headquarters. From the description of the tests, only breech face and firing pin marks were entered into the database. The 20 percent threshold (described in Section 4–D.2) was apparently left in effect: describing comparisons on a database with 792 entries, Tulleners (2001:C-1) writes that "the system was set up so that it could only rank to position 160," which is slightly more than 20 percent of the total database size. Spreadsheets of the test results indicate that any case where a breech face rank is listed as "Not in Selection" also has a firing pin rank "Not in Selection," and vice versa, suggesting that these are cases where an expected match did not survive the coarse comparison pass and 20 percent threshold. (The tests performed in the California evaluation, and the formal responses to the results of those tests, are summarized in the appendix to this chapter, Section 4–G.)

4–E.2 De Kinder et al. Analysis

In the wake of the California feasibility study, the lead author of the California technical evaluation and its independent reviewer collaborated on a follow-up study (De Kinder et al., 2004). This analysis responded to one principal criticism of the California study by including a wider range of ammunition, and it also used weapons of the more common (and commonly used in crime) 9mm caliber. For the purposes of this committee's work, the De Kinder et al. (2004) study is particularly important because NIST secured access to the original casings from that study; in Chapter 8, we describe work done by NIST on the committee's behalf to reanalyze some of these casings by two-dimensional photography, as well as original work with three-dimensional surface metrology techniques.

To create their exhibit set, seven cartridges were fired from each of 600 pistols used by the Sacramento and Modesto, California, police departments. All but 46 of the firearms were SIG Sauer P226 pistols; the 46 exceptions were of the SIG Sauer P225, P228, or P229 series, but "the general breech face, firing pin aperture, and extractor configurations are essentially the same" between the different models (De Kinder et al., 2004:208). Of the seven cartridges per pistol:

- two used Remington-Peters 115 grain FMJ (Remington) cartridges, one of which was entered into an IBIS station to create the test database and the second was retained for querying; and
- one shot each was made with each of five ammunition types: Winchester 147 grain JHP, Speer 115 grain FMJ, Wolf 115 grain FMJ, Federal 147 grain FMJ, and CCI 115 grain FMJ.

The cartridges to be fired were loaded into a magazine by a supervising criminalist before officers fired the rounds, but it is not known whether the same sequence of ammunition was used in each firing. It is also not stated whether the pistols were fired as new, or how they may have varied in age or use. In entering the exhibits into IBIS, the system defaults were not automatically accepted, and De Kinder et al. (2004:Table 2) list the frequencies with which manual corrections were made (the largest of which was adjusting the lighting for the breech face image, done in 37.7 percent of entries).

Breech face and firing pin images were acquired for all exhibits, and, in analyzing ranks, De Kinder et al. (2004) used the best rank on either of the two marks as the overall rank for an exhibit-to-exhibit match. A limitation of the study is that the IBIS staff entering test queries were instructed to consider and tabulate ranks within the top 30; any ranks higher than 30 were combined into a "More than 30" category. This decision is useful in that it arguably corresponds to a practical limit to the number of comparisons IBIS technicians might scroll through in a routine examination, if they look beyond the top 10. However, it does not provide insight into the number of possible matches that may be missed because the comparison fails to pass the coarse comparison and IBIS-default 20 percent threshold (under which the effective sample size would be somewhat more than 120). However, concerns about the 20 percent threshold were the focus of the George (2004a, 2004b) study, discussed in the next section.

With a quasi-RBID of 600 images, all of exhibits using Remington ammunition, De Kinder et al. (2004) performed a "best-case" matching exercise, querying the database using the second Remington casing for 32 randomly selected exhibits. Twenty-three of the 32 sister Remington images were found in the database in the top 10 ranks, and 18 of those matches were ranked number one. Eight of the possible matches ranked higher than 30 (or were eliminated by the 20 percent threshold). De Kinder et al. (2004:210) then drew 32 exhibits from each of the five non-Remington test firings and queried each of those against the database to try to locate the Remington casing from the same gun. All of the brands performed poorly relatively to the Remington-to-Remington comparisons; the Federal and Wolf firings fared particularly badly, with 24 (Wolf) and 27 (Federal) out of 32 searches ranking "more than 30." In total, only 21 percent of the comparisons found the sister Remington cartridge in the top 10 ranks.

Other tests performed in the study attempted to demonstrate degradation in ranks with database size and to estimate the time needed to perform a comparison as a database grows in size. A portion of the study also asked the IBIS operators to use the output to indicate which casing or casings they would recommend for manual examination by an examiner based on the IBIS output, to get some crude sense of the false negatives or false positives that might result from actual querying of an RBID.

De Kinder et al. (2004:214–215) concluded that "the results of our study illustrate that an RBID cannot adequately and efficiently compare specimens, leading us to conclude that such a database is unsuitable for law enforcement work. The current miss rate identified in this study is unacceptable for an RBID."

4–E.3 George Study

George (2004a, 2004b) conducted two experiments, both of which focused on concerns regarding the IBIS default coarse comparison pass and 20 percent cutoff for detailed scoring and ranking. George (2004a) suggested a high incidence of cases in which known exhibits from the same firearm, even in a relatively small database, were excluded from matching by the 20 percent threshold. A follow-up study (George, 2004b) makes a critical and unique contribution because, through arrangement with FTI, the analysis completely waived the coarse comparison and thresholding steps in IBIS processing.

Both George experiments made use of an exhibit set created due to the St. Louis County, Missouri, Police Department's requirement that test fires from every police officer's duty weapon be maintained on file and its 2003 decision to change the brand of its standard duty ammunition. Hence, more than 500 Smith & Wesson Model 4006 and 4013 .40 caliber pistols each had four consecutive shots fired through them—two using Remington 165 grain, Golden Saber Bonded JHP ammunition (the new duty ammunition) and two using Federal 165 grain tactical JHP. After firing, and prior to entry in IBIS, all four casings from a particular weapon were inspected using a comparison microscope "to ensure that a match was possible before being chosen as a candidate for the study" (George, 2004a:286). Only the cartridge cases were imaged, and the images were acquired so as to maximize uniformity; standard procedures for orienting the cartridges were followed, and all the exhibits were prepared and imaged by the same examiner. To be most favorable to IBIS' default settings, "the lighting was not secondarily adjusted from the automatic setting" suggested by the system. Though breech face and firing impressions were entered for the exhibits, the analysis of scores and rankings in George (2004a) use only the breech face mark.

Exhibits were entered into the database, and other casings from the same weapons used to query the database, in several stages; from the narrative in George (2004a), it is difficult to ascertain the exact content of the database at each particular instance when comparisons were run. Still, the basic conclusion reached by George (2004a) was that the default 20 percent threshold did hamper IBIS's ability to generate matches. In total, 183 comparisons were made between an "evidence" or "blind" exhibit and a database containing a sister image, from the same gun and using ammunition of a particular type. (In fact, due to the sequence by which the database was populated, there may have been two or three images from the same gun in the database, but each of the comparisons performed had a single "target" exhibit.) Of these 183 comparisons, 76 found the sister exhibit in the top-ranked position and an additional 13 in ranks 2 through 10. However, the 20 percent threshold excluded 64 known matches (35 percent) from final scoring and ranking, a seemingly high rejection rate. These dropouts due to the 20 percent threshold were concentrated among comparisons for which the ammunition type differed, trying to find a Federal-brand casing using a Remington exhibit and vice versa. Only 8 of 74 cross-ammunition-type comparisons returned ranked in the top 10 positions, while 54 (73 percent) were screened by the 20 percent threshold. By contrast, 81 out of 109 same-ammunition-type comparisons (74.2 percent) were found in the top 10 ranks.

George (2004b:290) extended this work, first by augmenting the exhibit set. Another 100 service weapons were test-fired and a third ammunition type—Winchester 165 grain Full Metal Jacket (FMJ) target—was added to the firing routine. Six firings were made from each of 100 additional service weapons, two of each of the three ammunition brands. One of the Federal-brand casings was imaged for each of the 100 guns; 25 of the guns were drawn at random and the five extra casings for each was entered. In this manner, "approximately 540 firearms have now been used to establish a database of 850 cartridge case exhibits." As in George (2004a), standard IBIS entry protocols were followed. Five images were taken of each casing—two of the breech face impression (including the optional side light image), one of the firing pin, and two of the ejector mark. However, only the breech face comparison scores were analyzed.

The results of this analysis are summarized in Table 4-1. Comparisons made between exhibits using the same ammunition type were more successful than comparison across ammunition brands: 56 percent of comparisons using the same ammunition found the desired sister image in the top 10 ranks, compared with 17.7 percent for cross-ammunition comparisons. The effect of ammunition choice on IBIS rankings is made vivid by George's full listing of the ranks; for a particular firearm, the set of 15 comparisons to find known exhibits from that same gun can provide matches within the top 10 (or top 5), but also ranks as low as 843 or 848 in an 850-element dataset.

Consistent with the earlier study, George (2004b) notes particular concern about the possible effect of the IBIS-default 20 percent threshold. In his analysis, George notes high percentages of cases with rank below 170, which is 20 percent of the database size; as shown in Table 4-1, the effective thresholded sample size is almost certainly higher than 170 because high-ranking exhibits from any of the three marks (breech face, firing pin, and ejector mark) are retained from the coarse comparison pass, and we use 190 as a tabulation comparison. In any event, the George data cannot speak directly to the number of cases that would be lost in a default IBIS

TABLE 4-1 Summary Results of George Study of IBIS Cartridge Case Comparison Performance

Ammunition Brand: "EVIDENCE" Casing to SISTER in Database	Rank					
	#1	#2–10	#11–25	#26–190	Below 190/ Threshold	Total
Federal to						
Federal	17	3	1	1	3	25
Winchester	5	23	4	10	8	50
Remington	0	6	1	13	30	50
Winchester to						
Winchester	8	5	1	6	5	25
Federal	3	7	7	20	13	50
Remington	2	2	1	13	32	50
Remington to						
Remington	3	6	3	9	4	25
Federal	1	1	2	11	35	50
Winchester	1	2	0	20	27	50
Same Ammunition	28	14	5	16	12	75
Different Ammunition	12	41	15	87	145	300
Total	40	55	20	103	157	375

NOTES: Comparisons were made to a database containing 850 exhibits, so that a strict 20 percent threshold would retain only 170 exhibits. However, firing pin and ejector mark images were acquired (even if the resulting scores on those marks were not used in the analysis), so the IBIS 20 percent threshold would include any exhibits in the top 20 percent by any of the three marks. Hence, the effective 20 percent threshold almost certainly involves more than 170 rankings; we use 190 as a rough approximation to the effective thresholded sample size.
SOURCE: Tabulations from a prepublication report made available in electronic form at the 2004 Association of Firearms and Tool Mark Examiners Training Meeting; as printed in George (2004b:Table 1), the table is missing three rows.

analysis because his data represents the entire correlation results using the full, detailed signature associated with image exhibits, and not the reduced, coarser signature typically used by IBIS in the thresholding step.

The data tables in George (2004b:295) also include a code (for each of the 375 performed comparisons) indicating a firearms examiner's quick visual assessment of "match" or "no match" based on the second breech face image, using side light illumination rather than center light. In total, 77 percent of the 375 side-light-to-side-light comparisons displayed "sufficient identifiable features . . . to warrant a microscopic examination." George argues that some use of the side light image in the correlation process "may be one way to increase the accuracy of the system" "given that in the present correlation system, 75% of the known matches [on 375 searches] failed to appear in the top 10 correlated positions."

4–E.4 Nennstiel and Rahm Studies

Nennstiel and Rahm (2006a, 2006b) authored two studies on the performance of IBIS comparison routines. The first study summarizes and suggests a common notation for direct comparison of the major previous studies of IBIS performance (the same studies we describe in this section). We focus here on the second study (Nennstiel and Rahm, 2006b), the results of their own experimental work with IBIS.

The work derives from the experience of the Federal Criminal Police Office (BKA) in Germany, which developed its initial IBIS database in 2000 and has added to it since 2001. The images in the BKA database are subject to a preselection bias, as departmental policy is to only enter into IBIS those exhibits that are deemed "suitable for comparison," a designation made by inspecting the casings and deciding whether sufficient markings exist so that there is a reasonably high probability that a match could be made by a "normal optical comparison" (Nennstiel and Rahm, 2006b:25). About 77 percent of cartridge cases processed by BKA are deemed suitable for comparison (the rest are labeled either partially suitable or unsuitable, and are not input into IBIS), but only 35 percent of bullets are considered suitable. It is also BKA's policy to enter "a maximum of two bullets and three cartridge cases" recovered as evidence from a crime scene and "one projectile and two cartridge cases (with the *most different* firearm markings)" from test-fired weapons, and to inspect the top five IBIS score results (Nennstiel and Rahm, 2006b:26).

Nennstiel and Rahm's analyses add new insight by considering two previously unexplored aspects of IBIS performance. First, as BKA populated its database in 2000, it not only acquired images for evidence in all open cases but also for "all crime links in the collection, known from pre-IBIS conventional microscopic comparison. This was performed to see whether known links would also result in a match with the IBIS" (Nennstiel and Rahm, 2006b:24–25). Specifically, 232 known hits using cartridge cases and 84 using bullets were reassessed, requiring "over 670 correlations with cartridge cases and 180 correlations with bullets" (Nennstiel and Rahm, 2006b:26). They report a success rate of 80.2 percent of finding the match in IBIS using cartridge cases, inspecting results for all three marks down to the fifth-ranked position; the rate increases to 85.8 percent for ranks in the top 10 by any mark (Nennstiel and Rahm, 2006b:29). They also conclude that considering all three marks is the best approach but that, considering each mark separately, the firing pin impression performed best for verifying the connections between cases.

The second innovation made by Nennstiel and Rahm (2006b) is that they also recorded attempts to use IBIS to verify "warm hits," instances in which police investigators suspected a link to other specific offenses already in the database. (This is in contrast to "cold hits," where there is no intelligence to suggest a connection between cases other than the similarity of the ballistic images.) For cartridge cases, these "warm hits" proved more amenable to IBIS confirmation than the larger set of previously known crime links, described above. A success rate of 93.9 percent of finding the suspected matches in the top five positions on any marking only increases by 0.9 percent by examining score lists to the top 10 positions.

Based on these analyses and other system tests (including known tests of multiple exhibits from the same firearm), Nennstiel and Rahm (2006b:28–29) conclude:

> When operating a collection of evidence ammunition [using IBIS], a success rate p in the area of 75–95% for cartridge case comparison and 50–75% for bullet comparison can be achieved in practice under certain conditions. A consideration of the [score] list elements up to $n = 5$ or $n = 10$ appears to be sufficient. Evaluations that go further increase the workload and contribute little to the improvement in the success rate.

4–E.5 FTI Benchmark Evaluation

As the developer and maintainer of IBIS, Forensic Technology WAI, Inc., enjoys unique advantages in testing the system's performance, including the ability to vary the level of thresholding used in the coarse comparison stage and to directly study the signatures derived from images. More directly, FTI's position offers great latitude with respect to one key performance variable: Because it can tap image data from IBIS installations worldwide, it can assemble larger image datasets than is possible for any particular agency, including large numbers of exhibits within particular caliber groupings. The images that can be assembled in this manner differ from what would be expected in a large-scale RBID—large numbers of exhibits from new guns, highly similar in class and possibly subclass characteristics—but the resulting datasets are arguably the best basis for assessing IBIS performance in the face of sheer sample size.

An FTI "benchmark evaluation" of IBIS performance for large databases proceeded in stages, taking as its base matched pairs of cartridge case exhibits provided by the Allegheny County, Pennsylvania, Coroner's Office; a sample of images from this base set is shown in Figure 4-3. Each pair had been fired from the same gun, but the set of guns included a variety of manufacturers and makes within each caliber. The ammunition used in the firings also varied widely, and in some cases the exact ammunition make is unknown; each pair of exhibits did not necessarily use the same ammunition. All images of these reference cases were acquired by FTI. Scores and ranks were generated against the sets of matched pairs themselves, as well as when they were combined with large numbers of completely unrelated exhibits from the same caliber pulled from IBIS sites worldwide. Initial results based on 9mm and .32 Auto pairs were presented by McLean (2004), and the 9mm results were also described by Nennstiel and Rahm (2006a). Results of the tests for other calibers were later summarized by Beauchamp and Roberge (2005).

The basic results of the FTI evaluation are summarized in Table 4-2. The flooding of the matched pair data with "noise" images from other sites did generally degrade the rankings, albeit not linearly. For instance, the nearly fourfold increase in the size of the .45 Auto database caused the chance of finding sister images to fall by 11–15 percent, while the 9mm database was increased to about 65 times its original size and yielded a comparatively smaller 21–28 percent reduction in performance. Comparisons of rimfire firing pin impressions from .22 caliber exhibits were effectively invariant to a tripling of database size. McLean (2004) concludes that the results underscore the importance of entering ejector marks into IBIS, along with the quicker-to-acquire breech face and firing pin impressions.

Though their IBIS analysis considered all of the casings, and not only ones that were visually reviewed and deemed to be "suitable for comparison" as in the BKA study, FTI did subsequently have a firearms examiner review each of the 434 9mm matched pairs and grade their ability to be successfully linked by optical examination. In all, 46 percent of the pairs of breech face images were judged "excellent," as were 54 percent of the firing pin images; 17 percent of breech face pairs and 11 percent of firing pin pairs were deemed "poor" or "no match" (Nennstiel and Rahm, 2006a: Table 6).

Beauchamp and Roberge (2005) extended the benchmark evaluation work, reporting the results of similar IBIS comparisons for two additional calibers. They also derive performance curves for IBIS comparisons, training or testing them on the images from the Allegheny County exhibits. Their work forecasts that—when searching a database of 1,000,000 exhibits—IBIS performance in detecting sister pairs within the top 10 ranks looking at both breech face and firing pin marks is on the order of 30–35 percent. Based on the smaller set of 9mm exhibits for which ejector marks were also considered, the estimated success at finding a known match in a 1,000,000-exhibit set is about 50 percent when all three marks are considered.

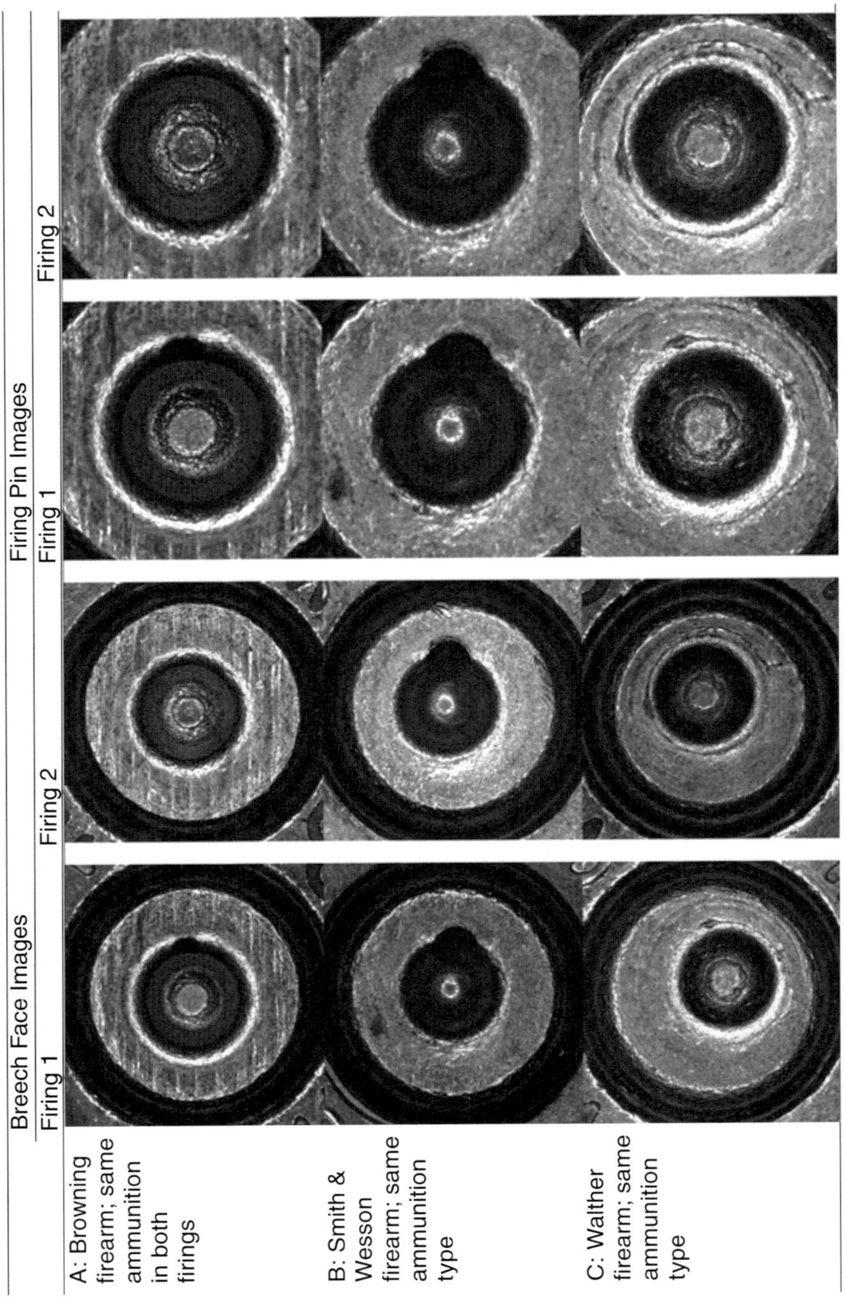

Breech Face Images
Firing Pin Images
Firing 1
Firing 2
Firing 1
Firing 2
A: Browning firearm; same ammunition in both firings
B: Smith & Wesson firearm; same ammunition type
C: Walther firearm; same ammunition type

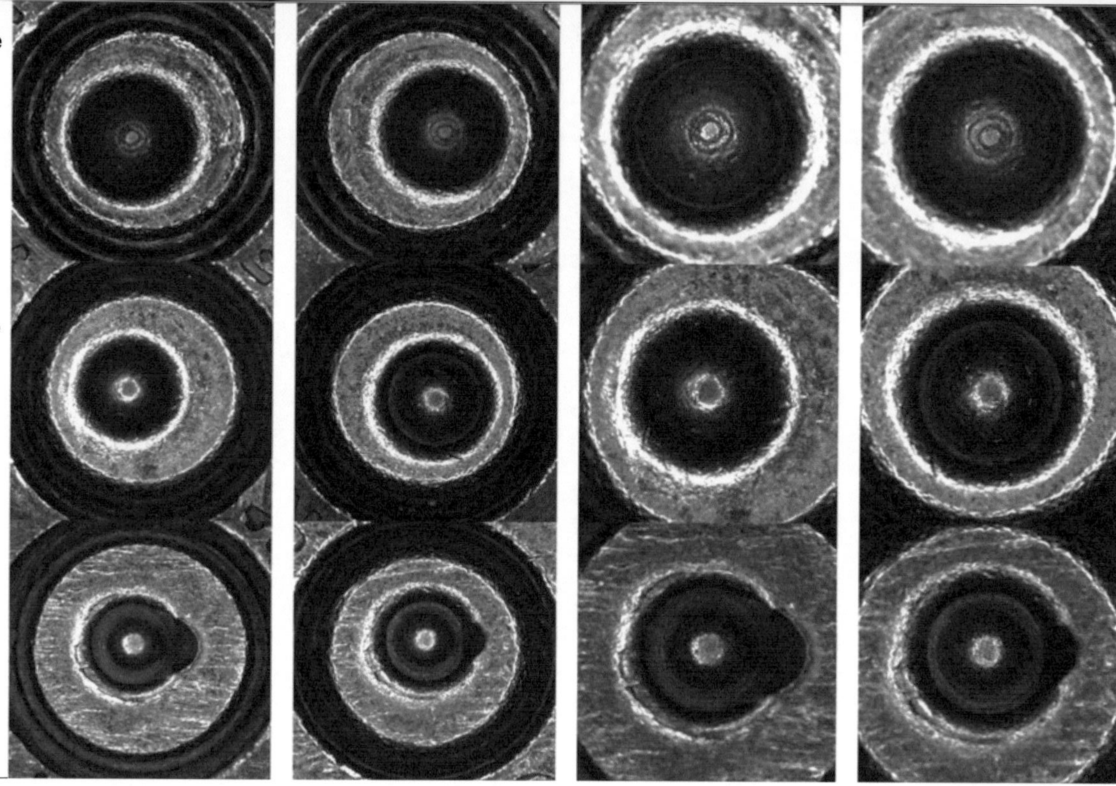

FIGURE 4-3 Sample matched pairs of breech face and firing pin images.
SOURCE: Images from Forensic Technology WAI, Inc., benchmark evaluation dataset of matched pairs of exhibits, shared with the committee.

TABLE 4-2 Summary Results of Forensic Technology WAI, Inc., Benchmark Evaluation

Caliber (No. of Pairs) and Database Size	Percentage of Success in Locating Sister Image, by Mark				
	BF	FP	BF+FP	EM	BF+FP+EM
9mm (434)					
868	53	74	84	—	—
56,000	39	53	66	—	—
9mm (78)					
4,030	51	56	82	46	94
.32 Auto (500)					
1,000	35	84	87	—	—
10,700	25	72	76	—	—
.45 Auto (474)					
948	55	57	73	—	—
3,535	47	49	65	—	—
.22 (500)					
1,000	—	—	—	87	—
3,070	—	—	—	87	—

NOTES: BF = breech face; FP = firing pin; EM = ejector mark or (for .22 caliber) rimfire firing pin impression. Sources vary on the standard used to define "success" in matching. Beauchamp and Roberge (2005) indicate that "success" refers to finding marks within the top 10 ranks, but Nennstiel and Rahm (2006a) note that comparison scores were reviewed down to 24 ranks.

SOURCES: Data from Beauchamp and Roberge (2005:11); see also McLean (2004) and Nennstiel and Rahm (2006a).

4–E.6 Other Studies

As is discussed further in Chapter 5, the Office of National Drug Control Policy (ONDCP) (1994) requested a benchmark comparison between the DRUGFIRE system and the early-IBIS BULLETPROOF systems, in the early days of ballistic imaging and as the potential for overlap became apparent. Though the hardware and software components of IBIS have improved since then, including the addition of BRASSCATCHER for imaging cartridge cases, this early examination is still noteworthy.

As its baseline database, the ONDCP used 150 matched pairs of both bullets and cartridge cases, collected from test fires of 30 weapons in each of five caliber groups (.25 Auto, .38 Auto, 9mm Luger, .38 Special/357 Magnum, and .45 Auto). These base data were then augmented with images acquired from other firearms, selected at random from exhibits in the existing FBI and ATF datasets and representing 100–500 additional weapons in each of the caliber groups. Tontarski and Thompson (1998:645) briefly summarized this benchmark evaluation in their overview paper of the new IBIS platform:

> During a series of stress tests, images were acquired outside the norms any trained operator would use. The tests included reducing and flaring the light sources, misplacing anchor lines, tilting the image during acquisition, incorrectly designating the striae angle, partially masking striae detail, and obliterating striae information by sanding a land engraved area. Even when combinations of mistakes were made, the system located the correct matching bullet among the top five candidates 85% of the time (22 out of 26 tests). A number of the tests included correlations where the images were acquired by two different operators.

More recently, smaller studies of IBIS performance have suggested possible improvements. Chan (2000) documented major changes in breech face and firing pin scores produced when a cartridge case is rotated by 90, 180, or 270 degrees from the FTI-suggested orientation. Staff of the Israel National Police have also generated a number of studies, based on experience in operating an IBIS installation since 1998. Argaman et al. (2001) document that department's policies for IBIS usage, including the entry of two or more cartridge casings when possible and the specification of manual date-limited queries in cases where information is known about the gun (e.g., the date it was known to be stolen). Silverwater and Koffman (2000) compare basic strategies for IBIS usage, including a strict policy to review the top five ranked results regardless of the score distribution and the entry of two cartridge cases when possible. Argaman et al. (2001) describe department policy for periodic reacquisition of cartridge case images—including entries from third or fourth firings, if possible—in order to get a sense of IBIS's reliability, while Giverts et al. (2002) suggest an "average phase" score for bullet comparisons. Schecter and Giverts (2005) suggest a workaround to improve IBIS performance when comparing Glock-type cartridge cases, for which the ejector mark impression lies within the casing's headstamp on the edge of the primer surface, and not on the outer rim of the casing. The suggested solution is to acquire the image of that region in the same manner as a single LEA on a bullet.

Fewer studies consider the impact of specific ammunition and firearms manufacturing processes on down-the-road IBIS performance. Hayes et al. (2004) tested whether the presence of a lacquer primer sealant over the entire primer surface (see Section 2–D.2) degrades IBIS scores in comparison with cases in which the sealant is removed. Sellier and Bellot 9mm rounds—known for a distinctive red lacquer coat over the entire primer surface—were fired through three makes of gun; several of the shells were cleaned with acetone prior to firing to remove the lacquer. Two lacquer-coated and two lacquer-stripped casings fired from each of three different guns were entered into the New York City Police Department's IBIS and scores were generated; at the time, the number of 9mm Luger, circular firing pin exhibits (the base set for this comparison) in the New York system was estimated at 5,700 images. Generally, guns known to produce clear characteristic breech face marks performed consistently regardless of the presence of lacquer, which is to say that pairs of lacquer-coated exhibits from the same gun were returned in the top ranks as were pairs of lacquer-stripped exhibits; guns known to produce fainter breech face marks produced lower-ranked matches, yet still generally in the top 10. However, matching lacquer-coated to lacquer-stripped exhibits from the same gun proved more problematic, apparently failing to clear the coarse correlation and 20 percent threshold steps for guns with weaker propensity to generate breech face marks (score reported as 0 and rank as "none"; Hayes et al., 2004:Table 1).

The IBIS function for comparing bullet evidence plays a prominent role in a multi-part examination of criteria for identifying bullet matches, and in particular standards for the number of groups of consecutive matching striations that can be said to define a match (Miller and McLean, 1998; Miller, 2000, 2004; see also Miller, 2001).

The committee's own experimentation, conducted by NIST under a separate contract with the National Institute of Justice, involved reanalysis of some of the De Kinder et al. (2004) cartridge casings as well as construction of a new 144-exhibit set of test-fired casings, varying ammunition brand and gun manufacturer. These casings were processed using both IBIS and three-dimensional metrology techniques, and were also run through IBIS waiving the coarse comparison and 20 percent threshold steps. We also performed limited IBIS experimentation using the New York CoBIS RBID and the independent IBIS database of the New York Police Department. We discuss the full details in Chapter 8; in brief summary, our own investigation corroborated the major findings of the predecessor studies described in this chapter.

4–F ASSESSMENT

The committee was charged to offer advice on the options of maintaining the current NIBIN program (limited to crime gun evidence) or enhancing it, and since NIBIN uses IBIS as its technical base, the evaluation of one requires evaluation of the other. Yet focusing too much on assessment of current IBIS is also somewhat unfair in light of the charge to our committee to evaluate the feasibility of a national RBID. As De Kinder et al. (2004:208) note, "currently, no technology has been perfected to deal specifically with very large databases of images of marks made by firearms." IBIS was developed to deal with smaller, regional "open case files" of images, and it is unreasonable to expect that the full system used to implement a national RBID would follow exactly the same lines as the current IBIS platform. However, an RBID system—perhaps streamlining the image acquisition process, allowing for mass entry of exhibits, and continuing to refine comparison procedures—would likely be based on IBIS, if only to maintain compatibility with NIBIN data.

As noted above, a subgroup of our committee discussed the IBIS comparison algorithm in detail with FTI staff under a confidential agreement. It is our judgment that the algorithm is generally quite sound, novel, and appropriate to the task of comparing images of ballistics evidence. Based on the era in which it was developed, IBIS is a valuable system that is fundamentally a vast improvement over relying on either human memory or the posting of Polaroids on the forensic laboratory bulletin board for deriving matches to evidence in open case files. Properly used—as we describe in Chapter 6—we believe that IBIS provides an adequate investigative tool for local and regional searches of ballistics evidence images. However, as we explain in fuller detail in Chapter 8, the review of past studies of IBIS performance and our own experimental work suggest that IBIS does not operate at the precision needed for a national RBID.

In its structure and implementation, the IBIS platform is a computerized version of the comparison microscope. This is beneficial in certain respects, in that it provides a familiar (albeit not exactly identical) interface for firearms examiners to review image data. Yet it is also, fundamentally, a limitation of the technology. Since its origins in the early 1990s, the progress in developing the existing IBIS platform for ballistic imaging has been evolutionary rather than revolutionary, in that it has remained anchored to the premise of emulating the functions of a comparison microscope. Direct pairwise comparisons of exhibits remain the heart of the process; IBIS was not designed to perform as a true image "search engine," indexing and comparing across large sets of images, as would be desirable in a national RBID implementation.

In its form and function, IBIS functions as a quick sorting and ranking mechanism: a tool for search, but not verification. There is great value in the sorting that is performed with relative ease and speed by IBIS. However, major problems arise when higher expectations are placed on the system than it was designed to accommodate. Users and policy makers bear a large part of the responsibility for "overselling" the system; it is unrealistic to expect "hits" on every database search, as effective use of the system depends as much or more on the timely entry of evidence into the system as on the ability of the system to detect a possible match. The system is also ill-served by the expectations of instantaneous and utterly definitive verification of evidence matches created by portrayals in popular media; Box 4-2 presents an example.

Overly high expectations and inaccurate portrayals have the unfortunate consequence of fueling the perception of ballistic imaging technology as a *test*—a source of verification—rather than a search tool. Most recently, this perception arose in litigation in Illinois (*People v. Pursley*, 341 Ill. App. 3d 230; 2003 Ill. App. LEXIS 784, 2003). In 2000, in light of exonerations due to DNA evidence, Illinois code was amended to give convicts the right to make a "motion for fingerprint or forensic testing not available at trial regarding actual innocence"—that is, to permit appeals for DNA testing. Invoking this provision, a man convicted in 1993 of first degree murder (and sentenced to life), largely on the basis of firearms identification evidence, "filed a motion . . . seeking an order requiring that his handgun be tested under the Integrated Ballistics Identification System (IBIS)." The appeals court ruled against the convict's motion for IBIS "testing," holding that the relevant statute was intended only to apply to fingerprint and DNA testing. Nowhere in the ruling (or, presumably, the motion) is it indicated what a "test under IBIS" might entail, how a comparison score might be interpreted, or against what database images should be searched. Only once (summarizing the state's motion to dismiss the convict's appeal) is it noted that "IBIS is not a new test but a new system for cataloging for ballistics information" and that "application of the IBIS would not produce new, noncumulative evidence."[7] Following the *Pursley* decision, Carso (2007) argued that the Illinois statute should be amended to include "ballistics testing" using IBIS but also does not describe what such a test would involve.

IBIS developers and proponents also bear responsibility for "over-

---

[7]Judge Gertner's ruling in *United States v. Green* (405 F.Supp. 2d 104; 2005 U.S. Dist. LEXIS 34273), described in Box 3-4, is also of interest because IBIS was used in the course of the investigation. It suggests that some basic concepts of IBIS scope and operation can be misconstrued. Section G of the ruling notes:

> [The sergeant/examiner] also used the Integratable [sic] Ballistic [sic] Identification System (IBIS) in his comparison, although the government represented that it would not offer IBIS results [as testimony]. A national computer database, IBIS allows examiners to identify the most likely matches for the evidence in a given case. IBIS uses a laser measuring device to evaluate shell casings and provides the examiner with a list of possible matches. . . . In fact, the IBIS system has been widely criticized. Its efficacy is limited by the detail with which police departments have scanned old shell casings into the computer and the accuracy of the mathematical algorithms used to compare casings. As with the individual examinations, no evidence was presented about the accuracy of the IBIS matches. . . . In any event, [the sergeant] acknowledged that even if the computer suggests numerous possible matches, he will not bother to check them all. That is, once he decides he has found a match, he will not eliminate all other alternatives by exhausting the IBIS-generated list of potential matches.

BOX 4-2
***CSI* Ballistic Imaging**

Firearms identification concepts and the use of ballistic imaging have periodically been referenced on forensic science-themed television shows. One such example is episode 307 ("Fight Night") of *CSI: Crime Scene Investigation*; this particular episode won an Emmy award for best writing. One scene finds a Las Vegas investigator talking with a firearms examiner who is peering intently into the microscope of what—externally—is a complete IBIS RDAS unit. The investigator asks, "Three guns found at the crime scene, none match the bullets recovered from the victim. What does that tell us?" "Shooter kept his weapon," the examiner replies. "Means he likes his gun, and may have used it before," says the investigator, as some part of the machinery makes a loud whirring noise. "Which is where the shell case and IBIS come in," says the examiner cheerfully. "I'll run it against the national database."

He wheels from the microscope to the keyboard and, off-camera, types a short sequence of characters. "Firing pin impressions and breech face marks—a closer look," muses the investigator; instantaneously, the system makes a loud shuffling sound and several beeps. The camera now shows the "IBIS" screen, which prominently shows a single image of the entire base of a cartridge, headstamp and all; some text indicating "Halo On" and "Magnification 150X," among other things, is superimposed over the corner of the image. Beside it is a four-column listing of "Case ID," "Exhibit Number," "Site Number," and "Firing Pin;" the entries are obviously not sorted in descending order by the purported firing pin score (that is, three digit "scores" are interspersed with two digit scores). The *middle* entry (clearly not the highest legible score, albeit close) flashes blue several times as the system beeps; at no point does a second, comparison casing image appear.

"Got us a hit," the examiner intones, now reading off of a new window that has popped up on screen. "Los Angeles County Sheriff's Department found . . . shell casings from the same gun . . . used in a gang murder two years ago." The investigator interjects, "They get a conviction on the suspect?" "No. Guy beat the rap," the examiner continues. "Timothy Fontaine, aka 'Tiny Tim' . . . member of the Snakebacks . . . current residence unknown." The "Criminal Records" window that appears on the screen also includes entries for a vehicle license number and the name of an arresting officer; unfortunately, the space clearly reserved for a photo of the person is labeled "NP AVAILABLE." The investigator says, "I bet I could find where he stays in Vegas," and the scene ends. The total elapsed time of the scene is 44 seconds.

promising" the system, in at least two crucial and related respects. The first is the pervasive mythology that has come to surround the "top 10" results in an IBIS search. The current IBIS provides as its default printed report a listing of the 10 highest scores by each type of marking, and IBIS training materials undercut guidance to consider gaps and features in the distribution of comparison scores by promoting the examination of the top 10 suggested matches. However, the implied physical or cognitive restriction to the top 10 results is not likely to be appropriate in all searches or all database sizes, and the focus on the top 10 results is inadequate for assessing the system's performance and for understanding the variability of scores by demographic characteristics (e.g., gun make and model). We know of no substantiated rationale for the ad hoc cutoff at rank 10; the resulting assumption that nothing outside of the top 10 ranked is valuable puts unduly high expectations on the system.

The second basic flaw is the use of the term "correlation" to describe the IBIS comparison process, which imputes to the system an unjustified air of technical exactness. The common, statistical use of the term implies a particular type of relationship and quantifies the strength of that relationship. In comparison, IBIS scores are described by the system's own training materials as having no intrinsic value, severely limiting the ability to express the strength of similarity between two exhibits and to compare results across different runs of the system. As we suggest in Chapter 6, we believe that the usefulness of IBIS is compromised unless some meaning can be imputed to its "correlation" scores—to make them function more like true statistical correlations.

4–G APPENDIX: SUMMARY OF PERFORMANCE TESTS IN THE CALIFORNIA EVALUATION OF A REFERENCE BALLISTIC IMAGE DATABASE

This appendix describes the tests performed by Tulleners (2001) in response to the California legislature's directive that the state's Department of Justice study the feasibility of a reference ballistic image database. We begin by profiling those tests that were actually completed; these summaries extract additional information from spreadsheet printouts that were included as an appendix to Tulleners (2001). We also describe those tests that were planned for the evaluation but were unable to be completed, and summarize the formal responses to and independent assessment of the California evaluation.

4–G.1 Completed Performance Tests

The Tulleners (2001) technical evaluation was based on the completion of five performance tests.

Test 1—Basic System Correlation

Two cartridges were fired from each of the 792 CHP pistols, one to be entered into a "test" database and the other retained as an "evidence" exhibit. All of these firings used the same Federal brand ammunition. The basic goals of this test were to assess the time required to enter specimens into a database and to test the accuracy of comparison as database size increases.

The first component of this test considered the basic ability of the system to find exhibits for guns known to be in the database. A sample of 50 test cartridges (the same-gun pairs of "evidence" entries already in the database) was drawn, and queries were made against the full database. Twenty-four (48 percent) of these test casings matched to their sister evidence casing as the first-ranked entry in either breech face or firing pin mark. However, a surprisingly high 19 of the comparisons (38 percent) did not find the sister casing within the top 10 ranked items in either breech face or firing pin,[8] of which 9 (18 percent) of these known-match comparisons failed to clear IBIS' coarse comparison and 20 percent threshold.[9] It does not appear that one mark was superior to the other in terms of generating possible matches: the 31 instances where the known sister was found in the top 10 by either mark are fairly evenly divided between cases where both marks were in the top 10 (10), only the breech face was in the top 10 (9), and only the firing pin was in the top 10 (12).

A second component of the test selected five of the "evidence" casings used in the first test that had low ranks on one or both markings; these were reacquired by a second IBIS operator and matched against smaller subsets of the data to see if those changes affected the rankings. In terms of comparisons to the full database, the rankings changed using the image from the second operator but not grossly so; no very low-ranked exhibits were converted to high ranks, although two of the casings apparently failed to clear the 20 percent threshold in the reacquisition.[10] The entries were compared against database subsets of size 100, 200, 300, 400, 500, 600, 700, and 792; generally, rankings degraded with the larger sample

[8]The main text of Tulleners (2001) indicates these figures as being searches for matches in the top 15 ranked items, but it can be verified from the "raw data" spreadsheets in Appendix C of the technical evaluation that the statements hold for the stronger (and more conventional) top 10 filter.

[9]Failure to clear the 20 percent threshold is assumed from the "Not in Selection" entry for both score types (breech face and firing pin) in the technical evaluation spreadsheets.

[10]One of these, labeled E44 in the first test and E152A in the reacquisition, appears to have had a significant difference in the acquisition of the firing pin image. The exhibit was ranked 45 on breech face and 1 on firing pin in the first analysis, but apparently failed to clear the 20 percent threshold and was excluded from listing in the reanalysis (Tulleners, 2001: Appendix C).

sizes, though very high-ranked exhibits tended to stay very high (e.g., a one-ranked exhibit on firing pin remained the number one rank for all the sizes, and a two-ranked exhibit for the 100-entry database slipped to rank six in the full 792 set).[11]

Test 2—Cartridges Not in Database

Ten cartridges were fired using the same Federal brand cartridges but using 10 pistols of the same make and model not from the new CHP order. The comparison scores for the best match on both marks were recorded and were judged to be consistent with the range of scores registered in Test 1, several with the high end of that range. However, the evaluation accepted FTI's advice that "a score is only relevant within a particular correlation" and that "the score cannot be used to compare the ranking of two correlations." The test was found to be inconclusive.

Test 3—Different Ammunition

During the test firing of the CHP pistols, 22 of the pistols were also used to fire rounds using batches of five different ammunition brands: PMC-Eldorado (.40 S&W 180 grain), CORBON (.40 S&W 165 grain), ARMSCOR (.40 S&W 180 grain), Remington (.40 S&W 180 grain), and Winchester (.40 S&W 180 grain). Not all of the ammunition types were fired from each of the guns; 72 cartridges were acquired in total. Each of these casings was then compared with the 792-exhibit set to test the ability of the system to find the Federal-brand test fire from the same gun in the database.

The test found poor results in finding matches to the images from Federal-brand ammunition using images from the other five brands. Sixteen of the 72 comparisons (22 percent) matched to the image from the same gun as the top-ranked result on either the breech face or firing pin impressions; in total, 21 of the comparisons (29 percent) had the known sister image occur in the top 10 ranks on either mark. Neither mark was better at generating matches; 13 top-10 matches were found on the breech face mark and 14 on the firing pin. No match was found in the top 10 ranks by either mark in 26 of the comparisons (36 percent), and 25 of the comparisons (35 percent) failed to clear the coarse comparison and 20 percent threshold.

[11]A third part of the test timed the comparison times for three selected exhibits for database subsets of different sizes (100, 250, 500, 792). From the results, Tulleners (2001:8-5) concluded that "correlation times are not a significant issue for a large database" although he assumed a strict linear interpolation in processing times.

Tabulations from Tulleners (2001:Appendix C) suggest that the ARMSCOR and Corbon ammunition proved particularly difficult to match. Out of 14 matches of ARMSCOR rounds to the Federal-brand images in the database by breech face, 6 failed to clear the coarse comparison step, and 8 ranked lower than 25; 13 Corbon comparisons were attempted, with 8 being rejected at the coarse comparison stage and only one ranking better than 25 (but out of the top 10). Results by firing pin were similar, with a few more rankings in the 11–25 range and one ARMSCOR round finding its Federal-brand sister as the top-ranked result. The Winchester rounds proved most amenable to matches in the 18 comparisons that were made: 7 found the Federal sister round in the top-ranked slot, with 1 ranking 11–25, 6 ranking below 25, and 4 missing the 20 percent threshold (see also De Kinder's [2002b:11] analysis of the same spreadsheet).

Test 4—Altered Breech Face

After firing the two Federal-brand cartridges for the "test" and "evidence" sets, the firing pin tip and breech face of one of the CHP pistols was subjected to "minimum file and sandpaper efforts" to attempt to change the firearm's individualizing marks (Tulleners, 2001:B-5). "This filing alteration took about three minutes using a standard file" (Tulleners, 2001:7-3). A second set of two test fires with Federal ammunition was then performed, one for entry in the database and the other used as an "evidence" query. The two sets of exhibits, before and after alteration, matched to each other well: the pre-alteration casings matched to each other in the top-ranked position on both firing pin and breech face and the post-alteration casings matched as the top-ranked pairing on firing pin (however, the rank was 35 on breech face). However, no match was possible from the pre-alteration to the post-alteration exhibits; in both cases, the technical evaluation's data appendix lists the matches as "not in selection list," suggesting that the deliberate alteration prevented the exhibits from clearing the IBIS coarse comparison pass.

Test 7—Breech Face Longevity Study

In a test intended to determine whether a breech face maintains individual marks over repeated firings, an independent laboratory was contracted to perform 600 test fires from each of two .40 caliber pistols; the make of one was described as a Glock type and the other as unknown (Tulleners, 2001:8-11). The Glock-type pistol was fired using CCI brand ammunition, and IMI ammunition was used in the unknown-make pistol. For each pistol, casings in the intervals 1–6, 101–106, 201–206, 301–306, 401–406, 501–506, and 595–600 were retained for analysis; one casing from each interval was used as the "test" database and the other as "evidence" entries. Ultimately, the Glock-type firings turned out to be unusable due to the lack of a larger database for comparison; none of the other CHP weapons have Glock type firing pins, so they could not be compared to the Glock firings due to IBIS' demographic filtering. Tulleners (2001:8-11) concluded that there were signs of "definitive ranking degradation" as the firings from later intervals were tended to rank lower than those from the earlier firings among the IMI cartridges. However, the evaluation suggested that "further tests need to be conducted in this area."

4–G.2 Incomplete Performance Tests

Tulleners (2001) was unable to carry out tests 5, 6, and 8 in his original slate of experiments. Test 5 was intended to assess IBIS performance using cartridges fired from SIG Sauer firearms, which are known among examiners for having minimal breech face characteristics. An extensive set of SIG Sauer test fires was subsequently used in Tulleners' joint study, De Kinder et al. (2004), described in the next section. Test 8 was meant to test the system using firearms known to have strong subclass characteristic carry-over, such as some Heckler and Koch and Lorcin firearms (see Section 3–B.1).

Test 6 "would have taken some test-fired cartridge cases from selected weapons, buried one of the cartridge cases in a large database and then observe the correlation on these cartridge cases" (Tulleners, 2001:7-3, 7-4). The California Department of Justice was unable to complete the test as planned, though it arranged for a limited test along the same lines to be conducted by the New York City Police Department (NYPD). The California Criminalistics Institute submitted eight casings each fired from two 9mm SIG Sauer pistols. In each set, two rounds used Remington-Peters ammunition, and the other firings used Winchester, Federal, Hornady Vector, Fiocchi, CCI, and Sellier and Bellot ammunition. One of the Remington rounds was retained as the "evidence" casing, so that for each of the two pistols, seven sister images were mixed into the NYPD's 9mm database, which then contained 3,673 items. For both pistols, four of the seven sister images were found in the top 15 ranks by either breech face or firing pin, and the second Remington round generally turned up as the top-ranked entry by either mark. The Hornady Vector, CCI, and Sellier and Bellot rounds "seemed to be the most difficult for comparison" (Tulleners, 2001:8-10).

4–G.3 Criticisms and Independent Review

Rebutting the California study on behalf of ATF, Thompson et al. (2002:15, 16) argued most stridently that "all of [the performance test results] are skewed due to the selection of Federal Brand ammunition." They argue that Federal is not the prescribed "ATF protocol ammunition in any of the calibers of interest, due to the primer surface generally being too hard in comparison to the ammunition being used in handguns." Instead, they suggested Remington-Peters ammunition as a more suitable medium. In his review, De Kinder (2002b:9–11) rejected this argument, citing research by the Forensic Institute in The Netherlands on IBIS score results using 18 common primers suggesting that Federal showed medium performance in registering marks. (Unfortunately, the Dutch study did not include Remington ammunition, as it is not common in Europe.) More directly, De Kinder noted that hardness properties of primers are not well known but hardness measures for the six types of ammunition used in California's Test 3 had been independently conducted by the Lawrence Livermore National Laboratory. The Federal brass primers were directly measured to be the least hard of the six (108 ± 5HV), including Remington-Peters' nickel primers (157 ± 12HV).[12]

In its rebuttal to the California study, FTI (2002:5) argued that "the *Evaluation* has an overly pessimistic view of automated ballistics technology that discredits its conclusions." In Test 1, FTI (2002:14–15), submits that too great a focus on the 38 percent of possible matches missing from the top 15 ranks unduly discounts the 48 percent that found the correct match in the top rank on one of the marks and the 62 percent that matched within the top 15 on either rank. "These results are sufficient to identify a significant number of cartridge cases that merit manual study and would have produced new cold hits." More fundamentally, FTI (2002:13, 14) holds that the IBIS system was held to an unfair standard in the test. A firearms examiner manually compared the cases for FTI and concluded that he could not certify a match between eight of the Test 1 pairs and that "approximately half had markings that were somewhat unfavorable." As a result, FTI suggested that at least the eight human-identified nonmatches be excluded from the statistics, arguing:

> It is immediately obvious that the performance of an automated examination could not, and should not, be more accurate than a microscope comparison by a firearms examiner. Thus, to the extent that the *Evaluation* included cartridge cases that had insufficient marks to be identified by a firearms examiner, the results cannot support the hypothesis, and the *Evaluation* must be without scientific value.

[12]De Kinder also noted that the criticism of Federal ammunition was unusual, given that Federal had been chosen for a similar study by several of the same ATF authors (Thompson et al., 1996).

On these points, De Kinder (2002b:14) concluded that the FTI arguments were an overreach. He countered that the passage quoted above "is the same type of expression as saying at the beginning of the 1990[s] that automated comparison of bullets and cartridge casings is impossible." He preferred instead the revised statement that "the current scientific knowledge and state-of-the-art technology does not allow one to be more accurate than a microscope comparison by a firearms examiner." De Kinder held that dropping the believed-"unmatchable" exhibits from analysis is "unacceptable," particularly given that the study was oriented to studying the feasibility of an RBID. "All data points have to be taken into consideration" because "the goal of [an RBID] is not restricted to those cartridge cases that can be identified by a trained firearm examiner."

Generally, De Kinder (2002b) indicated approval of the conduct and interpretation of the major performance tests in the California study. He suggested the need for further study in a variety of areas.

5

Current Ballistic Image Databases: NIBIN and the State Reference Databases

Computerized image analysis systems, such as the Integrated Ballistics Identification System (IBIS), brought the promise of overcoming some of the limitations of dealing effectively with open case files of ballistics evidence. Well utilized, a ballistic image database maintained by an individual law enforcement agency could now surpass previous limitations of time and human recall. "Human memory or selected bullet or cartridge casing photographs [were] the only tools normally available" to draw connections between ballistics evidence in different cases; "it [was] not normally feasible to be able to link cases beyond a few weeks or months unless investigative intelligence otherwise links the cases" (Tontarski and Thompson, 1998:642). But another vexing challenge to traditional examination remained: the ability to draw connections between cases between different law enforcement agencies and different geographic areas. To meet this need—to make it easier for agencies in a geographic region to submit evidence for imaging and comparison and to make it possible to highlight possible connections between cases across geographic lines—a wider network of ballistic imaging sites was necessary. Over the course of the 1990s, the National Integrated Ballistic Information Network (NIBIN) emerged and developed to meet this need.

In this chapter we describe the NIBIN program, two main policy options for which—maintenance as is or enhancement by various means—we are charged to assess. We describe the historical evolution of the program in Section 5–A and its current structure in Section 5–B. We then turn to various measures of the network's usage (5–C) and performance (5–D). Lastly, we describe in some detail in Section 5–E the existing reference ballistic image databases operated by the states of Maryland and New York. NIBIN and the state databases are decidedly not directly connected—as described in the section, the systems are physically walled off from each other as well as being distinctly different in their definition and composition. However, they are based on the same technical platform, and lessons from observing the state databases in operation can also inform possible enhancements for the NIBIN program. We return to the NIBIN policy options in Chapter 6. As with Chapter 4, a summary and our conclusions on the evidence in this chapter are in Chapter 6.

5–A EVOLUTION OF THE NIBIN PROGRAM

5–A.1 Early Development

The program that evolved into NIBIN began in 1992 with the development by the Bureau of Alcohol, Tobacco, Firearms, and Explosives (ATF) of the CEASEFIRE initiative, the objective of which was to "[enter] into a national computer system all data obtained from firearms seized as a result of a criminal investigation by ATF personnel" (NIBIN Program, 2001). Though oriented around a particular intervention by ATF personnel, the scope of the initiative was broader: "ATF intended to allow State and local law enforcement agencies to use and retrieve information for investigative purposes, and to submit information from their own firearms-related criminal investigations" (Thompson et al., 2002:10). Work on the database component developed in stages, beginning in 1993 with a partnering between the ATF National Laboratory Center in Ammendale, Maryland, and the Washington, DC, Metropolitan Police Department. This initial pilot work made it possible "to evaluate the impact of operator variability on image quality and matching, networking limitations, and ease of operator use for data entry, as well as correlations and system maintenance" (Tontarski and Thompson, 1998:646). The program grew to include other regional affiliations between ATF laboratories and major state and local law enforcement agencies: partnerships emerged between the ATF Atlanta laboratory and the Georgia Bureau of Investigation, and between the ATF Walnut Creek, California, laboratory to the Oakland Police Department and Contra Costa County Sheriff's laboratories. Also in 1993, the BULLETPROOF system—the bullets-only predecessor to IBIS (see Section 4–A)—was adopted as CEASEFIRE's hardware and software platform.

In 1995, ATF developed a set of criteria for participation in CEASEFIRE by state and local law enforcement agencies, including the population and firearms-related crime rates of areas; ATF also considered "known firearms trafficking routes that cross jurisdictional lines" in selecting sites (NIBIN Program, 2001:6). Priority was given to agencies that had demonstrated willingness to participate in joint investigative programs with the ATF. This initial set of criteria developed into the guidelines now used to evaluate new applicants to host NIBIN sites; see Box 5-1.

5–A.2 DRUGFIRE, Interoperability, and a Unified System

By the mid-1990s the looming problem of two potentially overlapping national databases became more apparent: the ATF continued to pursue development of CEASEFIRE at the same time that the Federal Bureau of Investigation (FBI) worked with law enforcement agencies to populate the DRUGFIRE database (see Box 5-2). The DRUGFIRE and CEASEFIRE systems were initially complementary, in that DRUGFIRE was focused on imaging cartridge case evidence and CEASEFIRE on imaging bullets. How-

BOX 5-1
Criteria for Participation in the NIBIN Program

To request participation in the NIBIN program, an executive of a state or local law enforcement agency had to submit a letter including the following information:

- the population of the area to be served by automated ballistics technology,
- the number of firearms-related violent crimes in the area serviced by the requesting agency,
- statistics on firearms-related assaults and homicides for the previous year,
- the number of firearms recovered by the requesting agency for the previous year,
- the number of firearms traced by the requesting agency during the previous year,
- whether the requesting agency had a firearms/toolmark examiner,
- whether the requesting agency would dedicate staff to support the data entry of ballistics information into the IBIS equipment,
- whether the requesting agency had a bullet and casing recovery system,
- whether the requesting agency had sufficient space that was climate controlled for placement of the equipment,
- whether the agency would allow other agencies to use the IBIS equipment if the requesting agency received it, and
- whether the agency would enter into a memorandum of understanding (MOU) with the ATF regarding the administration of the program.

SOURCE: Reproduced from U.S. Department of Justice, Office of Inspector General (2005:85–86).

BOX 5-2
DRUGFIRE

"Conceived by the FBI in 1991 as a part of the response to a call from the Office of National Drug Control Policy for an emergency action plan to help the Washington, DC Police cope with the rising tide of drug-related violence," the DRUGFIRE system was established in 1993 using a computer system developed by Mnemonics Systems, Inc. (Denio, 1999:383). DRUGFIRE differed from the successor IBIS in terms of which types of evidence were implemented first. IBIS began with BULLETPROOF (analyzing bullets) and later added the capacity to image cartridge cases (BRASSCATCHER). At the time of the Office of National Drug Control Policy (1994) benchmark evaluation of DRUGFIRE and BULLETPROOF, DRUGFIRE was solely limited to the analysis of cartridge casings; the ROTOSCAN add-on to acquire bullet images was developed around 1996 (Tulleners, 2001:2-2).

In their approach to acquiring and analyzing cartridge case evidence, DRUGFIRE and NIBIN diverge in two important respects. First, for purposes of comparison with other exhibits, DRUGFIRE "looked only at the breech face marks and not the firing pin impressions," while IBIS can separately generate scores and rankings by breech face, firing pin, and ejector marks. More fundamentally, DRUGFIRE used oblique illumination (side light), "much as used by firearms examiners at their comparison microscopes," while IBIS uses only radial illumination (center light) images for scoring purposes. The DRUGFIRE system typically required the acquisition of "two breech face images at 90-degree orientation" per exhibit (Tulleners, 2001:2-6).

Using DRUGFIRE technology, "cartridge cases are searched at approximately ten images per second; bullets are searched at approximately one image per second." Accordingly, "for large databases, users are encouraged to use filters based on class characteristics so that the number of images passed to the automated search is drastically reduced" (Denio, 1999:384).

As of May 1999, DRUGFIRE installations were located in 150 sites (Denio, 1999); Boesman and Krouse (2001) report that about 171 law enforcement agencies participated in DRUGFIRE between 1993 and 2001. Tulleners (2001: D-1) surveyed ballistic image database usage by a number of California law enforcement agencies, including the DRUGFIRE data collected from agencies in southern California (including the Los Angeles Police Department) and maintained by the Orange County Sheriff's Department. Across southern California, DRUGFIRE was credited with 431 cold hits on a total of 37,494 entries from centerfire weapons (about 78 percent of which were test fires from recovered firearms and 22 percent were evidence cartridges).

ever, as both systems continued to develop, and as the technology underlying both programs was upgraded to handle both bullets and cartridge cases, practical concerns about redundancy (the need to maintain two systems) and resources came into greater relief.

In 1995 the Office of National Drug Control requested an independent technical "benchmark evaluation" of the BULLETPROOF and DRUGFIRE technologies to inform a comparison between the systems. The tests performed during this benchmark evaluation suggested strengths in both systems. However, the evaluation concluded that "processing casings and projectiles on a common versatile platform would best fulfill ballistic imaging requirements." This recommendation added impetus to the development of BRASSCATCHER as a counterpart to BULLETPROOF, and the combined IBIS system became the norm in existing and new CEASEFIRE sites in 1996.

In January 1996 the FBI and ATF jointly agreed in a memorandum of understanding that IBIS and DRUGFIRE equipment should be made interoperable—specifically, that both systems "are able to (1) capture an image according to a standard protocol and in conformity with a minimum quality standard and (2) exchange images electronically in such a manner that an image captured on one system can be analyzed and correlated on the other" (NIBIN Program, 2001:7). The joint effort was dubbed the NIBIN system. Accordingly, a contract was established with the National Institute of Standards and Technology to study the technical interoperability of the two systems. Ultimately, however, true technical interoperability of the systems—converting the data in each system so that they would be used on both the DRUGFIRE and IBIS platforms—was not achieved. Instead, in 1999 a new memorandum of understanding established a partnership structure: the technical platform of the ATF program (IBIS) was adopted as the hardware/software standard, and the network would be constructed using the high-speed secure infrastructure maintained by the FBI.

The partnership between the FBI and ATF in building NIBIN was further cemented by the structure of the NIBIN executive board (consisting of one senior ATF executive, one senior FBI executive, and an executive from a state or local law enforcement agency) and its technical working groups. However, by October 2003, it was recognized that having two agencies responsible for different aspects of the same national program was an ineffective management arrangement. Accordingly, network responsibilities and authority were transferred from the FBI to ATF, and ATF became solely responsible for all aspects of the NIBIN program.

5–A.3 Full Implementation

State and local law enforcement agencies were added to the network in stages. An initial network connecting several northeastern agencies was set up in late 1998 (McLean, 1999:392), and the steps toward full rollout of the program were formalized in a strategic plan in 2000. The largest push in the rollout occurred during a 2-year deployment in 2001–2002, "in which 160 sites have received IBIS equipment," moving toward a "completed" network of "approximately 233 sites" (Thompson et al., 2002:11).

Thompson et al. (2002:11–12) note that "agencies may become part of the NIBIN program in two ways: through inclusion on the tentative deployment list or by nomination." In addition to signing a memorandum of understanding—agreeing to abide by ATF's regulations for use of the equipment including the entry of evidence from crime-related guns only (Thompson et al., 2002:12)—

> An agency must commit its own resources to the NIBIN program. . . . Agencies joining NIBIN must commit to maintaining adequate staff to support the program, and will need a comparison microscope and access to a bullet recovery system to testfire firearms. Agencies receiving a Remote Data Acquisition Station (RDAS) must have a firearms examiner available to evaluate correlation results; in some labs it is helpful to have trained technicians make entries into the IBIS system, freeing examiners to review results and confirm hits by examination of the original evidence. . . . Partner agencies must commit to entering as much crime gun evidence into the unit as possible, and to sharing intelligence information and evidence with other law enforcement agencies.

An audit report on the NIBIN program by the U.S. Department of Justice (DOJ), Office of Inspector General (2005) indicates that "the ATF has not made any plans to deploy IBIS equipment to additional agencies beyond [those] that have already received it," save for case-by-case requests by individual agencies and relocation of equipment from low-usage sites. However, the report suggests efforts to expand NIBIN technically by linking it with the ATF's N-Force case management system and to the National Tracing Center. "The ATF is also conducting a pilot program called 'COPS and DOCS,' which joins together health care and law enforcement professionals who recover firearms evidence and enter it into NIBIN. . . . When gunshot victims are brought into the hospital, bullets from wounds are packaged with identifying information and placed in an evidence box that is located in the hospital's operating room." The recovered bullets are then retrieved and entered into NIBIN by ATF (U.S. Department of Justice, Office of Inspector General, 2005:13–14).

5–B NIBIN CONTENT AND STRUCTURE

5–B.1 Regions and Partitions

As of December 2005, the NIBIN program included 228 partner sites representing 182 agencies. At least one NIBIN site is located in each state with the exception of Kentucky. The sites are grouped into 12 geographic regions, each of which is linked to servers in one of ATF's three national laboratories. Servers at the ATF laboratory in Ammendale, Maryland, are the central hub for NIBIN sites in the northeast and north central states; servers in Atlanta, Georgia, link the southeast United States and Puerto Rico; and Walnut Creek, California, is the focal point for NIBIN sites in Texas, the western United States, Alaska, Hawaii, and Guam. The geographic distribution of NIBIN sites and servers is illustrated in Figure 5-1.

The regional servers are central to the operation of NIBIN. They are not only the central data repository for the region—combining and archiving data from the distributed sites—but also the "correlation" servers for the region as well. That is, an exhibit entered into NIBIN in Idaho is uploaded to the Walnut Creek servers for comparison with other NIBIN exhibits; the correlation results are then sent back to Idaho for review. Batches of exhibits are transferred from the local sites to the regional servers at least once a day; the exhibits are compiled, comparison scores are generated, and results and images sent back to the local sites.

Each of the regional servers is divided into several partitions; these partitions are important because they define the range of automatic comparisons (versus those comparisons requested manually). For example, NIBIN region 1B covers central and southern California, and it is divided into three partitions (roughly, northern, central, and southern). The southern partition contains two NIBIN installations: the San Diego Police Department and the San Diego County Sheriff's Department. Hence, an exhibit entered into NIBIN by the San Diego County Sheriff's Department is automatically correlated against exhibits from both San Diego-area NIBIN sites (after uploading to Walnut Creek). However, searches against data from other sites—Los Angeles or Orange Counties, for example, or Yuma, Arizona—must be specially requested by a NIBIN operator. The Inspector General audit of NIBIN (U.S. Department of Justice, Office of Inspector General, 2005:110) notes:

> Although regional and national searches can be performed, they must be manually selected. To perform a regional search, the requestor must designate where to search from a map of the NIBIN regions. The requestor is then presented with a list of all the partner agencies in that region, and can either search against all the partner agencies shown or de-select those partner agencies that the requestor does not want included in the search.

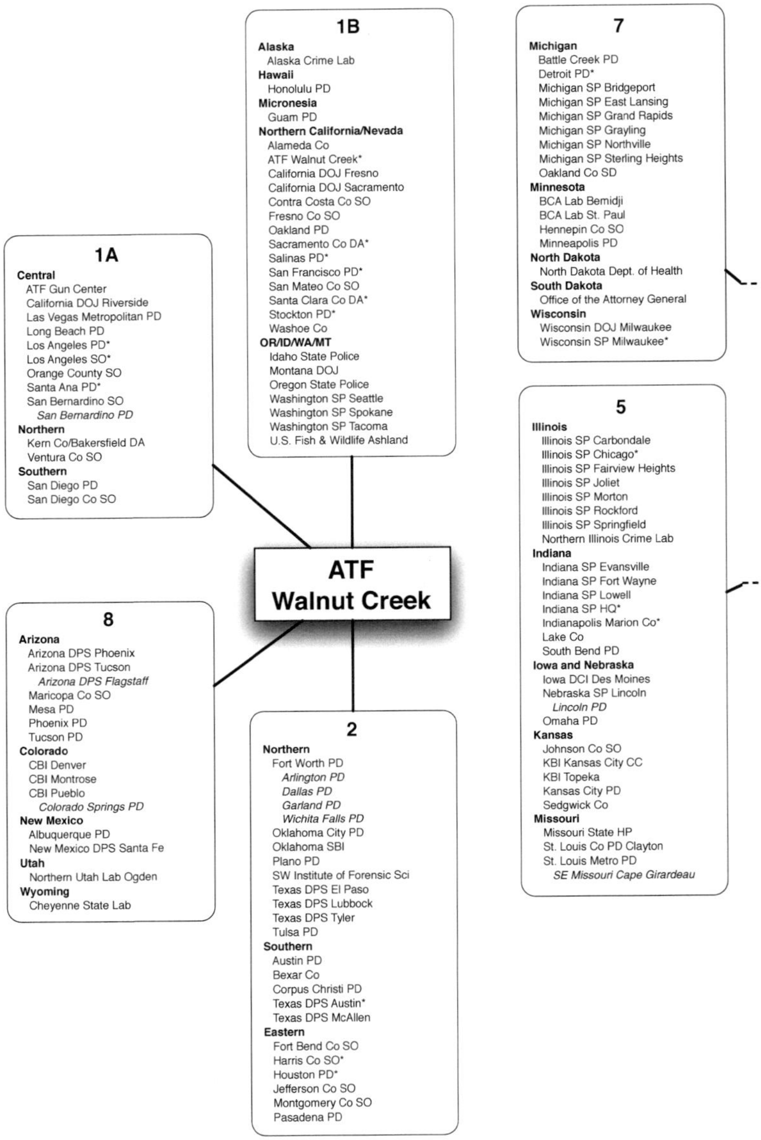

FIGURE 5-1 Geographic distribution of NIBIN sites.
NOTES: * indicates presence of more than one piece of equipment (e.g., multiple RDAS stations or combination of RDAS and Matchpoint viewers); see Chapter 4 for description of IBIS equipment. Region numbers are indicated at top of boxes; partitions are indicated in bold type; portable Rapid Brass Identification (RBI) units are indicated in italic, nested beneath their RDAS partner site.
SOURCE: U.S. Department of Justice Inspector General (2005:App.VI).

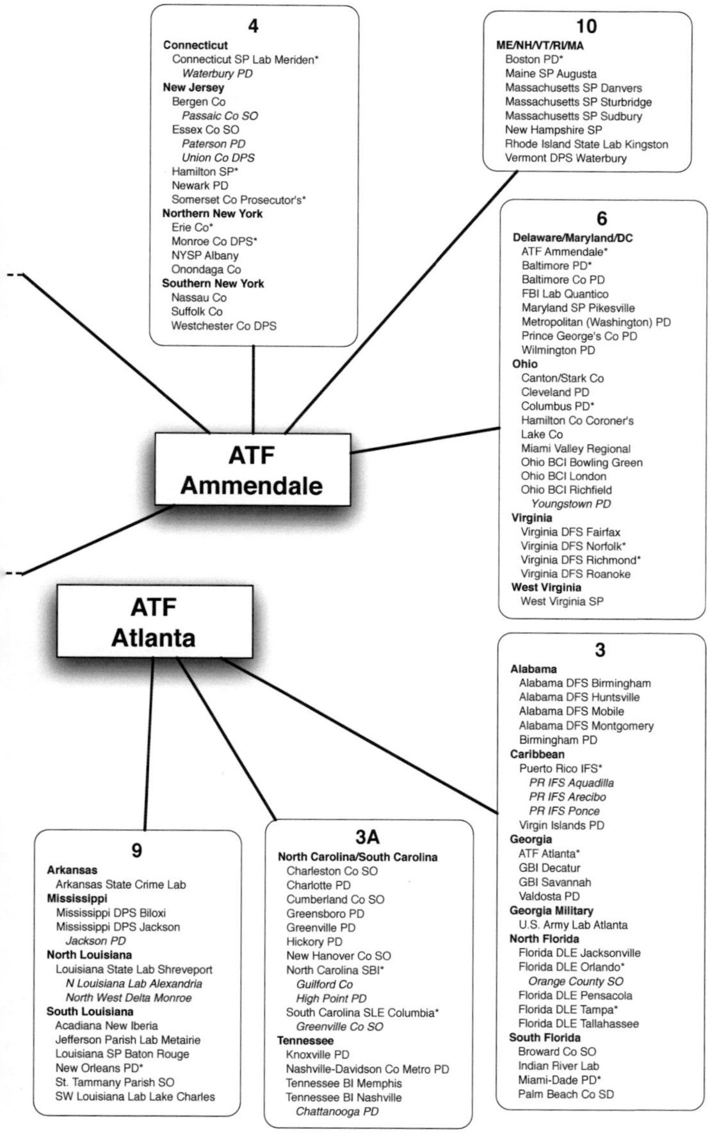
4
Connecticut
Connecticut SP Lab Meriden*
Waterbury PD
New Jersey
Bergen Co
Passaic Co SO
Essex Co SO
Paterson PD
Union Co DPS
Hamilton SP*
Newark PD
Somerset Co Prosecutor's*
Northern New York
Erie Co*
Monroe Co DPS*
NYSP Albany
Onondaga Co
Southern New York
Nassau Co
Suffolk Co
Westchester Co DPS
10
ME/NH/VT/RI/MA
Boston PD*
Maine SP Augusta
Massachusetts SP Danvers
Massachusetts SP Sturbridge
Massachusetts SP Sudbury
New Hampshire SP
Rhode Island State Lab Kingston
Vermont DPS Waterbury
6
Delaware/Maryland/DC
ATF Ammendale*
Baltimore PD*
Baltimore Co PD
FBI Lab Quantico
Maryland SP Pikesville
Metropolitan (Washington) PD
Prince George's Co PD
Wilmington PD
Ohio
Canton/Stark Co
Cleveland PD
Columbus PD*
Hamilton Co Coroner's
Lake Co
Miami Valley Regional
Ohio BCI Bowling Green
Ohio BCI London
Ohio BCI Richfield
Youngstown PD
Virginia
Virginia DFS Fairfax
Virginia DFS Norfolk*
Virginia DFS Richmond*
Virginia DFS Roanoke
West Virginia
West Virginia SP
ATF Ammendale
ATF Atlanta
3
Alabama
Alabama DFS Birmingham
Alabama DFS Huntsville
Alabama DFS Mobile
Alabama DFS Montgomery
Birmingham PD
Caribbean
Puerto Rico IFS*
PR IFS Aquadilla
PR IFS Arecibo
PR IFS Ponce
Virgin Islands PD
Georgia
ATF Atlanta*
GBI Decatur
GBI Savannah
Valdosta PD
Georgia Military
U.S. Army Lab Atlanta
North Florida
Florida DLE Jacksonville
Florida DLE Orlando*
Orange County SO
Florida DLE Pensacola
Florida DLE Tampa*
Florida DLE Tallahassee
South Florida
Broward Co SO
Indian River Lab
Miami-Dade PD*
Palm Beach Co SD
9
Arkansas
Arkansas State Crime Lab
Mississippi
Mississippi DPS Biloxi
Mississippi DPS Jackson
Jackson PD
North Louisiana
Louisiana State Lab Shreveport
N Louisiana Lab Alexandria
North West Delta Monroe
South Louisiana
Acadiana New Iberia
Jefferson Parish Lab Metairie
Louisiana SP Baton Rouge
New Orleans PD*
St. Tammany Parish SO
SW Louisiana Lab Lake Charles
3A
North Carolina/South Carolina
Charleston Co SO
Charlotte PD
Cumberland Co SO
Greensboro PD
Greenville PD
Hickory PD
New Hanover Co SO
North Carolina SBI*
Guilford Co
High Point PD
South Carolina SLE Columbia*
Greenville Co SO
Tennessee
Knoxville PD
Nashville-Davidson Co Metro PD
Tennessee BI Memphis
Tennessee BI Nashville
Chattanooga PD

In addition, the "national" scope of NIBIN—like the scope of a national reference ballistic image database (RBID)—suggests an ease in requesting a search against the entire nation that is not the case under the current NIBIN search. "To perform a national search, the requestor must repeat the regional search for each NIBIN region"—12 separate searches—"as the system will not search all regions at once" (U.S. Department of Justice, Office of Inspector General, 2005:110).

About 25 of the NIBIN installations may be considered satellite sites in that they possess only one or more Rapid Brass Identification (RBI) units, portable units for acquiring images from cartridge evidence. These RBI units must be connected with another site's full Remote Data Acquisition Station (RDAS) in order to transmit collected images to the regional server; "afterwards, the results are transmitted back through the RDAS unit to the RBI unit" (U.S. Department of Justice, Office of Inspector General, 2005:10). Some departments have experienced major problems with RBI units, including overheating and data transmission flaws; notably, the (non-NIBIN) Maryland RBID program ultimately returned the RBI it planned to use to permit the Baltimore Police Department to directly submit database entries after continued problems (Maryland State Police Forensic Sciences Division, 2003, 2004).

NIBIN sites are meant to provide regional access to ballistic imaging technology, and so individual law enforcement agencies within a region may partner with a NIBIN site to enter evidence as needed. Individual agencies in states with only one NIBIN installation (e.g., Iowa, Montana, and Wyoming) may route evidence through that site as they see fit. Several states have NIBIN sites at regional laboratories maintained by state police, which may be used by individual city departments, e.g., Virginia's distribution of NIBIN equipment in three regional state labs. Even some major city police departments do not have their own NIBIN sites and work through state or county NIBIN sites, such as Chicago, Atlanta, Milwaukee, Memphis, and Seattle.

Prominent among the law enforcement agencies that are not NIBIN participants is the New York City Police Department (NYPD). While NYPD does follow NIBIN program protocols for the entry of ballistics evidence, the department purchased and maintains its own IBIS equipment; it has not linked directly to NIBIN due to the desire to maintain the integrity of its own database (McCarthy, 2004). However, NIBIN and NYPD continue to work on limited ties between the two databases (e.g., mounting archive data tapes off-site from NYPD for comparison under NIBIN).

5–B.2 Legal Limitations on NIBIN Content

ATF maintains tight control on the content of the NIBIN database, limiting it only to pieces of evidence recovered at crime scenes or test fired from weapons recovered by the police. This prohibition on the entry of noncrime gun exhibits derives from the Firearm Owners' Protection Act of 1986 (18 U.S.C. 926), which prohibits the establishment of "any system of registration of firearms, firearms owners, or firearms transactions or dispositions." It also derives from ATF interpretation of language that is regularly applied to the agency's appropriations. For instance, the 2006 Science, State, Justice, and Commerce and Related Agencies Appropriations Act (P.L. 109-108) included 12 conditional clauses on the appropriated funds. First among these is the proviso that "no funds appropriated herein shall be available for salaries or administrative expenses in connection with consolidating or centralizing, within the Department of Justice, the records, or any portion thereof, of acquisition and disposition of firearms maintained by Federal firearms licensees." ATF has interpreted the acquisition of an image from a specimen fired from a gun for sale as such a "record," and hence excluded new guns from consideration in the database.[1]

5–C NIBIN USAGE

5–C.1 Deployment

One metric by which utilization of NIBIN can be assessed is the number of participating agencies relative to the number of eligible law enforcement agencies. Each piece of evidence entered in NIBIN is associated with its source agency through specification of an Originating Agency Identifier (ORI) code; ORIs are assigned by the FBI and are principally used to identify reporting agencies for the Uniform Crime Reports. In its audit, the U.S. Department of Justice, Office of Inspector General (2005:140), used the total number of ORIs predefined in NIBIN software (for selection by evidence-entry operators) as its measure of eligible agencies. Hence, they concluded that 231 of 38,717 agencies/ORIs were NIBIN partner sites. Responding to a draft report, ATF argued that the total number of ORIs is an inappropriate benchmark (U.S. Department of Justice, Office of Inspector General, 2005:130):

> ATF believes that it is misleading to use the number of ORIs as the statistical basis to evaluate technology allocation, program utilization, and performance because one single agency can have numerous ORIs assigned to it. By way of example, ATF alone has over 362 ORIs or about fifteen per field division. Similarly, many of the larger NIBIN State and local law enforcement partners have multiple ORIs within an agency, and all local law enforcement jurisdictions have at least one ORI number, regardless of size.

---

[1]Other clauses in the appropriation act limit the type of information that can be transferred or maintained in the standard gun tracing process and prohibit rules requiring a physical inventory of the stock maintained by firearms licensees.

Because the full set of ORIs also includes the police or public safety forces maintained by colleges and universities, state parks, and other agencies, ATF suggested 17,000 eligible agencies as a more valid figure, for a 1.3 percent utilization rate. The Inspector General's office could not find support for the 17,000 figure and continues to use 38,717 as the benchmark (U.S. Department of Justice, Office of Inspector General, 2005:140).

The Inspector General audit found that a total of 7,653 law enforcement agencies had contributed firearms evidence to the NIBIN system through the 231 agencies with IBIS equipment. The audit found 37 nonpartner agencies—which did not have a memorandum of understanding with ATF regarding the usage of IBIS equipment—contributed significant amounts of evidence to NIBIN through equipment provided to partner agencies. The audit also found that by November 2003 the NIBIN system had satisfied the goal of providing the capability to compare ballistic images at a national level, by performing several regional searches as described in Section 5–B.1.

5–C.2 Monthly Usage Statistics

To measure the utilization of the NIBIN-deployed IBIS equipment, ATF relies principally on system-generated operational data that are compiled monthly by polling the individual IBIS RDAS units. "The monthly acquisition report contains details of the number of bullets and cartridge casing entries that have been made, and the number of 'hits' that have resulted from such entries for each RDAS unit site. The activity of the [portable Rapid Brass Identification] units is rolled into the usage data for the RDAS unit where the RBI data is submitted" (U.S. Department of Justice, Office of Inspector General, 2005:11). These monthly data are reviewed and used to generate a quarterly "watch list" of low-usage sites.

NIBIN policy is to send a "Notice of Insufficient Usage" to agencies after the first quarter of low usage; if low usage persists the next quarter, ATF staff arrange a site visit to the location. If usage has not stepped up after a third quarter, the IBIS equipment is subject to removal and relocation to other agencies.

5–C.3 Inspector General Conclusions on NIBIN Usage

The Inspector General audit of NIBIN (U.S. Department of Justice, Office of Inspector General, 2005:20) analyzed 888,447 records of firearms evidence entered into NIBIN by 196 partner agencies as of October 22, 2004; it concluded that the IBIS equipment had not been effectively deployed at many NIBIN sites. First, the level of entry appeared to be disproportionate: the 30 highest-entry partner agencies (15 percent) accounted for 68 percent of the entries in the database; 36 percent of the agencies had entered fewer than 1,000 records, and 4 had entered fewer than 100 total records. Of the top 20 source agencies of entered exhibits, 7 were non-partner agencies that—not having an IBIS installation of their own—submitted their evidence to another agency for acquisition.

Second, certain agencies that received IBIS technology did not have or allocate adequate resources to properly run the systems. As a result, many partner agencies reported significant backlogs of firearms evidence that had not been entered into NIBIN. For example, at the time of the DOJ inquiry, the Prince George's County, Maryland, Police Department reported more than 1,000 recovered bullets and cartridge casings, and 269 test-fired bullets, cartridge casings, and guns were waiting to be entered into NIBIN.

Third, some agencies did not regularly review "high confidence" candidate matches identified by IBIS to determine whether a true ballistics match existed. For instance, at the time of the audit, the Georgia Bureau of Investigation had not examined any potential matches since January 2002 and had some 3,350 high-confidence candidates that had not been reviewed.

The audit also found that NIBIN's nationwide search capability is used extremely rarely, and that even regional searches were infrequent. Survey and site visit comments range from well-defined preferences for regional searches (e.g., one California laboratory that routinely performs checks against other California partitions) to indications that regional or national searches are not performed because the agency does not have a firearms examiner (it is not specified what that agency does with its local area searches). Several participating agencies indicated that they did not routinely perform regional or national searches due to the predominantly local nature of gun crime, though several indicated that they would conduct broader searches if conditions warranted or case agents specifically requested them. However, the survey of agencies also suggested a more fundamental reason for the lack of regional or national searches: more than one agency flatly indicated that they could not perform such cases because they do not know how to initiate them. (Excerpts from survey responses are reported in Appendixes XII–XIV of U.S. Department of Justice, Office of Inspector General, 2005.)

As of May 2006, the national database has grown to 926,000 imaged items and over 12,500 hits have been logged. Generally, growth in acquisitions has occurred as new sites have come on line rather than from expanded use of the system in existing sites (U.S. Department of Justice, Office of Inspector General, 2005). It is clear that resource problems in the partner sites make a significant contribution to the overall low hit rates in the partner sites, although a handful of sites have very respectable hit rates using NIBIN. Some of these problems may be caused by the relatively long evidence acquisition times witnessed by the committee and attested to by examiners from local sites the committee visited or heard from during its deliberations. Acquiring an image of a bullet or cartridge casing using NIBIN's automated microscope and digital imaging computer is estimated to take from 5 to 10 minutes depending on the quality of the evidence and the experience of the technician, but preparing the evidence for acquisition (test firing a confiscated weapon, for example, and filling out the required NIBIN and police department forms) and preparing the physical evidence for storage may add 10–45 minutes to the acquisition task. Some forensic laboratories told the committee that the use of their resources to clear up their DNA evidence backlog was more important than clearing out their ballistics evidence backlog.

5–D NIBIN PERFORMANCE

5–D.1 Case Experience: "Hits of the Week"

Arguably the best metric of the actual performance of the NIBIN system is the number and quality of the investigative leads arising from NIBIN queries. The purest of these leads are those arising from "cold hits," links suggested by the database search that might never have been detected were it not for the technology; statistics on these hits are systematically maintained by NIBIN managers. Yet it would also be beneficial to know of the usefulness of the system in confirming vague investigative connections, when a connection between cases is suspected but not yet confirmed; data on these "warm hits" are not regularly maintained, though NIBIN managers may glean some insight on their occurrence through discussions with local agencies. In both cases, a full evaluation of the program's performance would consider what happens after a "hit" is made using NIBIN—whether the information leads to an arrest or a conviction and how large a role the ballistics evidence "hit" played in achieving those results. Those "post-hit" data are apparently not maintained in any systematic collection.

As it is said, the plural of anecdote is not data, yet anecdotal information is effectively all that is available in getting a sense of the operational utility of NIBIN in active criminal investigations. The NIBIN program compiles such programs in its "Hits of the Week" releases, which—together with news accounts of individual cases—are suggestive of some aspects of the program's utility and ability to draw investigative connections in real cases.[2] The "Hits of the Week" releases from January 2002 through October 2006 contain 188 paragraph-length summaries of cases in which NIBIN played

[2]The NIBIN "Hits of the Week" archive is located at http://www.nibin.gov/nb_success.htm [11/1/06]. Postings on the site resumed in October 2006 after a 1-year absence.

a role in the investigation.[3] The nomenclature is deceptive in that a "Hit of the Week" is not necessarily—indeed, not often—a hit that was completed in that calendar week, but is rather a device for generating a NIBIN-usage profile on a weekly basis. The summaries reflect choices made by NIBIN management on which "hits" to profile and are not exhaustive of all the program's hits, yet they offer some interesting observations.

What is perhaps most striking from a review of the 188 "Hits of the Week" is that the "national" nature of the database never arises, and even instances of hits across multiple NIBIN sites are extremely rare. That is, the spotlighted "Hits of the Week" are generally instances in which leads are drawn between cases in the same city, county, or metropolitan area; very few of them are instances in which an exhibit from NIBIN Site A turns up as possibly linked to an exhibit entered at NIBIN Site B, elsewhere in the same state or across state lines. The hit profiled for June 10, 2002, is the only one where exhibits explicitly described as being entered at different NIBIN sites were connected, and that involved linkages drawn between multiple incidents in Houston and Harris County, Texas, with a homicide in Prairie View in neighboring Fort Bend County. Some of the reported hits do cover slightly larger geographic distances, but it is not clear that the evidence was entered at different NIBIN sites. For instance, the hit for June 30, 2003, linked a gun confiscated in Chicago with a homicide in McDonough County in western Illinois, but it is not indicated whether the evidence in question was processed by the same NIBIN site (i.e., the Illinois State Police crime laboratory in Chicago). Likewise, the hit profiled for March 1, 2004, linked a firearm from a shooting in Minneapolis to guns used in a homicide committed 3 months later and some 120 miles away in Redwood Falls, Minnesota, but the summary does not indicate which NIBIN site or sites acquired the evidence (or were credited with the hit).

We note that the "Hits of the Week" do not include cases where, for instance, evidence from a crime committed in Pennsylvania is found by a NIBIN query to be linked to cases in New York or Maryland. This is not to say that NIBIN hits are not cross-jurisdictional; indeed, the highlighted hits include numerous cases where separate police departments are able to generate links by submitting evidence to the same NIBIN site for acquisition and processing. For instance, the hit for March 18, 2003, indicates that multiple departments submit exhibits to the Essex County, New Jersey, Sheriff's Office for NIBIN entry, enabling links to be made between evi-

[3]Though there are 190 paragraphs, they appear to cover only 188 distinct "cases." The hit profiled for March 4, 2003, is an additional NIBIN-suggested link in a set of crimes first described the week before on February 25. The hits for January 19 and February 2, 2004, both describe linkages between four shootings in the Columbus, Ohio, area over a 6-week period; the paragraphs appear to cover the same incidents but are edited differently.

dence in cases being worked separately by the Linden and Kenilworth Police Departments. Similar hits across agencies in the same metropolitan area are described, e.g., between Dallas and Plano, Texas (March 28, 2005), and Atlanta and Alpharetta, Georgia (April 18, 2005).

The cases profiled in the "Hits of the Week" include instances in which the system performs as it is most commonly described, linking multiple open cases and providing investigators some new direction to pursue. For example, connections between bullet and casing evidence from two armed robberies in the Charlotte, North Carolina, area tipped investigators in the second incident to look more closely at the suspects in the first (November 25, 2002), and NIBIN comparisons of evidence from a series of 26 shootings over 2 years in Stockton, California, helped confirm gang involvement in the crimes (April 14, 2003).

What is remarkable about the "Hits of the Week" is the degree to which the NIBIN analysis provides links of a post hoc nature. In at least 154 of the 188 profiled cases (82 percent), NIBIN produced links based on test-fired exhibits—that is, cases where the firearm in question (and, in most instances, the suspect) has been recovered or seized by the police. In these cases, the NIBIN search has the effect of adding charges to suspects brought in or under investigation for other purposes, e.g., the weapon recovered from a person trying to pass off a counterfeit $100 bill in Los Angeles being linked to two fatal shootings in the preceding 4 weeks (September 23, 2002), the 9mm pistol recovered (along with several bags of marijuana) during a New Orleans traffic stop for equipment violations being linked to an unsolved homicide 5 weeks earlier (April 26, 2004), and the gun recovered from a person arrested after attempting to run a checkpoint for intoxicated drivers in Charlotte being linked to an armed robbery 2 months earlier (May 27, 2002).

The time between crimes connected through NIBIN searches on evidence varies greatly in profiled cases; the Denver example profiled for August 11, 2003, linked together five separate shootings over the span of 40 days, which had taken place as little as a few minutes and as much as 11 days apart. (When a gun was retrieved from suspects following a carjacking and police chase, test-fired evidence processed through NIBIN led to links between the gun and the five earlier incidents; the narrative is unclear whether NIBIN analysis suggested connections between the cases *prior* to recovery of the gun.) However, the most vivid of the NIBIN hit examples may be those that span months or years and resuscitate cold cases—where the sheer passage of time reduces the probability that an investigative lead could be made by traditional firearms identification:

- In Columbus, Ohio, a single shell casing was recovered from the scene of a murder where an elderly woman was slain during a purse snatching. Two weeks later, a man robbing a store fired his gun several times before fleeing, leaving shell casings at the scene. Three weeks after that, a casing was recovered from the scene of an armed robbery where the victim had been shot in the face. "As each entry was put into the NIBIN system, the latest entry revealed a match to the previous crime's evidence," but investigation yielded no suspects. The investigation remained stalled for 2 years, when police responded to a call from a city bus where a passenger was reported to be carrying a firearm. The gun was surrendered to police, and test-fired casings were linked using NIBIN to the earlier crimes; the bus passenger—"a convicted felon who had been arrested twice for possession of a handgun while on parole"—"was arrested and charged with firearms violations in addition to charges for the three violent crimes" (Hit of the Week for October 6, 2003).

- A drive-by shooting in Chicago that wounded two people yielded several cartridge casings and a bullet that were entered into NIBIN at the Illinois State Police Laboratory. Five years later, police in nearby Berwyn investigated a reported kidnapping; a woman was shot at and kidnapped by a man reported to be her boyfriend after the boyfriend accused her of stealing money. A shell casing was recovered from the scene and entered into NIBIN (the narrative does not indicate whether a possible match was detected on this entry); the suspect in the kidnapping and an associate were found and arrested, but no gun was found. Eleven days later, a Berwyn man mowing his lawn found a pistol in a plastic bag in his shrubs; a test firing from that gun matched to both the casing from the recent kidnapping and the aggravated assault 5 years earlier (Hit of the Week for June 20, 2005).
- Chicago and Illinois State police were also involved in a NIBIN hit that solved a crime that had been committed nearly 9 years earlier; this was not profiled as a NIBIN "Hit of the Week" but received other press coverage. On September 30, 1995, a 19-year-old Chicago factory worker was killed and another man wounded when a 9mm handgun was fired from a passing car into a small crowd. Ballistics evidence—the bullets recovered from the victims, other bullets that hit nearby parked cars, and six shell casings—was recovered from the scenes, but the investigation produced no immediate leads. The police recorded the images of the bullets and shell casings left at the scene and stored the images in their NIBIN database. Eight years later, on September 28, 2003, a car with a shattered back window was pulled over in a random traffic stop; a Glock Model 19 9mm semiautomatic pistol was found in the car and seized by Chicago police. On June 22, 2004, a NIBIN query made at the Illinois State Police crime laboratory using test-fired exhibits from the gun from the traffic stop suggested a link to the evidence from the 1995 killing; the news account of the investigation does not indicate the reason for the 9-month lag in processing

(Main, 2005). Based on the NIBIN lead, police used state databases to find the buyer of the Glock; the pistol had been sold the day before the drive-by killing; the buyer had purchased it for another person who was barred from making the purchase on his own because of a felony conviction. The buyer was able to provide a name for the shooter, and, after further research, the shooter was arrested and charged on May 18, 2005 (Main, 2005).

5–D.2 Analysis of NIBIN Operational Data

The committee asked ATF for a sample of the operational data that it uses to monitor NIBIN usage. We received 1 year's worth of monthly system reports, from May 2003 through April 2004. These were provided in the form of Microsoft Excel worksheets. The exact format and content in the spreadsheets varied, and there were sufficient inconsistencies in reporting agency names and identifiers to suggest that the reports are generated by hand (based on system queries of individual NIBIN sites) rather than being standard reports generated by the system's computer infrastructure. The worksheets included listings of agencies flagged as low users, site closures and installations, and other information. Though it is not directly linked to NIBIN, the NYPD's IBIS installation is included in these summaries.

The cover sheet in all these files conveys the same basic variables, per site:

- number of evidence bullets (e.g., recovered from crime scenes) entered this month;
- total number of evidence bullets entered, lifetime;
- number of nonevidence bullets (e.g., test fired from weapons recovered by or surrendered to the police) entered this month;
- total number of nonevidence bullets entered, lifetime;
- hits arising from bullets this month;
- total hits arising from bullets, lifetime; and
- the same set of variables, repeated for cartridge casings rather than bullets.

Consistent with the NIBIN program's definition of a hit (see Box 5-3), the hits tallied on the spreadsheets are those for which the physical evidence has been directly compared by a firearms examiner and the match confirmed. Also consistent with the program definition, only the NIBIN site confirming the hit is credited with the hit. These operational data contain no information on any NIBIN "results" short of a completed hit—that is, there is no information on the number of suspected matches for which the physical evidence was requested, nor is there information on the number of cases for which evidence was directly compared and found *not* to be a

BOX 5-3
NIBIN Definition of "Hit"

Definition of a Hit: A linkage of two different crime investigations by the user of the NIBIN technology, where previously there had been no known connection between the investigations.

A hit is a linkage between cases, not individual pieces of evidence. Multiple bullets and/or casings may be entered as part of the same case record, in this event, each discovered linkage to an additional case constitutes a hit.

A hit must be confirmed by a firearms examiner examining the actual specimens under a microscope.

Other NIBIN linkages derived by investigative leads, hunches, or previously identified laboratory examinations, are not "hits" according to this definition. Therefore, other linkages previously termed "warm hits" should not be counted as hits.

When an interagency hit occurs, the agency initiating and confirming the microscopic comparison will be credited for the hit.

Marking Hits in IBIS: Hits meeting the definition above should be linked in IBIS, using the procedures provided in instructional materials from Forensic Technology WAI, Inc. (FTI). Remember that if a link is confirmed between two cases, it is necessary to note this in each IBIS case record.

Linkages derived by investigative leads, hunches, or previously identified laboratory examinations should only be noted in the comments section of the IBIS screen. These linkages are not to be designated as hits.

When an interagency hit is confirmed, each involved site should mark the hit in IBIS, using procedures provided in instructional materials from FTI.

Statistical Reporting: For interagency hits, only the agency initiating and confirming the comparison should include the hit in its statistics reported to ATF NIBIN.

Please note in the current version of IBIS, the Crystal Reports function for generating hit statistics may not yield entirely accurate results and should not be used.

SOURCE: Reproduced from NIBIN Branch (2003).

hit. Hits are calculated in aggregate so that it is not possible to empirically determine how evidence and nonevidence entries compare in the propensity to generate hits.

A basic summary of the operational data is given in Table 5-1. Cartridge casings make up about 71 percent of the database entries; in turn, about 72 percent of those casings are "nonevidence" test fires (as opposed to "evidence" casings directly recovered at the crime scene). An even larger fraction—81 percent—of the bullets in the database are test fires. In this

TABLE 5-1 NIBIN Usage Data, May 2003–April 2004

	Casings					Bullets				
Month	Evidence (month)	Test Fire (month)	Total	Hits (month)	Hits (total)	Evidence (month)	Test Fire (month)	Total	Hits (month)	Hits (total)
5/03	2,682	7,410	441,636	166	6,331	546	2,765	195,382	3	293
6/03	3,206	6,471	451,006	160	6,514	637	2,387	198,355	6	299
7/03	3,435	7,423	461,669	190	6,828	727	2,506	201,525	1	300
8/03	2,757	7,169	471,009	160	7,026	554	2,209	204,172	2	302
9/03	3,030	7,672	481,465	250	7,372	607	2,095	206,842	1	298
10/03	2,998	7,069	491,182	204	7,592	506	2,188	209,415	2	300
11/03	2,747	6,990	500,786	156	7,776	543	2,275	212,169	0	300
12/03	2,544	7,206	510,383	201	7,977	507	2,221	214,869	2	302
1/04	2,544	7,129	520,447	207	8,184	680	2,156	217,627	7	305
2/04	3,167	7,549	530,978	147	8,332	543	2,579	220,676	1	306
3/04	3,465	9,662	520,257	249	8,570	625	2,880	223,930	14	316
4/04	3,062	8,606	554,578	228	8,910	510	2,694	226,830	72	388

NOTES: As of April 2004, 397,349 of the 554,578 total cartridge casings in the NIBIN database were from test fires, and 183,756 of the 226,830 bullets in the database were test fires. The apparent reason for the decline in the total number of casings in the NIBIN database between February and March 2004 is transcription error in the raw spreadsheets for several police departments in Michigan, particularly the Detroit Police Department (for which the reported total number of casings in February, March, and April 2004, are 19,342, 3,956, and 19,927, respectively). Returns for five Michigan State Police laboratories and the Oakland, Michigan, Police Department show similar one-time drops in total number of casings (albeit each with smaller counts than Detroit). Because the monthly totals can reflect deletions of exhibits as well as additions, we have not attempted to reconstruct the totals by adding from a May 2003 base and instead use the reported (albeit, for at least several agencies in March 2004, flawed) totals from the source spreadsheets.
SOURCE: Data from the Bureau of Alcohol, Tobacco, Firearms, and Explosives (personal communication).

sample of months, March 2004 was the peak month for entering both bullets and casings; for both types of evidence, entry was generally lower in November–January than in March–July. Absent information on the number of queries performed and more specifics on the nature of evidence entered, it is not clear why the number of hits on bullet evidence jumped from a seemingly steady state of less than 10 per month to 14 in March 2004 and then again to 72 in April 2004; casing hits were generated at an average of 193 per month.

The U.S. Department of Justice, Office of Inspector General (2005:25–26), audit of NIBIN had access to a snapshot of the NIBIN database as of October 2004, including 888,447 records of bullet and cartridge case evidence, 514,731 records of cases (groupings of exhibits), and 254,187 records of firearms. Just as analysis showed that a small percentage of sites accounted for a large share of evidence entered into NIBIN, high-entry sites also enjoyed the largest percentage of the hits made using the database. In all, 72 percent of the hits (both bullet and cartridge casings) were realized by the 20 percent of NIBIN partners who had input the most entries; the bottom 55 percent of entry-producing partners achieved only 9 percent of the hits (U.S. Department of Justice, Office of Inspector General, 2005:31).

Both our set of aggregate administrative data and the Inspector General's snapshot of the entire database provide some inkling as to the structure and composition of the database; still lacking is any ability to describe how the system is actually used and how it performs. The Inspector General audit attempted to get a basic sense of the system's utilization by comparing the number of evidence entries put into NIBIN by individual sites with the level of firearms-related crimes those agencies reported under the FBI's Uniform Crime Reporting (UCR) program. That analysis did not progress far; "meaningful comparisons were not possible based on the available data because of variables such as population size, population density, geographic location, and other demographic factors" (U.S. Department of Justice, Office of Inspector General, 2005:30). However, the report suggests that the major deployment of IBIS equipment to complete the planned NIBIN network had worked to narrow a broader gap between the number of NIBIN entries and the number of gun crimes.

We pursued a similar line of analysis in order to study whether a connection exists between success in generating hits and the level of crime in areas. This requires a linkage between the NIBIN usage data and the UCR data, and such a connection is fraught with complications more fundamental than the quote from the Inspector General audit admits. The Bureau of Justice Statistics (BJS) has compiled a "crosswalk" dataset, linking UCR ORI codes with BJS' Directory of Law Enforcement Agencies and data from the Census Bureau's Governments Integrated Directory (Lindgren and Zawitz, 2001) in order to estimate the service population of agencies reported in the UCR. However, defining the service population for a NIBIN site is complicated (as described in Section 5–B.1): NIBIN partner agencies process evidence submitted by other agencies because the number of NIBIN installations is relatively low. In states where NIBIN sites are located in laboratories of the state police (e.g., Wisconsin or Virginia), comparing NIBIN entries with crimes in the city where the NIBIN site is located is certainly inadequate, yet trying to associate each site with a proportionate share of the crimes in the entire state is likely inaccurate as well.

Due to these difficulties, we have treated our own attempts to link the NIBIN operational data with UCR figures as merely suggestive and in no way definitive; yet we judged it important to try to get some sense of whether high-crime areas are likely to benefit from hits achieved by ballistic image comparisons.[4] We erred on the side of simplicity by using crime data from the NIBIN site's home city as a proxy for the number of crimes committed in the site's service area, combining NIBIN entry counts in some cases where multiple installations are located in the same city. We also filtered cases to look only at NIBIN host cities with populations above 10,000. In this way, we augmented the NIBIN dataset with three variables for those sites for which we believed we could establish a pairing: population of the city in which the NIBIN site is located in 2003, average number of murders and non-negligent manslaughter incidents in 2002 and 2003, and total number of violent crimes (including, e.g., assault and forcible rape) in 2003.

After aggregating the information from sites located in the same city or town and deleting sites with missing information, our analysis dataset included 105 cases with complete NIBIN, population, and crime information. Of these, there were 33 NIBIN sites/localities at which at least one bullet hit had been obtained and 72 localities with no hits on bullets. The number of hits when using casings was significantly larger: at 85 localities, there was at least one hit on casings and there were only 20 localities at which no hits on casings were reported.

We analyzed bullets and casings separately. For each type of evidence,

[4]We also emphasize that this analysis is intended merely to be suggestive due to the limitations of the original operational dataset. As a record only of aggregate database additions and "hits," it is not as complete a resource for studying NIBIN system performance as would be desirable. In addition, as the note for Table 5-1 suggests, the operational data spreadsheets appear to be manual updates rather than system-generated tallies. A discrepancy in the cumulative count of cartridge casings from month to month led to the discovery of a significant error in reporting by Michigan agencies (particularly the Detroit Police Department), whose totals for 1 month were more than halved. Our analysis uses the year-end total entry and hit counts and so should not be affected by month-to-month discrepancies, but recording errors do apparently exist in the raw underlying data.

we constructed a binary variable: 0 indicated no hits, and 1 indicated at least one hit. We performed two basic analyses. First, we used logistic regression to model this binary response variable as a function of the number of NIBIN entries (four variables, including both evidence and test-fired bullets and casings), population size, and the two crime count variables. Second, we then restricted attention to only those localities where at least one hit was reported (for bullets or casings) and modeled the number of hits as the same function of potential predictors. Because the number of positive hits is not nearly normally distributed and because the number of sites reporting hits on bullets is very low (only 32 sites), we focused on modeling the number of hits on casings and used a log transformation to improve the distribution of the outcome variable.

Taking into account the contributions of the other predictors in the model, we found that the probability of a hit on cartridge casings increased as a function of the number of violent crimes in the NIBIN site locality during 2003 as well as on the number of evidence casings entered in the system. Likewise, the probability of a hit decreased with increased murder and non-negligent manslaughters in the locality and with the total number of bullets entered into the NIBIN system. The negative association between the probability of a hit on casings and the number of bullets in the NIBIN system at the site might be spurious and is likely attributable to correlation between the number of bullets and the number of casings, the latter of which makes a stronger contribution to the model. Alternately, it might be due to an unobserved underlying variable correlated with both the number of bullets in the system and the probability of a hit on casings. However, the probability of a hit on bullet evidence increased only as a function of the number of bullets collected as evidence that were entered into the NIBIN system; no other factor appears to be significantly associated to the probability that a bullet match will be found.

We checked the fit of the logistic regression models by considering the proportion of concordant pairs and by examining the chi-squared residuals (to identify influential observations and outliers). For bullets, the percent concordant pairs exceeded 90 percent, and for casings it was approximately 89 percent, indicating that the predictors in the model explain a significant portion of the between-locality variability in the probability of a hit.

Looking next at the 85 localities reporting at least one hit on casings, we fit a linear regression model to the rate of hits (computed as the number of hits divided by the total number of casings in the system) in the log scale. Predictors in the model included population at the locality, average number of murders and non-negligent manslaughters in the locality in 2002 and 2003, total number of violent crimes in 2003 in the locality, the total number of evidence casings in NIBIN, the total number of nonevidence (test fire) casings in NIBIN, and the total number of bullets entered in the NIBIN system at the locality. The log of the rate of casing hits was significantly associated with the number of evidence casings entered into NIBIN at the locality but was not associated with any other predictor. In particular, the association between the log rate of hits and the number of nonevidence casings in the system was negative, albeit not statistically significant.

We examined the fit of the linear model by inspecting residuals and estimating the degree of multicollinearity among predictors. All of the predictors in the model were positively correlated, which might partially explain the lack of statistically significant associations between the response variable and the predictors. A reasonable (43 percent) proportion of the total variability observed in the log probability of a casing hit was explained by the predictors in the model, and no outliers were detected when inspecting the standardized residuals from the regression. However, patterns in the standardized residuals plotted against the observed log probabilities of hits on casings do suggest that other, potentially important predictors are missing from the model.

The most basic interpretation we draw from this analysis, despite its limits, is the same reached by the Inspector General audit: the probabilities of getting a hit on either bullets or casings depend vitally on the number of entries entered into the NIBIN system at each locality. We observed the strongest connection to be with the counts of bullets or casings entered as evidence, whereas hit probabilities were negatively (but not significantly) associated with the number of nonevidence (test fire) samples entered into the system. This finding suggests that agencies might be better served by prioritizing entries so that evidence samples are entered into NIBIN most promptly.

5–E STATE REFERENCE BALLISTIC IMAGING DATABASES

The existing state reference ballistic image databases in New York and Maryland operate using the same IBIS computer and microscope image; their networks and correlation servers are entirely distinct, however, thus complying with the current prohibition on noncrime-gun evidence in the NIBIN database.

5–E.1 Maryland: MD-IBIS

As part of a larger gun legislation package, the Maryland Responsible Gun Safety Act of 2000 established a statewide database of images of cartridge cases test fired from every handgun sold, rented, or transferred by manufacturers in the state or whose products are sold in the state, under the premise that handguns are most frequently used in crimes. The database is known as Maryland-IBIS (MD-IBIS), was established under the Maryland

State Police, effective September 1, 2000. The database is not connected to the NIBIN network and is not networked to any other law enforcement agency in the state (though an unsuccessful attempt was made to permit entry of casings by the Baltimore city police; see Section 5–B.1). Casings for entry and comparison with MD-IBIS must be taken to the state police facility in Pikesville and processed there.

In September 2003 and September 2004 the Maryland State Police Forensic Sciences Division (2003, 2004) issued progress reports on MD-IBIS; the two reports were diametrically opposite in terms of supporting continued collection of image data. The first report (Maryland State Police Forensic Sciences Division, 2003:i) took an optimistic stance, arguing that the "time to crime" window—the length of time between the sale of a gun and its appearance as a crime gun—is roughly 3–6 years. Hence, the report argued that the MD-IBIS was just entering this period for guns sold in 2000 and that additional investigative "hits" would be forthcoming. The analysis drew from the example of the state's DNA database, which "was started in 1994 and obtained its first hit in November 1998." However, one year later, the Maryland State Police Forensic Sciences Division (2004:i) reversed course, citing "the failure of the MD-IBIS to provide any meaningful hits." The report found that the program "has not met expectations and does not aid in the Mission statement of the Department of State Police." It recommended that the data collection be suspended and that MD-IBIS staff be transferred to the DNA database unit. Both reports also commented on other problems involved with collections of data, including detected cases where the cartridge case sample packaged with a new firearm did not in fact correspond to that firearm; these arguments are discussed elsewhere in this report, particularly Section 9–C.2.

The 2003 report estimated the average annual cost of MD-IBIS operations over its then 3-year lifetime at $460,700, which included four staff members (technicians or firearms examiners), supplies, and service costs for the equipment. The 2004 report, which included initial capital to purchase the IBIS equipment, placed the cumulative cost of the database over 4 years at $2.6 million. Based on handgun sales data prior to the enabling law's passage, it was projected that cartridge casings for approximately 30,000 handguns would be entered into the system annually; actual entry had only been about one-third that amount, with 43,729 handguns in the database through 2004 (Maryland State Police Forensic Sciences Division, 2004:2) and only 49 of 215 handgun manufacturers had submitted casings for inclusion (Maryland State Police Forensic Sciences Division, 2003:2). Both reports attribute part of this shortfall to a general decrease in handgun sales in the state due to the full set of provisions in the 2000 act.

Of 208 police queries on the MD-IBIS database, six produced matches that were later determined to be hits. Two hits were produced in 2002 when ATF submitted two .45 caliber Taurus semiautomatic pistols whose serial numbers had been obliterated for comparison; matches were found to two pistols that had been stolen from the same dealership in December 2001. Two later hits also were found to two pistols (different manufacturers) that had been stolen from a common dealership; investigative leads were generated in a robbery and "a major burglary and assault case" (Maryland State Police Forensic Sciences Division, 2003:7). However, the Maryland State Police Forensic Sciences Division (2004:2) raised an important criticism of the MD-IBIS hits, which is that they generally "did not work according to the manner in which the system was designed." The underlying goal of an RBID is to generate an investigative lead to a point of sale *without* the need for the actual crime gun to be recovered; however, the gun in question was recovered and in police custody in five of the six confirmed hits. At the time of its publication, the Maryland State Police Forensic Sciences Division (2004:2) also critiqued the database's cost-effectiveness because "none of the 'hits' have been used in a criminal trial."

Following the 2004 review, the database's future appeared uncertain. In March 2005, the Maryland House Judiciary Committee held hearings on a bill to repeal the law establishing MD-IBIS (Butler, 2005). However, within a few weeks, one confirmed MD-IBIS hit that ran counter to both Maryland State Police Forensic Sciences Division (2004) criticisms—that the few hits being produced were in cases where the gun was already recovered and that none were being used in criminal proceedings—produced tangible results. On April 1, 2005, Oxon Hill, Maryland, resident Robert Garner was convicted of first-degree murder—in a case in which the critical investigative spark was provided by an MD-IBIS hit. As Castaneda and Snyder (2005) report:

> Although the [murder] weapon, a .40-caliber handgun, never was found, county police and prosecutors connected the firearm to Garner through 10 shell casings found at the scene. . . . The casings recovered at the murder scene matched a casing that was on file with Maryland State Police, showing that the weapon was purchased by Garner's then-girlfriend (now his wife) in a Forestville store about three weeks before the killing, according to trial testimony.[5] "That evidence was the cornerstone of our case," said Glenn F. Ivey, the Prince George's [County] state's attorney. "It was powerful evidence. I hope this verdict helps our efforts to have the [MD-IBIS database] continued and expanded."

[5]We note that this relatively quick 3-week span from sale to use in crime is inconsistent with the argument that RBIDs produce low numbers of hits due to a lengthy "time to crime."

This case appears to have won the system a temporary reprieve. The then-pending bill to scrap the MD-IBIS enabling legislation was not passed during the remainder of the 2005 legislative session; a similar bill was also introduced during the 2006 regular session but also was not enacted.

Along with the proposals to stop work on the database, recent sessions of the Maryland legislature have also raised possible modifications to MD-IBIS; none have moved beyond referral to committee. In the 2006 session, HB 1369 would have waived the requirement of image entry into MD-IBIS if a firearm's manufacture certified that microstamping was used on the gun's parts to impart markings on shell casings.

5–E.2 New York: CoBIS

The Combined Ballistic Identification System (CoBIS) is the state of New York's reference ballistic image database and is maintained by the New York State Police (NYSP) at its Forensic Investigation Center in Albany. The database began operation in March 2001, following the 2000 enactment of state legislation creating a "pistol and revolver ballistic identification databank."[6] The law required that any manufacturer shipping or delivering a pistol or revolver within the state include a shell casing from a round fired through that weapon. Firearms dealers are then required to forward the sample casing to the state police, or alternatively submit the weapon to be fired at a state police facility in order to collect a sample casing, when the gun is sold. Vendors at gun shows are dealers under this definition, and they are expected to comply with the law.

Many manufacturers or dealers comply with the law by performing test fires at their facilities and including the ballistic sample in an envelope. At the time of sale, this envelope containing the sample is sent to the Albany Forensic Investigation Center; the appropriate permit or license information is included on a slip of paper stapled to the envelope. CoBIS operators detach the permit slip and forward it to the appropriate branch of the NYSP; no information from the slip (e.g., name of buyer) is processed or entered in CoBIS. The envelope is checked-in and given a bar code or ID sticker and put into the queue for acquisition; the NYSP runs a backlog in acquiring these exhibits.

For the convenience of dealers in cases in which a ballistic sample is not included with the firearm, the NYSP maintains regional CoBIS centers at its six troop headquarters as well as a mobile center. Guns may be taken to any of these regional centers for test firing (using a water tank) and recov-

[6]The enacting legislation is codified as New York General Business Law, Article 26, Section 396-ff; the New York State Police subsequently published regulations on specific database operations as 9 NYCRR Section 493.1, Rule 18.

ery of a sample cartridge. At the regional centers, casings are collected and are checked in to the system (labeled and assigned a number), but ballistic images are only captured at the Albany headquarters.

The Albany Forensic Investigation Center includes four IBIS Data Acquisition Stations, purchased from FTI, dedicated to entry of CoBIS samples. An FTI correlation server is connected to these four stations, as is an IBIS hub/Signature Analysis Station for use in querying the database. The Forensic Investigation Center is also a NIBIN location; a separate IBIS hub—in a separate room from the CoBIS DAS stations—is used for NIBIN entries.

Any law enforcement agency in the state can submit exhibits for entry and comparison against CoBIS at no charge. At the time of the database's creation, plans suggested an average of 25–50 comparison requests per day, including requests against crime-scene evidence as entered in NIBIN; actual usage was much lower than expected. In a letter to this committee in December 2004, Zeosky (2005) wrote:

> Since its inception in March 2001, cartridge cases from more than 85,000 new handguns sold in New York have been submitted to CoBIS (14,590 from weapons test fired by the State Police and 71,346 provided by the manufacturers). To date there have been approximately 276 direct queries against CoBIS, with no "hits."

As of a 2005 visit by a subgroup of committee members to the CoBIS center, 400 internal NYSP queries had been made against the database, also with no hits.

Agreements have been made between the U.S. Department of Justice and the NYSP to arrange a one-way transfer of information. Specifically, ATF has provided the NYSP with NIBIN exhibits for other New York state law enforcement agencies, in the form of data tapes. With FTI assistance, these tapes have been used to run batches of requests on exhibits dating back to CoBIS' inception in March 2001. As of the subgroup visit, about 2,400 such queries had been run using NIBIN exhibits in CoBIS; one cold hit (unconfirmed by a firearms examiner) was found between a CoBIS exhibit and a NIBIN entry from Rochester.

Just as NYSP has arranged an indirect, loose tie between CoBIS and NIBIN, so too has limited connection been made between CoBIS and New York City's NIBIN-independent ballistic image database. As with NIBIN, the connection with New York City is one way and accomplished through transfer of tape archives. NYSP possesses a tape of all NYPD images; these remain to be sorted and filtered, limiting the focus to post-March 2001. CoBIS and the NYPD ballistic image database did have a previous connection; NYPD was linked on a one-time set-up for a preliminary test of 900 queries.

New York has not attempted any kind of audit of the manufacturer-supplied samples and exhibits from guns, though this is an acknowledged source of mix-ups. The basic logistical problem with such a hypothetical audit is that it would require voluntary cooperation by gun owners to turn over their firearms for new test firings. Likewise, CoBIS is limited in its capability to answer research question due to limitations on data collected. CoBIS personnel do not know how many guns recovered by the State Police were actually sold in New York State, since those data go through separate clearinghouses. Their rough impression is that the guns tend to not be "imports" from other states, but rather the use of old existing guns. Moreover, although information on the gun is recorded in the database, ammunition brand is not, though some technicians will enter that information in IBIS as comments if it is known. All that is generally recorded in CoBIS is make, model, serial number, and caliber; any other information is gathered by the permits office.

In the 2005 legislative session, bills offered in the New York State Assembly suggested a range of legislative responses to the CoBIS database, from a complete repeal of the enacting law (A05093) to multiple-phase expansions in scope to include additional classes of firearms and ballistic images of bullets for those weapons that do not eject shell casings (A00968, A06462). None of these was enacted. In the 2007 session, A07477 would expand CoBIS to include rifles and shotguns.

6

Operational and Technical Enhancements to NIBIN

As discussed in Chapter 1, the committee's interpretation of our charge is focused on offering advice on three basic policy options: *maintain* the National Integrated Ballistic Information Network (NIBIN) system as it is, *enhance* the NIBIN system in several possible ways (without expanding its scope to include new and imported firearms), or *establish* a national reference ballistic image database as a complement or adjunct to the current NIBIN. The first of these options may readily be viewed as something of a "straw man," particularly given the open-ended nature with which we were asked to consider enhancements or improvements to NIBIN.

No program is perfect: there is always opportunity for refinement and improvement, and such is the case with NIBIN. The underlying concepts of NIBIN are sound—facilitating transfer of information between geographically dispersed law enforcement agencies and giving those agencies access to technology that could generate investigative leads that would otherwise be impossible. However, the program falls short of its potential in several respects, and this chapter proposes some directions for improvement.

After briefly reviewing other perspectives that have been raised about improving the content and performance of the NIBIN system (Section 6–A), our comments focus on possible and suggested enhancements. The second section (6–B) considers operational enhancements, those that concern the administration of the program and the use of the system in general. The third section (6–C) considers technical enhancements, those that deal with the specific technology used by the NIBIN program; this section builds on Chapter 4's discussion of the current Integrated Ballistics Identification System (IBIS) platform.

In phrasing some of our recommendations, we opt for generic descriptions—"ATF and its NIBIN contractors" or the "NIBIN technical platform"—since they describe functionality that should apply regardless of the specific platform or vendor. One major possible enhancement of interest to the committee—a change in the basic imaging standard from two-dimensional photography to three-dimensional topography—is not discussed here; instead, we give the topic more detailed examination in Chapters 7 and 8.

6–A OTHER PERSPECTIVES ON NIBIN ENHANCEMENT

The Bureau of Alcohol, Tobacco, Firearms, and Explosives (ATF) and the NIBIN program have made strides to gather feedback on system procedures and performance from the user base, efforts for which they should be commended. Formally, forums for the gathering of feedback have included periodic meetings of the ATF-established NIBIN Users Congress since November 2002; users are also asked to serve as regional outreach coordinators, providing a sounding board for comments both informally and through the user group sessions. Based on the user group meetings, ATF and Forensic Technology WAI, Inc. (FTI), periodically update (and describe progress in addressing) a "top 10" list of user concerns and suggestions for improving NIBIN and the IBIS platform. In addition, NIBIN program staff periodically collect reports from the regions on indicators of system usage—e.g., cross-regional searches and number of correlation requests that have not been reviewed by local sites—that go beyond the monthly operational statistics.

The committee chair and staff attended the sixth NIBIN Users Congress meeting at FTI's U.S. training center in Largo, Florida, in October 2004. That session suggested a strong commitment among program managers and local users to making the system work more effectively as a key part of routine investigations. Concerns expressed at the meeting ranged from time-consuming software glitches (e.g., the focus jumping to the top of the list when an already-viewed comparison report is deleted rather than advancing to the next line) to serious interface issues (e.g., problems with the lighting filter on the microscope, particularly for side light images, that led some agencies to jury-rig fixes using Post-It notes to get acceptable images). This particular session came in the wake of the rollout of a new version of IBIS software meant to be compliant with federal government and Department of Justice cybersecurity requirements. The switch to the new version was problematic and debilitating in some sites, effectively shutting down evidence entry for days or weeks; user feedback helped assess the scope of the implementation problems and can suggest better practices for future major revisions. Some of the enhancements we suggest below reflect comments from the Users Congress meeting, as well as other observations from committee member visits to local NIBIN installations.

Another source of commentary on specific enhancements to improve NIBIN is the operational audit of the program conducted by the U.S. Department of Justice, Office of Inspector General (2005). The audit offered 12 formal recommendations to ATF; see Box 6-1. The audit included examination of a complete snapshot of the NIBIN database and its attempt to link NIBIN data to Uniform Crime Reports data based on Originating Agency Identifier (ORI) codes: hence the specific recommendations to ensure ORI

BOX 6-1
Recommendations from 2005 U.S. Department of Justice Inspector General Audit of NIBIN Program

Based on its review of NIBIN practices, the U.S. Department of Justice, Office of Inspector General (2005) offered 12 specific recommendations to ATF in its audit report:

1. Determine whether additional IBIS equipment should be purchased and deployed to high-usage nonpartner agencies, or whether equipment should be redistributed from the low-usage partner agencies to high-usage nonpartner agencies.
2. Provide additional guidance, training, or assistance to the partner agencies that indicated they did not perform regional or nationwide searches because they either lacked an understanding of the process or lacked manpower to perform such searches.
3. Ensure that NIBIN partner agencies enter the [Originating Agency Identifier (ORI)] number of the contributing agency for all evidence entered into NIBIN.
4. Resolve the duplicate case ID number issue in the NIBIN database for the Colorado Bureau of Investigation–Montrose; and the Rhode Island State Crime Laboratory.
5. Research the reasons why 12 agencies have achieved high hit rates with relatively low number of cases entered into NIBIN and share the results of such research with the remaining partner agencies.
6. Establish a plan to enhance promotion of NIBIN to law enforcement agencies nationwide to help increase participation in the program. The plan should address steps to: (1) increase the partner agencies' use of the system, (2) increase the nonpartner agencies' awareness and use of the system, and (3) encourage the partner agencies to promote the NIBIN program to other law enforcement agencies in their area.
7. Determine whether new technology exists that will improve the image quality of bullets enough to make it worthwhile for the participating agencies

reporting (about 55,000 records in the databases had missing ORI codes) and the specific identification glitch detected for cases in Colorado and Rhode Island. The Inspector General report also offers sound advice to evaluate the user base for the portable Rapid Brass Identification (RBI) units, which have the potential for permitting cartridge case entries by other agencies without a full IBIS set-up but which have been found to be problematic by previous users.

We generally concur with the Inspector General's recommendations and advance some themes from those recommendations in our own guid-

to spend valuable resources to enter the bullet data into NIBIN, and deploy the technology if it is cost-effective.

8. Perform an analysis of the current [Rapid Brass Identification (RBI)] users, and any other potential users, to determine if they would use an improved system enough to warrant the additional cost. If the analysis concludes that another system would be cost-effective, then ATF should pursue funding to obtain the system.
9. Provide guidance to partner agencies on the necessity to view correlations in a timely manner and to ensure that correlations viewed in NIBIN are properly marked.
10. Monitor the nonviewed correlations of partner agencies and take corrective actions when a backlog is identified.
11. Research ways to help the partner agencies eliminate the current backlog of firearms evidence awaiting entry into NIBIN. The research should consider whether the partner agencies can send their backlogged evidence to the ATF Laboratories or to other partner agencies for entry into NIBIN, and whether improvements to the efficiency of NIBIN would facilitate more rapid and easy entry of evidence.
12. Coordinate with Department of Justice law enforcement agencies that seize firearms and firearms evidence to help them establish a process for entering the seized evidence into NIBIN.

Asked to review a draft of the audit report, ATF noted its partial or full concurrence with every recommendation; the ATF response comprises Appendix XV of the audit report.

SOURCE: Text of recommendations excerpted from U.S. Department of Justice, Office of Inspector General (2005).

ance below. As noted in Box 6-1, ATF reviewed a draft of the Inspector General's audit and was asked for comment; the agency indicated partial or full concurrence with all 12 specific recommendations.

6–B OPERATIONAL ENHANCEMENTS

Suggesting operational enhancements to the NIBIN program is a complicated task due to the program's very nature. At its root, NIBIN is a grant-in-aid program that makes ballistic imaging technology available to law enforcement agencies to an extent that would not be possible if departments had to acquire the necessary equipment on their own. However, although ATF provides the equipment, the state and local law enforcement agencies must supply the resources for entering exhibits and populating the database. Accordingly, the incentive structures are complex: promoting top-down efforts by NIBIN administration to stimulate NIBIN entry necessarily incurs costs by the local departments. So, too, does suggesting that local NIBIN partners make concerted outreach efforts to acquire and process evidence from other agencies in their areas. The benefits that may accrue can be great, providing the vital lead that may put criminals in jail or generating the spark that may solve cold cases. Yet those benefits are not guaranteed, and the empirical data needed to inform the tradeoffs—on the number and nature of queries or on the success of NIBIN in making "warm" hits where there is some (but perhaps weak) investigative reason to suggest links between incidents—are not collected.

Accordingly, our suggested operational enhancements follow two basic themes. First, the process for acquiring evidence should be improved and, when possible, streamlined in order to promote active participation by NIBIN partners and to make ballistic imaging competitive for scarce forensic laboratory resources with DNA and other types of analysis. Second, the NIBIN management must have the information and resources necessary to allocate and reallocate equipment to agencies in order to maximize system usage.

6–B.1 Priority of Entry

In suggesting ways to improve the entry of evidence, a natural place to start is to suggest a prioritization or a structure for entry: which types of ballistics evidence, generally or from specific types of crimes, should be given top priority in order to maximize chances of obtaining hits and generating leads? On this point, the current composition of the NIBIN database suggests preferences that have emerged among partner agencies: more cartridge casings are entered than bullets and, in both instances, exhibits from test firings of recovered weapons are more frequently entered than individual specimens recovered as evidence from crime scenes. Recommendation 7 of the Inspector General audit of NIBIN (U.S. Department of Justice, Office of Inspector General, 2005) urges a general reconsideration of the imaging of bullets, motivated by survey responses from agencies about why they do not enter bullet evidence. Reasons cited for not entering bullets into NIBIN included the time-consuming and difficult nature of acquiring bullets, as well as a perceived low probability of success in generating hits. It has also become common practice by NIBIN users to acquire only firing pin and breech face images from cartridge casings and not the ejector marks when those are available. From observations of NIBIN sites, this seems to be largely due to the added time required to acquire that image (free-hand tracing of the region of interest), even though some research described in Section 4–E documents increased chances of generating hits when all three images are collected.

Understanding that decisions on entry priorities must be made at the local level, as determined by available resources, we suggest one basic ordering.

Recommendation 6.1: In managing evidence entry workload, NIBIN partner sites should give highest priority to entering cartridge casings collected from crime scenes, followed by bullet evidence recovered from crime scenes.

This recommendation is based in part on the findings of our study of completed hits in 1 year's worth of operational data from NIBIN; evidence suggests that the prompt acquisition and processing of cartridge case evidence results in the greatest number of hits. We do not discount the importance of the hits that arise from the entry of specimens test fired from firearms recovered by the police; links drawn to past cases (and past crimes) can be very useful in effective prosecution of criminal suspects. However, we believe that the system's greatest benefit may come from its use as a tool for working with active, open case files, generating investigative leads that may lead to the apprehension of at-large suspects rather than confirming other offenses associated with a gun (and suspect) already in police custody.

Though our committee's focus on a national reference ballistic image database has led us to focus more on the imaging of cartridge cases than bullets, we give the entry of evidence bullets a slight edge in priority over the entry of nonevidence (test-fired) cartridge casings. This again favors emphasizing the use of NIBIN in the most active crime investigations. However, this choice will ultimately be contingent on continuing improvements to the technology, streamlining the image acquisition process and improving comparison results for bullets. (We discuss related concerns on the tension between entering bullet and casing evidence in Section 6–B.3.)

A rough priority order for the entry of evidence would be the following: (1) cartridge case evidence recovered at crime scenes, (2) bullet evidence recovered at crime scenes, (3) casings test fired from weapons recovered by police that will not be destroyed or removed from circulation (i.e., must be returned to owner), (4) bullets test fired from weapons recovered by police that will not be destroyed or removed from circulation, (5) casings from weapons recovered at crime scenes that are to be destroyed, (6) bullets from weapons recovered at crime scenes that are to be destroyed, and (7) evidence entries that are archival in nature (e.g., working through and modernizing a backfile).

6–B.2 Expanding System Usage

Hits are only possible in the NIBIN system if evidence is entered into the database, and local departments will only put priority on entering evidence into NIBIN if they see tangible benefit in the form of hits. In this circle, we believe that it is important that the potential for NIBIN to generate active investigative leads be the primary emphasis; to the extent that NIBIN entry is viewed as drudgery or simply "feeding the beast" to no apparent end, participation will wane.

Recommendation 6.2: In order to promote wider use of NIBIN resources and to ensure that entry of ballistics evidence into NIBIN is a high priority, ATF should work with state and local law enforcement agencies to encourage them to incorporate ballistic imaging as a vital part of the criminal investigation process. This work should include early and continued involvement of agency forensic staff in working with detectives on cases involving ballistics evidence and regular department reviews of NIBIN-related cases.

This kind of promotion should include encouragement of programs like the Los Angeles Police Department's "Walk-In Wednesdays," a designated time for detectives to consult with firearms examiners and IBIS technicians, enter evidence into NIBIN, and analyze resulting comparison results. The lessons learned in areas like Boston (as described in Appendix A), where cross-jurisdictional NIBIN searches have proven highly successful, should also be studied and disseminated to the broader NIBIN partner base.

Through its "Hits of the Week" program, the central NIBIN program administration has provided limited anecdotal data on the system's performance in jurisdictions and in solving a variety of crime types. These kinds of case stories can serve to instill confidence in the system and promote continued "buy-in" by NIBIN partner sites. As described in Chapter 5, though, the "Hits of the Week" most often chronicle cases in which NIBIN analysis is only brought into play when a firearm—and frequently a suspect—is in custody. The "Hits of the Week" that speak to links between evidence casings and bullets are less satisfying as short anecdotes because they typically have to be left unresolved, noting that "investigation is continuing" or that leads are being followed up. The NIBIN program would be well served by adding to the staccato "Hits of the Week" more detailed investigative studies of completed cases that describe the contribution of NIBIN-generated leads.

On the subject of hits, the NIBIN program has the capacity to make a simple change that may help participation by overcoming an odd quirk and subtle disincentive in the current structure.

Recommendation 6.3: A separate count variable of cross-jurisdictional hits should be added to the system's basic operational statistics, crediting both the originating jurisdiction of linked evidence and the site that confirms the hit.

As described in Box 5-3, the NIBIN program currently credits completed "hits" to the site that actually completes the microscopic examination that confirms the match. In many cases, matches will be made between pieces of evidence within the same agency and the same NIBIN site. However, other hits may be made locally (including evidence from nonpartner agencies submitting evidence to a NIBIN site), regionally, or cross-regionally. Both agencies are instructed to *mark* completed hits in their system, but only the agency confirming the hit is supposed to *report* it to NIBIN management. Moreover, "if a hit occurs between two sites, the information is not transferred to the other site by the system. Rather, the other site must be [separately] notified to create the hit in its own database" (U.S. Department of Justice, Office of Inspector General, 2005:110).

It is a serious impediment that data on interagency hits are not automatically or systematically recorded as part of the NIBIN program's default operational statistics; without that information, it is difficult to have a complete sense of the system's usage. But the current asymmetric definition of a hit also sharply undercuts the "network" aspect of NIBIN: Agencies that serve as good partners (or who take the trouble to route evidence to NIBIN partners in their area) by entering their data in a timely fashion should receive credit when their effort bears fruit, even if the hit is actually made in another place. Ideally, tabulations should be made not only of hits across NIBIN sites but across different ORI codes as well, in order to better detect current nonpartners who might benefit from NIBIN equipment installation.

Alternatively, the NIBIN definitions of a "hit" could be revised to be symmetric, creating both the source(s) and the verifier of evidence matches. However, this change is undesirable because it would double-count (or more) the number of NIBIN-generated investigative leads.

6–B.3 Improving Image Entry Protocols

The acquisition of evidence into NIBIN can be very time consuming, particularly for bullet evidence. Even for cartridge casings, the mechanics of positioning evidence under the microscope and taking the images is only a part of the time demand. The time needed to collect the images may be topped by the time needed to clean, prepare, and mount the evidence; the time to prepare necessary paperwork, notes, and reports on entry; the time to prepare written reports on possible and completed hits; and the filing (or refiling) of evidence into storage. There is a need for the acquisition process to be routinized and rigorous; analysis is for naught if anything in the acquisition process compromises the chain of evidence and renders the exhibits inadmissible in court.

When local agencies have affirmed a commitment to ballistic imaging as part of their analyses and revised procedures for the entry and filing of evidence, streamlined procedures have been developed to make NIBIN entry more rapid. A notable example of this type of procedural review was completed by the New York City Police Department (NYPD), which reviewed its evidence processing routines and revamped them into the "Fast Brass" system (see Box 6-2). Building from models like the New York example, other departments may find ways to work through existing backlogs and realize more benefits from their NIBIN participation.

Recommendation 6.4: State and local law enforcement agencies should be encouraged to streamline the ballistic image acquisition process and reporting requirements as much as possible, in order to facilitate rapid data entry and avoid evidence backlogs.

The California technical evaluation of a potential state reference ballistic image database made reference to low levels of bullet hits achieved by the NYPD. The ATF critique of the technical evaluation attributed this to one part of the Fast Brass process: the department's policy of entering only casings if both bullets and casings are recovered from the same crime scene. Thompson et al. (2002:17) commented that "ATF utilizes both the bullet and cartridge casing entry aspects of IBIS, and we recommend that our NIBIN partner agencies do the same in entering their crime gun evidence." They argue that the NYPD policy jeopardizes the chances to

BOX 6-2
New York City Police Department "Fast Brass" Processing

The New York City Police Department policy is to enter ballistics evidence into its IBIS within 24 to 48 hours of its delivery to the department's crime lab. A typical IBIS entry workload is on the order of 10–40 bullets and 100–150 cartridge casings per week.

In 2002, faced with an IBIS entry backlog of about 1,300 cases, the department sought to streamline its entry process to eliminate redundancy. The resulting "Fast Brass" process pared the inventory and case note report filed for ballistics evidence to a limit of one page and required a full report (of less than five pages) only for IBIS-generated hits. In cases in which multiple bullets or casings were recovered and all were of the same type and caliber, the Fast Brass rules put priority on immediately entering only one of the exhibits (presumably, the one judged to have the clearest toolmarks).

Phased in over the course of 2003, the new Fast Brass protocols succeeded in eliminating the IBIS entry backlog; about 9,650 items were entered into IBIS, and 310 hits were achieved in 2003, compared with 8,400 items and 195 hits in 2002.

Another evidence protocol maintained by the NYPD is based on a prioritization of resources and assessment of current system performance: if both bullets and casings are recovered from the crime scene and they are of the same caliber, only the casings are entered into IBIS. Of the nearly 1,400 IBIS hits obtained by the NYPD from October 1995 through December 2004, fewer than 10 were generated by bullet evidence—hence a higher priority on cartridge case entry.

SOURCE: McCarthy (2004).

make hits in crimes where casing evidence is not likely to be recovered: "drive-by shootings in which the bullets are found at the scene but the casings remain in the shooter's vehicle, for example." It is impossible to fully evaluate the tradeoff between entering bullets and entering casings without a line of empirical research that is lacking at present: When both casings and bullets are recovered from the same scenes or collected in test firings and both are entered into NIBIN, how do relative scores and ranks on the cartridge case markings compare to those for bullets? Further work in this area could also help finalize a priority for exhibit entry, as described in Recommendation 6.1, suggesting whether potential gains in generating hits compare with resource efficiencies inherent in favoring the entry of casings over bullets.

6–B.4 Formalize Best Practices

One of our committee's plenary meetings was held in the Phoenix metropolitan area, where several NIBIN sites at various levels of jurisdiction—state police, county sheriffs, and municipal police departments—are clustered. Another of our meetings included presentations by the NYPD and officials from the Boston area, commenting on usage of ballistic imaging technology in that area. In addition, each member of the committee and its staff visited at least one NIBIN site or IBIS installation. Our discussions at these sites corroborate what is evident from NIBIN operational data, including the analysis done in the Inspector General audit of NIBIN (U.S. Department of Justice, Office of Inspector General, 2005). That is, active participation in NIBIN and image entry into the system spans a continuum, from vigorous users who put high priority on use of the system to agencies for which data entry (like the resulting number of hits) is much more limited.

In the preceding sections we have touched on some of the reasons for this variability, including the time-consuming nature of bullet entry and perceptions of limited payoff in terms of confirmed hits; our recommendations in the rest of this chapter try to address some other points of aggravation by NIBIN users. As we noted above, ATF has done a commendable job in soliciting feedback from its users, and it is important that this continue. But we also believe that it is important that—drawing on local users' experience—NIBIN management take a detailed look at sites that have most successfully and productively used the system. Through such a review, it would be useful to distill "best practices" by high-achieving agencies—for example, means of obtaining high-level commitment by agency officials, methods for working through returned lists of comparison scores, or interacting with detectives and beat officers—for dissemination to all NIBIN partners.

Recommendation 6.5: Local NIBIN experience should be a basis of research and development activities by ATF, its contractors, and the National Institute of Justice. Local experience could usefully contribute to such efforts as "best practices" for image acquisition, investigative strategies, data archiving standards, and the development and refinement of NIBIN computer hardware and software.

6–B.5 Entry of Multiple Exemplars

Although many of our recommendations are intended to make NIBIN image acquisition less burdensome, there is one point on which we believe that a slight loss in efficiency will ultimately lead to greater effectiveness in producing investigative leads. This point is the question of what evidence should be entered into NIBIN when multiple exhibits are possible, whether this is because multiple pieces of evidence are recovered from the same crime scene or because a gun is recovered by police (and hence can be test fired more than once). In some instances, this may also include crimes for which a firearm is left at the crime scene, as well as spent bullets or casings, but a suspect may not yet be apprehended. For expedience, some agencies may only enter a single exhibit that a firearms examiner or an IBIS operator judges to be the "best" marked of the exhibits; we have observed this kind of assessment at individual law enforcement agencies, and it is also the standard practice for New York's Combined Ballistic Identification System (CoBIS) reference database when more than one casing is included as the required ballistic sample.[1]

A recurring message from the studies of IBIS performance reviewed in Chapter 4—as well as our committee's own experimental work, discussed in Chapter 8—is that ammunition type is extremely consequential in obtaining high-probability matches. The NIBIN program maintains a list of standard protocol ammunition for various firearms calibers. This protocol ammunition is meant to provide the best conditions for depositing toolmarks, and that is an important consideration. However, George (2004a:288) phrased a fundamental point most clearly and bluntly: "criminals do not feel obligated to use the ammunition our laboratory equipment may prefer, and firearms submitted at a later date may have a different brand of ammunition than was used at earlier, unknown, crime scenes." Based on the sizable impact ammunition type appears to play in IBIS comparison scores, and on the inherent variability in the production of marks from shot to shot, we conclude that the NIBIN system's ability to generate hits is hindered by policies of including only a single exemplar for cases.

Nennstiel and Rahm (2006b:29, 30) noted the tension inherent in this choice. Concluding that IBIS comparison performance degrades with database size, they argued that the size of a caliber group in a database "should be achieved as small as possible"; in addition to basic database filtering, they suggested that this could be achieved by rotating evidence out of the database after a certain time period. That said, they argued, "multiple ammunition specimens of the same test firearm should be used for an electronic comparison," as their study indicated that this increases the success rate in finding hits. Moreover, "if available, there should be more than one

---

[1]On one of our site visits, we discussed some archival cases and retrieved some exhibits from the archives for reanalysis. For one of these instances, both a firearm and a spent casing were recovered from a crime scene; only the casing obtained by test firing the weapon (using department protocol ammunition) had been entered into NIBIN, not the actual crime scene evidence.

single (two, or, better yet, three) specimens of the same unrecovered firearm included in the setting up of the open case databases"; they acknowledge that this directly contradicts the guidance to keep databases as small as possible, but that the gain in performance merits the additional entry.

De Kinder (2002a:200) reached the same conclusion. Although his remarks apply specifically to the construction of a reference ballistic image database, they apply equally to NIBIN. Entry of more than one specimen per firearm, when possible, accounts for the variability inherent in firings using different ammunition makes.

> In regular casework [in Belgium], we use about two to three different brands of ammunition to account for a different metallic composition of the primer (brass and nickel) and the bullet (brass, nickel and lead). This will substantially ease later microscopic comparisons. It also accounts for some variation in the ductility of the primer material. As the presence of a good quality mark out of the headstamped areas is needed, three cartridges are fired with each brand of ammunition. More experience has to be acquired with automated comparison systems to see what number of test firings has to be performed.

Argaman et al. (2001:270) documents similar protocols used by the Israel National Police, entering two cartridge casings when possible and possibly more. "Although inputting two [casings] almost doubles entry time and increases workload, the authors believe that the benefits outweigh the costs." "The two [casings] entered into the system should differ from each other as much as possible" in order "to increase the chances of finding a match (a possible hit) and for better evaluation of the correlation results."

The ATF critique of the California technical evaluation (see Section 4–G) discounted the findings of a strong ammunition effect. "It is worth noting that ammunition difference is not necessarily prohibitive to the discovery of a hit; most of the hits at ATF labs are between evidence from different ammunition manufacturers" (Thompson et al., 2002:16). No exact data was provided in support of this assessment. However, disputing an assertion that large databases necessarily drown out potential hits by forcing potential matches lower in the list of rankings, Thompson et al. (2002:19) commented that, "in actual fieldwork, IBIS correlation scores seem to actually improve with 'sister' test casings acquired, as the computer refines its search capability."

Practically, of course, there is a limit to how much data local agencies should (or will want) to enter for particular cases; in a shooting incident involving a semiautomatic firearm, where a dozen or more casings may be recovered from the scene, basic resource constraints will preclude entering all of the possible evidence into NIBIN. However, it makes intuitive sense to include more than one to maximize the chances of finding connections to other incidents that might involve the same gun. Likewise, in test firing a weapon in police custody, all manner of variations are possible, and we do not suggest that agencies try to anticipate every possible shooting condition. What we do suggest is that more than one exhibit be put into NIBIN, ideally representing some span of ammunition makes.

Recommendation 6.6: The NIBIN program should consider a protocol, to be recommended to partner sites, for the entry of more than one exhibit from the same crime scene or test firing when more than one is available. For crime scene evidence, more than one exhibit—but not necessarily all of them—should be entered, rather than having examiners or technicians select only the "best" exemplar. For test-fired weapons, it is particularly important to consider entering additional exhibit(s) using different ammunition brands.

To be truly effective, this recommendation necessarily incurs a basic technical enhancement to the current IBIS platform; see Recommendation 6.10; some of the usability enhancements suggested in Recommendation 6.13 also complement the notion of multiple exemplars.

6–B.6 Reallocation of NIBIN Resources

The final operational enhancement we suggest is an echoing of Recommendation 1 in the Inspector General audit of NIBIN (U.S. Department of Justice, Office of Inspector General, 2005). The NIBIN program does have procedures in place for monitoring low-usage sites and sending warning messages. As ATF commented in its reply to a draft of the audit report, "consideration must be given to the availability of IBIS technology to law enforcement agencies that reside in regions that historically have low usage based on the amount of firearms crimes" (U.S. Department of Justice, Office of Inspector General, 2005:131). That is, ATF is aware that a strict quota of evidence entries per month is an unfair benchmark, since agencies vary in the number of gun crimes (and hence the number of possible NIBIN entries) they encounter. That said, systemic low usage should be grounds for reallocation of scarce program resources to other agencies who can be more effective partners in the system.

Recommendation 6.7: Priority for dispensing NIBIN system technology should be given to high-input environments. This entails adding machines (and input capacity) to sites that process large volumes of evidence and especially to sites that lack their own NIBIN installations but that routinely and regularly submit evidence to regional NIBIN

sites for processing. For NIBIN partner agencies with low volume of entry of crime scene evidence, the ATF should continue to develop its procedures for reallocating NIBIN equipment to higher performance environments.

6–C TECHNICAL ENHANCEMENTS

Several of them deal with the specific functionality and interface of the current IBIS platform; others are broader in scope and speak to the type of information that should be recorded for the NIBIN system as a whole. Put another way, these recommendations are not a "to do" list for the current IBIS or its developers, but will require collaboration between system developers, NIBIN management, and the program's user base.

A common theme of our technical recommendations extends from our general assessment of the IBIS platform in Section 4–F: that it is a sorter and a tool for *search* that is commonly, and unfortunately, confused with a vehicle for *verification*; the two are very different functions. The recommendations we offer are meant to improve the system's effectiveness as an engine to search and process large volumes of data and to give its users more flexibility to explore possible connections between cases.

6–C.1 The Language of "Correlation"

We begin with a matter that is inherently technical, even though it does not deal directly with computer hardware or software: It is an issue of nomenclature, of what to call the basic process performed by the IBIS technology. As described in Chapter 4, Forensic Technology WAI, Inc., and the IBIS user base describe the process as "correlation," even though system training materials repeatedly stress that the actual correlation "scores" are of little consequence and that what matters is the rank of particular exhibits. We avoid using "correlation" throughout this report, describing the algorithm and process as "comparison" instead. In statistics, and as has seeped into common parlance, the correlation coefficient measures the strength of linear association between two random variables. Scaled to fall between 0 (no relationship) and 1 (perfect linear relationship), the correlation coefficient provides a clear and easy to understand measure of association. That IBIS uses the same term in labeling its scores imparts to the process—however subtly—an undue degree of quantitative confidence. This is not to say that the IBIS procedures are either unreliable or unsophisticated; indeed, we argue quite the opposite in Chapter 4.

To fully warrant the term correlation, the scores reported by ballistic imaging systems would have the same easily understood interpretation as a correlation coefficient; this is almost certainly an unrealizable goal. Absent that, what would be helpful is any kind of benchmark or context that can be attributed to system-reported scores.

Recommendation 6.8: Normalized comparison scores—such as statistical correlation scores, which scale to fall between 0 and 1—are vital to assign meaning to candidate matches and to make comparison across searches. Though current IBIS scoring methods may not lend themselves directly to mathematically normalized scores, research on score distributions in a wide variety of search situations should be used to provide some context and normalization to output correlation scores. Possible approaches could include comparing computed pairwise scores with assessments of similarity by trained firearms examiners or empirical evaluation of the scores obtained in previous IBIS searches and confirmed evidence "hits."

6–C.2 Collecting the Right Data

Audit Trail

As discussed in Chapter 5, it is impossible to make a full evaluation of the NIBIN program and its effectiveness because the data that are systematically collected on system performance is far too limited. The monthly operational reports that are reviewed by the NIBIN program consist of basic counts of evidence (entered that month and cumulative) and of completed hits. Even within this extremely limited set of variables, the information collected is not rich enough to answer important questions, such as whether hits are more often realized when connecting two pieces of crime scene evidence or in linking a crime scene exhibit to one test fired from a recovered weapon. Completely absent from the standard operational statistics are any indicators of the searches performed by the system (save for the fact that the entry of every piece of evidence should incur a local search by default).

Certainly, some of the data that one would like to have to evaluate the system's effectiveness are not items that can or should be maintained within the IBIS platform; these items include any of the indications of the quality of the investigate leads generated by completed hits, whether an arrest was made in a particular case (or cases), and whether convictions are achieved. But we believe that IBIS at present is too "black box" in nature and that it is not amenable to analysis or evaluation; the system should be capable of generating a fuller audit trail and operational database than the inadequate monthly summaries currently generated and assembled by NIBIN program staff.

Recommendation 6.9: ATF should work with its NIBIN contractor to ensure that the system's hardware and software systems generate an audit trail that is sufficient to adequately evaluate system usage and effectiveness. In most cases, these data should be generated automatically by the software; however, others will require changes to the software so that data may be entered manually (as is currently the case with the recording of hits). The data items that should be routinely tallied and evaluated include (but are not limited to):

- **counts of manually requested database searches, such as those against other regions or the nation as a whole;**
- **information on the origin of the case with which a hit is detected (not just the case number and agency that detects and verifies the hit); and**
- **characteristics of cases in which a possible match is deemed sufficiently strong to request the physical evidence for direct comparison by an examiner, including the "correlation" scores and ranks for the match, an indicator of which image(s) motivated the request, and an indicator of the disposition of the case (either a hit or a nonhit).**

Ammunition Type

The previous recommendation addressed our concern that the NIBIN machinery does not currently produce the right operational data, for effective analysis. We now turn to how the system could benefit from collection of a fundamental variable during the demographic entry stage of image acquisition. In our observations of IBIS at work, a major deficiency in the current set-up is the inability to specify what is known about the ammunition used in the exhibit. Some information about ammunition make can be entered in a "notes" field on the demographic entry screen, but ammunition brand and type should be a standard variable that agencies can use in filtering or sorting their comparison score reports (see Recommendation 6.13). It could also be used as a presorting variable to narrow down the search space before initiating a manual search, as might be desirable in following up a series of shootings for which links and common features are suspected in advance. In Recommendation 6.6, we urge the entry of multiple exemplars, particularly involving the use of multiple ammunition types when test firings from a weapon are possible. Having ammunition as a viewable variable would be invaluable in interpreting the results of comparison runs in cases where multiple exemplars are in the database.

In offering this recommendation, we recognize that it is not as simple a fix as it may appear. To promote more consistent entry, headstamp information would likely have to be entered using a drop-down list, which could be lengthy and would have to adjust to changes in the ammunition market (as is the case with built-in lists of firearms manufacturers). The best way to implement this change, including the easiest spot in the data entry process in which to insert the new item, should be determined on the basis of feedback from NIBIN users.

Recommendation 6.10: ATF and its technical contractors should facilitate the entry of ammunition brand information for exhibits, when it is known or apparent from the specimens. In consultation with its NIBIN user base, ATF should also consider allowing entry of other relevant fields, such as the composition of the primer and the nature of the jacketing of the bullet.

6–C.3 Improving Search Strategies and Server Workload

Refinement to the image acquisition process—making it more accurate and less burdensome—is critical to full use of NIBIN resources. So, too, are refinements to the nature of searches conducted. To be most effective, searches have to be easy to specify (if they are not automatic) and must be relevant and important to the local law enforcement agencies using the system.

We do not suggest or advocate that nationwide searches against the whole NIBIN database should be routine and default, but we do concur with the Inspector General audit of NIBIN that it is important that agencies have the knowledge and training to initiate nationwide searches if conditions in a case warrant a sweeping search. It is not surprising that agencies rarely conduct national searches given that, at present, a national search must be carried out by searching each NIBIN region separately. What is disturbing about some agency responses to the Inspector General's survey is that some partners use only the default local search because they do not know how to initiate wider searches or because they consider those searches irrelevant. Accordingly, we echo the Inspector General's Recommendation 2 and amplify it. As a matter of routine, we believe that NIBIN management should periodically conduct national or multiregional searches on samples of evidence, both to get a sense of the ease with which those searches can be conducted and to determine whether the searches indicate possible (or spurious) matches.

Recommendation 6.11: Even though national or cross-regional searches against the NIBIN database may be rare, the capacity for such a search to be conducted should exist and should be well communicated

to NIBIN partner agencies. A protocol for national or multiregion searches, whether initiated by individual agencies or in regular system checks by ATF, should be promulgated, with an eye toward providing some investigative spark in open but cold crime investigations.

In consultation with its user base, the NIBIN program should also work to ensure that the default searches performed by the system are adequate for user needs. This entails periodically reviewing the region and partition structure of the NIBIN database; it may also involve working with IBIS developers to define easily accessible "shortcut" searches, rather than work through display maps and a drop-down list every time a certain search region is desired.

Recommendation 6.12: Based on information from NIBIN users, ATF and its technical contractors should:

- **regularly review the partition structure of the NIBIN database (which defines the default search space for local agencies) for its appropriateness for partner agencies' needs, and**
- **develop methods for flexible and user-designed searches that may be more useful to local agencies than the default partitions. These types of searches could be based on the frequency of contacts between local law enforcement agencies or intelligence on the nature and dynamics of known gun market corridors, among other possibilities.**

Additional flexible search possibilities could include searches in areas of known gang activity or between jurisdictions where connections were successfully made in previous investigations.

A peculiar and disturbing finding from the U.S. Department of Justice Inspector General audit of NIBIN is that there are NIBIN partner agencies that enter exhibits into the database but do not regularly (or ever) review the comparison scores that are returned by the NIBIN regional servers. It is difficult to say why this is the case. In part, though, it may be due to the structure of the NIBIN database itself, funneling all evidence and comparison requests through IBIS correlation servers at three ATF laboratories. It is unrealistic to expect completely instantaneous results, even if each site had its own servers (which we do not suggest). Yet the distributed nature of the network necessarily involves some considerable amount of waiting: waiting for new images and requests to be uploaded to the servers, waiting for comparison routines to be performed, and waiting for comparison scores and images to be pushed back to the local installations.

Our committee and staff site visits included trips to two of the ATF laboratories; at both we saw the general slow-down at IBIS stations when the local NIBIN sites were "polled" for new images and processing was being performed. Given the time involved, it is not difficult to imagine local agency staff moving on to other duties rather than waiting on returned results. Again, we do not suggest that there is necessarily anything wrong with the NIBIN program's strategy of consolidating servers at a limited number of sites, and we do not suggest that this strategy and the waiting time that it incurs is the complete, direct cause of agencies not following up comparison score results. What we do suggest is that NIBIN management must also periodically consider whether the regional server workload is balanced so that the time from image acquisition to comparison score results is as small as possible for NIBIN users.

6–C.4 User Improvements for NIBIN as a Search Tool

As we discuss in Section 4–F and above in this chapter, we think that the NIBIN program and the IBIS platform would be best served by breaking away from a strict top-10, verification-focused posture; it is best conceived as a tool for search, analysis, and discovery. The current IBIS is fairly rigid in its structure, affording users little or no flexibility in defining the reports that are generated by the system or the interface they view on screen. Comparison scores are repeated in a basic spreadsheet layout, and users are effectively limited to choosing which column to sort, which row to highlight, and which row (exhibit-to-exhibit) comparison to pull up for viewing. No graphical indication of the distribution of scores is provided (as might be useful to see clear "breaks" or gaps in the scores), and it can be difficult to see where a particular exhibit (or set of exhibits) fall in the rankings across the different scores.

As another example, the IBIS Multiviewer interface allows users to see several exhibit-to-exhibit comparisons at once, showing the images in an array; however, useful text or labels of what exhibits or cases are currently being shown in the Multiviewer are lacking. Moreover, the Multiviewer comparisons are anchored to the reference exhibit that was run in the comparison request; as examiners peruse multiple images, it would be useful to pull up pairs of nonreference exhibits from the score results for closer examination, to find possible "chains" of three or more same-gun exhibits found in the same set of scores. The enhancements we suggest include some user-interface modifications that would make the IBIS platform more useful for analysis, but is not meant to be exhaustive of all such modifications.

Recommendation 6.13: To enhance the NIBIN technical platform as an analytical tool, ATF and its technical contractors should:

• allow users to filter and sort the returned lists of comparison scores and ranks by such variables as gun type, ammunition type, reporting agency, and date of entry;

• use persistent highlighting or coloring to allow users to readily see the relative positioning of specific exhibit(s) across the rankings for different marks (e.g., to be able to see where the top five exhibits by breech face score fall in the rankings by firing pin, or to see where multiple exhibits from the same case lie in any of the rankings);

• use visual cues to alert reviewers of comparison scores that exhibits have already been physically examined and deemed a hit (or examined and found not to be a hit);

• permit flexibility in the Multiviewer screen (on which multiple images can be displayed in an array) so that two nonreference exhibits can easily be compared side by side, thus permitting easier examination of chains of potentially linked exhibits; and

• permit flexibility in specifying the printed reports produced by the system so that listings of multiple exhibits are more informative than the current exhibit/case number and score layout.

6–C.5 Side Light Images

Although IBIS computes comparison scores for breech face impression using an image taken using a center ring light, examiners generally prefer visually examining the alternative image taken using a side light when reviewing potential comparisons. The side light image is a representation more akin to what examiners are able to see looking directly at a cartridge casing through a microscope; the side light adds contrasts that give a better sense of depth and of the texture of the primer surface. Given this preference, George (2004a:288) argued for additional work on imagery akin to the side light image: "[FTI] needs to develop images which are more compatible with those the user actually views on the comparison microscope. The user must be able to **visually** eliminate or associate candidates in order to have any level of confidence that a match is not being overlooked."

We agree that users should have a clearer visual benchmark to consider when examining comparison score results, even if the actual image acquired by the system for use in deriving signatures and computing scores is different and taken under conditions most favorable to the comparison process. However, we also suggest that IBIS developers explore ways to make use of the auxiliary information collected in the side light image: Methods for computing an alternative comparison score based on the side light image should be developed and tested to see how they perform relative to the IBIS-standard methodology using the center light image.

Recommendation 6.14: Because the side light image of the breech face impression area is more consistent with firearms examiners' usual view of ballistics evidence—and may be the basis for pulling potential matches for direct physical examination—the side light imagery should be a more vital part of the NIBIN process. Users should have the option to view (if not actually capture) the side light image before acquiring the center light image, for easier inspection of the casing's alignment and basic features. IBIS developers should experiment with comparison scores and rankings based on the side light image, and compare those with scores using the standard center light image.

6–C.6 Operator Variability

In the current IBIS system, users entering images into the system are confronted with several system-computed default suggestions—on image focus, image lighting, and the suggested placement of region-of-interest delimiters. Users have the capacity to adjust or override these defaults. In our site visits, we observed a variety of such adjustments, less on image focus but much more frequently on the intensity of lighting. At some sites, operators would increase the lighting slightly because their firearms examiners found the slightly brighter images easier to work with; at other sites, operators would do exactly the opposite. The exact placement of region-of-interest delimiters is obviously crucial to subsequent comparisons, as it dictates the image content used to derive a mathematical signature, but the effects and tolerances on the other user-adjustable parts of the acquisition process are not well documented.[2] Research on these lines—for instance, looking at the impact on scores when comparison images are lightened or darkened by degrees—should be conducted and used to promulgate best practices throughout the NIBIN system.

FTI is continuing to develop a new system, dubbed BrassTRAX, that is very literally more of a "black box" than the current IBIS/BRASSCATCHER

[2]On a site visit to the New York Police Department, we had opportunity to try one such adjustment. We requested that an examiner acquire breech face and firing pin images from the same image three times. Twice, the examiner entered the image as normal, adjusting the lighting slightly if he deemed it appropriate; this allowed us to see a near-perfect match (and resulting score). The third acquisition was set several steps brighter than the examiner would ordinarily prefer, though it was far short of complete saturation and a pure-white image. Both scores were fairly robust to the lighting change; the two normal-lighting images were returned as the top-ranked pair on both scores, with breech face and firing pin scores of 315 and 351, respectively. The scores against the over-bright image only degraded slightly for the breech face but more so for firing pin—302 and 282, respectively—but they were still comfortably the number-2 ranked comparison.

platform; as described in Box 4-1, the system is already being positioned as the next-generation IBIS. Physically, the unit is a box with only one spot for entry or adjustment: A cartridge casing is inserted into the tray at one corner of the box. The equipment then automatically handles all parts of image acquisition (save for demographic data entry), including the alignment and rotation of the casing. Development of such a platform is intriguing, but—consistent with Recommendation 6.14—it is important that users also be comfortable with viewing and interpreting the imagery generated by the system.

As complete automation of the image acquisition process continues to evolve—reducing the effect of operator variability—it is particularly important that systems be developed with procedures for routine calibration and validation. System performance over time in processing known, standard exhibits should be a regular part of system monitoring, and the capacity for logging these calibration data in a simple and recoverable manner (for subsequent analysis) should be a priority. Further specification of calibration and validation routines should make use of exhibits that can be entered and compared at different points in time and at different NIBIN sites, including ongoing efforts by the National Institute of Standards and Technology to develop a "standard bullet" and a "standard casing" as known measurement standards.

6–C.7 Revisiting the Comparison Process and 20 Percent Threshold

Finally, we turn to a critical part of the current process: the coarse comparison pass, in which all eligible exhibits are compared with the reference exhibit using a rougher comparison score, and only the top 20 percent of scores (for any of the types of markings) are retained for subsequent processing. As discussed in Chapter 4, this threshold was originally intended as a computational aid, restricting the pool of candidates for more detailed comparison beyond the prefiltering imposed by subsetting the database by demographic data (e.g., incident date and caliber family). However, the major analyses of IBIS performance described in Chapter 4—particularly the George (2004a, 2004b) studies, in which the coarse comparison step was completely waived—demonstrate that the sharp thresholding does cause known sister exhibits to be excluded from consideration. We see the same behavior in our own analyses in Chapter 8. In some of the experiments we performed, loss of potential matches was virtually guaranteed: The database was small and heavily concentrated with sister exhibits from the same guns, and so the imposition of any threshold or removal of exhibits from final consideration would incur some losses. But we also observed known sister exhibits to be screened out by the coarse comparison pass in runs against much larger segments of the New York CoBIS database.

Figure 4-2 shows the basic printed report generated by IBIS, the top 10 ranked pairings by the different cartridge case markings. Reported prominently on the sheet is a sample size of 12,353. In discussing this type of report with other parties—such as investigating detectives, departmental superiors, and legal counsel—the meaning of "sample size" can be explained relatively easily as (roughly) the subset of the database matching the reference exhibit in caliber. But no information is readily provided on the *effective* sample size that is most relevant to the scores presented on the page—the number of exhibits retained after the coarse pass, for which the full scores were computed. That this effective sample size can be as small as 2,470 would be surprising, and potentially misleading, to observers without a detailed knowledge of all the steps in the IBIS comparison process.

We do not argue that there is anything inherently wrong with a first, coarse cut of the database or the specific method used; however, research should still be done to determine whether 20 percent is an appropriate measure, balancing gains in processing time with the potential to miss hits. We also believe that NIBIN users should have the capacity to easily adjust the threshold level in regenerating comparison score results. Particularly if circumstances lead to court trials where an IBIS-suggested linkage is the primary (or very important) evidence, it would behoove agencies and examiners to be able to demonstrate that the suggested pairing came about in a process where all eligible exhibits were subjected to the same score and rank, rather than roughly 20 percent of them. As with national and cross-regional searches, we also suggest that 100 percent full-comparison requests (that is, waiving the coarse comparison entirely) should be performed by NIBIN management as a matter of routine research and evaluation.

Recommendation 6.15: In light of improvements in computer processing time, the relatively *ad hoc* choice of 20 percent of potential exhibit pairs from the coarse comparison step should be reexamined. IBIS developers should consider removing the 20 percent threshold restriction or revising the percentage cut if it does not seriously degrade search time over moderate database sizes. In any event, IBIS developers should make it easier for local agencies to adjust the threshold level or to waive the coarse comparison pass altogether if specific investigative cases warrant a full, unfettered regional search of evidence at the expense of some processing speed.

7

Three-Dimensional Measurement and Ballistic Imaging

The striations on the edges of fired bullets and the textures impressed on the primer surface of a cartridge casing are, in their own right, *images*: representations of physical objects (imperfections and textures in a firearm's barrel, breech face, and firing pin) depicted in a medium. These physical "images" are also inherently three-dimensional, produced by cutting, scraping, and etching. Part of the tension that has accompanied the use of photography in forensic firearms identification (see Section 3–F) arises from the fact that flat, two-dimensional representations of tactile, three-dimensional features is necessarily somewhat dissatisfying. Though it could be argued that any of the instantaneous views of bullet or cartridge case evidence through a comparison microscope is a two-dimensional perception, the ability to directly manipulate the exhibits—to alter their rotation and lighting—gives a three-dimensional experience that any single two-dimensional freeze-frame would lack.

The basic objective of any ballistic image database is to collect some accurate representation of cartridge cases and bullets, derived so that entries can be compared and scored for similarity with others. The presence of an electronically coded representation of the physical objects obviates the need for direct access to the physical objects for comparison (though they would have to be directly examined for final confirmation). In theory, then, a three-dimensional model of a cartridge case or bullet—accurately conveying fine differences in depth but still capable of mathematical processing—would be ideally suited to the task.

As advances have continued in the field of surface metrology in recent years, applications in the three-dimensional measurement of ballistics evidence have begun to emerge. As part of our charge to consider technical enhancements to the present National Integrated Ballistic Information Network (NIBIN) system—and to ballistic imaging, generally—consideration of three-dimensional measurement versus two-dimensional photography as the imaging standard was a natural pursuit. As Thompson (2006:10, 12) suggests, fully exploiting the three-dimensional aspects of the toolmarks left by firearms raises new levels of complexity relative to two-dimensional photography. "Striated [three-dimensional] toolmarks would be easy to match if, from the beginning to the end, they always stayed the same," but they do not. Indeed, even fine striations—colloquially referred to as lines—do have a third dimension, depth, that can be appreciated "by using higher magnification"; ultimately, computer-based systems for analyzing striations will have to contend with the problem of deciding whether the different depths of "lines" convey any special significance. Moreover, Thompson (2006:12) notes:

> The dynamics of a bullet going down the barrel of a firearm, the downward movement of a fired cartridge case against the breech face of a Glock pistol, or the movement of a screwdriver across a door strike plate all leave 3-dimensional toolmarks that can change considerably in a short distance. . . . These features, toolmark angle, ammunition variability, [and] tool/barrel wear are features that an examiner considers during an examination and none of these can be [fully] captured in a [two-dimensional] photograph.

In Chapter 8, we discuss experiments conducted on the committee's behalf by the National Institute of Standards and Technology (NIST) using a prototype three-dimensional sensor on cartridge cases. This chapter provides basic background for that discussion, beginning with a discussion of the conceptual differences between two-dimensional and three-dimensional image acquisition technologies (Section 7–A). Previous efforts in three-dimensional measurement of ballistics evidence are described in Section 7–B, along with currently emerging three-dimensional products (7–C).

7–A ACQUISITION TECHNOLOGIES

7–A.1 Two-Dimensional Acquisition

A two-dimensional approach to pattern comparison uses a photographic image of the object as the basic element. In considering the impact of two-dimensional imaging on the comparison process, there are several key factors—all driven by the fact that the image is a projection of light reflected off of three-dimensional objects onto a two-dimensional acquisition plane. These factors generally separate into geometry and photometry.

The basic process of two-dimensional image formation involves several steps. Light rays are emitted from a source (or sources) located at specific geometric spots relative to the object and the sensor. Those rays follow standard optics as they emanate from the source to the object. When each ray strikes the object, it interacts with the surface of the object. There are several effects, depending on the material properties of the object. If the object is purely specular (a mirror), the ray is reflected back into the world at an orientation governed by the local geometry of the surface. More generally, however, the ray interacts with the surface. Some of the energy of the ray will be absorbed by the material, thus diminishing the total energy reflected back into the world. In addition, the microstructure of the surface will typically cause the ray to diffract, meaning that the amount of energy retransmitted off of the surface will vary as a function of the angle of emittance relative to the surface normal at the point. For example, in a purely matte surface, the amount of energy reflected from the surface varies as a cosine law. These effects are generally captured by the photometry of the situation, and techniques such as the bi-directional reflectance distribution function (BRDF) can be used to very accurately capture the reflectance properties of a material. Of course, this works for ideal materials, or materials whose properties can be measured in isolation. In more general settings, one uses approximations to capture the BRDF of a material.

Once the light energy is reflected off of the surface, it obeys standard optics laws, and is captured by a sensor (camera). Here, the geometry of the situation will influence how many photons are captured at a single image element—the distance of the camera from the surface (typically not an issue in close-range imaging), the orientation of the cameras optics system and acquisition plane relative to the incoming rays, as well as other effects.

In general, one can characterize several factors that influence the amount of light captured at a pixel (picture element) in a standard imaging device:

- position and strength of the light source;
- physical extent of the light source (assuming it is not a point source);
- use of multiple light sources;
- geometry relating light source positions to the surface material of the object being sensed;
- geometry of the object itself (see below);
- material properties of the object (this includes both changes in the material across the object, which will change the amount of light reflected independent of geometry (e.g., dirt or other defects may reduce the light and

thus the appearance of a particular pixel) and the manner in which light, independent of the total incoming amount, is reflected from the surface); and

- geometry of the sensor relative to the object being sensed.

Clearly, the overall orientation of a local patch of an object, both relative to the sources and to the sensor, is a major factor in determining how much light is reflected to the source. A naïve analysis, however, assumes that the object is spherical or cylindrical, that is, that all incoming rays strike the object and there is no occlusion. When the object has a more intricate surface, however, the situation gets more complex. This is especially true if there can be self-occlusion, that is, that some light rays may not reach part of the object because they are reflected by other parts of the object—casting self-shadows.

Given all of these factors, one can see that there is a fundamental issue in comparing an image of a probe object against an image of a target object—one needs to ensure that the comparison of intensities in an image, or of some other feature extracted from the intensities, is actually reflecting the shape of the underlying object, and not some other factor. Many of these elements can be controlled. For example, using the same strength of light source, and fixing the position of the light source relative to the object will keep these factors constant across images. Normalization of the image intensities can also remove effects of the elements. Ensuring that the objects are cleaned in a consistent manner will remove material property changes from the images.

Because of the shapes of bullets and shell casings and because their surfaces can be highly reflective (and hence high-glare), the geometry of the acquisition setup is very important. Keeping the orientation of the object the same with respect to the camera across acquisitions is very important. Given that one is primarily measuring striations on the surface of the object, self-shadowing and angle of reflectance effects are very critical, in order to ensure that the striations are both visible and have the same effect on intensities in the two images. One way to deal with this issue is to use multiple light sources—effectively to bathe the object in light from multiple directions. A standard technique is to use a ring of light sources surrounding the camera itself. This tends to reduce self-shadowing effects and reduces the impact of the specular reflection properties of metal objects. An alternative is to use multiple sources but to sequence them—that is, to take multiple images in the same geometry but illuminated from different directions. This can highlight striation patterns in one of the images that might get washed out in a bathing scenario.

Other actions can be taken to reduce image variations not related to surface variations. In addition to controlling the lighting effects, the resolution of the image acquisition device, relative to the size of the object, is important. Since one is typically trying to capture image information about small markings on the object, there is a danger that those markings will get blurred out. Consider the geometry of the situation. While idealistically each light ray is reflected from a different infinitesimal patch of the surface, so that surface patches from the interior of a striation will reflect a different ray than a nearby unmarked surface patch, at some point all of those rays are captured by a patch of an acquisition device (leading to a pixel or picture element). If the pixels are small in comparison with the object size, then nearby rays—one from a striation, one from the nearby surface—will be captured by different pixels. However, if the pixels are too large, then these rays may project to and be integrated out by the same pixel. This blurring of the image can be crucial in this setting, so it is important to determine the size of standard striations and to ensure that the camera device is sufficiently high resolution to capture these changes in surface shape.

7–A.2 Three-Dimensional Acquisition

Since the goal is to compare physical shapes of specimens—the probe object against a stored target object—an alternative is to try to directly measure the three-dimensional shapes. In other words, rather than trying to control or factor out all of the components that affect the image of an object, an alternative is to directly measure the shape. If one can do this, then the comparison can take place on shapes, rather than on image appearance of shapes, and all of the light interaction issues no longer matter.

Three-dimensional surface measurement techniques have developed to include both contact and noncontact methodologies. A contact probe, such as a stylus, can directly measure the three-dimensional position of a point on a surface relative to a fixed coordinate frame. Repeated passes of such a contact probe can be used to more fully reconstruct a three-dimensional shape, and these direct surface measurements can be directly compared against other exemplars. In the particular context of ballistics evidence analysis, however, contact methods are problematic for several reasons. One problem is the size of the object being studied—a bullet or a casing. Most contact probes do not have the level of resolution necessary to build a sufficiently detailed three-dimensional reconstruction. As described more fully in the next section, a more fundamental difficulty is the potential for the evidence bullet or casing to be scratched or otherwise damaged using contact methods, potentially jeopardizing the chain of evidence.

Noncontact methodologies have emerged that do have high resolution, certainly sufficient for the task of working with bullet or casing evidence. These noncontact methodologies include confocal microscopy, interferometry, or laser scanners. Each of these methods can be used to capture the three-dimensional shape of an object, without being subject to nonlinear intensity effects due to light reflection properties, or to self-shadowing effects. The main advantage, therefore, is being able to capture and directly compare three-dimensional shape information. However, the use of these highly sensitive methods can incur some disadvantages, chief among them:

- *Cost*—such sensors are usually much more expensive than optical camera systems.
- *Speed*—such sensors are typically much slower, taking orders of minutes or tens of minutes to acquire a three-dimensional image, rather than a fraction of a second.
- *Noise*—it is important to characterize the noise in the acquired measurements. If the noise is on the order of the depth of the striations, this will render the approach ineffective.

In Chapter 8 we consider the performance of confocal microscopy, which operates on the principle of focusing a point of light on parts of a surface separately and measuring the intensity of returned rays of light rather than a pure reflectivity approach of illuminating the whole surface at once. In particular, light is concentrated through a pinhole aperture to reach the surface, and reflected rays pass through a second pinhole in order to filter out rays that are not directly from the focal point. A three-dimensional reconstruction can be built by varying the height of the pinhole apparatus, thus creating a series of thin two-dimensional slices from which three-dimensional heights can be derived by considering the vertical level at which the maximum level of light was reflected back from a particular point (Semwogerere and Weeks, 2005). The particular microscope tested in Chapter 8 makes use of a Nipkow disk, a spinning disk consisting of multiple pinholes, in order to collect information more rapidly from a wider lateral surface.

7–B PAST EFFORTS IN THREE-DIMENSIONAL IMAGING OF BALLISTICS EVIDENCE

Seeking a way to reinforce firearms identification with a quantifiable and objective basis, Davis (1958) developed an instrument he called a "striagraph." The striagraph recorded measurements from a stylus riding around the circumference of a recovered bullet as the bullet was rotated, providing three-dimensional surface measurement of the path around the bullet. The striagraph was never developed commercially, in part because of two key limitations that continue to affect the use of stylus methods for forensic analysis today: The method was not applicable to deformed or fragmented bullets (as are not uncommon at crime scenes), and the direct contact of the stylus could scratch or mark the bullet, corrupting the evidence (Gardner, 1979). A similar stylus method, dubbed the Balid system, was described in a conference presentation and summarized in the second issue of the *AFTE Newsletter* in 1969. The destructive nature of stylus profiling methods was later demonstrated by Blackwell and Framan (1980), using scanning electron microscopy to illustrate the deformation caused by using a stylus-based "Profilcorder" to trace the circumference of several bullets.

Though stylus methods are infeasible for forensic analysis, methods for *profilometry*—the generation of one-dimensional vectors of height information—of ballistics evidence were pursued by later researchers. De Kinder et al. (1998) and De Kinder and Bonfanti (1999) analyzed bullet striations using three-dimensional profilometry; their scope used a reflected laser as a sensor and was capable of measuring height differences to 1 µm. De Kinder et al. (1998:299) performed preliminary analysis on 9mm Para bullets (including bullets from unfired rounds), as well as those fired through a Fabrique Nationale High Power pistol and recovered using either a water tank or cotton wool. They concluded by noting that "we hope to reduce [the disadvantage of lengthy data capture times] by setting up a procedure to extract a feature vector. This will probably no longer necessitate us to record the whole surface of a bullet, but only a few circumferences to obtain a representative data set of the surface topology."

De Kinder and Bonfanti (1999) extended this work, taking 151 scans (0.05 cm apart) beginning approximately 1mm from the end of the bullet, thus giving a set of profiles along a 7.5mm patch. (The first 34 scans were later found to be relatively noninformative and were dropped from analysis.) Each circumference measurement was taken with an overlap to account for striations split by the initial starting point. Data capture time was 4–5 hours per bullet, "which will be reduced by optimising the definition of the feature vector" (De Kinder and Bonfanti, 1999:87). To compare bullets, they constructed a correlation matrix consisting of the correlations between feature vectors for each of the land impressions (the bullets they studied had six land engraved areas). They took the trace of the resulting matrix as a summary measure for that specific alignment between the bullets; the six traces that arise from reordering the matrix for different land impression alignments were collected. They then compared the maximum value (the presumptive best match) to the average of the traces for non-corresponding alignments. So, for one case involving two bullets from the same gun, they found that the "sum of the correlation coefficients for corresponding striation marks" was 64 percent "higher than the average value for non-corresponding match." In the sole case where they compared bullets from two different guns, the same factor came to 11 percent. They concluded that, of six cases where two bullets from the same gun were compared, "a well founded positive answer can be provided for about one in four cases, while for the two other comparisons, no clear answers can be given" (De Kinder and Bonfanti, 1999:92). In correlating the series acquired at different heights from the bullet base, they found that, "contrary to our expectations, optimal results (correlation coefficients larger than 80 percent) were not obtained for the scans closest to the back of the bullet, but for lines 80 to 100, corresponding to a distance to the base of about 2mm" (De Kinder and Bonfanti, 1999:89–90).

Also focused on the problem of analyzing bullet striations, Bachrach (2002) developed SciClops to acquire profiles of bullet striations. This platform used confocal microscopy to derive a linear, topographic trace around the circumference of a bullet. This work would ultimately be extended to include analysis of a rich set of test-fired bullets, using gun barrels from nine different manufacturers and including more than 200 firings through each (the barrels were cleaned at one point in the firing, to determine the effect of that action on observed striations). The research suggested a three-way gradation in terms of the propensity of manufactured barrels to leave detectable and reproducible marks. A middle range of barrels and manufacturers worked best for toolmark deposition. At one extreme were relatively cheap firearms barrels whose less precise manufacturing standards added randomness to the observed markings and precluded easy matching; at the other were extremely high-end barrels that were so finely polished and machined as to render toolmarks too subtle to readily distinguish.

Banno et al. (2004) acquired images from bullets (two from a Tanfoglio GT27 automatic pistol and another from a Browning model 1910 7.65mm) using a Lasertec HD100D-A confocal microscope. This microscope is capable of measuring a 3.2mm × 3.2mm patch with 450 × 450 pixels, with 0.02 μm height resolution. Images of land engraved areas were generated by connecting a 4 × 4 set of separate patches. Software aligned the different three-dimensional renderings, and similarity was assessed by differencing the aligned images and visualizing the results, shaded to indicate whether differences were within a 0.015mm tolerance. Images for the bullets fired from the same Tanfoglio pistol showed generally strong similarity, with higher differences generated when comparing features from the Tanfoglio and Browning test fires. Banno et al. (2004:240) illustrate but do not extensively analyze use of this measurement for other surfaces, including cartridge case markings. "This algorithm did well" in comparing firing pin impressions for two cartridges from the same weapon; though there is difference in texture along the wall of the firing pin impression, the hollows of the interior of the marks overlap almost exactly.

Zographos et al. (1997) and Evans et al. (2004) advanced the "Linescan" system, a revised methodology for obtaining a composite two-dimensional image around the edge of cylindrical shape, such as a cartridge case or bullet. The system acquires images in a small window while the object is turned, resulting in a continuous imaging process rather than a stitch-together of related images.

7–C EMERGING PLATFORMS FOR THREE-DIMENSIONAL IMAGING OF BALLISTICS EVIDENCE

In the past few years, Forensic Technology WAI, Inc. (FTI) has developed a bullet-only three-dimensional imaging system, dubbed BulletTRAX-3D.[1] This new system "acquires two-dimensional and three-dimensional data in digital form from the entire bearing surface of a fired bullet to obtain its digital 'signature', specifically, a map of its surface topography" for a band around the bullet (Dillon, 2005:5). This differs from the standard Integrated Ballistics Identification System (IBIS) entry that requires operators to specify and image the separate land engraved areas. Graphically, this image data can be rendered onscreen in layers and, notably, as a planar surface that can be rotated and lit (altering both direction and type of simulated lighting) to see striations in relief. A software module also attempts to detect and display bands of consecutive matching striations, an emerging standard for quantifying bullet comparisons (see Section 3–B.3). Like its two-dimensional counterpart in IBIS, the comparison algorithm utilized by BulletTRAX-3D is proprietary information.[2] As such, it is unknown how it differs from the standard two-dimensional IBIS in its comparison routines. However, a reading of Roberge and Beauchamp's (2006) analysis, described below, suggests that the types of scores returned by BulletTRAX-3D are similar to those returned by IBIS.

Roberge and Beauchamp (2006) report success in using FTI's BulletTRAX-3D platform in a complicated test of bullet matching, making use of a set of 10 consecutively manufactured Hi-Point barrels. These button-rifled barrels are known to create major problems for direct visual comparison (see Section 2–D.1). Four bullets were fired through each barrel, and these were grouped into pairs; the objective was to match one

---

[1] The exact rendering of the name of the system varies. The promotional brochure for the system uses a logo that depicts the "3D" part of the name in superscript—BULLETTRAX^{3D}—but describes the system in text as BULLETTRAX-3D. However, Dillon (2005) and Roberge and Beauchamp (2006) used mixed case, calling it BulletTRAX-3D.

[2] Dillon (2005:15) makes the remarkable statement that "the search algorithms employed . . . are proprietary in nature and not of direct interest to the firearms examiner." Dillon suggests that "the examiner is less concerned with the search algorithms and much more concerned with the bottom line represented by the system's list of high probability associations with other cases," though how one can be confident in the "high probability" of suggested associations without any understanding of the algorithm's process is not specified.

group of 10 pairs (labeled 1–10) to the second (labeled A–K; an 11th pair with a different number of land impressions was inserted in this group). Roberge and Beauchamp (2006) exploited the pairwise nature of the test samples to create a training set of known matches; this gave them a sense of optimal "Max Phase" scores (see Chapter 4) to use as a decision rule and assign matches. Following the training phase, the testing was performed stage-wise—performing a set of comparisons, applying decision rules to pick out matches, removing those elements from the dataset, and repeating—until all assignments were made.

Though a caption in Dillon (2005:10) touted BulletTRAX-3D (and its companion MatchPoint Plus display stations) as "the latest configuration of IBIS"—suggesting a replacement of IBIS—the system was originally positioned as a counterpart to IBIS. However, FTI has recently indicated a shift of its product line to focus on three-dimensional platforms, shifting the two-dimensional system currently deployed as the base for the NIBIN-system as the "IBIS Heritage" branch (see Box 4-1). Promotional materials for the three-dimensional systems emphasize that the three-dimensional systems are backward-compatible with the older two-dimensional systems; photographs are taken during the two-dimensional acquisition process and are offered as a layer that can be viewed onscreen in the three-dimensional system, so that photographs can presumably be subjected to the existing two-dimensional comparison process. It is unknown what changes have been made to account for three-dimensional measurement information in generating comparison scores in these new systems.

PART III

Implications for a National Reference Ballistic Image Database

8

Experimental Evidence on Sources of Variability and Imaging Standards

The performance studies of the Integrated Ballistics Identification System (IBIS) platform—the current standard for ballistic imaging—summarized in Section 4–D provide context for the committee's own analyses. The core of the experimental work performed by the committee was coordinated by the Office of Law Enforcement Standards of the National Institute of Standards and Technology (NIST), with whom the National Institute of Justice executed a separate contract to perform analyses at the committee's direction.

Given the committee's basic charge, an ideal test would involve the creation of a prototype national reference ballistic image database (RBID), exceeding the size of the De Kinder et al. (2004) exhibit set, and thus getting a direct impression of automated systems' ability to detect sameness amidst a vast array of exhibits with highly similar class characteristics. However, such a massive collection was clearly beyond the scope of our available resources. Working with NIST, and recognizing the work in previous studies, we judged it best to focus our analyses on narrower objectives. Our experimentation was aimed at generating an exhibit set that—although small in size—could facilitate studies of system performance when both firearm and ammunition type are varied. Significantly, a main objective of our work was to study the effectiveness of one possible enhancement to the current National Integrated Ballistic Information Network (NIBIN) or, alternately, a possible design choice for a new national RBID: a switch from two-dimensional photography to three-dimensional surface measurement as an imaging standard. When NIST and the committee began its work, three-dimensional profilometry analyses had been performed on bullets but had not yet been attempted on cartridge case markings; our experimental work was intended to shed light on the tradeoff between two-dimensional and three-dimensional imaging in computer-assisted firearms identification.

An important set of caveats is in order at the outset regarding this work. Since NIST and the committee began its work, Forensic Technology WAI, Inc. (FTI) has refined its BulletTRAX-3D offering, and an FTI system for three-dimensional analysis of cartridge casings is in production; see Box 4-1 and Chapter 7. The three-dimensional analyses described in this chapter and expressed fully in NIST's report (Vorburger et al., 2007) do *not* make use of FTI's three-dimensional software and systems, although they do share common technology. Indeed, since our three-dimensional analyses are exclusively focused on cartridge case markings, using the FTI three-dimensional equipment was not possible since its cartridge case system was not in production during the committee's period of analysis. In this chapter, we do make reference to performance comparisons between NIST's three-dimensional system and "IBIS," referring to the standard IBIS two-dimensional-photography-based product, even though FTI has branded its three-dimensional systems with the IBIS name. As described in Box 4-1, this nomenclature and comparison is appropriate since it is the two-dimensional version of IBIS that is currently used by the NIBIN program, which is central to our charge.

Although construction of a full-fledged national RBID prototype was not within our committee's resources, we did wish to do the next best thing: namely, work with data from the existing state-level RBIDs. We accepted an invitation from the New York Combined Ballistic Identification System (CoBIS) RBID to perform limited data entry and experimentation at its Albany headquarters location.

The design of the exhibit sets studied in this chapter is described in Section 8–A, as well as the process used to acquire three-dimensional topographic images. Section 8–B summarizes the work done on the committee's behalf by NIST and concentrates on the comparison between two-dimensional and three-dimensional performance. The results of limited experimentation with the existing New York RBID are described in Section 8–C. Overall conclusions from this work are not presented in this chapter, but are rather deferred to Chapter 9's discussion of the advisability of a national RBID.

8–A DATA SOURCES, DESIGN, AND IMAGE ACQUISITION

The committee's experimental work relied principally on two sets of cartridge case exhibits: an extract of casings from the De Kinder et al. (2004) study of large image database performance and a new set of test firings commissioned by the committee and collected by NIST. We describe these sources below, along with the steps taken to acquire two-dimensional and three-dimensional images and measurements; for ease of reference, the basic design of the exhibit sets is summarized in Box 8-1.

BOX 8-1
Design of Test-Fire Cartridge Sets

DKT (De Kinder et al., 2004) Exhibit Set

- *Firearms Used:* 600 California Highway Patrol service pistols, all generally of the same SIG Sauer P226 make. Forty-six of the pistols were of the P225, P228, or P229 series, but these models were judged to be consistent in breech face and firing pin configurations with the P226.
- *Ammunition Used:* Six brands—CCI, Federal, Remington, Speer, Winchester, and Wolf.
- *Firing Protocol:* A set of seven cartridges—two using Remington ammunition, and one each from the other five ammunition brands—were loaded into a magazine and fired from each pistol. It is not known whether the same ammunition sequence was used in each of the firings.
- *Analysis Set:* NIST obtained access to the full set of 4,200 casings. At the committee's direction, 10 of the 554 guns known to be of the P226 make were selected at random and the 7 casings from those guns were extracted to form a 70-element analysis set.

NBIDE (Vorburger et al., 2007) Exhibit Set

- *Firearms Used:* 12, 4 from each of 3 brands, purchased as new by NIST from standard vendors. Makes were chosen to try to obtain a range of known quality and tooling, subject to constraints on NIST's ability to purchase from available dealers. Only 9mm caliber firearms were considered, for simplicity. Chosen makes were Ruger P95D, SIG Sauer P226, and Smith & Wesson 9VE. The SIG Sauer pistols bore consecutive serial numbers; the Ruger pistols bore closely proximate serial numbers; the Smith & Wesson pistols included 3 with close serial numbers.
- *Ammunition Used:* Four brands, all 115 grain and full metal jacketed. Chosen brands were PMC Eldorado, Remington, Speer, and Winchester. All but the Winchester have nickel-plated primers, while the Winchester is brass.
- *Firing Protocol:* The firearms were inspected and cleaned prior to test firings. One set of repetitions was performed on each of three days. The 12 pistols were fired in randomly chosen order using one ammunition type before going on to the next ammunition brand; the order in which the ammunition brands were handled was varied across the 3 days. After the full set of cartridge casings was collected and labeled, a new randomization was performed and new labels assigned before the casings were analyzed.
- *Analysis Set:* The full exhibit set has 144 casings (4 guns × 3 gun brands × 4 ammunition brands × 3 ammunition repetitions). Due to time constraints, NIST only processed 108 casings—excluding the Speer-brand firings—using three-dimensional surface measurements.

8–A.1 DKT: De Kinder et al. (2004) Exhibit Set

NIST staff obtained access to the 4,200-element exhibit set analyzed by De Kinder et al. (2004), representing firings of seven cartridges in each of 600 SIG Sauer pistols. From the pistols known to be of the SIG Sauer P226 model (some of the 600 pistols were very similar to the P226 but not that exact model), the committee randomly selected 10 pistols; all 7 casings for each of those guns were extracted from the exhibit set for further analysis. For convenience, we refer to this sample of 70 casings as the DKT exhibit set (using the initials for the first two authors).

8–A.2 NBIDE: NIST New Test-Fire Exhibit Set

The De Kinder et al. (2004) analysis made use of a natural opportunity for test firing many similar weapons—a large order of new firearms for a law enforcement agency. In addition to the advantage of database size, it is also strong due to its attention to varying one major factor in the quality of ballistic toolmarks as registered by photographic techniques, namely ammunition type. Strong though it is, it is also limited by its focus on only one firearm type or brand. It is also somewhat limited by its lack of repetitions within firearm and ammunition combinations; only two of the seven firings from each pistol repeated the same combination of major factors (i.e., the same firearm using two rounds of Remington-Peters ammunition); hence, it is limited in its ability to study shot-to-shot variability between firings. Working with NIST, the committee sought to develop a small exhibit set addressing both of these limitations that could then be subjected to both two-dimensional and three-dimensional analysis. NIST used the terminology "NIST Ballistics Identification Designed Experiment" to describe its work, and so we use the label NBIDE to refer to the experiment and the new test-fire exhibit set produced for it.

For simplicity, we restricted attention to a single caliber of firearms—9mm. Moreover, absent the ability to obtain firearms with consecutively manufactured parts or to acquire guns direct off the production line—which was not within our resources—we elected to focus on firearms purchased as new from standard dealers. Within those constraints, the intent for the NBIDE exhibit set was to select several gun models representing a range of perceived quality and precision tooling. The Smith & Wesson 9VE and Ruger P95D were identified as choices, Smith & Wesson being a relatively finely tooled weapon and Ruger being a perceived mid-range choice. However, acquiring as-new firearms on the low end of that continuum—for instance, the relatively inexpensive Lorcin or Bryco firearms that still show up among the most traced guns even though the manufacturers are now out of business—proved difficult for NIST to procure. We opted instead to add another relatively high-end firearm model: the same SIG Sauer P226 model used in the De Kinder et al. (2004) study. This serves to give us a point of comparison with that study, albeit adding more repetitions using the same ammunition. For each of these three brands, four new guns were purchased. All four Ruger P95D firearms and three of the four Smith & Wesson 9VE guns bore close serial numbers (within eight units of each other); three of the SIG Sauer P226 guns bore consecutive serial numbers.

Like the choice of gun make and model, the selection of ammunition masks or subsumes other individual factors affecting the marks left on fired rounds and the ability to detect them through imaging. These individual factors include variation in such areas as the plating of the primer, the presence of nonfiring manufacturing marks, or the presence and thickness of lacquer on the primer. For the NBIDE exhibit set, we elected to retain three of the ammunition brands used by De Kinder et al. (2004)—Remington, Winchester, and Speer—while adding another, PMC (Eldorado) brand ammunition. All the selected ammunition had the same powder charge, 115 grain.

The full NBIDE exhibit set has 144 elements: three repetitions of each of four ammunition brands, fired through four guns from each of three makes. However, the NIST analysis (Vorburger et al., 2007) uses only a reduced 108-element subset of the exhibits, excluding the Speer brand ammunition firings from analysis. This reduction in size was done to reduce the analysis burden, when it was unclear how time consuming three-dimensional surface measurement would be. Although only the 108-element set was subjected to three-dimensional analysis, all 144 exhibits were later analyzed using the current IBIS system.

Prior to test firing, the firearms were inspected and cleaned: in particular, excess oil left inside the weapons at the factory was removed. The test firings were completed over the course of 3 days inside a range facility at NIST's Gaithersburg, Maryland, campus. Only the cartridge casings were retained during firing, caught in a windsock-type attachment after each shot was fired; bullets were fired into a destructive, scrap rubber-type trap. One set of repetitions was performed each day; the ordering of guns and ammunition was randomized across the 3 days.

After the test firing was complete, the 144 exhibits were re-randomized and labeled (though this was done so that the Speer rounds could be separated out for NIST's three-dimensional measurement purposes). The exact mapping of exhibits back to their parent gun was sealed and kept unknown to NIST's analysts, so that they were blind to the true results until imaging and processing was complete.

8–A.3 Image Acquisition

Three-dimensional surface measurements of the firing pin, breech face, and ejector mark impressions on the DKT and NBIDE (108) casings were gathered using NanoFocus μSurf microscopes. Measurements were made using a microscope at NIST's Gaithersburg campus and one at the Rockville, Maryland, facilities of Intelligent Automation, Inc., with whom NIST subcontracted on this work. Each of the microscopes were checked for calibration on a daily basis during the measurement acquisition process, making use of the "standard bullet" and prototypes of a "standard casing" under development under separate studies as NIST-designated reference measurement standards (see Vorburger et al., 2007:Section 4.2).

Subsequently, the DKT and NBIDE (144) casings were submitted to the Bureau of Alcohol, Tobacco, Firearms, and Explosives (ATF) National Laboratory at Ammendale, Maryland, for entry on an IBIS station. The two batches were processed separately; that is, an IBIS comparison request was generated for each of the 70 DKT casings, comparing each entry against the other 69 in the set. Similar work was done for each of the 144 NBIDE casings. By default, each of these comparison runs produced a hard-copy cover sheet returning the "top 10" comparison results, such as that illustrated in Figure 4-2. Through arrangement with FTI, NIST and the committee were able to obtain additional information from each of the two exhibit sets:

- For the DKT casings, the raw IBIS images—including the placement of region-of-interest delimiters on the standard center-light images as well as the side-light image—were extracted and provided in electronic form.
- For the NBIDE (144) casings, FTI performed a complete comparison that waived the 20 percent threshold and coarse comparison steps, generating the IBIS correlation scores for each casing against the remaining 143 elements, and provided those scores in electronic form.

Figure 8-1 contrasts the greyscale photographic images collected by the current IBIS platform with representations of three-dimensional surface measurement data, for both the breech face and firing pin markings of a particular cartridge casing. The raw data for the three-dimensional surface measurements are just that—numeric distance measurements over a fine array of spatial coordinates; for graphical purposes, these can be rendered in many ways, using colors to suggest "height" or "depth" or simulating lighting from any desired angle. The two three-dimensional plots in Figure 8-1 use different color and texture schemes to approximate the appearance of the surfaces.

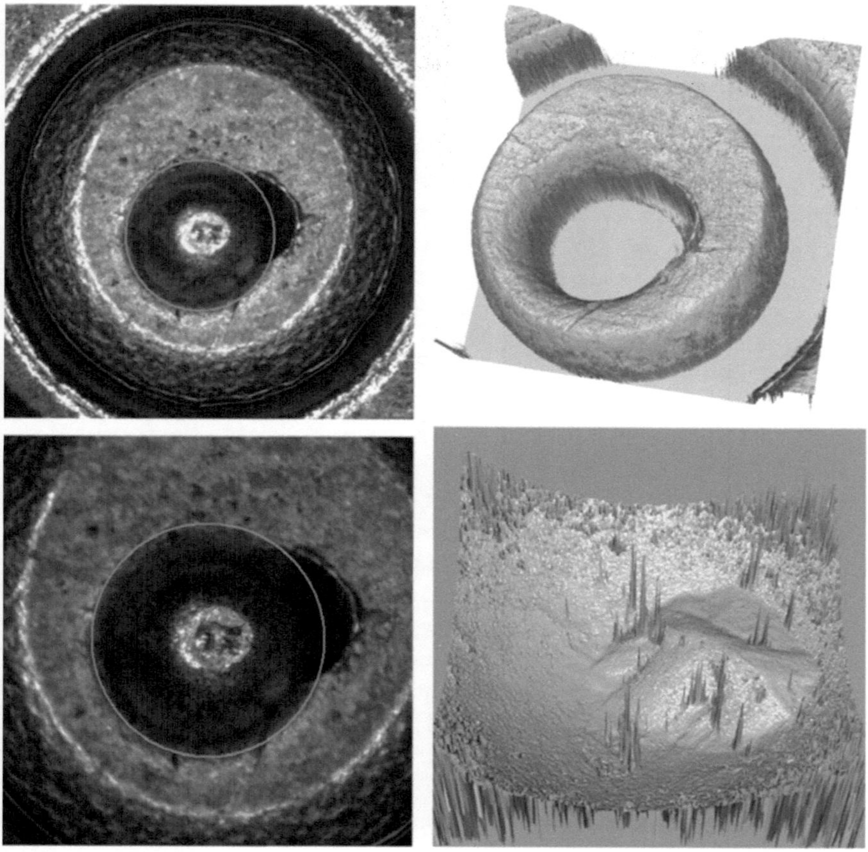

FIGURE 8-1 IBIS two-dimensional images and rendered three-dimensional surfaces, breech face, and firing pin impressions from one casing.
NOTES: Breech face images in row 1; firing pin images in row 2. Images are from the DKT exhibit set, the Federal casing from pistol number 535. The region-of-interest delimiter circles are superimposed on the IBIS images.

8–A.4 Processing Steps and Similarity Measures for Three-Dimensional Measurement Data

Vorburger et al. (2007:Section 8) describe the data processing steps for NIST's topographic measurements in considerable detail. Here, we describe the basic steps:

- *Data trimming and thinning:* Alone, the sheer size and detail of the topographic measurement datasets make the cross-comparison of three-dimensional "images" a time- and computer-intensive activity. For breech face impressions in particular, where measurements may be picked up on the cartridge rim, some data are trimmed so as to include only the primer surface. NIST also worked with algorithms for thinning the data, reducing the lateral resolution of breech face images from on the order of a 2,600 × 2,600 grid of data points to 650 × 650. (Measurements for firing pin impressions were not thinned, however.)

- *Removal of dropout and outlier points:* Good though a three-dimensional sensor may be, it does ultimately provide only an *estimate* of height or depth; there are individual spatial points that the sensor may simply fail to acquire (dropouts) and others where the estimate is made with appreciable noise or inaccuracy (outliers). Code developed by NIST analyzed the three-dimensional measurement datasets for these problematic points and interpolated new values from nearest neighboring points.
- *Filtering:* As a rough means to try to emphasize individual characteristics rather than class characteristics in the three-dimensional images, NIST applied standard filters in noncontact optical profilometry, based on spatial wavelengths in the topographic image data. Spatial wavelength calculations are based on distance between consecutive peaks after subtracting out a mean surface depth; in this particular case, both very short and long wavelengths are subtracted out, removing effects that can be thought of as corresponding to system measurement noise and broad structural features (class characteristics), respectively. This filtering adjustment stops short of true feature extraction, using algorithms to try to detect and highlight particular image features.
- *Registration:* Finally, the adjusted topographic image is processed by another program, intended to find the rotation and horizontal/vertical shift that gives best correspondence between images.

To compare images, NIST used areal cross-correlation functions, as are common in spatial statistics. Like the standard statistical correlation score, the cross-correlation scores are scaled; two topographic images that are exactly the same would yield an areal cross-correlation of 1.0. As the measures are computed, the functions used by NIST are very slightly asymmetric—that is, the cross-correlation of image A compared with image B can be slightly different from the results when image A is used as the reference and compared with image B. Noting that the standard IBIS two-dimensional comparison score is similarly asymmetric, NIST judged the discrepancies to be generally insignificant (Vorburger et al., 2007:126–127).

8–B ANALYSIS OF TWO- AND THREE-DIMENSIONAL IMAGE DATA

In this section, we describe the results of analyzing the DKT and NBIDE datasets using both two-dimensional image data (e.g., the current IBIS platform) and three-dimensional topographic data (using NIST's acquisition protocols and algorithms). With specific regard to the DKT data (and, perhaps, to the firings from SIG Sauer pistols in the NBIDE dataset), these analyses are partly meant to assess the consistency of our results with those by De Kinder et al. (2004), as described in Chapter 4. But—in addition to getting a sense of the capability of the current IBIS to detect known "sister" casings from the same gun—this work is also meant to shed some light on the tradeoff between two-dimensional and three-dimensional measurement, to see whether the latter offers clear-cut advantages over the former.

In what follows, we rely heavily on "top 10" analyses, looking at the 10 highest-ranked possible matches by different markings. This is somewhat unfortunate given our assessment in Section 4–F that there is no special magic in the top 10 as a cutoff (and, indeed, that the focus on the top 10 in current training and IBIS reports has the effect of overpromising the system). However, it is a practical limitation necessitated by a desire to stick to standard IBIS analysis and experience as much as possible: that is, we look principally at the top 10 because generation of the top 10 cover sheet scores is the system default, and we confine ourselves to the top 10 ranks using three-dimensional measurements for consistency. A fuller analysis would have considered larger cuts at the rankings, such as the top 50—more than the strict limit of the top 10, but still within the number of results a human examiner might reasonably routinely scroll through onscreen to find potential matches. However, as we will discuss, we did obtain a full set of comparison scores for the full NBIDE dataset and discuss those results as well.

8–B.1 Two-Dimensional and Three-Dimensional Performance, DKT Data

As shown in Box 8-1, each exhibit in the DKT exhibit set has six possible same-gun matches. Table 8-1 summarizes the same-gun entries found in the top 10 rankings in a standard IBIS search against the 69 other DKT exhibits, and Table 8-2 provides the same results based on NIST's analysis of three-dimensional topographic data.

On firing pins, the two-dimensional and three-dimensional systems do comparably well. While the three-dimensional system does a much better job at finding the casings from pistols 375, 430, and 535, the two-

TABLE 8-1 Number of Same-Gun Matches Found in Top 10 Ranks, Two-Dimensional/IBIS Analysis of DKT Exhibit Set

Mark and Ammunition Type	Sample SIG Sauer Pistol Number										
	7	9	117	139	213	215	314	375	430	535	Avg.
Firing Pin											
CCI	4	3	3	3	1	1	4	3	2	1	2.5
Winchester	5	0	0	3	4	2	2	3	0	4	2.3
Speer	6	4	5	3	3	1	2	5	3	3	3.5
Wolf	6	4	5	2	3	1	3	4	3	2	3.3
Federal	6	4	5	1	1	2	3	4	2	2	3.0
Rem-1	6	2	4	4	4	3	5	4	3	1	3.6
Rem-2	6	4	3	3	0	2	3	4	5	2	3.1
Average	5.6	3.0	3.6	2.7	2.3	1.7	3.1	3.9	2.6	2.1	3.1
Breech Face											
CCI	0	0	1	0	2	1	2	3	1	0	1.0
Winchester	0	0	0	1	0	0	0	0	0	1	0.2
Speer	1	1	1	2	0	0	2	2	1	0	1.0
Wolf	1	0	1	0	1	2	1	1	1	0	0.8
Federal	2	1	0	1	0	0	1	2	1	0	0.8
Rem-1	2	0	2	2	2	1	1	2	2	3	1.7
Rem-2	1	2	1	3	2	1	1	2	1	2	1.6
Average	1.0	0.6	0.9	1.3	1.0	0.7	1.1	1.7	1.0	0.9	1.0

NOTES: Rem = Remington-Peters. Cell entries are the number of casings fired from the same pistol found in the top 10 comparison results, using the cartridge of the row ammunition type as the reference; the maximum possible score is 6.

dimensional analysis outperforms the three-dimensional on pistols like 139, 213, and 314—ones for which both systems appear to have trouble finding the same-gun casings even in a small dataset, and thus ones that may be tougher challenges for firearms identification generally. The gains from two-dimensional to three-dimensional analysis are quite strong for breech face marks; this is particularly true for pistols 117 and 215, which go from averaging less than one sister pair found in the top ranks to four. This success in finding sister pairs by breech face is largely responsible for the summary result: on average, looking in the top 10 ranks by either breech face or firing pin, the three-dimensional system finds 4.7 out of 6 same-gun pairs while the two-dimensional system finds 3.3.

Though the DKT data provide a glimpse at only one firearm type—SIG Sauers—Tables 8-1 and 8-2 do underscore variability—in propensity to leave clear, identifiable, and computer-matchable marks—from gun to gun and across ammunition types. The firing pins from pistol 7, for instance,

TABLE 8-2 Number of Same-Gun Matches Found in Top 10 Ranks, Three-Dimensional/NIST Analysis of DKT Exhibit Set

Mark and Ammunition Type	Sample SIG Sauer Pistol Number										
	7	9	117	139	213	215	314	375	430	535	Avg.
Firing Pin											
CCI	4	5	1	1	0	3	1	6	5	5	3.1
Winchester	6	1	3	0	0	0	0	6	6	6	2.8
Speer	6	5	4	0	0	3	2	6	6	6	3.8
Wolf	5	5	4	0	0	1	1	6	6	6	3.4
Federal	5	5	3	0	0	2	2	6	6	6	3.5
Rem-1	6	5	2	0	1	0	0	6	6	6	3.2
Rem-2	6	5	0	0	0	1	0	6	6	6	3.0
Average	5.4	4.4	2.4	0.1	0.1	1.4	0.9	6.0	5.9	5.9	3.3
Breech Face											
CCI	2	2	5	4	4	6	4	1	5	3	3.6
Winchester	1	0	1	1	0	4	0	2	2	2	1.3
Speer	0	0	3	3	3	4	2	0	1	3	1.9
Wolf	1	1	4	2	3	3	1	2	4	2	2.3
Federal	1	3	4	5	1	3	0	1	3	2	2.3
Rem-1	2	4	5	3	5	6	4	2	6	3	4.0
Rem-2	4	3	6	5	5	5	4	4	5	3	4.4
Average	1.6	1.9	4.0	3.3	3.0	4.4	2.1	1.7	3.7	2.6	2.8

NOTES: Rem = Remington-Peters. Cell entries are the number of casings fired from the same pistol found in the top 10 comparison results, using the cartridge of the row ammunition type as the reference; the maximum possible score is 6.

provided little challenge for either the two-dimensional or three-dimensional analyses, while the scores on pistols 139, 213, and 314 are generally poor by either mark on either system. Similarly, Winchester ammunition seemed to impair the ability to match on either system (especially by breech face), and the CCI ammunition provided particular difficulties in the two-dimensional images.

8–B.2 Two-Dimensional and Three-Dimensional Performance, NBIDE Data

Tables 8-3 and 8-4 summarize the results of two-dimensional and three-dimensional analyses of the NBIDE exhibit set. Again referring to the design in Box 8-1, and given that NIST withheld casings from one ammunition type (Speer) from its analysis, comparisons were run using the two-dimensional IBIS and NIST's three-dimensional system on each of 108

TABLE 8-3 Number of Same-Gun Matches Found in Top 10 Ranks, Two-Dimensional/IBIS Analysis of NBIDE Exhibit Set

	Gun Type														
Mark and	Ruger					SIG Sauer					Smith & Wesson				
Ammunition	R1	R2	R3	R4	Avg.	S1	S2	S3	S4	Avg.	SW1	SW2	SW3	SW4	Avg.
Firing Pin															
Winchester	4.3	4.7	2.3	6.7	4.5	2.0	3.0	4.7	5.0	3.7	6.0	3.0	4.7	2.0	3.9
Remington	0.7	4.3	3.0	2.3	2.6	2.0	2.0	4.0	4.0	3.0	3.3	2.0	5.3	3.7	3.6
PMC	5.0	5.0	3.0	6.0	4.8	2.3	2.7	4.0	4.3	3.3	6.0	3.0	5.0	3.0	4.3
Average	3.3	4.7	2.8	5.0	4.0	2.1	2.6	4.2	4.4	3.3	5.1	2.7	5.0	2.9	3.9
Breech Face															
Winchester	5.7	5.7	5.0	6.3	5.7	4.0	4.0	7.0	4.0	4.8	6.7	6.7	5.7	4.7	5.9
Remington	3.0	6.0	4.7	6.0	4.9	3.3	3.3	6.0	3.0	3.9	5.7	6.0	5.7	4.3	5.4
PMC	2.0	6.0	4.7	6.7	4.8	4.7	3.7	5.0	4.0	4.3	6.7	7.3	6.3	5.7	6.5
Average	3.6	5.9	4.8	6.3	5.1	4.0	3.7	6.0	3.7	4.3	6.3	6.7	5.9	4.9	5.9

NOTES: PMC = PMC Eldorado. Cell scores are averages over three repetitions of the same gun-ammunition combination. Maximum possible value is 8.

TABLE 8-4 Number of Same-Gun Matches Found in Top 10 Ranks, Three-Dimensiona/NIST Analysis of NBIDE Exhibit Set

	Gun Type														
Mark and	Ruger					SIG Sauer					Smith & Wesson				
Ammunition	R1	R2	R3	R4	Avg.	S1	S2	S3	S4	Avg.	SW1	SW2	SW3	SW4	Avg.
Firing Pin															
Winchester	6.7	8.0	4.7	7.3	6.7	4.0	2.7	6.0	5.7	4.6	7.3	4.3	7.3	4.7	5.9
Remington	6.7	8.0	4.7	5.0	6.1	3.3	2.3	6.7	3.3	3.9	7.7	3.3	5.7	3.7	5.1
PMC	6.7	8.0	5.3	7.7	6.9	4.7	3.0	8.0	6.3	5.5	8.0	5.3	6.3	4.3	6.0
Average	6.7	8.0	4.9	6.7	6.6	4.0	2.7	6.9	5.1	4.7	7.7	4.3	6.4	4.2	5.7
Breech Face															
Winchester	8.0	8.0	8.0	8.0	8.0	8.0	8.0	7.7	7.7	7.8	7.7	8.0	7.3	8.0	7.8
Remington	8.0	8.0	8.0	7.7	7.9	8.0	8.0	8.0	8.0	8.0	7.7	8.0	8.0	8.0	7.9
PMC	8.0	8.0	8.0	8.0	8.0	8.0	8.0	8.0	8.0	8.0	8.0	8.0	8.0	8.0	8.0
Average	8.0	8.0	8.0	7.9	8.0	8.0	8.0	7.9	7.9	7.9	7.8	8.0	7.8	8.0	7.9

NOTES: PMC = PMC Eldorado. Cell scores are averages over three repetitions of the same gun-ammunition combination. Maximum possible value is 8.

casings against the 107 other casings. Accordingly, each comparison was against a database containing 8 same-gun matches (three ammunition types × three repetitions – one) and 99 nonmatches (11 other firearms × three ammunition types × three repetitions). The cell counts in Tables 8-3 and 8-4 indicate the number of same-gun matches for each firearm and ammunition combination, averaged across the three repetitions.

For the pure SIG Sauer DKT exhibit set, both the two-dimensional and three-dimensional systems appeared to do a better job at finding same-gun matches using the firing pin mark than the breech face; the opposite appears to be true for the NBIDE dataset. The success of the three-dimensional system in finding the same-gun matches in the top 10 ranks on breech face is excellent; indeed, it is near perfect. For the two-dimensional systems, the success rates on breech face generally exceeded those for firing pin; the two-dimensional scores are not weak (averaging about six of eight same-gun matches detected for the Smith & Wesson pistols, and doing less well—about four of eight—on the SIG Sauers), but they do not approach the high success of the three-dimensional analysis.

On firing pins, the scores corresponding to the SIG Sauer firings are generally lower than those for the Ruger and Smith & Wesson guns. The second of the SIG Sauer pistols seems particularly difficult, yielding less than three out of eight same-gun matches on either the two-dimensional or three-dimensional systems. As suggested in the DKT analysis above, ammunition seems to have a strong effect, with the Remington ammunition producing consistently fewer matches than the PMC or Winchester rounds. Overall, the three-dimensional analysis appears to outperform the two-dimensional, particularly for the Ruger firings and the second Ruger pistol.

Some further insight into the two-dimensional/IBIS performance on this dataset can be had by considering a complete set of scores and rankings—waiving the coarse comparison and 20 percent threshold steps—that was prepared for the committee by FTI. Table 8-5 summarizes the distribution of the ranks of matching exhibits in these complete score lists; for this analysis, we include the Speer casings and use the complete 144-element NBIDE set. The table combines the 144 separate comparison reports, indicating the distribution of all 144 × 143 = 20,592 pairwise comparisons, of which 1,584 were between exhibits that were fired from the same gun. Out of 1,440 possible top-10-ranked positions by breech face, across the 144 different comparisons, about 57 percent were between reference and test exhibits from the same firearm; 33 percent were from different firearms but the same gun brand, while 10 percent were from exhibits from completely different gun brands. On the firing pin impression alone, the share of top-10 positions filled by same-firearm matches dips to 42 percent while the share from same-brand-but-different-firearm comparisons grows to 43 percent.

TABLE 8-5 Summary of IBIS Comparisons for Full 144-Exhibit NBIDE Set

Relationship of Reference To Test Casing	Ranks of Matching Exhibits in Complete Score List											
	Breech Face Only				Firing Pin Only				Breech Face or Firing Pin			
	#1	#2–10	#11–29	#30+	#1	#2–10	#11–29	#30+	#1	#2–10	#11–29	#30+
Different Gun Brand												
Different Ammunition	0	71	602	9,695	6	140	640	9,582	6	210	1,182	8,970
Same Ammunition	0	70	383	3,003	0	71	286	3,099	0	133	615	2,708
Same Gun Brand												
Different Specific Firearm												
Different Ammunition	1	181	960	2,746	13	347	1,064	2,464	14	502	1,613	1,759
Same Ammunition	11	288	451	546	8	256	426	606	19	450	522	305
Same Specific Firearm												
Different Ammunition	49	553	303	391	55	373	281	587	92	678	336	190
Same Ammunition	83	133	37	35	62	109	39	78	115	118	30	25

NOTES: Tabulations are from score lists generated by Forensic Technology WAI, Inc., waiving the coarse comparison pass and 20 percent threshold. Each of the 144 casings was compared with the 143 other exhibits in the set, for a total of 20,592 comparisons. The cutoff at rank 29 corresponds to a strict 20 percent threshold on a sample size of 143; the actual effective sample size for any of these comparisons in a standard IBIS run would be somewhat larger because both breech face and firing pin images are considered, but we use the 29 cutoff for simplicity. For purposes of generating ranks, tie scores in the score lists are assigned final ranks by sorting by the NIST-assigned ID number for the test (in-database) exhibits. This is tantamount to a random assignment of ranks for tie scores because the ID numbers were randomly mixed prior to analysis.

8–B.3 Analysis of Matching and Nonmatching Distributions of Similarity Scores

Extending beyond analysis of ranks—as in Table 8-5 for the two-dimensional IBIS data—the NIST study (Vorburger et al., 2007:Section 9.5) derives an *overlap metric* to assess its cross-correlation similarity scores for three-dimensional topography data.

The empirical distribution of the cross-correlation scores can be derived separately for the matching (same-firearm) and nonmatching pairwise comparisons in a dataset of topographic "images"; Figure 8-2 illustrates such a distribution for the scores generated from the firing pin scores using the NBIDE exhibit set. Continuous distributions can then be estimated for the matching and nonmatching comparisons, with the intent of calculating the degree of overlap between them. Ideally, the matching and nonmatching distributions would have no overlap and be wholly distinct from each other,

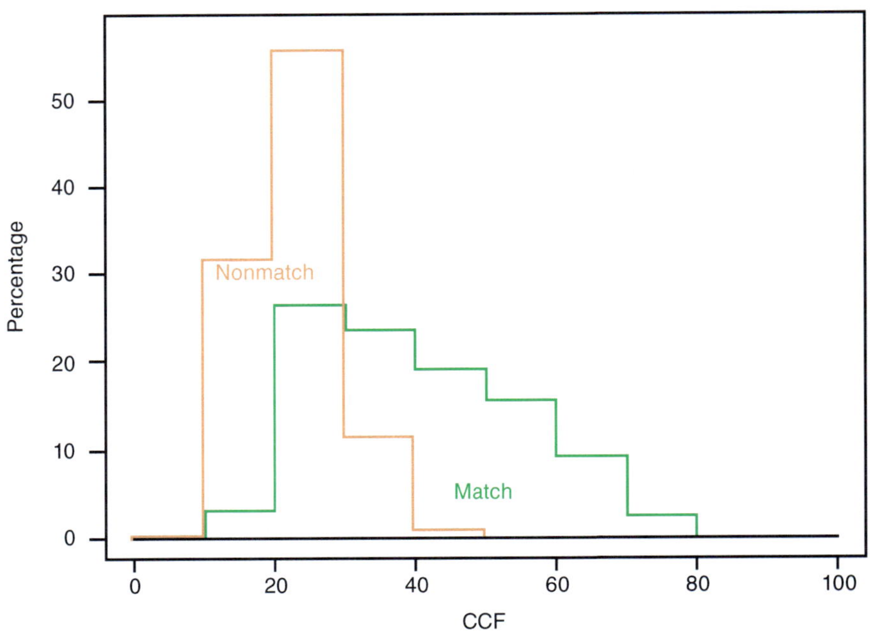

FIGURE 8-2 Empirical distribution of matching and nonmatching pairwise comparisons.
NOTE: Data used are the scores from comparisons of the three-dimensional topographic measurements of firing pin impressions using the NBIDE exhibit set.
SOURCE: Vorburger et al. (2007:Fig. 9-16).

with the matching scores at the high end of the range and nonmatching scores concentrated near 0. The more the matching and nonmatching distributions overlap, the greater the degree of false matches may be expected since matches and nonmatches become harder to distinguish. The extent of overlap can be summarized by estimating p, the probability that the similarity score (maximum cross-correlation) of a randomly chosen element of the nonmatching distribution is larger than a randomly selected member from the matching distribution. In the ideal separation described above, p would be 0; in a completely overlapping distribution, p would be 0.5.

This same logic can be applied to an exhibit set as a whole (to provide a single estimate of p) or on subsets: specific values of p could be derived for particular firearms or particular casings. For instance, for the 108-element NBIDE dataset (excluding the Speer firings), a casing-specific p can be derived from the 107 pairwise comparisons using that casing as the reference, 8 of which are same-gun matches and 99 of which are nonmatches.

Table 8-6 summarizes estimates of casing-specific values of p from the DKT and NBIDE exhibit sets. The table confirms the three-dimensional system's strong performance on breech face measurements for the NBIDE exhibits, with 90 percent of the casing-specific estimates of p being less than 0.001. For the NBIDE firing pin measurements, separation was less clear; only 18 percent of the p estimates were less than 0.001. The degree of overlap is more pronounced for the DKT data; the maximum estimated p for the DKT firing pin comparisons was 0.415, quite close to complete overlap.

TABLE 8-6 Summary of Overlap Metrics for Three-Dimensional Images

	Proportion of $p \leq$		
Image Type	0.001	0.01	0.1
DKT Data			
Firing Pin	0.09	0.21	0.45
Breech Face	0.01	0.03	0.21
NBIDE Data			
Firing Pin	0.18	0.25	0.56
Breech Face	0.90	0.95	1.00

NOTE: The table summarizes the proportion of casing-specific estimates of p falling below a particular value, where $p = 0$ indicates perfect separation of matching and nonmatching distributions; see text for further derivation.

8–B.4 General Assessment

Although we defer our main conclusions from this experimental work to our discussion of a national reference ballistic image database in Chapter 9, some comment is in order here on the trade-off between two-dimensional photography and three-dimensional surface measurement as an imaging standard, particularly as a possible technical enhancement to the current NIBIN system.

We conclude that NIST's work on the committee's behalf on a prototype three-dimensional ballistics evidence comparison system suggests that such a system has strong merit. Although in early development, NIST's version of a three-dimensional analysis system produced results on par with—and, for some markings, outperformed—the current two-dimensional system in detecting same-gun sisters. That it did not consistently produce same-gun match rates that exceed the two-dimensional system—for instance, that it did not always do best at handling breech face markings—suggests that there is room for improvement and refinement. Much work also remains to done on streamlining the acquisition and data processing steps. As a first foray—one geared to ensuring proper calibration of equipment and to testing different algorithms and computer programs for generating comparison scores—the data acquisition process was time consuming and comparisons took many hours to run to completion. In both respects, the specific three-dimensional system developed by NIST is unsuitable for deployment and immediate use. We have no information on the performance of the new Forensic Technology WAI, Inc., three-dimensional-based IBIS for cartridge casings and hence cannot comment on it. However, we are confident that three-dimensional surface measurement of ballistics evidence can be made to be tractable; though not ready for immediate implementation, three-dimensional measurement and analysis of bullet and cartridge evidence should be a high priority for continued research and development.

8–C BASIC EXPERIMENTATION WITH NEW YORK CoBIS DATABASE

A subgroup of committee members and staff made two visits to the New York State Police (NYSP) Forensic Investigation Center in Albany in March and July 2005 to see a state RBID in operation and to perform some small-scale tests of system performance. Our analysis was deliberately limited in nature, so as to avoid unduly interfering with the center's operations for part or all of a day. The exploration we pursued consisted in part of entering a subsample of exhibits from the DKT set, for which we also had (independent) IBIS analysis by ATF and three-dimensional measurement by NIST. We also drew a sample from past CoBIS caseload for reacquisition and analysis, and observed the entry of new exhibits waiting in the queue for entry.

In advance of the visits, committee staff asked NYSP for a basic breakdown of gun makes in the CoBIS dataset, to get a sense of high- and low-frequency cases. Casings from 9mm pistols make up the largest portion of the CoBIS data (about 38 percent of the total); of the 9mm pistols, Glock pistols are most highly represented (46.5 percent), followed by Smith & Wesson (18 percent). The second-most represented caliber group are 40 caliber firearms, followed by .22 caliber; Glock and Smith & Wesson are the largest entrants among .40 caliber arms, while Kimber and Ruger firearms are the largest constituent parts of the .22 caliber database.

We selected four manufacturer-and-caliber combinations, including both high-frequency cases and very-low-frequency cases. For the latter, we selected Kimber 9mm, a group for which only 23 exhibits, of the entire 29,355-element 9mm pool, were known to be in the database. The other combinations we sought were Glock 9mm (the single largest component of the database), Beretta .22, and Smith & Wesson .357.

For each of these groups, one exhibit was retrieved arbitrarily from storage (archive) and one from waiting caseload (new).[1] The "new" exhibits were checked in and entered into CoBIS as usual, and the envelopes retained so that they could be reentered later. As the exhibits were being processed, we learned of Glock's practice of including two casings in the sample envelope packaged with its new guns. In standard CoBIS practice, the IBIS technician briefly looks at both casings and chooses one as the "best" casing for entry. Only the casing deemed to be the best for entry was reacquired into the system, but we generated comparison scores using both casings as references to see if the second casing matched well with the best. The technician-determined best casing was labeled 1, and the second was labeled 2. Only the breech face and firing pin images were acquired; one of our chosen weapons, the Beretta .22, is a rimfire firearm, and so its single mark is acquired in the free-hand trace method usually used for ejector marks.

This set of casings was supplemented by a small extract of eight casings from the DKT exhibit set.[2] Two DKT pistols (numbers 535 and 68)

---

[1]For the archive cases, exhibits were drawn from 2004 forward, since boxes containing those exhibits were accessible near the IBIS entry room. As described below, we had occasion to retrieve one specimen from CoBIS pre-2004 archive. One of the casings used as a "new" was extremely new; it was from a firing performed on-site on the morning of our visit, when a dealer brought in a gun for firing and cartridge collection prior to sale.

[2]Our analysis set also had one other unplanned addition. The very first comparison score results to be returned on screen were for NYSP05, a "new" casing from a Smith & Wesson .357 model 640 revolver; that casing had a CoBIS ID with stub 05-05061 (05 indicating 2005 and the last five digits being a sequential ID number). It turned out that the highest-

were chosen; both Remington casings plus the CCI and Speer casings were selected from gun 535, and both Remington casings plus the Wolf and Federal casings were selected from gun number 68. These were entered into the system as new evidence, labeled NAS01 through NAS08, respectively. The workload for entering the NAS exhibits and the "new" caseload exhibits was divided among four CoBIS operators; however, when exhibits were entered for querying the database, all entries were made by the same person. The exhibit set analyzed in Albany is summarized in Box 8-2.

8–C.1 Basic IBIS Results, NAS Exhibits

Table 8-7 reports the IBIS breech face and firing pin scores and ranks for the eight NAS exhibits, extracted from the DKT exhibit set. Practically, these comparison runs looked at the performance of the current IBIS in finding elements of an eight-exhibit set, nested within a database of effective sample size 15,082 of casing images from new firearms of the same caliber and basic demographic characteristics.

The first thing that is evident from Table 8-7 is that the system did effectively find matches between images of the absolute highest similarity: different image entries of the exact same casing, differing only (possibly) by the operator who acquired the images. These exact image repetitions are the top-ranked possible match on both the breech face and firing pin marks, and the raw scores dwarf the others.

The second finding shown in the table is that performance on these exhibits is far from the ideal, which is that each exhibit (when used in the reference) would find its three known "sister" casings from the same gun as very highly ranked possible matches, and that the four NAS-labeled exhibits known to be from a different gun would not be highly ranked. For only one of the exhibits—NAS05—do all three of the casings known to be from the same gun even appear on the "full" IBIS comparison score report: the others are rejected in the coarse comparison and 20 percent threshold steps described in Chapter 4. Out of 24 possible same-gun matches (eight exhibits times three "sisters" from the same gun):

ranked possible match by breech face—other than the known image in the system, already entered—bore the ID stub 01-05061, a casing from 2001 bearing the same ID number as the new 2005 case. The breech face score (60) was not exceptional relative to the rest of the distribution, and indeed, visual examination of the images suggested nothing close to a true match. But the happenstance of having a very similar revolver (same manufacturer, slightly different make) from 4 years prior show up at the top of the correlation heap raised some curiosity (was the system somehow sorting on ID?), so the 2001 exhibit was pulled from deep storage for direct examination.

BOX 8-2
Exhibit Set Tested in Work with CoBIS Database

DKT (De Kinder et al., 2004) Exhibit Set Extract: All cartridges are firings from SIG Sauer P226 pistols and represent a subset of the DKT data analyzed by NIST.

- NAS01: Pistol #535, Remington-Peters casing 1
- NAS02: Pistol #535, Remington-Peters casing 2
- NAS03: Pistol #535, CCI casing
- NAS04: Pistol #535, Speer casing
- NAS05: Pistol #68, Remington-Peters casing 1
- NAS06: Pistol #68, Remington-Peters casing 2
- NAS07: Pistol #68, Wolf casing
- NAS08: Pistol #68, Federal casing

CoBIS Extract: For each gun type, one "new" case was selected from casings awaiting entry in the database and one "archive" case drawn from the past 1–2 years of entered exhibits.

- NYSP01: Beretta .22, new
- NYSP02: Beretta .22, archive
- NYSP03-1: Glock 9mm, new, "best" of the two sample casings included in envelope by manufacturer
- NYSP03-2: Glock 9mm, new, second sample casing from manufacturer
- NYSP04-1: Glock 9mm, archive, "best" of the two sample casings included in envelope by manufacturer
- NYSP04-2: Glock 9mm, archive, second sample casing from manufacturer
- NYSP05: Smith & Wesson .357 640 revolver, new
- NYSP06: Smith & Wesson .357 640 revolver, archive
- NYSP07: Kimber 9mm, new
- NYSP08: Kimber 9mm, archive

- Only 3 are found are in the top 11 ranks by either breech face or firing pin (11 is used because of the presence of the image from the exact same exhibit that is always the #1 entry). These are NAS01 to NAS02, NAS02 to NAS01 (on firing pin only), and NAS06 to NAS05—all three casings using the same ammunition (Remington-Peters) as well as the same gun.
- Half (12) had a best ranking (between the breech face and firing pin) that was less than 11—none of these lower than 27, and most of them greater than 100—but still merited inclusion in the "full" correlation report.
- The balance, 9, failed the coarse comparison pass and 20 percent threshold.

TABLE 8-7 IBIS Comparison Results, DKT Exhibit Set Extract in CoBIS Database

Reference ID (# of results)	Test ID	Breech Face Score	Breech Face Rank	Firing Pin Score	Firing Pin Rank
NAS01 (1,014)	NAS01	229	1	226	1
	NAS02	29	11	101	2
	NAS04	10	728	61	86
	NAS05	12	641	55	199
	NAS06	7	861	50	340
NAS02 (1,106)	NAS01	26	279	106	2
	NAS02	249	1	366	1
	NAS04	22	594	52	160
	NAS05	25	342	49	225
	NAS06	11	838	46	338
NAS03 (1,024)	NAS02	15	641	41	177
	NAS03	280	1	253	1
	NAS04	25	339	28	657
NAS04 (987)	NAS03	36	69	43	645
	NAS04	273	1	299	1
	NAS08	12	711	65	288
NAS05 (1,039)	NAS01	17	637	54	305
	NAS04	25	143	58	175
	NAS05	275	1	226	1
	NAS06	15	676	63	69
	NAS07	4	1,013	55	251
	NAS08	14	706	65	48
NAS06 (1,048)	NAS01	15	655	70	37
	NAS02	11	763	60	140
	NAS04	22	167	60	139
	NAS05	33	3	99	2
	NAS06	190	1	203	1
	NAS08	18	484	60	138
NAS07 (1,018)	NAS05	4	899	63	27
	NAS07	275	1	253	1
	NAS08	1	1,001	51	724
NAS08 (1,049)	NAS02	20	486	36	761
	NAS04	21	409	60	337
	NAS05	23	281	63	215
	NAS08	169	1	276	1

NOTES: All exhibits are of the same 9mm caliber, and so all had the same effective sample size of 15,082 exhibits. The (# of results) entries represent the number of entries included in the "full" IBIS comparison report and are the number of exhibits that survive the coarse comparison and 20 percent threshold steps (see Chapter 4). NAS01–04 are from the same SIG Sauer P226, De Kinder et al. (2004) pistol 535; NAS01 and 02 use the same Remington ammunition. NAS05–08 are from the same SIG Sauer P226 pistol, De Kinder et al. (2004) pistol 68; NAS05 and 06 use Remington ammunition.

NAS-labeled exhibits from a different gun than the reference exhibit did appear in the full comparison reports. In fact, when NAS06 was used in the reference, three NAS exhibits from the other SIG Sauer pistol could be found in the comparison report compared to two sister entries from the same pistol. However, none of these comparisons yielded scores that cracked the top 11 rankings by either mark.

With CoBIS staff, we examined the firearms makes and models for the 16 highest-ranked possible matches, on the breech face and firing pin lists, for each of the NAS-labeled exhibits. A wide variety of 9mm pistols appear throughout the listings, including Smith & Wesson, Beretta, and Taurus arms, with smaller numbers of Kahr, Springfield, and Keltec guns. Other SIG models are not uncommon in the listings, but the highest ranks are not dominated by them. It is of interest that some of the NAS casings do frequently match to casings from two runs of near-consecutive serial numbers and, consequently, near-consecutive CoBIS IDs. These likely correspond to large batch sales, such as police department orders. For instance, for the NAS02 casing, the top 16 ranks by firing pin include four entries from one of these runs, entered in 2003 (two other nonrelated SIG exhibits from 2001 are also highly ranked on firing pin); however, none of these pistols appears in the highest ranked possible matches by breech face.[3]

Independently, a committee subgroup visited the New York City Police Department forensic laboratory and ran tests on NAS01–NAS04; the Albany test had the effect of seeing how these same-gun casings were handled in an RBID of images from new firearms, while the New York City test contrasted that with performance in a large database of crime scene evidence. The results were very consistent with those reported in Table 8-7, against a crime-evidence database of 12,427 exhibits after demographic filtering.[4]

8–C.2 Basic IBIS Results, NYSP Exhibits

Our work with the NYSP-labeled exhibits described in Box 8-2 was similar to that done for the NAS-labeled exhibits. "New" exhibits were entered into CoBIS, and then subsequently re-imaged for comparisons.

---

[3]Another oddity that shows up in the top 16 rankings is that the NAS01 and NAS02 casings, in particular, find three test casings—apparently entered by FTI in setting up and maintaining CoBIS' IBIS equipment—among the top ranks by breech face. The make and model of these test rounds (which stand out in the listings because they, like the NAS-labeled exhibits, do not use the typical CoBIS naming conventions) are unknown. It should be emphasized, though, that although they appear in the high ranks, the actual scores and visual match on the images are unremarkable.

[4]Specifically, when NAS01 was used as the reference, NAS03 was again excluded by the coarse comparison pass; NAS02 was nearly top-ranked on firing pin (but low-ranked on breech face), and NAS04 ranked 90th on firing pin and 673rd on breech face.

We were interested in determining whether the system reliably found this exact same image—differing only by acquisition at different times, possibly by different operators—in databases of different effective sample sizes (between 5,312 and 15,082) after the standard filtering. The Glock entries (NYSP03 and NYSP04) provided the opportunity to see where casings in the same manufacturer-supplied envelope related strongly to each other. And, on a follow-up visit to the NYSP Forensic Investigation Center, the makes and models for the top 10 results by both breech face and firing pin were recorded to see whether like models dominated the top rankings.

As with the NAS-labeled exhibits, the current IBIS system had no problem detecting the "needle"—a new instance of the same exhibit image—in "haystacks" of varying sizes, with one prominent exception. That exception was NYSP01, a "new" Beretta 9mm; because it is a rimfire weapon, image entry is done by manually tracing the region of interest (see Section 4–B.2), and a single ejector mark/rimfire impression score is returned by the system. For this exhibit, the image on file in CoBIS—acquired that same morning—appeared as the 137th ranked possible match; its score was 328, compared to the top score (to another Beretta pistol, entered in 2004) of 571. The effective sample size was 8,106, so the link from NYSP01 to itself was not in great danger of being excluded by the coarse comparison and 20 percent threshold steps. Visual examination of the surface images suggest a curious ridge-like structure in the rimfire impression that apparently registers differently under slightly discrepant lighting and orientation. NYSP02, the "archive" Beretta casing, encountered no such difficulty; the original image from 2004 was found in the #1 position with score 2,631, with the score dropping to 444 for the #2 entry.

For each of the Glock exhibits, the second casing in the manufacturer-supplied envelope could be found as a match in the top 10 by one of the marks. When NYSP03-2 was used as the reference, NYSP03-1 was returned as the #4-ranked entry on breech face (raw score 61, relative to a maximum of 64) but was not within the top 10 on firing pin. When NYSP04-2 was the reference, NYSP04-1 was the top-ranked potential match by firing pin (score 168, with an unrelated Glock scoring 163 as the #2 possibility) but dropped out of the top 10 on breech face. In all these cases, the demographic filtering by Glock firing pin gave an effective sample size of 12,353 casings.

For the remaining NYSP-labeled exhibits, the same-gun image was very comfortably returned as the #1-ranked entry on both the breech face and firing pin scores, with wide separations between it and the remaining entries. The top 10 lists for each exhibit are most populated by guns by the same manufacturer and the same model, except for the Kimber exhibits (NYSP07 and NYSP08), for which none of the less-than-30 Kimbers in the CoBIS system were returned as top-10 candidates by either score.

9

Feasibility of a National Reference Ballistic Image Database

In the formative era of modern firearms examination, Hatcher (1935:291–292) noted a development that he interpreted to be suggestive of the adage that "a little knowledge is a dangerous thing." "Certain very well-intentioned individuals recently came very near having a federal law enacted to require every maker of a pistol or revolver to fire and recover a bullet from each gun made, and to mark that bullet with the number of the gun, and keep it for reference by the legal authorities in case a crime should later be committed with a gun of that caliber." Hatcher argued against this forerunner of a national ballistic toolmark database (if not a national reference ballistic image database), citing the complexity of the task and the workload burden it would create:

> In the first place, it is by no means certain that a bullet fired through the same gun several years later would match the one kept for record, for the barrel may have rusted or otherwise changed during the interval. In the second place, the matter of the classification of bullets so as to lighten the labor of looking for the right one of the thousands of record bullets has not, and probably never can be, solved, for the fine scratches, parallel to the rifling marks, on which this identification depends, have nothing by which they can be sub-classified. [Although fingerprints can be classified by general shape patterns, bullets can] be roughly classified by caliber, number of grooves, direction of rifling, etc.; but there is no method of sub-classification. Suppose, for example, that the maker produces only 1000 .38 Special caliber guns in the same year. There will be five or six grooves on each bullet, say 5000 groves to be compared in trying to match the murder bullet to only one year's production of guns of only one maker. It

> may take from fifteen minutes to one hour to compare each groove, and looking searchingly into the comparison microscope is impossible for more than about three hours a day, otherwise the operator is likely to suffer severely from eye-strain, fatigue, and headache. At this rate, it would take one operator something like four or five years to search one manufacturer's record bullets for one year's production of one caliber of gun.

More than 70 years later, ballistic imaging technology has demonstrated its capacity to address some of these concerns, providing an initial analysis and sorting of massive volumes of evidence that—now, as then—are impossible for a human examiner to process. The question is whether the technology has advanced to the point that a massive, national database of exhibits and images from new and imported firearms is any more tractable than the collection Hatcher described as well intentioned but dangerous.

In this chapter, we present the argument from the preceding chapters in order to answer the primary, titular question of our study: Is a national reference ballistic image database (RBID) a feasible, accurate, and technically capable proposition? In Section 9–A, we discuss the basic question of how many guns would be included in a national RBID, followed in Section 9–B with an outline of other general assumptions on the shape and content of a national RBID. Subject to those assumptions, we consider in Section 9–C the technical aspects of establishing such a database from the information management and manufacturing perspectives, the statistical feasibility of such a database, and other perspectives on the issue. Section 9–D presents our general conclusions. We then discuss the implications of our conclusions on subnational, state-level RBIDs that currently exist or that may be created (Section 9–E). This is important because conclusions for or against a national RBID impact not only state RBIDs but—depending on the weight placed on supporting arguments—on the long-term viability of a crime-evidence database like the National Integrated Ballistic Information Network (NIBIN) as well. Some detailed probabilistic calculations related to the statistical feasibility of an RBID are laid out more fully in the appendix to this chapter, in Section 9–F.

9–A A NATIONAL REFERENCE DATABASE: HOW MANY GUNS?

An important consideration in evaluating the feasibility of a national RBID is the magnitude by which ballistic imaging workload would increase: How many guns would have to be entered into such a database?

Yearly firearm production figures compiled by the Bureau of Alcohol, Tobacco, Firearms, and Explosives (ATF) reveal that domestic firearms manufacturers produce between 3–3.5 million firearms per year (see Table 9-1). Approximately one-third of these, on the order of 1 million,

TABLE 9-1 Firearms Manufactured in and Exported from the United States, 2002–2004

Firearms	2002	2003	2004*
Manufactured			
Handguns	1,088,584	1,121,024	1,022,610
Pistols	741,514	811,660	728,511
Revolvers	347,070	309,364	294,099
Rifles	1,515,286	1,430,324	1,325,138
Shotguns	741,325	726,078	731,769
Miscellaneous	21,700	30,978	19,508
Total	3,366,895	3,308,404	3,099,025
Exported			
Handguns	56,742	42,864	39,081
Pistols	22,555	16,340	14,959
Revolvers	34,187	26,524	24,122
Rifles	60,644	62,522	62,403
Shotguns	31,897	29,537	31,025
Miscellaneous	1,473	6,989	7,411
Total	150,756	141,912	139,920

*The cover sheet for the 2004 report indicates that 26 percent of manufacturers did not file reports for 2004. No such response or compliance rates are indicated in the 2002 and 2003 reports.

SOURCE: Data from Bureau of Alcohol, Tobacco, Firearms, and Explosives Annual Firearms Manufacturing and Export Reports, 2002–2004.

are handguns; rifles are the modal category, constituting 35–40 percent of annual domestic firearms production. Relatively few of these firearms—only about 150,000—are exported from the United States. By comparison, tabulations from the U.S. Census Bureau's Foreign Trade Division (see Thurman, 2006) indicate that 844,866 handguns were imported to the United States in 2004, most from Austria (29 percent), Brazil (24 percent), and Germany (17 percent). Nearly twice as many handguns were imported to the United States as rifles (489,740); an additional 71,625 shotguns and combination guns were imported in 2004 (Thurman, 2006).

However, the enabling action for entry in a national RBID is not the production of a firearm or its arrival in the United States; rather, it is the *sale* of a firearm. The previously cited firearms manufacture statistics do not directly correspond to annual sales to individual customers; they include production for military and law enforcement purposes, and they include guns that may sit in inventory rather than be quickly sold. The ATF estimates about 4.5 million "new firearms, including approximately about 2 million handguns, are sold in the United States" each year (U.S. Bureau of Alcohol, Tobacco, and Firearms, 2000:1). It is important to remember that these figures—and the coverage of a national RBID—include only the primary gun market, which covers sales from licensed dealers to consumers. Cook and Ludwig (1996) estimate that about 2 million secondhand guns are sold each year in the United States, from a mixture of primary and secondary sources (where the secondary gun market includes transactions by unlicensed dealers).

The answer to the question of how many guns would have to be entered into a newly established national RBID each year depends crucially on the exact specification of the content of the database—whether the database is restricted to handguns and whether imported firearms from foreign countries are required to be included. As we discuss further in the next section, we generally assume that a national RBID would—at least initially—focus on handguns, and hence an annual entry workload of 1–2 million firearms per year, depending on whether imports are included.

9–B ASSUMPTIONS

In Box 1-3, we describe some basic assumptions about the nature of a national RBID, with particular regard to the wording used in past legislation and in the enabling language of the currently operational state RBIDs. It is useful to begin the assessment of the feasibility of a national RBID by revisiting those assumptions. Fundamentally, we assume that a national RBID would—at least initially—be tantamount to a scaled-up version of the current state RBIDs.

First, we assume that the "ballistic sample" required for entry in the database would consist of expended cartridge cases and not bullets. Though the enabling legislation in Maryland and New York was vague on this point, the only operationally feasible approach was to restrict attention to casings. It takes more operator time (and money) to enter bullet evidence into a system such as the Integrated Ballistics Identification System (IBIS) than casings, and requiring recovery of a bullet specimen at the end of the manufacturing process would be unduly burdensome. That would require firing into a water tank or other nondestructive trap; as in test firings conducted by the police, firings into a tank must be done one at a time—and the bullet retrieved from the tank between each firing—in order to prevent damage to the specimens and to ensure that recovered bullets are identified as coming from the proper gun. Collecting cartridge casings also involves additional time—the protocol must allow for a casing to be attributed to the correct gun source—but the ejected casing is more amenable to rapid recovery than spent bullets that must be separately fished from a tank.

Second, we assume that the focus of a national RBID would be on handguns, as the major gun class used in crime. Expanding state RBIDs to include long guns has been contemplated by legislation in Maryland but not enacted. These first two assumptions—cartridge cases only and a restriction to handguns—combine to limit the ability of the national RBID to generate "cold hits" to one group of firearms: revolvers, which do not automatically expel cartridge casings and, hence, would leave casings at a crime scene only if the gun user manually emptied them at the scene (e.g., to reload). However, we believe that the assumptions are realistic to make the program tractable at the outset.

Third, we assume that the actual process of generating samples and acquiring images from them would follow very closely the New York Combined Ballistic Identification System (CoBIS) model: that is, that most of the burden of generating the sample of cartridge casings would fall on firearms manufacturers, who would include the sample in the firearm's packaging. The burden of actually acquiring images and entering them in the database would be done by another entity, and the envelope containing the sample would be sent for imaging (along with related information) at the point and time of sale. In principle, images could be acquired by manufacturers, but the approach poses major problems both operationally and conceptually.

In terms of operations, it would require the placement of at least one IBIS-type installation at every manufacturer's location and require trained operators, a very costly proposition. Technology for mass batch capture of images from cartridge cases could be developed—Forensic Technology WAI, Inc. (FTI), continues to develop a prototype, which it dubs the Virtual Serial Number System—but the technology is not yet mature, and working with large batches of samples simultaneously exacerbates the problem of ensuring that the sample packaged from a gun was actually fired from that gun (see Section 9–B.2).

Conceptually, imaging by the manufacturer is problematic because it is a step removed from the objective of an RBID, connecting ballistics evidence with a point of *sale* and not the point of *manufacture*. Achieving the link to point of sale would require a further database of sales, presumably to be merged periodically with the image database using the firearm serial number and other data.

Imported firearms are particularly tricky in this regard because they raise potential problems of differential compliance. U.S. legislation to establish a national RBID could compel manufacturers to include test-fired exemplars with newly shipped firearms, for entry into the database, but foreign manufacturers might not be so bound. Hence, imported firearms may involve the additional workload of test firing before sale, in addition to acquiring images.

A critical assumption that underlies much of the political debate over a national RBID deals with the information entered into the database along with exhibit images: Should information on the firearm's *purchaser* be logged in the database, rather than just information on the firearm? The extent to which personal information is recorded raises the question of whether implementation of a national RBID is tantamount to establishing a national gun registry. Again, we assume that the New York CoBIS model would hold. In New York, licensing information completed at the time of sale is sent along with manufacturer-supplied casing samples to the state police headquarters for processing. However, that personal (purchaser) information is immediately separated from the ballistic image processing and forwarded to another agency, and it is not entered into the CoBIS database. We interpret the goal of a national RBID as suggesting an investigative lead to the point of sale. This is obviously not as direct a lead as could be the case, and requires that investigators follow up with seller records to progress further (akin to the standard gun tracing process described in Box 9-1), but it could still provide

BOX 9-1
Tracing Guns

The Gun Control Act of 1968 (18 U.S.C. 922(a)) established the legal framework for regulating firearms transactions in the United States, requiring that any individual engaged in the selling of guns in the United States must be a federal firearms licensee (FFL). Significantly, the act also established a set of requirements—a paper trail—designed to allow the tracing of the chain of commerce for any given firearm, from its manufacture or import through its first sale by a retail dealer. Each new firearm, whether manufactured or imported, must be stamped with a unique serial number (27 CFR 178.92; ATF Ruling 76-28). Manufacturers, importers, distributors, and FFLs are required to maintain records of all firearms transactions, including sales and shipments received; FFLs must also report multiple handgun sales and stolen firearms to ATF and provide transaction records to ATF in response to firearms trace requests. When FFLs go out of business they are required to transfer their transaction records to ATF, which then stores them for use in tracing.

Local law enforcement agencies may initiate a trace request by submitting a confiscated gun and associated information to the ATF's National Tracing Center (NTC); in addition to descriptors of the gun itself, this associated information may include the location of the recovery of the gun, the criminal offense associated with the recovery, and the name and date of birth (if known) of the firearm's possessor. The NTC searches this information against its in-house databases—the records of out-of-business FFLs and the records of multiple handgun sales. If no matching information is found from these queries, NTC agents contact the manufacturer or importer and begin following the chain of subsequent transfers until they identify the first retail seller and (through that FFL's records) the first buyer of the gun.

The table below summarizes gun trace results in 1999, omitting on the order of 11,000 trace requests from foreign agencies (summary counts and percentages are recomputed from the cell entries in the original table).

some spark to criminal investigations that may otherwise grow cold. The assumption that purchaser information would not be recorded in an RBID is consistent with the federal law that prohibits the establishment of "any system of registration of firearms, firearms, owners, or firearms transactions or dispositions" by federal or state agencies (18 U.S.C. 926(a)).

We also assume that the user interface to a national RBID would mirror—and likely build on top of—the current interface of the NIBIN program. Specifically, we assume that queries on the database would be initiated by state and local law enforcement agencies, who would acquire images from evidence they wished to compare and send them over a network for comparison. (Doing this on NIBIN-supplied IBIS equipment, and effectively using the existing NIBIN terminals as the interface to the RBID, would obviously require changes in legislation—which currently limits

Trace Result	Count	Percent
Completed Traces (by method)	82,669	52.9
Out-of-business FFL records	13,167	8.4
Multiple sale reports	3,627	2.3
FFL record	60,526	38.7
Other	5,349	3.4
Incomplete/Not Traced (by reason)	73,690	47.1
Too old	16,192	10.4
Serial number problem	16,920	10.8
Error on trace request	17,588	11.2
Dealer record problem	15,123	9.7
Other	7,867	5.0
Total	156,359	100.0

SOURCE: Cook and Braga (2001:Table 1).

Of the guns submitted for tracing in 1999, slightly more than half were successfully traced to the point of origin. Trace failures may be caused by the age of the gun (e.g., manufactured before 1968 and hence exempt from serial numbering and recordkeeping), or because of problems with the serial number, the submission form, or the information on file with the FFL where the gun was first sold.

"End to end" or investigative traces—completely documenting the chain of possession from manufacture or import through the most recent owner—are considerably more expensive and are not routine. However, under the Youth Crime Gun Interdiction Initiative, ATF does perform "end to end" tracing for all firearms recovered from people under 21 years old.

NIBIN to crime-scene evidence—and in the memoranda of understanding with partner sites.) A partial explanation for the scarcity of hits from the current state RBIDs in Maryland and New York is a relative scarcity of searches performed on the system, and a key reason for that lack of queries is that questioned evidence must be transported to a specific site for entry on RBID-specific equipment. To promote usage of the system, we assume that ways would be found to allow local law enforcement to directly query the database without turning over the physical evidence to other agencies, thus raising concerns about the chain of custody of that evidence. In articulating this model, we further assume that possible high-probability matches on the national RBID would be returned to those localities for their review and, if desired, for them to subsequently request pieces of physical evidence to confirm a hit.

A technical assumption—and a difference between a national RBID and the existing NIBIN system—concerns the performance of automatic comparison requests. In the current NIBIN framework, any new piece of evidence entered into the system incurs an automatic comparison against all evidence entries within that NIBIN site's partition, and the results of that comparison are returned to the local site after processing at one of the three ATF national laboratories. (Manual comparison requests can also be initiated.) This default behavior is sensible for a database like NIBIN, which is assumed to consist exclusively of case-related evidence and for which the interrelationship between entries is of interest. In a national RBID, however, the interrelationships between entries in the database are not of direct interest (since there is no reason to expect a match between two newly manufactured or imported guns), and performing comparison requests as each new entry is added only serves to increase the computational demands on the system infrastructure.[1] What is interesting in the RBID setting is the comparison results that are obtained when a piece of crime scene evidence is entered and compared against the RBID. Hence, we assume that comparison requests in a national RBID would be manually generated or automatic when it is known that a new image being acquired comes from crime scene evidence.

[1]This is not to say that interrelationships between RBID entries—and what comparison scores say about them—are *uninteresting*; indeed, an RBID provides ideal opportunities for studies of system performance in a large database of known nonmatches. Hence, comparison requests of RBID entries against the balance of the database are of great potential research interest, but are logically unnecessary as part of the data entry process.

9–C TECHNICAL FEASIBILITY

9–C.1 Information Management Perspective

At one basic level, a national RBID is technically feasible: Current and projected computer capabilities can handle the information flows associated with such a database. In our assessment, a national RBID would be a sizable but not insurmountable computational challenge and would be within the capacity of existing technology. The human workload necessary to process exhibits and acquire images would be formidable, but possible. In this section we describe this conclusion using basic calculations that—although "back of the envelope" in nature—are meant to be "worst case" projections.

We include computational, networking, staffing, and physical requirements, and impose a number of stricter assumptions (beyond the general nature of the database) in making this analysis. These additional assumptions include:

1. *The work of collecting test-fired exhibits and acquiring images from them will be distributed across a small number of geographic sites.* In this, we diverge from the New York CoBIS and Maryland MD-IBIS models, where routing of all database entries through a single site is tractable, and move toward the existing NIBIN model where computational infrastructure is divided across three sites (and entry dispersed over more than 200 localities). Economies of scale are maximized if the workers and machines are clustered into a dozen or less geographic centers. We will assume that there are 10 such data acquisition centers.
2. *Assume a data entry rate of samples from 1 million guns per year, and that image acquisition itself takes approximately 5 minutes.* The 5-minute mark follows from our high-level assumption that cartridge cases, and not bullets, are to be imaged into the system, and is a plausible assumption with the current two-dimensional imaging standard. However, it may be an overly optimistic assumption for three-dimensional surface measurement, as it has developed to date (see Chapter 7), if that emerges as the imaging standard for the database. That said, the time needed to acquire three-dimensional measurement data has decreased significantly from the earliest efforts at imaging three-dimensional contours of bullets; with further refinement and automation, a 5-minute acquisition time is not unreasonable in the long run.
3. *Allow 5 minutes per entry for associated tasks, such as barcode reading, preparing and mounting the exhibits, and transporting exhibits between physical storage areas.*
4. *Data collection for this national system would run 24 hours a day,*

7 days a week. Timeliness of searches on the database requires round-the-clock operation.

Under these assumptions, six guns or exhibits can be processed by a human operator each hour. Multiplied by 2,000 hours per year, this implies 12,000 guns processed per operator per year, and hence a human staff of at least 84 operators. A three-shift staff of 84 requires 28 data entry terminals; to allow headroom for maintenance (or equipment failures), this could be expanded to 40–42 data entry terminals.

The rate at which queries are made of the national RBID—that exhibits are entered by state and local law enforcement agencies for comparison purposes with the database—will depend on local law enforcement acceptance and staff limitations. As described in previous chapters, large differences between jurisdiction in the effective use of the existing NIBIN system depends on differences in acceptance of the technology, hence the set of recommendations in Chapter 6 to enhance NIBIN by making it a more vital part of the investigative system. The actual use of New York's CoBIS database, in terms of queries made, has been vastly short of expectations. Still, we have to assume that the presence of a national RBID would lead to the desire to conduct searches against it, as the technology is accepted and such searches become routine. Hence, for the purposes of this section, we assume 1,000 query exhibits are entered (nationwide) each day.

It is expected that these searches will be done on an ad hoc basis, rather than in large batches. A reference image will be sent in parallel to a collection of geographically dispersed servers, over conventional networking, for comparison against stored images. The system's ability to handle this throughput depends on the speed of the comparison process and the size of the database against which the reference image is compared. As we reiterate later in this chapter, a common logical flaw in considering a national RBID is looking at the large number of new guns produced annually (that would have to be entered in the database) and assuming that the system will automatically be swamped by the computational demands of performing one-against-millions comparisons. However, one would never do a straight comparison of one image against the *entire* database; like the current IBIS and NIBIN setup, some demographic filtering will inevitably be done to reduce the size of the comparison set. In addition to demographic filtering, similar subsetting may be done on the shape of the firing pin, gun entry and crime occurrence dates, gross features of the casing, and (perhaps) geographic region and proximity. Exactly how much of a reduction can be expected is an open question and would impact the computational requirements. If it can be assumed that reference images can be compared against stored images at a rate of 30 per second (on a PC-class machine), and that demographic subsetting can whittle down the comparison set of images to

1/20 of the full database size, then—in aggregate—comparing a reference image to 1 year's worth of RBID data would mean performing 50 million pairwise comparisons per day. This would require 20 PC-class machines as comparison servers. If one plans for a factor of three in "headroom," then 60 machines are required. Each year that the system is in operation, 60 additional machines must be purchased (or the original 60 replaced by ones that are twice as fast).

Storage space, both electronic and physical, is a significant "wild card" in implementing the technical infrastructure for a national RBID. In terms of electronic storage, the per-casing disk storage for two-dimensional greyscale images as currently done by the IBIS platform is on the order of 1 megabyte. At 1 million casings per year, the aggregate system must be capable of storing 1 terabyte of information during the first year, and then to add 1 terabyte per year thereafter. Given modern computing environments, this is certainly feasible. However, these demands would have to be scaled upward with a change in imaging standard, either to finer-resolution two-dimensional photography or to three-dimensional imaging. The per-casing storage would also increase if practices such as those we recommend for the NIBIN program—entering of more than one exemplar per gun, particularly one of a different ammunition type—are used as standard protocols for a new national RBID. Physical storage of the casing exhibits is also an important consideration. We expect that human firearms examiners would still be needed to confirm "hits" on the national RBID through direct comparison; hence, the physical casings must be retained and must remain accessible. They must be filed in such a way that they can be retrieved with ease, that they are not damaged, and that there is minimal risk of being exchanged or confused with exhibits from a different firearm. Hence, simply packing envelopes of exhibits in large boxes and warehousing them is not a viable option, and the physical structure would have to be designed accordingly.

The computing and network assumptions sketched above suggest that the informational throughput in one direction—submitting an inquiry to the database for processing—is manageable. However, care would have to be taken in specifying the reciprocal flow of comparison results back to requesting sites. Though we critique the IBIS 20 percent threshold elsewhere in the report and recommend that it be revisited (Recommendation 6.15), the threshold does serve the purpose of limiting the amount of image and score data that must be pushed back from regional correlation servers to NIBIN partner agencies for every comparison request. Some limit on the number of results routinely returned on comparison requests would likely have to be established to keep transmission times in check.

The preceding is a somewhat simplified list of concerns from the information management perspective; practically, the implementation of a national RBID would raise related—and complex—concerns. Of these, access control—how and from which locations an RBID search can be initiated and who is enabled to edit records—is a particularly significant one. Computer security and database encryption are also not built directly into the preceding assumptions, but would involve cost and computational burden, as well as maintaining compliance with relevant regulations at the federal level and at access points (e.g., state law enforcement agencies). Policies on "sunsetting" of exhibits and procedures for removing entries (e.g., if a gun is known to have been recovered by police and destroyed) would have to be considered in assessing the growth of the database.

9–C.2 Manufacturing Perspective

Just as we conclude that a national RBID is, strictly speaking, technically feasible from the information management perspective, we conclude that it is generally feasible from the manufacturing perspective. Like the information management question, though, this assessment is very much conditional on some details in the implementation of the RBID. Specifically, the specification of the database content and the question of how images are to be acquired and entered into the system are critical in judging how disruptive—and costly—RBID implementation would be to firearms manufacturers.

At the most basic level, the collection of exhibit casings from newly manufactured firearms should be relatively tractable because, conceptually, all it would require is a systematic, cross-manufacture standardization of current practices of test firing for quality control. Manufacturers routinely test (or proof) fire new firearms to assess product safety issues; the needed change in procedures would be to recover the casing(s), label them, and keep them associated with the correct firearm through the remaining parts of the manufacture process (e.g., packaging and shipping). There is cost associated with reconfiguring the late stages of production to accommodate this process and in providing adequate personnel to keep the process moving, and there is cost associated with the slowing of production—however slight that might be—to ensure that the casing collection is done accurately.

The accurate connection between a newly manufactured firearm and the exhibit casings packaged with it has emerged as an issue with the existing state RBIDs. Tew (2003) noted a problem with the sets of two fired cartridge cases included with new Glock firearms, part of a large batch purchase by the Scottsdale, Arizona, Police Department. Two casings each were retained for 15 of the new pistols during the department's qualification shooting, and these casings were compared against each other and with the casings in the envelope provided by the manufacturer. Examiners determined that only 2 of the 15 guns had manufacturer-provided casings that could be matched to the new post-purchase test firings; for 2 other guns, a match was possible with one of the provided casings but not the other. The remaining 11 appeared to have manufacturer-provided samples that were not from the actual gun that was sold; worse, in 6 cases, the two packaged casings were determined to be from two different firearms, neither of which were the sold gun. The Maryland State Police Forensic Sciences Division (2003:8) noted a similar problem, also with a Glock firearm. Evidence from a gun known to have been sold in Maryland was matched against the Maryland RBID, but no good matches were found: When the crime gun in question was later recovered, it was found that the casing entered in MD-IBIS did not appear to have been fired from that gun. "Glock has since taken measures to correct this problem on their end," the report observed.

During one of the committee's site visits to manufacturers, personnel from Beretta USA estimated that their per-gun charge to perform test firings (and thus comply with Maryland's MD-IBIS database) is about $7.[2] But this is for a relatively limited number of guns; if manufacturers were required to perform shell casing capture for compliance with a national database, some efficiencies would doubtless be realized. Still, it must be recognized that implementation of a national RBID would, in at least the short term, detrimentally affect manufacturers' production schedules and thus result in a commensurate increase in product costs. There is also a likely significant detrimental effect on the profitability of the companies because the delivery schedule for products plays such an important role in capturing overhead and fixed costs.

Collecting test-fired exhibits from newly manufactured firearms raises one set of logistical issues; collecting such exhibits from newly *imported* firearms poses similar problems. Foreign manufacturers could not be directly bound to supply test-fired exemplars with their weapons, so the process of unpackaging, test firing, cleaning, and repackaging imported firearms would likely be shifted to domestic distributors.

For both newly manufactured and newly imported firearms, a critical question that would have to be addressed is exact specification of the conditions under which test fires are to be performed and the number of firings that must be completed before designating one or two casings as the ballistic sample. As described in Section 3–D.3, the concept of a "settle-in" effect would be a greater concern if bullets were used as the sample rather than casings; in that event, the prevailing view among firearms examiners would hold that the gun must be fired 8–10 times before its unique markings stabilize. However, as mentioned in Section 3–D.3, structural features like paint on the breech face can lead to early shot-to-shot variability in

[2]Beretta USA is headquartered in Accokeek, Maryland, hence the immediate need to comply with Maryland statute.

cartridge case markings. New York CoBIS personnel have partnered with manufacturers to consider a related problem, which is the effect (if any) of the cleanliness of a new firearm on the first cartridges fired through the weapon. Specifically, it remains an open question whether the presence of heavy grease or oil when weapons are pulled from the assembly line for test firing diminishes the breech face or firing pin impressions on recovered cartridges. One firearms manufacturer the committee visited suggests that they fire up to three rounds; if there is some ground to doubt the clearness of marks on the very first firing(s), and it is necessary to fire more rounds through each weapons, the cost of RBID compliance (in both time and money) would ratchet up accordingly.

9–C.3 Statistical Perspective

Following the logic of the preceding sections, a national RBID is technically implementable; we now turn to the fundamental question of the overall feasibility and accuracy of such a database in providing investigative leads.

A useful framework is to consider the basic problem in working with ballistic image databases probabilistically. Define a true match to be the case when a firearms examiner confirms a suggested possible match from an image database query. One can decompose the probability of a true match into a number of conditional probabilities that capture the various stages involved in getting a true match:

$$
\begin{aligned}
\Pr(\text{true match}) &= \Pr(\text{true match} \mid \text{potential match with item based on images}) \\
&\times \Pr(\text{potential match with item based on images} \mid \text{item in top } K) \\
&\times \Pr(\text{item in top } K \mid \text{item in database}) \\
&\times \Pr(\text{item entered in database} \mid \text{item submitted to database}) \\
&\times \Pr(\text{item submitted to database} \mid \text{item collected in field}) \\
&\times \Pr(\text{item collected in field})
\end{aligned}
$$

All but one of the components in this expression involve human and not algorithmic issues:

- Pr(true match | potential match with item based on images) measures the concordance of physical evidence similarity (as determined by the firearms examiner through direct physical comparison) with similarity based on database images.
- Pr(potential match with item based on images | item in top *K*) measures whether the human firearms examiner can pick out a potential match when images are ranked as highly similar in a list of possible matches.

- Pr(item in top K | item in database) measures the ability of the algorithm to rank the item in the top K results.
- Pr(item entered in database | item submitted to database) measures the chance that the item was entered into the database as opposed to not being entered (e.g., caught in a backlog).
- Pr(item submitted to database | item collected in field) measures the chance that the item was submitted for further processing.
- Pr(item collected in field) measures whether the evidence was collected at the time of manufacture or sale (for an RBID) or whether it was found and recoverable at a crime scene (for a NIBIN-type database), and whether it was damaged or otherwise rendered unfit for analysis.

These are the major components to determining how good the overall ballistics identification *system* is. The technical, algorithmic component of this expression—Pr(item in top K | item in database)—is an important one; it is the focus of the major studies outlined in Section 4–E, the experimental work described in Chapter 8, and the balance of this section. It is important to remember, though, how that component fits in the whole system; that single probability can be quite high—even 1—and yet a ballistics identification system could be judged a failure, depending on the other components.

The discussion of overlap metrics in Section 8–B.3 suggests a way of framing the problem using a simple binomial model; the appendix to this chapter, Section 9–F, develops a model in fuller generality.

Suppose one compares a reference casing with N guns in an image database; for simplicity, assume that there is one correct casing (gun) in the database that matches this reference exhibit and that all the other entries are nonmatches. Also assume that the ballistics identification system yields a single list of ranked exhibits; this is tantamount to looking only at one type of marking on the casings, which is generally not advisable, but is a useful simplification for these approximate calculations. Let the overlap metric be p, the probability that the similarity score for a correct casing will be smaller than that for the nonmatches. Assume that all of the N comparisons are independent (see the appendix, Section 9–F, for more elaborate structures). If X is the number of casings in the database that yield a higher similarity score than the correct match, then X follows a binomial (n,p) distribution. One can use this to assess the likelihood of the correct match being in a top 10 list of ranked probable matches (akin, in this model, to flipping N coins, each with probability p of turning up tails, and calculating the probability of getting nine or fewer tails). This simple probability model can be used to make approximate statements on how good the identification system's similarity scores and overlap metrics have to be in order to have effective identification. For instance, suppose that the database against which a reference casing is to be compared has 10,000 elements; how small does p have to be in order to have the correct casing appear in the 10 highest rankings at least 99 percent of the time? In probabilistic terms, how small does p have to be so that $Pr(X < 10) \geq 0.99$?

As a rough calculation, the properties of the binomial distribution are such that if $Np = 10$, then the probability of the matching casing being in the top 10 is only around 0.46. Therefore, as N gets very large, p has to be accordingly small. In fact, p needs to be approximately $4/N$ to get the correct match in the top 10 rankings 99 percent of the time. To get in the top 10 rankings 90 percent of the time, p can be around $6.2/N$. In a comparison database of 100,000 images/guns, then p needs to be on the order of 6.2×10^{-5} to have a 90 percent chance of the correct matching casing in the top 10.

The estimated overlap metrics in Table 8-6 can be used to assess the feasibility of databases of different sizes. These specific metrics correspond to calculations using the analysis of three-dimensional topographic data by the National Institute of Standards and Technology (NIST), and not the current two-dimensional IBIS system, but they are instructive nonetheless because we found the three-dimensional system to perform comparably with IBIS. For a moderate database of size $N = 100{,}000$, the only estimated values of p small enough are those that are zero. However, one can see from Table 8-6 that, with the exception of breech face measurements on the NBIDE exhibit set, the overlap metrics are all too large to be adequate. Even if N is as small as 100, the success rate for top 10 lists for the DKT exhibit sets are still less than 0.5. The success rate would only be slightly higher (56 percent) for the NBIDE firing pins.

The breech face measurements on the NBIDE exhibits stand out as being excellent. Under the most optimistic scenario (grouping by casing), for a database of size $N = 100{,}000$, the success rate is about 90 percent. If, instead, there is grouping by guns, then the success rate is only 50 percent. Under the pessimistic scenario of a single group, p needs to be on the order of 6.2×10^{-5}, so that the estimate of $p = 0.002$ is over 30 times too large, despite being orders of magnitude smaller than anything else.

The above analysis was just for a single casing. When there are multiple firings from each gun, one can form separate matching and nonmatching distributions for each gun, resulting in a different p for each gun. In general, having more numerous and more refined groups will lead to more optimistic conclusions, while having fewer groups that are pooled will lead to more pessimistic conclusions. That is, success in a very large database demands a very small value of p. Thus casings that are not very distinguishable will tend to increase the estimated p of their member group to unacceptably high levels. Having a smaller group limits the damage done by a single casing.

9–D CONCLUSION

Conclusion: A national reference ballistic image database of all new and imported guns is not advisable at this time.

Three lines of reasoning have particular salience for this conclusion. The first has to do with the general use and role of ballistic imaging technology. *The current technology in use for automated toolmark comparison, based on two-dimensional greyscale images, can be useful for gross categorization and sorting of large quantities of evidence. However, it appears to be less reliable for distinguishing extremely fine individual marks as is necessary to make successful matches in RBIDs, where large numbers of exhibits on file would share gross class and subclass characteristics.*

Throughout the report, and particularly in Chapter 4, we make it clear that we view ballistic imaging as a form of computer-assisted firearms identification and advise against practices—like overreliance on "top 10" comparisons—that impute to ballistic imaging an unwarranted level of precision for identifying matches. The temptation to expect too much from a national RBID—to expect "hits," and investigative leads to points of sale, with high frequency—is misguided given that the event of a single, particular new gun being used in committing a crime is relatively rare. The difficulty in achieving matches in an RBID is compounded by the gross sameness—in class and subclass characteristics—of large segments of the database exhibits. Ballistic imaging can be an effective tool for screening and filtering, and can be 70–95 percent successful in finding same-gun matches using cartridge case markings, as Nennstiel and Rahm (2006b:28) concluded. This is very good performance, but De Kinder et al. (2004) compellingly demonstrate that this performance can degrade in databases flooded with same-class-characteristic images; we saw much the same thing in our limited work entering exhibits in the New York CoBIS database (described in Chapter 8).

The second salient argument concerns the capacity of ballistic imaging systems to distinguish true matches from nonmatches, as described in Section 9–B.3 and Chapter 8: *Basic probability calculations, under reasonable assumptions, suggest that the process of identifying a subset of possible matches, that contains the true match with a specified level of certainty, depends critically on as-yet-underived measures of similarity between and within gun type. The process may return too large a subset of candidates to be practically useful for investigative purposes.*

We emphasize that we do not frame this argument strictly as a "breakdown" or massive degradation in matching capability with database size. Pure reliance on a numeric breakdown argument maligns all forms of ballistic imaging—a national RBID most immediately, due to the large number of guns involved. But such arguments would apply in short order to state RBIDs, to the national-level NIBIN crime scene evidence database, and, ultimately, to individual databases maintained by metropolitan police departments (particularly for popular caliber families). What we do comment on is accuracy of making matches within some range of possible matches and with a specified level of probability; the experimental work described in Chapter 8 suggests that the existing imaging methodologies (including NIST's three-dimensional-topography prototype) do not have the discriminatory power needed to reliably place true matches in the top rankings using imaging comparisons.

Though there is no special magic in the top 10 ranks, there is also a practical limit in the number of potential matches that any human examiner or operator is likely to page through and consider in his or her work; though the existing methods can be made to work well, they simply do not work well enough to make a national RBID practical. De Kinder (2002a:202) reached a similar conclusion in his assessment of implementing national RBIDs, generally:

> The goal of the [RBID] is to identify a cartridge case or bullet found at the crime scene. Let us try to evaluate the effort needed to find a cartridge case of caliber 9mm PARA in a relatively small ballistic fingerprinting database of 400,000 entries, containing a single cartridge case per firearm. A preselection on the caliber has to be performed first. For bullets, a further pre-selection on the general rifling characteristics can be performed. The general occurrence of this caliber is about 30%. [We] define the discriminating power of an automated comparison system as the percentage of the hit list you have to examine manually in order to have an acceptable probability of 99.99% of including the correct firearm. The current computing time needed to perform the comparisons and set up a hit list is still acceptable, as it can be run overnight. A discriminating power of 1% corresponds to 120 cartridge cases. All of them have to be manually compared with the questioned cartridge case using a comparison microscope. This is a substantial task, as the traces on the cartridge cases will be much alike. . . . This number is, at its very best, linear in the number of firearms contained in the ballistic fingerprinting database. This means that higher performances of the comparison algorithm are needed in order to perform comparisons in a feasible way.

A common argument against a national RBID is the perceived ease with which such a database could be "defeated" by replacing firearms parts (like the firing pin) or taking deliberate action to alter the individual markings of firearms. Defeat is perhaps too strong a word, but the third salient point that has particular weight is a potentially much easier (and likely more unintentional) way of dampening an RBID's ability to find matches—the choice of ammunition used in shooting. *The potential large influence of ammunition type and variability is a significant source of error in identification. A standard, protocol type of ammunition could be specified in an RBID (as it is in NIBIN), but it may not correspond with the ammunition used in crime; the choice of protocol ammunition, or a requirement to use multiple ammunition types, could have significant financial implications for both ammunition and firearms manufacturers.*

In addition to these three core arguments against a national RBID, other supplemental arguments contribute to our assessment that a national RBID is inadvisable. As indicated in Sections 9–B.1 and 9–B.2, too much remains unknown about the real costs of implementing collections for such a database in the context of the existing firearms manufacturing environment. Furthermore, the means for ensuring that the sample of casings included with a newly manufactured gun actually originated from that gun lies at the heart of the enterprise; the issue of chain of custody of the test fires in order to provide a legal linkage is a daunting challenge.

De Kinder (2002a:199–200) adds another argument against a national RBID, which is that—by construction—the content of an RBID is not truly representative of the firearms used in crime, the set with which RBID entries would ultimately be compared. Specifically, De Kinder reports the results of a limited test in Belgium, in which for 1 year police processed and imaged all ballistics evidence acquired by the police in one section of the country, crime-related and noncrime-related. The "firearms not directly related to crime" included "firearms which are in illegal possession for failing to comply with the current firearms law and firearms which were proactively seized after family problems." This type of test is substantially weaker than the creation of a pure RBID—in the U.S. context, it would correspond to a relatively modest expansion of NIBIN's scope rather than the imaging of all new and imported firearms. Still, the composition of the dataset after 1 year suggests a basic difficulty: the resulting set of images is inherently "bias[ed] towards other types of guns than those normally used at crime scenes." That is, even when restricting searches by caliber and other demographic information, an RBID necessarily overrepresents some types of guns (e.g., those from smaller manufacturers, possibly more expensive and intricately machined guns) relative to their use in crime. The Maryland State Police, Forensic Sciences Division (2003:9–10), made the same observation based on the first 3 years' experience of the Maryland RBID, comparing the common makes of guns entered in the RBID with ATF gun trace statistics. In particular, several revolvers are among the most frequently traced guns in Maryland (including the most frequently traced gun, a Smith & Wesson .38 revolver), which is inherently problematic for RBIDs since "revolvers are less likely to leave cartridge casings at crime scenes than are pistols."

9–E IMPLICATIONS FOR STATE REFERENCE BALLISTIC IMAGE DATABASES

Having concluded that a national RBID is inadvisable at this time, a natural follow-up question is what this conclusion means for the state-level RBIDs currently in operation in Maryland and New York and as may be implemented by other states. Although the core arguments that can be made against a national RBID can be applied to a state RBID, we conclude that the smaller-scale state databases are critically important proving grounds for improvements in the matching and scoring algorithms used in ballistic imaging. Indeed, they provide an ideal setting for the continuing empirical evaluation of the underlying tenets of firearms identification in general. The state databases can be a critical, emerging testbed for research in ballistic imaging and firearms identification.

Early in ATF's work with the IBIS platform, Masson (1997:42) observed that as ballistic image databases grew in size, the IBIS rankings tended to produce suggested linkages that might look promising on-screen—and might also be tricky to evaluate using direct microscopy:

> As the database grew within a particular caliber, 9mm for instance, there were a number of known non-matched testfires from different firearms that were coming up near the top of the candidate list. When retrieving these known non-matches on the comparison screen, there were numerous two dimensional similarities. When using a comparison microscope, these similarities are still present and it is difficult to eliminate comparisons even though we know they are from different firearms.

Far from undermining the utility of the system, Masson (1997:43) argued that this finding presented a critical learning opportunity. "In the past, best examples of known nonmatched agreement were collected from casework and thus, surfaced sporadically;" in addition to the potential for generating hits, Masson suggested value in studying misses. "Firearms examiners should take advantage of this current expanded database to fully familiarize themselves with the extent of similarities found in many non-identifications in order to hone their criteria for striae identification" because the "examiner's power of discrimination can be heightened because of the experience."

Even in the best of operational circumstances, RBIDs should not be expected to produce torrents of hits or completed matches. They are, at root, akin to detecting low-base-rate phenomena in large populations, and present particular difficulties because—by construction—such large populations contain a great many elements that are virtually identical in all but the tiniest details. A major reason that the current state databases have underperformed in generating hits is that they have been undersearched. As put most bluntly, in a discussion of the MD-IBIS hit that yielded a criminal conviction, by a critic of the current implementation, "If you don't use the system . . . it isn't going to work" (quoted in Butler, 2005). The utility of state-level RBIDs will depend on how often the database is actually queried in the conduct of investigations and how investigative leads are followed up. The design of the current databases, and the need to ensure a firewall from NIBIN data due to the legal restrictions on NIBIN content, have made the databases inconvenient to search: exhibits must be transported to specific facilities for acquisition and comparison. To that end, mechanisms for encouraging searches of state RBIDs by law enforcement agencies in the same state or region should be developed and the results evaluated. To the extent that law permits and arrangements can be made, broader research involving the merging and comparison of state-level RBID images with NIBIN-type evidence would also be valuable.

9–F APPENDIX: MODELS OF HYPOTHESIZED SYSTEM PERFORMANCE

Throughout this appendix, we restrict the discussion to cartridge casings; however, the same problem formulation would apply to bullets.

Suppose one has a database that consists of N images of casings, where N is a large number. These images may correspond to D different types of (new) guns. For each gun type, there are n_d different images, from different guns of the same type or various gun and ammunition combinations, etc. So the database has a total of $N = \sum_{d=1}^{D} n_d$ images. Consider now a newly acquired casing from a crime scene. One wants to compare the image of the new casing with the N images in the database and find the best K matches. The top K matches will then be scrutinized by a firearms examiner, and a direct physical comparison made will be to verify any hits.

Assume that the database does in fact contain a casing fired from the particular crime gun. Then, the statistical feasibility of the problem depends on whether the correct image will be among the top K matches, when K is a reasonably small number (top 10, top 50, or even top 100) even though N, the size of the database, is very large—on the order of millions.

Specifically, some of the statistical questions of interest are:

1. What is the probability that the correct image from the database (the one that corresponds to the crime gun) will be in the top K? How does this probability decrease with N? What are the critical factors that affect it?
2. How large should $K = K(\alpha)$ be if we want to be certain that the correct image is in the top K with probability at least $(1 - \alpha)$? How does this depend on the size of the database and other factors?

9–F.1 A Simple Formulation

For a particular combination of image capture technology and algorithm, the comparison of a newly acquired casing with the N images in the database yields comparison scores $X_1, \ldots, X_N$. (The scores themselves are functions of the comparison algorithm but are considered variable—and subject to a probability distribution—because of the variability in the markings of the newly acquired casing, because the arrival of a new casing can be seen as a draw from an underlying distribution, and because of variability in the image capture process.)

Assume throughout that a high score implies a good match; furthermore, as stated above, assume that there is a casing in the database that corresponds to the crime gun (so that there is a true or "right" match). To be specific, let X_1 be the score obtained for the "right" match.

Suppose the scores $X_1, \ldots, X_N$ are independent. (See the end of this section for a discussion of this assumption.) Let X_i be distributed according to $F_i(x)$, $i = 1, \ldots N$. Furthermore, let

$$I_j = I\left[X_j > X_1\right]$$

denote the indicator of the event that the score from one of the wrong casings has a higher score than X_1, the right match. Note that the I_j's are dependent since X_1 is common to all of them. Let

$$p_j = E\left(I_j\right) = P\left(X_j > X_1\right), j = 2, \ldots N.$$

One can compute p_j using the expression

$$p_j = \int\left[1 - F_j\left(x\right)\right]dF_1\left(x\right) = \int F_1\left(x\right)dF_j\left(x\right).$$

The key random variable of interest for our problem is

$$T = \sum_{j=2}^{N} I_j,$$

the number of scores that are ranked higher than the true match X_1.

The questions of interest can be answered if one can compute the distribution of T. For example, the probability that the score of the true casing is in the top-K matches is obtained by computing $P(T < K) \geq 1 - \alpha$: that is, the probability that the total number of wrong matches is strictly less than K. Similarly, the question of how large should K be chosen to ensure that this probability is at least $(1 - \alpha)$ is answered by choosing K so that $P(T < K) \geq 1 - \alpha$. Analyzing this distribution will also show how the probability and $K = K(\alpha)$ vary with the size of the database and what other factors influence them. It is clear that they depend critically on p_j's, the probabilities. (Other important parameters are discussed below.)

If the X_j's are independent, then in the simple case where all the p_j's are the same and equal p, T will have a binomial distribution with parameters N and p. However, the X_j's are not independent; in this case, with a single p, T has a correlated binomial distribution with a simple correlation structure. In our application, however, the p_j's will all be different, and the distribution of T is more complicated. But one can still write down expressions for the distribution of T. For example, the probability that X_1 is the top score is

$$P(T=0)=\int\prod_{j=2}^{N}\left[1-p_j(x)\right]dF_1(x)$$

where $p_j(x)=P(X_j>x)$. Expressions for $P(T=k)$ and $P(T\leq k)$ can be similarly written down. However, one will have to resort to numerical or other kinds of approximation to compute the required probabilities.

Since N is very large, a normal approximation is the simplest and most natural. It is easy to see that

$$E(T)=\beta=\sum_{j=2}^{N}p_j.$$

For computing the variance, since the I_j's are dependent (due to common X_1), we have to take the covariances into account. The variance of T is

$$Var(T)=\gamma^2=\sum_{j=2}^{N}\sum_{k=2}^{N}\left[p_{jk}-p_jp_k\right]=\gamma^2=\sum_{j=2}^{N}p_j\left(1-p_j\right)+2\sum_{j>k}\left[p_{jk}-p_jp_k\right],$$

where $p_{jk} = p_j$ if $j = k$ and

$$p_{jk}=P\left(X_j>X_1,X_k>X_1\right)=\int\left[1-F_j(x)\right]\left[1-F_k(x)\right]dF_1(x),j\neq k.$$

One can now approximate the distribution of T by a normal distribution with mean β and variance γ^2. Based on this, the probability of having the correct match being in the top-K scores can be approximated as

$$P(T\leq K)=\Phi\left(\frac{K-\beta}{\gamma}\right).$$

Furthermore, to ensure that this probability of the correct one being in the top-K scores is at least $(1-\alpha)$, i.e., $\Phi\left(\frac{K-\beta}{\gamma}\right)\geq 1-\alpha$, we must take $K\geq\beta+\gamma\Phi^{-1}(1-\alpha)$.

The key factors underlying these are β and γ, which depend on the p_j's and the p_{jk}'s. To see more clearly what influences these p_j's and p_{jk}'s, suppose the distributions of the X_i's are all Gaussian, that is, $F_1(x)$ is $N\left(\mu_i, \sigma_i^2\right), I = 1, \ldots, N$. (One can just as easily consider any other parametric distribution.)

9–F.2 Calculations and Insights

In the rest of this appendix we take the X_i's to be independent and normal with mean μ_i and variance σ_i^2. Then

$$p_j = P\left(X_j > X_1\right) = \Phi\left(\frac{\mu_j - \mu_1}{\sqrt{\sigma_1^2 + \sigma_j^2}}\right), j = 2, \ldots, N.$$

Furthermore,

$$p_{jk} = P\left(X_j > X_1, X_k > X_1\right) = \int \Phi\left(\frac{\mu_j - \mu_1 - \sigma_1 z}{\sigma_j}\right) \Phi\left(\frac{\mu_k - \mu_1 - \sigma_1 z}{\sigma_k}\right) \phi(z)\, dz,$$

where $\phi(z)$ is the standard normal density. These correspond to probabilities of quadrants of bivariate normal random variables and have to be calculated numerically.

We offer two general observations. First, the Gaussian case is much more general than it seems at first. The rankings of the scores are invariant under any monotone transformations of the X_i's, i.e., $I\left[X_j > X_1\right] = I\left[h\left(X_j\right) > h\left(X_1\right)\right]$ for any monotone increasing, continuous function $h(\cdot)$. Thus, assuming a lognormal distribution, for example, is equivalent to assuming a normal distribution.

Second, recall the assumption that the scores, $X_1, \ldots, X_N$'s, are independent. Since these are all matches to the same casing from the crime scene, a natural question is whether this will induce dependence among the X_i's and if so how will the assumption of independence affect the results. Statistically speaking, what is the difference between treating the image of the crime scene casing as fixed versus random? It turns out, however, that if the effect of the common source of dependence is the same on the X_i's, it does not matter. Specifically, suppose $X_i = Y_i + Z$ for $i = 1, \ldots, N$ where the Y_i's are independent and Z is the common source of dependence for the X_i's due to the crime scene casing. Then, it is easy to see that $I\left[X_j > X_1\right] = P\left(Y_j > Y_1\right)$, where the Y_i's are independent. The dependence can be more than additive, as long as it is additive up to a monotone increasing transformation.

More specifically, if $X_i = h(Y_i + Z)$ for a monotone increasing function, then $I[X_j > X_1] = I(Y_j > Y)$ where the Y_j's are independent. It is possible that the "effect" of the common source (i.e., the crime scene casing) is not the same on the different images, in which case the analysis will be more complicated. We will not deal with this case here.

For two cases, we compute the probabilities of interest under several scenarios to see how they vary with N and the parameter values μ_j's and σ_j's of the Gaussian distribution.

Case 1

We start with the simple case where there is only one gun type, $D = 1$, and all the images correspond to different guns of the same type. In some sense, this is the make-or-break case, since there has to be enough separation of the images that correspond to guns of the same type. One has the matching image X_1 from the crime scene gun and the others $X_2, \ldots, X_N$ that are all from different guns but of the same type. To keep things simple, assume that $X_2, \ldots, X_N$ all have the same distribution with parameters μ_2 and σ_2. Let μ_1 and σ_1 be the mean and standard deviation of the matching image. The computations depend only on $\mu_1 - \mu_2$, so one can assume without loss of generality that $\mu_1 = 0$. We consider different values for N and $\Delta = \mu_1 - \mu_2$ in the calculations.

In this analysis, we address only the second question that is posed in the introduction: What are the values of $K = K(\alpha)$ needed to ensure a confidence level of at least $100(1 - \alpha)\%$, that is, that a correct image is found in the top K with at least the specified probability? The tables below give the number K of matches we need to examine to ensure that the true casing is in the top K for a given size of the database and parameter configurations. We also give K corresponding to 50 percent even though a 50 percent confidence level would commonly be viewed as unacceptable; the main reason for giving it is because it corresponds to the mean of the random variable T. It provides a (conservative) lower bound to the value of K under various assumptions about the variances of the X_j's.

Optimistic Scenario It turns out that the values of $K(\alpha)$ depend greatly on the ratio of σ_1 to σ_2, that is, the variability of the true match to that of the wrong matches. First take the extreme case where $\sigma_1 = 0$, i.e., X_1 has zero variance. Recall that one is interested in the random variables $I_j = I[X_j > X_1]$ and $T = \sum_{j=2}^{N} I_j$. If X_1 has zero variance, then the I_j's are independent. Furthermore, in this special case where $X_2, \ldots, X_N$ have the same distribution, T has a binomial distribution.

TABLE 9-2 Values of $K(\alpha)$ for Various Configurations of N and α for the Optimistic Scenario

		Confidence Level			
Δ	$N - 1 = n_1 - 1$	50%	75%	90%	99%
2	1,000	23	26	29	34
2	10,000	228	238	247	262
3	10,000	14	16	19	23
3	100,000	135	143	150	163
4	100,000	4	5	6	8
4	1,000,000	32	36	39	45
4	10,000,000	317	329	340	359
5	10,000,000	3	5	6	7
5	100,000,000	29	33	36	42

Table 9-2 gives the values of $K(\alpha)$ for various combinations of N and Δ that might be of interest. For example, if $\Delta = \mu_1 - \mu_2 = 4$ and there are about 100,000 images from the same type of gun in the database, and one wants a 99 percent confidence level, then one needs to look at the top $K = 8$ matches. If N increases to about 1,000,000, then one needs to look at the top $K = 45$ matches.

The situation considered here—that variance of X_1 is zero or very small relative to that of the other matches—is a very optimistic scenario. The required number of matches will be much larger when the variance of X_1 is of the same order of magnitude as that of the other X_j's. We turn to this comparison next. But a caveat is in order first: the confidence levels in Tables 9-2 through 9-5 refer only to the probability of the true match being in the top K. They do not say anything about the correct one being actually identified in practice, which would depend on a firearms examiner reviewing the results of all K matches and finding the correct one (retrieving the physical evidence for a direct comparison). This may or may not actually happen.

Pessimistic Scenario This scenario considers exactly the same setup as before except that $\sigma_1 = \sigma_2$. The results depend only on the ratios, so one might as well take them to equal one.

For the computations in Table 9-3, we used Monte Carlo simulation to approximate the probabilities

$$p_{jk} = P\left(X_j > X_1, X_k > X_1\right) = \int \Phi\left(\frac{\mu_j - \mu_1 - \sigma_1 z}{\sigma_j}\right)\Phi\left(\frac{\mu_k - \mu_1 - \sigma_1 z}{\sigma_k}\right)\phi(z)\,dz.$$

TABLE 9-3 Values of $K(\alpha)$ for Various Configurations of N and α for the Pessimistic Scenario

		Confidence Level			
Δ	$N - 1 = n_1 - 1$	50%	75%	90%	99%
2	1,000	79	165	245	380
2	10,000	787	1,660	2,450	3,815
3	1,000	17	50	80	130
3	10,000	169	500	800	1,310
4	1,000	2	12	20	33
4	10,000	23	110	190	325
4	100,000	233	1,110	1,900	3,255
5	10,000	2	18	33	60
5	100,000	20	190	340	600
5	1,000,000	203	1,875	3,380	5,970
6	100,000	1	23	43	76
6	1,000,000	11	230	430	770
6	10,000,000	110	2,310	4,280	7,680
7	1,000,000	1	25	45	80
7	10,000,000	4	230	430	775
8	10,000,000	1	10	20	40

Even though the simulation error was less than 10^{-8}, the error in the standard error of T can be large when the database size N is of the order of 10^6 or bigger. Recall that there are roughly N^2 covariance terms. So there is large variability in the values of K in Table 9-3 for large N, and for these cases, they should be interpreted only as providing approximate guidelines.

Several features are of interest in Table 9-3. First, the values of K are much larger than in Table 9-2. The reason for the larger values of K is that the mean of T is smaller since $p = \Phi\left(-\Delta/\sqrt{2}\right)$ instead of $\Phi(-\Delta)$ in the earlier case. Furthermore, the variance of T is now much larger due to the positive correlation among the $I_j = I\left[X_j > X_1\right]$'s. This dependence gets larger with the ratio σ_1/σ_2, i.e., the variance of X_1 relative to the others.

A particularly discouraging feature is that, for fixed Δ and α, the values of K scale up almost linearly in the size of the database N. In the independent case in Table 9-2, the standard deviations were scaling up in terms of $\sqrt{N}$. But here they are scaling up linearly due to the covariances. More specifically, there are $(N - 1)(N - 2)$ covariance terms, and these are

TABLE 9-4 Values of $K(\alpha)$ for Various Configurations of $n_1 - 1$, n_2, Δ_1, Δ_2, and α for the Optimistic Scenario

				Confidence Level			
Δ_1	$n_1 - 1$	Δ_2	n_2	50%	75%	90%	99%
2	1,000	3	1,000	25	28	31	36
2	1,000	4	10,000	24	27	30	35
2	1,000	5	100,000	23	26	29	34
2	1,000	5	1,000,000	23	26	29	34
3	10,000	4	100,000	17	20	22	27
3	10,000	4	1,000,000	46	50	54	61
4	1,000,000	5	1,000,000	32	36	40	46
4	1,000,000	5	10,000,000	35	39	43	49

about the same order as the variance of I_j, so the standard deviation of T is now increasing linearly with N; this is troublesome as it leads to much larger values of K.

Case 2

We now consider situations in which there is more than one gun type in the database. The essence of the problem can be captured by just two types, so we restrict attention to this case. Again, assume that X_1 has mean μ_1 and variance σ_1^2, all the X_j's corresponding to the same gun type as X_1 have common mean μ_2 and variance σ_2^2, and finally all the X_j's corresponding to the second gun type have common mean μ_3 and variance σ_3^2. Tables 9-4 and 9-5 give the values of $K = K(\alpha)$ for various values of $\Delta_1 = \mu_1 - \mu_2$, $\Delta_2 = \mu_1 - \mu_3$, n_1, and n_2.

Table 9-4 corresponds to the optimistic scenario where the variance of X_1 is zero. Recall that the I_j's are all independent in this case. Table 9-5 corresponds to the pessimistic case where the variance of X_1 is the same as the variance of the other X_j's. The calculations in Tables 9-4 and 9-5 suggest that—as in the simpler one-gun case—values of K can quickly grow to levels of practical implausibility from the perspective of reviewing database comparison reports, particularly for low Δ values and less-clear separations between gun types. However, they also illustrate the importance of the degree of mean separation between the images from different gun types (akin to the discussion of overlap metrics in Section 9–C.3). Notice in Table 9-5 that if Δ_2 is 2 units bigger than Δ_1 and $n_1 = n_2$, the values of K in Table 9-5 are about the same as that in Table 9-3. A similar conclusion

TABLE 9-5 Values of $K(\alpha)$ for Various Configurations of $n_1 - 1$, n_2, Δ_1, Δ_2, and α for the Pessimistic Scenario

				Confidence Level			
Δ_1	$n_1 - 1$	Δ_2	n_2	50%	75%	90%	99%
3	1,000	5	1,000	17	52	82	135
3	1,000	6	10,000	17	51	82	135
3	1,000	7	100,000	17	51	81	133
4	10,000	6	10,000	24	113	192	330
4	10,000	7	100,000	24	112	192	330
4	10,000	8	1,000,000	24	112	190	325
5	10,000	7	10,000	3	20	35	60
5	10,000	8	100,000	3	20	35	62
5	10,000	9	1,000,000	3	19	35	61
6	100,000	8	100,000	2	25	50	85
6	100,000	9	1,000,000	2	24	44	76
6	100,000	10	10,000,000	2	26	50	80
7	1,000,000	9	1,000,000	1	30	50	90
7	1,000,000	10	10,000,000	1	26	48	85

holds if Δ_2 is 3 units bigger than Δ_1 and $n_2 = 10n_1$ or if Δ_2 is 4 units bigger than Δ_1 and $n_2 = 100n_1$. So, for instance, the ability to detect matches in a relatively small database containing equal numbers of moderately distinct images ($\Delta_1 = 4$, $\Delta_2 = 6$; 10,000 each) is comparable to that when one small set of images ($\Delta_1 = 4$; 10,000) is flooded with 1,000,000 images that are vastly different in mean ($\Delta_2 = 8$).

PART IV

Future Directions

10

Microstamping: Alternative Technology for Tracing to Point of Sale

Contemporary firearms identification and ballistic imaging techniques are predicated on the deposition of markings on evidence as a result of random variation in key processes—the manufacturing of firearms and ammunition parts and the mechanical operations and controlled explosions involved in the firing of a gun. The main objective of a national reference ballistic image database (RBID) is to use an image catalog of these markings to provide an investigative linkage between evidence collected at a crime scene and the original point of sale of the weapon. However, it may be useful to consider a completely alternative approach to arriving at the same goal: altering firearms so that, on every firing, they impart a known, unique, and unalterable marking on spent casings, rather than relying on the toolmarks generated by the firing process.

If such known markings—for instance, a gun-specific alphanumeric code—are logged at the point of sale, the same goal as a national image database would be achieved: a spent casing recovered at a later crime scene could be rapidly traced back to the point of sale by reading the etched marking. Likewise, known and individual markers could be placed directly on individual pieces of ammunition; again, if the component codes in a box of ammunition are logged at the point of sale, investigative leads could result later in time when pieces of stamped ammunition are found at crime scenes. The question is whether these alternatives compare favorably to a national RBID, in terms of cost, accuracy, or time savings.

This kind of technology—known as microstamping—has become a prominent part of the contemporary debate on "ballistic fingerprinting" and enhancing forensic identification technology. In October 2007 legislation requiring microstamping on internal parts of new semiautomatic pistols was signed into law in California, to take effect in 2010. It is also telling that long-proposed (but never enacted) federal legislation calling for the creation of a national RBID was revised in the 109th Congress to require microstamping instead. Because microstamping has become so enmeshed in the policy debate, we describe the technology and consider its development. However, because it is not a direct task of this study, we refrain from offering formal recommendations or findings specific to microstamping.

This chapter begins by describing the concept of tagging as a form of identification from a historical and technical perspective (Section 10–A) before describing current proposals for microstamping related to ballistics evidence (10–B), including the California law. Sections 10–C and 10–D focus on specific technologies for microstamping firearms parts and ammunition, respectively; brief general commentary is offered in Section 10–E.

10–A TAGGING AS A MEANS OF IDENTIFICATION

Identification tagging or "labeling" crafted or manufactured items has its origins in antiquity when the first artist signed his or her work or a person wished to uniquely identify an object to reflect its point of origin, manufacture, or ownership. Unique "signatures," either literal or representative symbols, have continued to be used for these purposes to the present day. Such markings of authorship or origin remain one of the evidentiary links used to identify art objects, for example, or to link "lost" masterpieces to their creators over the years.

Over time, manufacturers transitioned from simple graphic insignia to digital serial numbers to uniquely track their goods for a variety of reasons: the increasing scale of mass production, the need for accurate sequential tracking of goods during manufacture, and the necessity of monitoring lot specificity and quality in response to legal oversight. The manner by which serial numbers are applied to objects is as varied as the products produced. Whether bar-coded, machined, cast, painted, or laser-engraved, serial numbers provide a readily discernable means to uniquely mark an object to provide provenance of an object.

Because serial numbers can link manufactured objects to their owners, they provide a valuable tool to law enforcement in developing leads in criminal cases. Two well-known illustrations of the utility of serial numbers in investigating criminal cases—the bombings of the World Trade Center in New York in 1993 and of the Alfred P. Murrah federal office building in Oklahoma City in 1995—involved the use of vehicle identification numbers (VINs). A car's VIN is roughly the automotive equivalent of human

DNA: although it can be altered, it generally sets a vehicle apart from the millions of other vehicles in circulation. U.S. automobile manufacturers began stamping and casting identifying numbers on cars and their parts in the mid-1950s. Originally developed to give an accurate description of the vehicle as mass production increased, the use of VINs grew in the early 1980s when the National Highway Traffic Safety Administration (NHTSA) required that all road vehicles must contain a 17-character VIN (Insurance Information Institute, 2006). The required VIN number identifies the country of manufacture, the manufacturer, the vehicle type, and specific descriptors of the individual vehicle (49 U.S.C. 565); as a unique DNA-style number for each individual vehicle, it can be used to track recalls, registrations, warranty claims, thefts, and insurance coverage.

Investigators sifting through the rubble in the parking garage under the World Trade Center following the 1993 bomb explosion found fragments bearing a VIN corresponding to the number of a missing van. Tracing the van to a Ryder truck rental agency led to the arrest of a suspect in the bombing; leading in turn to the capture of additional suspects (Parachini, 2000). In the 1995 Oklahoma City case, a VIN—along with a partial license plate—were recovered at the scene of the explosion; this led to the determination that the explosive was contained in a 1993 Ford rented by Ryder in Junction City, Oklahoma. Subsequent contact with the rental agent allowed investigators to develop a composite drawing of a suspect; combined with other evidence, this was instrumental in the arrest and conviction of Timothy McVeigh for the bombing (Michel and Herbeck, 2001). In addition to the utility of unique tagging marks in furthering investigations, these examples are also illustrative in the context of firearms evidence for another reason: they suggest the remarkable retention of engraved serial numbers on metallic components subjected to explosive impact.

10–B ID TAGGING IN FIREARMS IDENTIFICATION

As manufactured goods, both firearms and ammunition are already subject to conventional serial numbering. The serial number imprinted on the frame of a firearm can be traced to a point of sale if the weapon is recovered; methods for the restoration of serial numbers that have been defaced by filing or other means are an important part of forensic analysis. Similarly, boxes of ammunition also bear serial numbers, which may be useful in quality control and in identifying defective rounds. What is novel in contemporary discussion of microstamping or "ballistic ID tagging" is the potential for generating investigative leads early in the investigative process: the new technology is meant to link expended rounds of ammunition to a point of sale *without* requiring the recovery of the gun itself.

10–B.1 Microstamping Proposals in California, 2005–2006

The idea of a large-scale reference ballistic image database became very prominent when the most populous state, California, considered the feasibility of implementing the technology. Likewise, the issue of direct tagging or microstamping of firearms and ammunition has grown in prominence due to developments in California. Microstamping had been referenced as an "intriguing alternative," possibly an economical one, in the California Department of Justice report on a state RBID (Lockyer, 2003:6). Microstamping was also raised as a question by De Kinder (2002b:22) in his independent review of the California technical evaluation of a proposed state RBID. Subsequently, it was recommended as a research topic by De Kinder et al. (2004:215).

The emerging discussion of microstamping sparked the introduction of two bills in the California legislature in spring 2005. The first bill, Assembly Bill (AB) 352, would have expanded the provisions of California's penal code relating to handguns that are "unsafe" and hence illegal for sale. Specifically, the bill would declare as unsafe:

> semiautomatic pistols that are not designed or equipped with a microscopic array of characters that identify the make, model, and serial number of the pistol, etched or otherwise imprinted onto the interior surface or working parts of the pistol, and which are transferred by imprinting on each cartridge case when the firearm is fired.

AB 352 passed the General Assembly in 2005 and moved to the Senate for consideration; it failed passage in the Senate in September 2005 but was made open for reconsideration.[1] After a hiatus, the bill was amended in June 2006 to address some points of concern that had arisen in debate—specifically, that the "technology to create the imprint, if reliant on a patent, [must be] available to more than one manufacturer" and that the state attorney general has the authority to decide whether different methods for leaving such unique imprints on cartridge cases are "equally or more reliable and effective" and, hence, could be used for the same purpose. The bill received high-profile endorsements from the mayor and police chief of Los Angeles (Newton, 2006), as well as several county sheriffs (Sanchez, 2006), and the Senate passed its amended bill 22–18 in late August 2006. However, the Assembly and Senate could not agree on a conference version of the bill before the end of the 2006 legislative session.

The second bill, Senate Bill 357, would have required all handgun ammunition manufactured or imported into California for sale or personal

[1]The roll call on the vote was 20–19 in favor, but 21 votes are needed for passage in the 40-member Senate.

use be "serialized"—uniquely identified in a manner that permits visual inspection, in a manner so that the identifier is maintained "subsequent to the discharge of the ammunition and subsequent to the impact of the bullet"—based on standards to be prescribed by the California Department of Justice. In other words, the mark must be capable of surviving the firing of the gun and the impact of the bullet with the target. The unique identifiers on each piece of ammunition were to be coded or affixed to the box in which the ammunition is packaged. At the point of sale, then, the identifier on a box of ammunition (and all the individual identification codes contained therein) could be linked to information on the purchaser, such as name, driver's licensee or other identification number, and date of birth. The bill required the justice department to establish a registry of ammunition vendors and manufacturers and permitted the assessment and collection of fees associated with the registration program. In addition to transmitting the sales information to the state department of justice, the bill required ammunition vendors to maintain records of sales on the premises for 7 years. The bill carved out some exemptions to the use and movement of serialized ammunition, including crime laboratories and the transfer of properties from the estate of a deceased person. Attempts to remove or obliterate identifiers on ammunition was made a criminal offense. To support the operational and administrative costs of maintaining the sales registry, the bill suggested a registration fee of $50 for handgun ammunition vendors and a user fee (not to exceed $0.005 per bullet or round of ammunition).

Senate Bill 357 was passed by the Senate in June 2005 and sent to the General Assembly's public safety committee. However, that committee referred the measure to the appropriations committee due to uncertainty regarding the costs of implementing the technology. No further action was taken on the bill during the legislative session.[2]

Though the California legislature did not adopt microstamping during its 2005–2006 session, it did stimulate interest in the idea elsewhere in the country; see, e.g., Tsai (2006:1) on interest expressed by New Jersey law enforcement officials in microstamping of firing pins.

[2]Though the microstamping proposal was not enacted, Senate Bill 357 was in fact passed into law; in August 2006, the bill was amended to strike the entire text relating to microstamped ammunition and was replaced with language on collective bargaining with state employees.

10–B.2 The California Crime Gun Identification Act of 2007

Though the ammunition microstamping bill was not revived in 2007, the firearms microstamping bill was reintroduced as AB 1471.[3] Microstamping remained a high-profile issue through endorsements of the technology by local officials—at least 60 municipal police chiefs and the mayors of Los Angeles, San Diego, and San Francisco were indicated as supporters of the bill in the legislative analysis that preceded the state Senate's vote, with 14 county sheriffs listed in opposition—as well as other reports.[4]

AB 1471 set January 1, 2010, as the effective date of requirements that semiautomatic pistols bear microstamped identifiers. As it developed through the legislature, the bill was amended several times. One change was cosmetic in nature, labeling the bill the "Crime Gun Identification Act of 2007," but other amendments were substantive:

- The "microscopic array of characters" identifying the make, model, and serial number of the semiautomatic pistol were now required to be etched "in two or more places on the interior surface or internal working parts" of the gun, for transference to the cartridge case upon firing.
- The state Department of Justice is required to certify that the microstamping technology put into use "is available to more than one manufacturer unencumbered by any patent restrictions," or to substitute methods "of equal or greater reliability and effectiveness" that are unencumbered by patent restrictions.
- Specific clarification was added that the microstamped identifier envisioned by the new legislation is not the same as existing identifier marks (e.g., manufacturer's number or serial number) required by law.

---

[3]The main content of the new bill and its 2005–2006 predecessor remained the same. However, the new AB 1471 omitted some portions of the previous legislation that explicitly required a certification program to ensure that some existing handguns meet or exceed the new standards, including the microstamping provision.

[4]On May 3, 2007, the University of California, Davis, issued a press release profiling a new study from the California Policy Research Center (a center affiliated with the University of California system). The report described the performance of microstamped firing pins when fit into California Highway Patrol-issue Smith & Wesson .40 caliber pistols and fired up to 2,500 times. The study concluded that the principal markings on the stamped firing pins remained legible on repeated firings but that finer markings (e.g., striations left by a barcode etched on the side of the firing pin) were subject to wear; microstamping was said to hold promise but required further research. However, the report had not undergone review at that time, and the press release implied that the study was commissioned by the legislature and linked to AB 1471; UC Davis chancellor Larry Vanderhoef circulated a letter on May 15, 2007, to AB 1471 sponsor Mike Feuer and other legislators, apologizing for the premature release of the report and errors in the press release.

Having passed the General Assembly, AB 1471 was approved by the Senate on September 10, 2007 (see, e.g., Sweeney, 2007), and signed into law by California Governor Arnold Schwarzenegger on October 13, 2007. The governor's signing measure on the bill reads:[5]

> While I appreciate and understand that this technology is not without limitations, I am signing this bill to provide law enforcement with an additional tool for solving crimes committed with semi-automatic handguns in California.
>
> Public safety is one of the most important roles of government and I encourage all stakeholders to work on improving this technology so that it may become an even more effective crime fighting tool.

10–B.3 Proposed Federal Legislation

At the federal level, the proposed Technological Resource to Assist Criminal Enforcement (TRACE) Act has been offered in the past several U.S. Congresses, but has not advanced beyond subcommittee referral. In the 109th Congress, the act was substantially revised to implement microstamping rather than a national RBID. Specifically, the proposed legislation would forbid the manufacture or import of any "firearm that is not microstamped or a microstamped firearm that does not transfer the array of characters constituting the microstamp onto the cartridge case of any ammunition fired from the firearm." The bill, H.R. 5073, specifically defines a microstamp as "an array of characters which identify the make, model, and serial number of the firearm" that is "etched into the interior surface or internal working parts of the firearm." Although it no longer called for creation of an image database, the new legislative text retained language from previous versions that requires "ballistics testing of any firearm in the custody of the Federal Government" and establishment of "an electronic database containing records of the results of the testing" that can be accessed by state and local law enforcement agencies. The bill was not enacted in the 109th Congress, and the same legislative text was introduced in the House of Representatives in the 110th Congress in April 2007.

10–C MICROSTAMPING OF FIREARMS PARTS

The basic concept of microstamping firearms parts is to etch identifier codes into the hard metal components of guns so that—when they are fired—the markings are impressed on the relatively softer cartridge case or

---

[5] See http://gov.ca.gov/pdf/press/2007bills/AB 1471 Signing Message.pdf [accessed February 2008].

bullet. The early work that has been done in the area has focused on the etching of alphanumeric symbols on the tip of the firing pin. The identifying mark is created when the pin hits the primer surface of the cartridge, and the "image" of the microstamp marking can be read in the base of the firing pin impression on the recovered casing.

The microstamped markings are created by ultraviolet (UV) photoablation by means of a high-power laser.[6] As currently developed, UV radiation from an excimer laser or a frequency-tripled solid state yttrium aluminum garnet (YAG) laser is used to remove material from the firing pin tip according to a predefined pattern. The microstamp is created by illuminating the surface of the firing pin with the laser beam, either through a lithographically prepared mask or by a maskless procedure in which the beam is positioned by a system of computer-controlled movable mirrors. This latter procedure is significantly cheaper than the former.

The individual symbols in the microstamped marking can range from a few microns tall to several hundred microns, with the optimum size range being 50 to 100 microns per character. A smaller size compromises the mechanical strength of the individual symbols. Due to the high intensity of the UV beam, the material is removed from the firing pin in a very short time, typically about 200 milliseconds. To increase the strength of the characters in the microstamp, a thin (1 micron) diamond or titanium carbide layer can be evaporated onto the stamp.

To maintain the functionality of the firing pin, the material between the characters making up the code is removed only inside a circular area, so that the characters are raised against a background, but the character tops are flush with the original surface of the firing pin. This ensures that the overall tip shape is maintained. It also makes it much harder to remove the marking without rendering the firing pin useless. When the firing pin hits the primer, an imprint of the microstamp is left at the bottom of the impression. This imprint consists of depressions corresponding to the stamp characters or symbols. The tip of the firing pin is not the only part of a firearm that could be microstamped so that known markings are recovered on evidence fired in that weapon; however, the other possibilities remain more speculative and untested at this time. (We discuss one such idea—the etching of markings in the barrel of a gun, so that a known "barcode"-type identifier is formed on the soft bullet as it grips the rifling and exits the barrel—in Section 10–C.1, below.) Alternately, known markings could be imparted on cartridge casings by placing one or more microstamped patches on the breech block of the firearm, surrounding the firing pin hole; the mark would then be created as the soft primer surface is forced outward by the ignition of powder and

---

[6]The process is similar to the photokeratectomy process (commonly known as LASIK) used in eye surgery to adjust the shape of the cornea.

expansion of gases. It may also be possible to place a microstamp identifier on the firearm's ejector mechanism or elsewhere on the inside of the chamber (in the latter case, leaving a mark on the side of the cartridge brass). It is also reasonable to assume that, as the technology matures, multiple microstamped markings could be put on the same firearm, which would serve as a countermeasure against the defacing or attempted removal of one of the marks. However, this conceptual approach raises logistical concerns as well as technical: Would the individual markings or codes have to be identical at all places on the gun or could they be allowed to vary? The former raises potential problems in coordinating interchangeable parts with the same identifiers on the manufacturing line; the latter presents the problem of having to log all the constituent identifiers at the time of sale.

10–C.1 Research Studies

In addition to experiments performed by the microstamping technology's developer, the present technology for microstamping the tip of firing pins has been tested by two firearms examiners. Haag (2004) submitted four firing pins to the developer—NanoMark Technologies, then known as NanoVia—for microstamping: three of them were for a machine gun or automatic rifle, intended to test the durability of the microstamp engraving over large numbers of firings. In these test cases, the microstamp took the form of an eight-character alphanumeric code; firings using the treated firing pins were conducted using a mix of military and commercial cartridges that varied in primer hardness and the presence of a lacquer coat on the primer.

Haag (2004) found that the marks were generally durable and left readable codes after 2,500 firings. The microstamp also left readable codes on misfired cartridges, where the pin only struck the primer lightly and the bullet was not discharged. In some instances, the presence of a red lacquer coat over the primer surface—which might be hypothesized to absorb impact and degrade the markings left on the primer—actually served to accentuate the alphanumeric code.

The fourth firing pin submitted for microstamping was from a Glock pistol, and was so chosen due to the distinctive scraping (and resulting scrape mark) known to occur in the firearm; this provided the opportunity to test the durability of the stamp given the additional wear caused by scraping. A variety of ammunition was run through the Glock with the microstamped pin, including lacquered primers and casings with pronounced nonfiring manufacturing marks. After more than 1,400 rounds, Haag (2004) concluded that the firing pin scrape in the Glock did not degrade the microstamped identifier and that neither lacquered primers nor variation in primer finish and hardness affected the microstamp's ability to impart a fixed marking.

However, Krivosta (2006) offered cautionary notes based on work with microstamped barrels prepared at the request of the Rhode Island Crime Laboratory. He observed that "a number of test fires" from a Remington .22 Long Rifle semiautomatic rifle—a rimfire weapon, rather than centerfire—were "illegible." The microstamped marking did not register well in the hard brass of the cartridge rim, and marks were further obscured by repeated (and overlapping) strikes of the pin against the cartridge during the same firing sequence (Krivosta, 2006:42). He also questioned the explicit provision in then-proposed state legislation that the microstamped identifier on firearms include the gun's make, model, and serial number—a large number of characters for a small surface area. Specifically, he referred to firings involving two Colt .45 pistols with different microstamp configurations—one with an eight-character alphanumeric code in "large," block capital letters and the other showing the name "NanoTag™" surrounded by the digits 0–9 and the full English alphabet in smaller "type." With the latter microstamped engraving, "the vast majority of this pin's characters were never visualized in the firing pin mark of any of the [ten] expended cartridge cases generated and examined" (Krivosta, 2006:42). Krivosta (2006:43) subjected a microstamped firing pin to "intentional defacement:" a process "easily accomplished in approximately one minute's time" using a sharpening stone and a portable drill. The removal of the microstamped identifier in this case did not impede the ability of the gun to fire: the mechanics of the gun are such that "the pin could have easily been shortened by 0.030 inch or more . . . and the weapon would have still functioned."

Although much of the initial work done to date has focused on placing microstamped identifiers on firing pins (thus marking cartridge casings), parallel work has continued on placing known identifiers on other parts of the firearm. In particular, Carr and Fadal (1997) and Fadal and Nuñez (2003, 2006) describe efforts by one manufacturer, Glock, to develop an alternative rifling technique to impart "readily identifiable" marks on bullets as they pass through the barrel. The introduction of such a technique is particularly significant since Glock's use of polygonal rifling has traditionally made bullets extremely difficult to match in the past. The work was initiated through a special order by the Miami Police Department, and so the efforts are described in the literature as "the Miami barrel"; Glock has also referred to the modified barrels as the Enhanced Bullet Identification System, or EBIS.[7]

[7]The "Miami barrel" followed another Glock experimental effort, the "New York barrel"; under a special order from the New York City Police Department, Glock produced a set of barrels for testing using conventional rifling rather than the company's usual hammer-forged hexagonal rifling (Carr and Fadal, 1997:233).

Fadal and Nuñez (2006:98) cite Glock as stipulating that "their patented tooling method may be manipulated to create 80,000 possible different combinations per caliber," using a "finger-like tool" to etch cuts in the barrel wall. The markings intended to be replicated with every firing by the Miami barrels include both gross characteristics that may appear the same across guns (subclass characteristics) and fine individual detail. Up to 3,000 rounds were fired through the latest iterations of the Miami barrel; "the gross and individual characteristics changed slightly between test firings as may be expected with wear (e.g., test from 500th shot as compared to test from 2000th shot)," and test bullets were still distinguishable after 3,000 firings (Fadal and Nuñez, 2006:97).

10–C.2 Advantages

Conceptually, the microstamping of firearms parts so that a known, unique, and repeatable identification tag is imparted on each cartridge case (or bullet) passing through a weapon has several potential advantages for forensic identification.

- Assuming that the microstamped identifier is clearly impressed on spent casings, no special equipment is needed to read the identifier code; it can be viewed using microscopes already present in standard laboratories. Conceivably, some identifiers could even be read at crime scenes using a hand magnifying lens, saving considerable time. Again assuming a clear impression, identification based on a microstamped marker is also easier to explain and interpret, as it does not require the subjective judgment that is now central to the interpretation of toolmarks left on a spent cartridge case.
- The fixtures used to hold and manipulate the various firearms components during the etching of the microstamp would be specialized equipment, but the machinery used to perform the etching is not highly specialized. To the extent that microstamping is performed on modular parts of a firearm—for instance, on firing pins that are manufactured and tooled independent of other parts and then assembled on the production line—the process need not be disruptive of the whole firearms production cycle. Also, each individual imprint can be created in a short time—typically around 200 milliseconds—so that the additional overhead in the firearms production process is small.
- More than one microstamped identifier could be placed on different areas of the gun's firing assembly to increase the likelihood that at least one identifiable mark will be imparted on cartridge case or bullet evidence and recoverable by investigators. As noted above, though, multiple identifiers raise the issue of coordination, ensuring either that the same identifier

is placed on all parts in the same gun or that all the individual identifiers are cataloged and linked to the same gun.

- Placing recessed characters on the firing pin, and perhaps adding a microstamped identifier elsewhere, would make it more difficult to deface or remove the identifiers without rendering the gun inoperable.
- As observed by Haag (2004), microstamped identifiers on firing pins appear to work in some instances where difficulty would naturally be expected, such as ammunition with lacquered primers or misfired cartridges. In the latter example, though, the markings may require more advanced equipment and microscopy to read the marking.
- Microstamping of firearms parts is akin to—and can be perceived as an extension of—the known and accepted practices of placing a serial number on all guns sold in the United States and logging that serial number at the time of sale.

10–C.3 Disadvantages

There are also important conceptual disadvantages of microstamping firearms parts, particularly the firing pin.

- Firearms microstamping shares a critical liability of an RBID: Barring a radical (and likely untenable) legislative requirement prohibiting use of any firearm without a microstamped identifier, the coverage of firearms microstamping would include only new firearms. Hence, the millions of firearms currently in circulation would not be affected. Thus, a resource such as the existing NIBIN database would still be necessary to assist examiners with finding links to crime guns that come from the existing stock of guns.
- Like a national RBID—for which the focus would likely be on cartridge casings rather than bullets, due to the time necessary for nondestructive test firings to obtain bullet specimens—microstamping strategies that only impart identifiers on cartridge casings would not be effective in solving crimes involving revolvers. Similarly, such strategies would also be hindered in instances in which suspects remove spent casings from crime scenes.
- Firing pins can be replaced with relative ease, so a single microstamped identifier could be defeated by swapping in a new pin. Working around this would require that newly manufactured firearms *parts* have to bear an identifier, and that this information would have to be logged at time of sale and maintained on file.
- Estimates of the per-unit cost to place a microstamp tag vary widely. Proponents of microstamping suggest that the cost of marking a firing pin would be between $0.50 and $1.00 (Tsai, 2006), with some

estimates as low as $0.15. However, opponents claim the cost to be closer to $150 (Tsai, 2006), perhaps taking into account the initial capitalization needed to obtain and operate the equipment or to change production flows so that component parts are stamped.

- As discussed by Krivosta (2006), microstamped identifiers may be difficult to use effectively in rimfire weapons and in low-pressure firings.
- A database associating microstamped identifier codes with purchase information would need to be constructed. Populating this database would require coordination at the federal and state levels to manage input from individual firearms dealers. Politically—as is the case with a national RBID—the question of whether information on the *purchaser*, and not just the point of sale, should be logged in the database would have to be addressed. Although the task of setting up and maintaining such a database would not be exceptionally difficult, it would still be a large database and would take resources to manage, purge, secure, upgrade, and operate. However, it is worth noting that this database would avoid some costs associated with a large-scale RBID, such as the manpower requirements to acquire images and the storage and preservation of physical exhibits.

10–D MICROSTAMPING OF AMMUNITION

As described above, the microstamping of firearms—as currently conceived—is principally about imposing marks on expended cartridge casings. Hence, as would be true in a cartridge case-only national RBID, it would not work in settings in which casings are not expelled at crime scenes (e.g., revolvers are used) or are removed from the scene. A different approach to microstamping focuses on *bullets*. Conceptually, the microengraving of individual markers on every bullet offers one prominent advantage over other identification technologies, which is that—in time—it would aid in criminal investigations involving guns that are already in circulation. Ammunition can be a durable commodity but it is, ultimately, exhaustible, and new (microstamped) ammunition would eventually replace it.

10–D.1 Ammunition Microstamping Process

There are multiple points in a single ammunition cartridge that could, conceivably, be engraved using microstamping. However, as experienced in the analysis of bullet striations, the sides of a (relatively soft) bullet can warp or distort on impact, and fragmentation of the bullet is also possible. In what follows, we outline the approach that was advocated by Ammunition Coding System (ACS), the firm (and prospective vendor) that was the focus of attention during debate on the California microstamping legislation.

For maximum survivability, the ACS proposal centers on the etching of microstamped identifiers on the *base* of the bullet. In initial work, the identifier is a six-character alphanumeric code. The code is not engraved a single time on the base but, rather, repeated several times, in an array over the surface of the bullet base. The goal of this repetition is to "allow law enforcement personnel to identify the bullet code in cases where as little as 20% of the bullet base remains intact after recovery" (http://www.ammocoding.com [February 2008]).

Though placing the marker on the base of the bullet may enhance its survivability, it does raise a basic logistical and physical problem at the time of manufacture: the base of a bullet is no longer visible once the bullet is seated in the cartridge. Hence, the assembly line process for bullets must be reengineered so that—at a minimum—the code etched on the bullet in a single cartridge is known when that cartridge is put in a box or that the same code is etched later in the process on a visible part of the cartridge (e.g., the side of the bullet or the exterior of the cartridge case). This concern is addressed in part by the etching of the identifier, once, on the surface of the bullet near the tip. In addition, ACS prototyped a process wherein a camera records the code marking on the bullet base immediately prior to its being seated in the cartridge; based on the camera reading, the assembled cartridge is cycled through additional machinery so that the same code on the bullet is etched on or near the bottom of the cartridge case. (As a late-in-the-stage process, care is obviously required in devising this process and creating the printed code since the propellant and primer would already be in place in the cartridge.) Once marked, the rounds are packed in a cardboard box; a scanner would then read the codes on all the individual rounds in the box and generate a barcode label to be placed on the box. This single, exterior barcode would then be scanned at the time of retail purchase. Later, when a microstamped bullet is recovered at a crime scene, the individual bullet code would be read and matched to an exterior box code; that box code would in turn provide the lead to the point of sale.

ACS-marked ammunition was subjected to two tests by California law enforcement personnel. In April 2004 the San Bernardino County Sheriff's Department test fired 25 rounds of microstamped ammunition, including both .45 caliber and 9mm ammunition, firing into media including plywood, rubber, and a steel door. Three of the bullets were unrecoverable; of the 22 that were recovered, an identifier code could be read on 21.[8] The California Department of Justice conducted further testing on 200 rounds of microstamped ammunition in September 2004. In addition to firings

[8]The exception was a 9mm round fired from 25 yards into 1.5 inches of rubber; only two small fragments could be recovered, but apparently not enough of the base endured in order to preserve the code.

into the side of a car door and standard wall material (plywood, insulation, and drywall), rounds were fired into gelatin to replicate the consistency of human bodies. When the bullet was recoverable—in 181 of the 200 firings—the code was again readable in all but one instance.[9]

10–D.2 Advantages

There are at least five advantages to microstamping ammunition.

- Fully implemented, microstamped ammunition can provide valuable investigative leads from evidence recovered at crime scenes to the point of sale, and perhaps to the original purchaser.
- As described at the beginning of this section, a key conceptual advantage of ammunition microstamping is that it would, eventually, be applicable to the existing gun stock. Though ammunition may be stockpiled and can be durable with proper storage, it is possible that much of the existing ammunition stock would turn over in 3–5 years, and that new (microstamped) ammunition would gradually replace it.
- Microstamping ammunition overcomes a limitation of a national RBID based on cartridge case evidence, in that bullets are almost always "left" at a crime scene.
- The base of a bullet—the proposed area for the microstamped identifiers to be located—is more likely to avoid warping or deformation when the bullet hits a target, relative to the striation marks on the side of the bullet.
- The process of reading a code on a recovered bullet is a relatively quick one, and in some cases may be possible at the crime scene itself. The key time limitation would be in extracting the bullets from wherever they may be lodged. As with marks from microstamped firearms parts, the identifiers can be read without specialized training or equipment.

10–D.3 Disadvantages

There are also significant disadvantages to microstamping ammunition.

- Although markings on the base of a bullet have proved to be durable in testing in some highly demanding situations—firing into wood or a car door, for example—the durability and survivability of markings on the bullet are still major concerns. Bullets would also be likely to suffer

[9]The exception occurred in firings of 30 rounds of .38 Special ammunition into a car door from 10 yards: 22 of the 30 bullets were recoverable, and it was one of these bullets that was unreadable.

the corrosive effects of blood and other substances (and the potential for damage in cleaning them).

- The investigative lead generated by recovering a microstamped bullet from a crime scene would be between a crime-related bullet and its purchaser; as is true with a national RBID, this stops short of directly linking ballistics evidence to the particular person who fired the shot. Moreover, in complex crime scenes where multiple firearms are discharged, microstamped bullet markings could not directly lead to connections between specific bullets and the guns that fired them.
- Though individual records would be much simpler than in an image database, ammunition microstamping would require a new database of massive scope, providing the mapping from codes on individual rounds of ammunition to the code on the box of ammunition that contained them. This new database would rely on collection from ammunition manufacturers and would grow by billions of records (one per piece of ammunition) each year.
- In the discussion of ammunition microstamping in California, a perceived advantage was that the second critical data-gathering activity—logging the ammunition box codes at the point of sale—would require little or no new resources. Because the technical infrastructure to scan both ammunition-box barcodes and the barcodes on purchasers' driver's licenses is already in place among the state's ammunition vendors. However, in other states, barcode reading and ammunition sales databases may not be standard, and practices for examining or recording driver's license or firearm owner's identification card information may also vary. In such states, a new system would have to be developed to capture codes at the point of sale.
- As is the case with firearms microstamping, cost estimates vary widely, and the inability to peg down a per-unit cost factored into the inability to pass the California legislation. In terms of initial capital costs to ammunition manufacturers, Ammunition Coding System stipulated that "reliable estimates for a complete set of engraving/material handling equipment range from $300,000 to $500,000 each." However, "since approximately 10 billion bullets are sold in the United States alone each year, equipment costs, once amortized over the number of bullets produced and sold are not significant" (http://www.ammocoding.com [February 2008]). While proponents of microstamping argued that the per-bullet cost would amount to 1 cent or less, ammunition manufacturers countered that the per-unit cost would be measured in dollars (Yamamura, 2005b). A further sticking point in the California legislation was the provision for a licensing fee—per round of ammunition—to be paid, in addition to the cost of making the laser engravings. Research on the costs associated with retooling existing manufacturing plants would have to be conducted as a supplement

to implementation estimates being offered by vendors. The per-round costs were raised as a particular concern for high-volume ammunition purchasers such as police forces (Yamamura, 2005a) and the military.

- The proposed laser marking proposed by Ammunition Coding System involves evaporation of lead, as well as laser marking on live ammunition and the use of lasers where explosive compounds are present. Extensive research would be required to resolve environmental and safety concerns.

10–E COMMENTARY

It is not within the committee's purview to offer formal recommendations on microstamping technologies—to suggest microstamping as a more reliable, less expensive, or generally better alternative than imaging technologies applied to ballistics evidence, or vice versa. However, we find that both the microstamping of firearms parts and ammunition possess the formidable conceptual advantage of imposing discernible and objective uniqueness on bullet or cartridge case evidence. Thus, microstamping could provide a stronger basis for identification based on the evidence than the status quo, positing that uniqueness arises from random microscopic phenomena and assuming that unique features manifest themselves in different imaging media. However, it is also abundantly clear that substantial further research would be necessary to inform a thorough assessment of the viability of microstamping either gun parts or bullets. Particularly necessary would be credible estimates of the real cost of implementation, separating initial configuration costs from other life-cycle costs, that accurately take into account the reengineering of existing firearms and ammunition production lines.

The emergence of microstamping suggests a theme that we explore further in the next chapter. In microstamping—as in the early days of computer-based ballistic imaging—there has arguably been a push to legislate on the basis of the claims and competences of one or two vendors. We do not challenge the work done by the vendors who have suggested microstamping to date; they have made solid and worthwhile contributions. Microstamping may indeed be a viable future for firearms identification, and we strongly encourage continuing research in this area. However, we do conclude that state and federal law enforcement would be better served by new technologies and systems developed through richer and more open competitions, by multiple vendors and research teams and with fuller appreciation for the integration of new systems with existing manufacturing practices.

11

Best Standards for Future Developments in Computer-Assisted Firearms Identification

The technology of the Integrated Ballistics Identification System (IBIS) provides a significant benefit in reducing the time it takes to identify a match and increasing the overall capacity of toolmark examiners to find matches and to link crimes committed with the same gun. Properly used, the committee believes that the current National Integrated Ballistic Information Network (NIBIN) can be a valuable investigative tool, providing important leads to law enforcement through searches of ballistics evidence images stored in a database. However, a mature scientific approach is required to improve the reliability of automated searches and, if possible, ultimately to reduce costs, particularly labor costs associated with acquisition and search. Neither the current system, nor newer technologies under development, have demonstrated the ability to operate with the precision, safety, and cost effectiveness needed for a national reference ballistic image database (RBID).

The current system has been designed to support the traditional task of having a firearms examiner confirm that a particular cartridge was fired from a particular gun or that two or more cartridges were fired from the same gun. Chapter 6 provides a number of recommendations regarding the kinds of operational and technical improvements that are needed to smooth the progress of this task using the current system. However, the enormous number of firearms crimes committed annually in the United States with their accompanying toll of serious injury and death would seem to call for a far more robust research enterprise in the area of firearms identification than exists in the nation today. This chapter discusses what the government can do to advance the science in acquisition technology, search, and pattern recognition to improve the specific performance of technologies designed to assist in firearms identification and to address systematically the problems that prevent current technologies from being scaled up.

11–A VERIFICATION, SEARCH, AND THE CHALLENGE OF SCALE

Forensic analysis of firearms has traditionally been a process in which an expert examiner is charged with the task of matching spent cartridge cases or bullets with a particular firearm or linking evidence from different crimes to a particular weapon. This is fundamentally a process of verification, in which a hypothesis—that the same firearm was used in two firings—is accepted, rejected, or found to be inconclusive. This judgment is made on the basis of physical markings on the cartridge case or bullet, generally observed visually by the firearms examiner with the assistance of a microscope. An examiner must usually support the judgment of a match in court and thus seeks considerable evidence of a match in order to reach the conclusion of a definitive match.

In considering the development of ballistic image databases, it is critically important to distinguish this traditional process of verification, in which there are external reasons that lead investigators to ask whether two bullets or casings were fired by the same firearm, from the process of search in which a number of cases are compared with the goal of finding possible reasons to tie them together. In verification, one is validating or rejecting a specific hypothesis on the basis of additional data, in this case forensic evidence. In search, one is trying to come up with potential hypotheses by filtering through potentially large amounts of data. In general, search tasks are considerably more difficult than verification tasks. This same distinction arises in a number of areas other than ballistics, most notably biometrics. For instance, it is a considerably easier task to determine whether two particular fingerprints match each other than it is to find potentially matching fingerprints from a large database.

A central distinction between verification and search is that in a verification task one can be quite conservative, not accepting a match unless there is overwhelming evidence. In law enforcement this is ensured by the courts and expert testimony. In fingerprint-based security systems, this is ensured by requiring a very high-quality match of an individual's stored fingerprint to the one read by a scanner, even if that requires several attempts by a user to have the print correctly read. In contrast, for a search task, if a system is too conservative it does not generate any useful potential matches, or hypotheses, to consider. Yet if a search system is not conservative enough, it generates too many useless hypotheses or false leads. Neither of these approaches is very useful. Thus, for search-based tasks, such as a ballistic image database, it is very important that the system have both a low false alarm rate (reporting of incorrect matches) and a high true detection rate (reporting of correct matches).

Simultaneously achieving a low false alarm rate and high true detection rate is well known in the statistics and pattern recognition scientific literatures to be challenging, although for many tasks not insurmountable. A given false alarm rate and true detection rate may even produce acceptable performance for a particular database size but still not scale up effectively to larger databases. For instance, if a database grows by a factor of 100, for a given false alarm rate the number of incorrect matches reported will also be expected to grow by a factor of 100. This may simply be too many potential leads to follow up on. Thus, as a rule of thumb, the false alarm rate often must get better (lower) as the database size increases, while at the same time maintaining the true detection rate.

Early ballistic image "databases" consisted of photographs of bullets and shell casings hanging on the wall. These photographs were taken with a camera attached to a forensic microscope. For unsolved cases these photographs served as reminders in the event that an examiner encountered other evidence that could possibly be tied to these cases. Ballistic image database systems, such as NIBIN, can be viewed as a means of automating this manual process of hanging photos on the wall, enabling investigators to potentially tie cases together based on images of a larger number of bullets and shell casings than can be considered by manual inspection. These systems are now routinely used to handle much larger databases of ballistic images than one could hang on a wall, and in several law enforcement jurisdictions have been effective for finding "cold hits" or links between cases that were not otherwise known.

One can thus view NIBIN as an illustration of the potential that an automated image database search has to increase the capacity to tie cases together in comparison with the manual examination of images (or evidence itself). However, as detailed throughout this report, there is a finite limit on the extent to which such a database can be scaled up and still prove useful. This is both an empirical fact for the particular technologies used by the NIBIN system and a question of both theory and experimentation for other imaging technologies and other pattern recognition techniques. In this chapter we briefly review some of the relevant technologies and techniques and offer suggestions for improving the system.

11–B VISUAL PATTERN RECOGNITION

The goal of visual pattern recognition methods is to find possible matches between images. Pattern recognition methods can be used as part of either a verification or a search task. As discussed above, the former involves validating a particular hypothesis, in this case assessing a potential match between a particular pair of images, and search involves matching a query or probe image against a potentially large set of other images to find potential matches. Pattern matching techniques used for search are generally specifically designed in order to be able to efficiently consider a large number of images. Search techniques generally also provide a ranking of how well each potential image matches the query (such rankings for collections of text are now widely familiar in web search engines).

There are typically two parts to the pattern recognition process: how to compare a single pair of a probe and a target image and how to structure a search over a large set of targets. Clearly, the search element incorporates the comparison stage as part of its process. The comparison step further typically involves two key elements: what features, signature, or other representations of the image content are to be used in the actual comparison operation and what measure is used to compare these features. Associated with the measure will often be a set of allowable transformations: for example, objects may be allowed to translate, rotate, or scale without penalty, or they may be allowed to deform in certain other ways without penalty. These transformations are often not only geometric in nature, but also include transformations that might result from other sources of variation, such as changes in lighting.

Search-based pattern recognition methods involve a broad range of possible techniques. The most straightforward are sequential searches and rankings that in effect verify a match between the query image and each image in the dataset. However, this kind of approach only works for relatively small datasets. More sophisticated methods include hierarchical search methods, in which one first uses a coarse set of features to roughly rank the targets and then a refined comparison is performed only on the top few selections, or hashing function methods, in which a small set of features are used to index into a precomputed arrangement of the targets, focusing on a small set of most likely matches.

Fingerprints are a good example with which to illustrate these tradeoffs. There are many choices of possible features. One could use minutiae (i.e., sets of distinctive local points in the pattern of lines, based on sharp changes in curvature). One could use a broader distribution of the overall orientation of the lines in the pattern, or the density of lines in the pattern, such as histograms of orientation. One could use a learned representation of distinctive features (that is, a set of local features that have been learned as distinctive for this particular print by a series of trials against a large database). Or one could use model-driven features, in which an analysis of the process of generation of fingerprints or an analysis of a particular pattern is used to determine which specific features are distinctive (such as using a local feature focus method).

Thus, in matching fingerprints, images of two fingerprints are not compared directly, pixel for pixel: instead, each fingerprint image is preprocessed to extract certain features. These features are then compared. Human fingerprint experts use features such as minutiae. Pattern recognition systems use features or signatures that are derived mathematically or with machine learning techniques. For automated pattern recognition systems, such formally derived features generally work better than do features that are used by human experts. A recent study by the National Institute of Standards and Technology (NIST) on the accuracy of fingerprint recognition systems found that the best pattern recognition methods are able to achieve a 98.6 percent correct detection rate using a single finger and a 99.9 percent correct detection rate using four fingers, with a false alarm rate of 0.01 percent (Wilson et al., 2004). That is, such a system will correctly match two fingerprints from the same person much of the time while only incorrectly saying there is a match (when there is none) only 1 in 10,000 times (for details, see, e.g., http://www.sciencedaily.com/releases/2004/07/040716080142.htm [February 2008]).

When considering possible comparison measures, there is again a broad range of options. Again we use fingerprints as an example. One approach is simply to measure the degree of overlap between two patterns—that is, search over all possible alignments of the features or signature (query for a particular target) and count something, such as the number of pixels in the query and target, to find pairs that have the same value or values within some tolerance. Note that inherent in this definition is the notion of allowable transformations between the probe and the target, which may be abstracted out in the feature extraction process, part of the matching process, or a mixture of both.

11–C BEST PRACTICES FOR LESS MATURE TECHNOLOGIES

Current NIBIN technology has been developed using a single vendor approach. This kind of approach is common when the technological problem to be solved—in this case, automating the search function in firearms identification—seems to be straightforward and the market for the resulting product is limited. However, any vendor must necessarily choose a particular approach based on its best judgment as to what is most feasible and cost effective. The kinds and scope of empirical questions involved in advancing the technologies and improving performance and scalability are difficult for a single vendor to address. The challenge, then, is how to divide the task so that particular pieces of the application can be addressed through a competitive research and development process.

There are two recent examples of government mandated large-scale system developments based on (initially) nonmature technologies: fingerprint identification and facial recognition. Both systems required the creation of dedicated pattern recognition algorithms, similar to the requirements of the proposed RBID. Instead of relying on a single system produced by a single vendor, both systems were organized as competitions between vendors. In the following sections, we first describe the two competitions and then extract best practice suggestions from those experiences.

11–C.1 Fingerprint Identification

The statutory mandate of NIST under Section 403c of the USA PATRIOT Act requires that NIST examine and certify biometric technologies that may be used, among others, in the U.S. Visitor and Immigrant Status Indication Technology (VISIT), formerly known as the U.S. entry-exit system. The Fingerprint Vendor Technology Evaluation (FpVTE) 2003 was conducted on behalf of the Justice Management Division of the Department of Justice in the fall of 2003, to evaluate the accuracy of commercial fingerprint matching, identification, and verification systems (Wilson et al., 2004; see also http://fpvte.nist.gov [January 15, 2007]).

FpVTE 2003 was designed to assess the capability of fingerprint systems to meet requirements for both large-scale and small-scale real-world applications. FpVTE 2003 consists of multiple tests performed with combinations of fingers (e.g., single fingers, 2 index fingers, 4 to 10 fingers) and different types and qualities of operational fingerprints (e.g., flat livescan images from visa applicants, multifinger slap livescan images from present-day booking or background check systems, or rolled and flat inked fingerprints from legacy criminal databases).

FpVTE 2003 was among the most comprehensive evaluations of fingerprint matching systems ever executed, particularly in terms of the number and variety of systems and fingerprints: 18 companies participated, with 34 systems tested. The test used 48,105 sets of flat slap or rolled fingerprint sets from 25,309 individuals, with a total of 393,370 distinct fingerprint images. The tests revealed that, when four fingerprints were used for matching, the most accurate fingerprint system tested always had a true accept rate that was higher than 99.9 percent with a false accept rate of 0.01 percent.

The evaluations were conducted to (1) measure the accuracy of fingerprint matching, identification, and verification systems using operational fingerprint data; (2) identify the most accurate fingerprint matching systems; (3) determine the effect of a wide variety of variables on matcher accuracy; and (4) develop well-vetted sets of operational data from a variety of sources for use in future research. As such, the fingerprint identification system is considered to be a system in continuous evolution. As better algorithms become available, the system can be updated to improve the identification success rate.

The use of a systematic competitive test between vendors ensures that the best possible algorithms are developed and used. In addition, the effects of various external factors on the accuracy of the identifications can be quantitatively addressed. For instance, it was shown unambiguously that the variables that had the largest effect on system accuracy were the number of fingers used and fingerprint quality. A national RBID would require a similar systematic study of the effect of external variables on the accuracy of matching for both cartridge cases and bullets.

11–C.2 Facial Recognition

The U.S. Department of Defense Counterdrug Technology Development Program Office began the Face Recognition Program (FERET) in 1993 and sponsored it through its completion in 1998. Total funding for the program was a little over $6.5 million. The goal of FERET was to develop automatic face recognition capabilities that could be employed to assist security, intelligence, and law enforcement personnel in the performance of their duties. FERET consisted of three major elements. First, the program sponsored research that advanced facial recognition from theory to working laboratory algorithms. Many of the algorithms that were developed in FERET form the foundation of today's commercial systems. Second was the collection and distribution of the FERET database, which contains 14,126 facial images of 1,199 individuals. (The FERET database is currently maintained at NIST.) The development portion of the FERET database has been distributed to more than 100 groups outside the original program. The final, and most recognized, part of the FERET program involved the FERET evaluations that compared the abilities of various facial recognition algorithms using the FERET database.

A standard database of face imagery was essential to the success of FERET, both to supply standard imagery to the algorithm developers and to supply a sufficient number of images to allow testing of these algorithms. Before the start of FERET, there was no way to accurately evaluate or compare facial recognition algorithms (see http://www.frvt.org/FERET/default.htm [February 2008]). FERET set out to establish a large database of facial images that was gathered independently from the algorithm developers. The database made it possible for researchers to develop algorithms on a common database and to report results in the literature using this database.

The results reported in the standard literature did not provide a direct comparison among algorithms because each researcher reported results using different assumptions, scoring methods, and images. The independently administered FERET evaluations, using well-defined and published evaluation methodologies (Phillips et al., 2000), allowed for a direct quantitative assessment of the relative strengths and weaknesses of different approaches. One of the most important aspects of the use of this database was that the variability of the data could be controlled (e.g., images of a person taken on the same day under different lighting conditions, images taken on different days or a year apart, and so on). It is only after the intrinsic variability of the data is explicitly taken into account that a facial recognition system can function reliably. The FERET database has been used in two face-recognition vendor tests (FRVT), one in 2000 and 2002, and a face-recognition grand challenge in 2004–2006. The grand challenge was motivated by advances in computer vision techniques, computer design, and sensor design that held the promise of reducing the error rate of the present systems by an order of magnitude (see http://www.frvt.org/FRGC/ [February 2008]).

The use of a standardized evaluation method also allows for a comparison of different systems, in this case of the accuracy of the fingerprint systems and the facial recognition systems. It was concluded that leading contemporary fingerprint systems are substantially more accurate than the face-recognition systems tested in 2002 (Wilson et al., 2004).

11–D BEST PRACTICES

Both of the systems discussed in the preceding sections share several commonalities with the proposed national RBID:

- Fingerprint, facial recognition, and ballistic imaging all use images as input.
- There is considerable variability between the images in each of these areas.
- All three systems have potentially large databases that must be searched with high accuracy and within a reasonable search time.

One important distinction between the three systems is that fingerprint and facial recognition attempt to directly connect an image with a person but the proposed national RBID connects an image to a weapon, not to a person. A second important distinction emanates from the stochastic nature of ballistics: that is, noise and variation in fingerprints comes from acquisition; in ballistics there is the additional process of generating the physical characteristics that are then going to be acquired changes each time.

Just as automated fingerprint and facial recognition systems were considered to be nonmature technologies in the 1990s, automated ballistic imaging can today be considered as a nonmature technology. The use of large-scale evaluations of the fingerprint and face recognition technologies through controlled competitive vendor tests has advanced those technologies tremendously. The committee believes that it is likely that a similar competitive research program for ballistic imaging—involving university, federal and state agencies, and industrial researchers—would lead to significant improvements in image matching algorithms. The research could be partitioned into separable components that have applicability across a wide range of research applications. For example, image acquisition could be investigated separately from search and pattern recognition. In addition, the competitive vendor tests approach could be used to test the safety, durability, and cost-effectiveness of engraving identifiers on firearms parts and or bullets and cartridge cases, such as the microstamping approaches discussed in Chapter 10.

Given the cost of the current system, the need for improved performance of the system documented in this report and elsewhere, the costs to society of crimes committed with firearms, and the clear interest of state legislatures and Congress to make improvements in firearms identification, the committee believes that such an investment in research to support the development of technologies to assist in firearms identification is critically important.

References

AFTE Criteria for Identification Committee (1992). Theory of identification, range of striae comparison reports and modified glossary definitions—An AFTE criteria for identification committee report. *AFTE Journal 24*(3), 336–340.

American Institute of Applied Science (1982). Firearms examination, lessons 1–3. *AFTE Journal 14*(2), 16–86.

Argaman, U., E. Shoshani, and G. Hocherman (2001). Utilization of the IBIS™ in Israel. *AFTE Journal 33*(3), 269–272.

Bachrach, B. (2002). Development of a 3D-based automated firearms evidence comparison system. *Journal of Forensic Sciences 47*(6), 1253–1264.

Banno, A., T. Masuda, and K. Ikeuchi (2004). Three dimensional visualization and comparison of impressions on fired bullets. *Forensic Science International 140*, 233–240.

Beauchamp, A., and D. Roberge (2005). Model of the behavior of the IBIS correlation scores in a large database of cartridge scores. Unpublished manuscript provided to the committee.

Biasotti, A.A. (1959). A statistical study of the individual characteristics of fired bullets. *Journal of Forensic Sciences 4*(1), 34–50.

Biasotti, A.A. (1970). A proposal for a computer based firearms class characteristics information system. *Newsletter of the Association of Firearm and Tool Mark Examiners* (5), 12–16.

Biasotti, A.A., and J.E. Murdock (2002). Firearms and toolmark identification—Scientific issues. Pp. 205–230 (Chapter 4, Section 4-2) in D. Faigman, D.H. Kaye, M.J. Saks, and J. Sanders (Eds.), *Modern Scientific Evidence: The Law and Science of Expert Testimony.* St. Paul, MN: West Group Publishing Company.

Blackwell, R., and E. Framan (1980). Automated firearms identification systems afids: Phase I. *AFTE Journal 12*(4), 11–37.

Blumstein, A. (1995). Youth violence, guns, and the illicit-drug industry. *Journal of Criminal Law and Criminology 86*, 10–36.

Boesman, W.C., and W.J. Krouse (2001). *National Integrated Ballistics Information Network (NIBIN) for Law Enforcement.* (CRS Report for Congress #RL31040.) Washington, DC: Congressional Research Service.

Bonfanti, M.S., and J. De Kinder (1999a). The influence of manufacturing processes on the identification of bullets and cartridge cases—A review of the literature. *Science & Justice 39*(1), 3–10.

Bonfanti, M.S., and J. De Kinder (1999b). The influence of the use of firearms on their characteristic marks. *AFTE Journal 31*(3), 318–323.

Braga, A.A. (2003). Serious youth gun offenders and the epidemic of youth violence in Boston. *Journal of Quantitative Criminology 19*(1), 33–54.

Braga, A.A., and G.L. Pierce (2004). Linking gun crimes: The impact of ballistics imaging technology on the productivity of the Boston Police Department's ballistics unit. *Journal of Forensic Sciences 46*(4), 701–706.

Braga, A.A., D.M. Kennedy, and G.E. Tita (2002). New Approaches to the strategic prevention of gang and group-involved violence. Pp. 271–285 (Chapter 17) in C. Ronald Huff (Ed.), *Gangs in America III.* Thousand Oaks, CA: Sage Publications.

Braga, A.A., D.M. Kennedy, E.J. Waring, and A.M. Piehl (2001). Problem-oriented policing, deterrence, and youth violence: An evaluation of Boston's Operation Ceasefire. *Journal of Research in Crime and Delinquency 38*(3), 195–225.

Brundage, D.J. (1998). The identification of consecutively rifled gun barrels. *AFTE Journal 30*(3), 438–444.

Burd, D., and P. Kirk (1942). Tool marks—Factors involved in their comparison and use as evidence. *Journal of Criminal Law and Criminology 32*, 679–686.

Burrard, G. (1962). *The Identification of Firearms and Forensic Ballistics.* New York: A.S. Barnes and Company. (First American edition; originally published in United Kingdom in 1934.)

Butler, A. (2005, March 10). House weighs ballistics database: State police head testifies to committee on report calling system ineffective. *Baltimore Sun*, p. 2B.

Butterfield, F. (2002, October 24). The hunt for a sniper: Technology—Now, 4 states look to start tracing shells and bullets. *New York Times.* Available: http://query.nytimes.com/gst/fullpage.html?res=9D06E6D8123CF937A15753C1A9649C8B63 [accessed April 2008].

Campbell, D.T., and J. Stanley (1966). *Experimental and Quasi-Experimental Designs for Research.* Chicago: Rand McNally.

Carr, J., and T. Fadal (1997). The Miami barrel. *AFTE Journal 29*(2), 232–234.

Carso, K.E. (2007). Symposium: Is the rule of law waning in America? Twelfth Annual Clifford Symposium on Tort Law and Social Policy: Comment: Amending the Illinois postconviction statute to include ballistics testing. *DePaul Law Review 56*(695).

Castaneda, R., and D. Snyder (2005, April 2). Ballistics database yields 1st conviction: Oxon Hill man tied to murder weapon. *Washington Post*, p. B1.

Champod, C. (2000). Identification/individualization—Overview and meaning of ID. Pp. 1077–1084 (Volume 3) in J.A. Siegel (Ed.), *Encyclopedia of Forensic Sciences.* London: Academic Press.

Champod, C., D. Baldwin, F. Taroni, and J. Buckleton (2003). Firearm and tool marks identification: The Bayesian approach. *AFTE Journal 35*(3), 307–316.

Chan, R. (2000). The relationship between acquisition positions of cartridge cases and discrepancy in correlation scores on IBIS. *AFTE Journal 32*(4), 337–341.

Churchman, J. (1981). The reproduction of characteristics in signatures of Cooey rifles. *AFTE Journal 13*(1), 46–52.

Collins, J.M. (1997). Manufacturing the Lorcin L380 and corresponding characteristics. *AFTE Journal 29*(4), 498–502.

Cook, P.J., and A.A. Braga (2001). Comprehensive firearms tracing: Strategic and investigative uses of new data on firearms markets. *Arizona Law Review 43*(2), 277–309.

Cook, P.J., and J.H. Laub (2002). After the epidemic: Recent trends in youth violence in the United States. Pp. 117–153 in M. Tonry (Ed.), *Crime and Justice: A Review of Research*. Chicago: University of Chicago Press.

Cook, P.J., and J.O. Ludwig (2000). *Gun Violence: The Real Costs*. New York: Oxford University Press.

Cook, P.J., and J.O. Ludwig (2002). The costs of gun violence against children. *The Future of Children 12*(2), 87–99.

Cook, T.D., and D.T. Campbell (1979). *Quasi Experimentation: Design and Analytical Issues for Field Settings*. Chicago: Rand McNally.

Davis, J. (1958). *An Introduction to Tool Marks, Firearms, and the Striagraph*. Springfield, IL: Charles C. Thomas.

De Kinder, J. (2002a). Ballistic fingerprinting databases. *Science and Justice 42*, 197–203.

De Kinder, J. (2002b, December). Review—AB 1717 report, technical evaluation: Feasibility of a ballistics imaging database for all new handgun sales. Independent review for California Department of Justice, National Institute for Forensic Science, Belgium.

De Kinder, J., and M. Bonfanti (1999). Automated comparisons of bullet striations based on 3D topography. *Forensic Science International 101*, 85–93.

De Kinder, J., P. Prevot, M. Pirlot, and B. Nys (1998). Surface topology of bullet striations: An innovating technique. *AFTE Journal 30*(2), 294–299.

De Kinder, J., F. Tulleners, and H. Thiebaut (2004, March 10). Reference ballistic imaging database performance. *Forensic Science International 140*(2–3), 207–215.

Denio, D. (1999). Drugfire: The Federal Bureau of Investigation which is a participant in the National Integrated Ballistic Information Network (NIBIN). *AFTE Journal 31*(3), 383–385.

Dillon, Jr., J.H. (2005). *BulletTRAX™-3D, MatchPoint Plus™ and the Firearms Examiner: A Practical Application of Forensic Science, Technology and Engineering to Case Linkage in Shooting Incidents Not Previously Related by Investigative Personnel*. Independent report commissioned by Forensic Technology WAI, Inc.

Ethridge, M.W. (1998). The ATF National Firearm Examiner Academy—A new part of ATF's integrated firearm enforcement strategy. *AFTE Journal 30*(4), 703–704.

Evans, J.P.O., C.L. Smith, and M. Robinson (2004). Validation of the linescan imaging technique for imaging cylindrical forensic ballistics specimens. *AFTE Journal 36*(4), 275–280.

Fadal, Jr., T.G. (1995). One striker leaves two different firing pin impressions. *AFTE Journal 27*(1), 38–39.

Fadal, Jr., T.G., and A. Nuñez (2003). The Miami barrel saga continues. *AFTE Journal 35*(3), 290–297.

Fadal, Jr., T.G., and A. Nuñez (2006). Glock's new "EBIS" barrel: The finale to the Miami barrel story. *AFTE Journal 38*(2), 96–100.

Flater, J.A. (2002). Manufacturing marks on Winchester USA brand 9mm Luger primers. *AFTE Journal 34*(3), 315.

Forensic Technology WAI, Inc. (2001). *IBIS User Guide, Version 3.3*. Montréal: Forensic Technology WAI, Inc.

Forensic Technology WAI, Inc. (2002a, March). Comments of Forensic Technology, Inc., on the technical evaluation: Feasibility of a ballistics imaging database for all new handgun sales. Response to California Department of Justice evaluation.

Forensic Technology WAI, Inc. (2002b). *IBIS Version 3.4 Training Course: Student Book*. Montréal: Forensic Technology WAI, Inc.

Frost, G.E. (1990). *Ammunition Making: An Insider's Story*. Washington, DC: National Rifle Association of America.

Gardner, G.Y. (1979). Computer identification of bullets. *AFTE Journal 11*(2), 26–33.

George, W. (2004a). A validation of the Brasscatcher™ portion of the NIBIN/IBIS™ system. *AFTE Journal 36*(4), 286–288.

George, W. (2004b). The validation of the Brasscatcher™ portion of the NIBIN/IBIS™ system part two: "Fingerprinting firearms" reality or fantasy. *AFTE Journal 36*(4), 289–294.

Giverts, P., U. Argaman, E. Shoshani, and O. Aharon (2002). An average phase scoring for bullets, in the IBIS™ correlation results. *AFTE Journal 34*(2), 199–202.

Glass, S., and W. Gibson (1997). Firearms factory tours. *AFTE Journal 29*(4), 487–493.

Goddard, C.H. (1980). A history of firearms identification. *AFTE Journal 12*(4), 38–57. [Reprinted from *Chicago Police Journal*, 1936.]

Goddard, C.H. (1999). History of firearms identification to 1930 [reprint of 1953 address]. *AFTE Journal 31*(3), 225–241.

Goebel, R., K. Gross, H. Katterwe, and W. Kammrath (1980). The comparison scanning electron microscope: First experiments in forensic application. *Scanning 3*, 193–201.

Grooß, K. (1995). The "hammer-murderer." *AFTE Journal 27*(1), 27–30.

Grove, C., C. Judd, and R. Horn (1972). SEM—A new technique for firearms examination. *Newsletter of the Association of Firearm and Tool Mark Examiners* (18), 19–21.

Grzybowski, R.A., and J.E. Murdock (1998). Firearm and toolmark identification—Meeting the Daubert challenge. *AFTE Journal 30*(1), 3–14.

Grzybowski, R., J. Miller, B. Moran, J. Murdock, R. Nichols, and R. Thompson (2003). Firearm/toolmark identification: Passing the reliability test under federal and state evidentiary standards. *AFTE Journal 35*(2), 209–241.

Haag, L.C. (2004). Ballistic ID tagging. Presentation to the Committee on the Feasibility, Accuracy, and Technical Capability of a National Ballistics Database, December.

Hall, E.E. (1983). Bullet markings from consecutively rifled Shilen DGA barrels. *AFTE Journal 15*(1), 33–53.

Hamby, J.E. (1974). Identification of projectiles. *AFTE Journal 6*(5–6), 22.

Hamby, J.E., and J.W. Thorpe (1999). The history of firearm and toolmark identification. *AFTE Journal 31*(3), 266–284.

Hatcher, J.S. (1935). *Textbook of Firearms Investigation, Identification and Evidence* (First Edition). Marines, NC: Small-Arms Technical Publishing Company.

Hayes, C.S., M. Basoa, and R. Freese (2004). Reduction of characteristic breechface marks due to primer sealants. *AFTE Journal 36*(2), 139–146.

Heard, B.J. (1997). *Handbook of Firearms and Ballistics: Examining and Interpreting Forensic Evidence*. Chichester, England: John Wiley and Sons.

Hess, P.A., and B. Moran (2006). The removal of superficial rust/corrosion from the working surfaces of firearms for the purpose of revealing their potentially identifiable signature and an application of this technique in a firearms identification. *AFTE Journal 38*(2), 112–132.

Insurance Information Institute (2006). Hot Topics and Issue Updates: Auto Theft. Available: http://www.iii.org/media/hottopics/insurance/test4/ [accessed February 2008].

Kennedy, D.M., A.M. Piehl, and A.A. Braga (1996). Youth violence in Boston: Gun markets, serious youth offenders, and a use-reduction strategy. *Law and Contemporary Problems* 59(1):147–196.

Kennington, R.H. (1992). *The Matrix, 9mm Parabellum: An Empirical Study of Type Determination*. Miami: R.H. Kennington.

Kennington, R.H. (1995). 9mm arcology: Arch contenders. *AFTE Journal* 27(3), 213–219.

Kirk, P. (1963). The ontogeny of criminalistics. *Journal of Criminal Law, Criminology, and Police Science 54*, 235–238.

Konior, T. (2006). Identification based on breech face markings on the head of a discharged cartridge case. *AFTE Journal 38*(3), 242–244.

Kopel, D., and H. Burnett (2003). *Ballistics Imaging: Not Ready for Prime Time*. (Policy Backgrounder No. 160.) Dallas, TX: National Center for Policy Analysis.

Kreiser, J. (1995). Primer "flowback" is not always due to high pressure. *AFTE Journal 27*(1), 1–4.

Krivosta, G.G. (2006). NanoTag™ markings from another perspective. *AFTE Journal 38*(1), 41–47.

Lardizabal, P.P. (1995). Cartridge case study of the Heckler & Koch USP. *AFTE Journal 27*(1), 49–51.

Larrison, R.M. (2006). Degradation of fired bullets and cartridge cases in different environmental mediums. *AFTE Journal 38*(3), 223–230.

Lindgren, S.A., and M.W. Zawitz (2001). *Linking Uniform Crime Reporting Data to Other Datasets*. NCJ185233. Washington, DC: U.S. Department of Justice.

Lockyer, B. (2003, January). *Feasibility of a California Ballistics Identification System: Assembly Bill 1717 (Hertzberg) (Stats. 2000, ch. 271)—Report to the Legislature*. Sacramento: California Department of Justice.

Lomoro, V. (1974). Class characteristics of 32 SWL, F.I.E. Titanic revolvers. *AFTE Journal 6*(2), 18–21.

Ludwig, J.O., and P.J. Cook (2001). The benefits of reducing gun violence: Evidence from contingent-valuation survey data. *Journal of Risk and Uncertainty* 22(3), 207–226.

Lutz, M.C. (1970, August). Consecutive revolver barrels. *Newsletter of the Association of Firearm and Tool Mark Examiners* (9), 24–28.

Main, F. (2005, May 31). Cops: Bullet database cracks '95 murder. *Chicago Sun Times*.

Maruoka, R.K. (1994a). Guilty before the crime? The potential for a possible misidentification or elimination. *AFTE Journal 26*(3), 206–213.

Maruoka, R.K. (1994b). Turning unknowns into knowns: Linking cartridge cases to the firearms and suspects to crime scenes. *AFTE Journal 26*(3), 214–215.

Maruoka, R.K., and P. Ball (1995). Guilty before the crime II. *AFTE Journal 27*(1):20–21.

Maryland State Police, Forensic Sciences Division (2003, September). *Maryland-IBIS (Integrated Ballistics Identification System)*. Pikesville, MD: Maryland State Police.

Maryland State Police, Forensic Sciences Division (2004, September). *MD-IBIS Progress Report #2*. Pikesville, MD: Maryland State Police.

Masson, J.J. (1997). Confidence level variations in firearms identification through computerized technology. *AFTE Journal 29*(1), 42–44.

Matty, W. (1985). A comparison of three individual barrels produced from one button rifled barrel blank. *AFTE Journal 17*(3), 64–69.

Matty, W. (1987). Primer composition and gunshot residue. *AFTE Journal 19*(1), 8–13.

Matty, W. (1999). Lorcin L9MM and L380 pistol breechface toolmark patterns. *AFTE Journal 31*(2), 134–137.

Matty, W., and T. Johnson (1984). A comparison of manufacturing marks on Smith & Wesson firing pins. *AFTE Journal 16*(3), 51–56.

McCarthy, D.M. (2004). The NYPD ballistic image database. Presentation to the Committee on the Feasibility, Accuracy, and Technical Capability of a National Ballistics Database, December.

McLean, D. (1999). Examiners make explosive gains in the ballistic labs; productivity rockets to levels unheard of before. *AFTE Journal 31*(3), 386–392.

McLean, M. (2004). Initial results: Large database study and new firing pin algorithm. Presentation to the Committee on the Feasibility, Accuracy, and Technical Capability of a National Ballistics Database, May.

Michel, L., and D. Herbeck (2001). *American Terrorist: Timothy McVeigh and the Oklahoma City Bombing*. New York: ReganBooks.

Miller, J. (2000). Criteria for identification of toolmarks part II: Single land impression comparisons. *AFTE Journal 32*(2), 116–131.

Miller, J. (2001). An examination of the application of the conservative criteria for identification of striated toolmarks using bullets fired from ten consecutively rifled barrels. *AFTE Journal 33*(2), 125–132.

Miller, J. (2004). Criteria for identification of toolmarks part III: Supporting the conclusion. *AFTE Journal 36*(1), 7–38.

Miller, J., and M. McLean (1998). Criteria for identification of toolmarks. *AFTE Journal 30*(1), 15–61.

Molnar, S. (1970, December). What is a firearms examiner—Some provocative thoughts. *Association of Firearm and Tool Mark Examiners Newsletter* (11), 36–39.

Molnar, S. (1977). Notes on breech face marks and fouling. *AFTE Journal 9*(1), 21.

Moran, B. (2000). Firearms examiner expert witness testimony: The forensic firearms identification process including criteria for identification and distance determination. *AFTE Journal 32*(3), 231–251.

Moran, B. (2002). A report on the AFTE theory of identification and range of conclusions for tool mark identification and resulting approaches to casework. *AFTE Journal 34*(2), 227–235.

Moran, B. (2003). Photo documentation of toolmark identifications—An argument in support. *AFTE Journal 35*(2), 174–189.

Moran, B., and J. Murdock (2002). *Joseph Ramirez vs. State of Florida* [Supreme Court decision, December 20.] *AFTE Journal 34*(2), 215.

Murdock, J.E. (1981). A general discussion of gun barrel individuality and an empirical assessment of the individuality of consecutively button rifled .22 caliber rifle barrels. *AFTE Journal 13*(3), 84–95.

Murray, K. (2004). Toolmark identifications on unfired primers: More Fiocchi manufacturing marks. *AFTE Journal 36*(4), 313–314.

Nagin, D. (1998). Deterrence and incapacitation. Pp. 345–368 in M. Tonry (Ed.), *Oxford Handbook of Crime and Punishment*. New York: Oxford University Press.

National Research Council (1996). *The Evaluation of Forensic DNA Evidence*. Committee on DNA Forensic Science: An Update. Commission on DNA Forensic Science: An Update. Washington, DC: National Academy Press.

National Research Council (2005). *Firearms and Violence: A Critical Review*. Committee to Improve Research Information and Data on Firearms. C.F. Wellford, J.V. Pepper, and C.V. Petrie (Eds.). Committee on Law and Justice, Division of Behavioral and Social Sciences and Education. Washington, DC: The National Academies Press.

Nennstiel, R., and J. Rahm (2006a). An experience report regarding the performance of the IBIS™ correlator. *Journal of Forensic Sciences 51*(1), 24–30.

Nennstiel, R., and J. Rahm (2006b). A parameter study regarding the IBIS™ correlator. *Journal of Forensic Sciences 51*(1), 18–23.

Newton, J. (2006, August 10). Mayor, police chief endorse bullet-identification measure. *Los Angeles Times*, p. B5.

NIBIN Branch (2003, May). NIBIN News: Guidance for Hit Reporting. Available: http://www.nibin.gov/documents/0503hitdefinition.pdf [accessed February 2008].

NIBIN Program (2001). *The Missing Link: Ballistics Technology That Helps Solve Crimes*. (Publication ATF P.3315.1.) Washington, DC: U.S. Bureau of Alcohol, Tobacco, Firearms, and Explosives.

Nichols, R.G. (1995). Glock versus Smith & Wesson model SW40F: Comparison of markings on fired cartridge cases. *AFTE Journal 27*(2), 133–139.

Nichols, R.G. (1997). Firearm and toolmark identification criteria: A review of the literature. *Journal of Forensic Sciences 42*(3), 466–474.

Nichols, R.G. (2003). Consecutive matching striations (CMS): Its definition, study and application in the discipline of firearms and tool mark identification. *AFTE Journal 35*(3), 298–306.

Nichols, R.G. (2004). Firearm and tool mark identification: The scientific reliability and validity of the AFTE theory of identification discussed within the framework of a study of ten consecutively manufactured extractors. *AFTE Journal 36*(1), 67–88.

Nichols, R.G. (2005). The scientific foundations of firearms and tool mark identification—A response to recent challenges. Available: http://www.nibin.gov/documents/120299mou.htm [accessed March 2008].

Office of National Drug Control Policy (1994, November). *Benchmark Evaluation Studies of the BULLETPROOF and DRUGFIRE Ballistic Imaging Systems: A Technical Evaluation with Recommendations for Action.* (Counterdrug Technology Assessment Center). Washington, DC: Executive Office of the President.

Ogihara, Y., M. Kubota, M. Sanada, K. Fukuda, T. Uchiyama, and J. Hamby (1989). Comparison of 5000 consecutively fired bullets and cartridge cases from a 45 caliber M1911A1 pistol. *AFTE Journal 21*(2), 331–343.

Parachini, J.V. (2000). The World Trade Center bombers (1993). Chapter 11 in J.B. Tucker (Ed.), *Toxic Terror: Assessing Terrorist Use of Chemical and Biological Weapons*. Cambridge, MA: MIT Press.

Phillips, P.J., H. Moon, S.A. Rizvi, and P.J. Rauss (2000). The FERET evaluation methodology for face-recognition algorithms. *IEEE Transactions on Pattern Analysis and Machine Intelligence 22*, 1090–1104.

Rector, M. (2002). Effects of ultrasonic cleaning of bullets on IBIS correlation scores: A preliminary report. *AFTE Journal 34*(2), 165–168.

Reitz, J.E. (1975). Unfired cartridge phenomenon. *AFTE Journal 7*(2), 103–104.

Rinker, R.A. (2004). *Understanding Firearm Ballistics* (Fifth Edition). Clarksville, IN: Mulberry House Publishing.

Roberge, D., and A. Beauchamp (2006). The use of BulletTrax-3D in a study of consecutively manufactured barrels. *AFTE Journal 38*(2), 166–172.

Robinson, M.K. (1996). Another manufactured toolmark. *AFTE Journal 28*(3), 164–165.

Rosenberry, J.L. (2003). Firearm/toolmark examination and the *Daubert* criteria. *AFTE Journal 35*(1), 38–48.

Rowe, W.F. (1991). Statistics in forensic ballistics. Pp. 168–177 in C.G.G. Aitken and D.A. Stoney (Eds.), *The Use of Statistics in Forensic Science*. New York: Ellis Horwood Ltd.

Saks, M.J., and J.J. Kohler (2005, August 5). The coming paradigm shift in forensic identification science. *Science 309*(5736), 892–895.

Sánchez, G.B. (2006, September 11). Tracking crime gun by tracking ammo: One bill to do that failed in legislature. *Monterey County Herald*, p. A1.

Schecter, B., and P. Giverts (2005). An additional method of using the IBIS algorithm for comparison of Glock type cartridge cases. *AFTE Journal 37*(1), 27–31.

Schecter, L., L. Nedivi, and G. Hocherman (1996). Changing the individual characteristics of the Sig-Sauer pistol. *AFTE Journal* 28(2), 97–103.

Schwartz, A. (2005). A systemic challenge to the reliability and admissibility of firearms and toolmark identification. *Columbia Science and Technology Law Review VI*, 1–42.

Semwogerere, D., and E.R. Weeks (2005). Confocal microscopy. In G. Wnek and G.L. Bowlin (Eds.), *Encyclopedia of Biomaterials and Biomedical Engineering*. New York: Taylor & Francis.

Silverwater, H., and A. Koffman (2000). IBIS™ correlation results—Improvements. *AFTE Journal 32*(1), 32–39.

Smith, E.D. (2004). Cartridge case and bullet comparison validation study with firearms submitted in casework. *AFTE Journal 36*(4), 130–135.

Smith, L.L. (1971, February). Jokers in the field of firearms examination. *Association of Firearm and Tool Mark Examiners Newsletter* (12), 12–22.

Stoney, D.A. (1991). What made us ever think we could individualize using statistics? *Journal of the Forensic Science Society 31*(2), 197–199.

Sweeney, J.P. (2007, September 11). Handgun stamping bill sent to governor. Copley News Service. Available: http://www.signonsandiego.com/news/state/20070911-9999-1n11gunstamp.html [accessed February 2008].

Tam, C.K. (2001). Overview of manufacturing marks on center fire cartridges. *AFTE Journal 33*(2), 112–115.

Tew, J.D. (2003). Incorrect manufacturer supplied test fire cartridge cases. *AFTE Journal* 35(2):195–196.

Thompson, E. (1996). False breech face ID's. *AFTE Journal 28*(2), 25–26.

Thompson, E. (2006). Editorial: Two-dimensional versus three-dimensional characteristics. *AFTE Journal 38*(1), 10–13.

Thompson, R.M. (1998b, November). Automated firearms evidence comparison using the Integrated Ballistic Identification System (IBIS). Pp. 94–103 in *Part of the SPIE Conference on Investigation and Forensic Technologies.* Boston, MA: International Society for Optical Engineering.

Thompson, R.M., M. Desrosiers, and S. Hester (1996). Computerized image analysis for firearms identification: The Integrated Ballistic Identification System (IBIS) Brasscatcher performance study. *AFTE Journal 28*(3), 194–203.

Thompson, R.M., J. Miller, M.G. Ols, and J.C. Budden (2002, May). Ballistic imaging and comparison of crime gun evidence by the Bureau of Alcohol, Tobacco, and Firearms. Response to California Department of Justice evaluation, Bureau of Alcohol, Tobacco, and Firearms.

Thornton, J.I. (1978). Some historical notes on the comparison microscope. *AFTE Journal 10*(1), 7–10.

Thornton, J.I., and J.L. Peterson (2002). The general assumptions and rationale of forensic identification. Pp. 1–49 in D.L. Faigman, D.H. Kaye, M.J. Saks, and J. Sanders (Eds.), *Science in the Law: Forensic Science Issues.* St. Paul, MN: West Group Publishing Company.

Thurman, R. (2006, July). A business in transaction: Industry embarks on a period of growth. *Shooting Industry*, 30–43.

Tontarski, R.E., and R.M. Thompson (1998). Automated firearms evidence comparison: A forensic tool for firearms identification—An update. *Journal of Forensic Sciences 43*(3), 641–647.

Tsai, J. (2006, September 25). Etched bullets interest law enforcement; lasering may help solve gun crimes. *Bergen County Record*, p. A1.

Tulleners, F.A. (2001). *Technical evaluation: Feasibility of a ballistics imaging database for all new handgun sales.* (Attachment to Lockyer [2003]); Evaluation for California Department of Justice.

Uchiyama, T. (1986). Similarity among breech face marks fired from guns with close serial numbers. *AFTE Journal 18*(3), 15–52.

Uchiyama, T., N. Igarashi, and M. Nagai (1988). The frequency of occurrence of individual characteristics of firearms on fired bullets and cartridge cases. *AFTE Journal 20*(4), 376–390.

U.S. Bureau of Alcohol, Tobacco, and Firearms (2000). *Commerce in Firearms in the United States.* Washington, DC: U.S. Department of the Treasury.

U.S. Department of Justice, Office of the Inspector General (2005, June). *The Bureau of Alcohol, Tobacco, Firearms and Explosives' National Integrated Ballistic Information Network Program.* (Audit Division, Audit Report #05-30.) Washington, DC: U.S. Department of Justice.

Vinci, F., R. Falamingo, C.P. Campobasso, and J.A. Bailey (2005). Morphological study of class and individual characteristics produced by firing 2500 cartridges in a .45 caliber semi-automatic pistol. *AFTE Journal 37*(4), 368–373.

Vorburger, T., J.H. Yen, B. Bachrach,T.B. Renegar, J.J. Filliben, L. Ma, H.-G. Rhee, A. Zheng, J.-F. Song, M. Riley, C.D. Foreman, and S.M. Ballou (2007). *Surface Topography Analysis for a Feasibility Assessment of a National Ballistics Imaging Database.* (NISTIR 7362; revision December 26, 2006.) Report prepared for the Committee to Assess the Feasibility, Accuracy, and Technical Capability of a National Ballistics Database under National Institute of Justice Grant 2003-IJ-R-029 with the NIST Office of Law Enforcement Standards. Gaithersburg, MD: National Institute of Standards and Technology.

Wellford, C., and J. Cronin (1999, October). *An Analysis of Variables Affecting the Clearance of Homicides: A Multistate Study.* Washington, DC: Justice Research and Statistics Association.

Wellford, C., and J. Cronin (2000). Clearing up homicide clearance rates. *NIJ Journal* (April), 3–7.

Wilson, C., R.A. Hicklin, H. Korves, B. Ulery, M. Zoepfl, M. Bone, P. Grother, R. Micheals, S. Otto, and C. Watson (2004). *Fingerprint Vendor Technology Evaluation 2003: Summary of Results.* (IR 7123.) Gaithersburg, MD: National Institute of Standards and Technology.

Yamamura, K. (2005a, August 25). Bullet serial number proposal is tabled. *Sacramento Bee*, p. A5.

Yamamura, K. (2005b, May 1). Marking bullets would help cops, supporters say. *Sacramento Bee*, p. A3.

Yborra, L.F., and J.R. McClary (2004). Toolmarks on Remington 9mm luger caliber ammunition. *AFTE Journal 36*(4), 308–310.

Zeosky, G.F. (2005, December). Letter to staff of the Committee on the Feasibility, Accuracy, and Technical Capability of a National Ballistics Database.

Zographos, A., M. Robinson, J. Evans, and C.L. Smith (1997). Ballistics identification using line-scan imaging techniques. Pp. 82–87 in *Proceedings of the Institute of Electrical and Electronics Engineers 31st Annual 1997 International Carnahan Conference on Security Technology.*

Appendix A

Gun Enforcement and Ballistic Imaging Technology in Boston

Anthony A. Braga[*]

In March 1995 Boston was one of the first major cities to receive Integrated Ballistics Identification System (IBIS) ballistic imaging technology from the Bureau of Alcohol, Tobacco, Firearms, and Explosives (ATF). The system was considered fully implemented when the Boston Police Department (BPD) ballistics unit made its first IBIS match in July 1995 (Braga and Pierce, 2004). Prior to the adoption of IBIS, BPD ballistics operations usually consisted of manually matched bullets and cartridge casings recovered at a crime scene to determine whether the bullets or casings were fired from a suspect's firearm. Firearms examiners in the ballistics unit did not systematically compare bullets and casings from one scene to ballistics evidence recovered at other crime scenes to determine whether separate gun crimes were linked. When BPD firearms examiners did attempt to make such matches, known as making "cold hits," it happened in one of

---

[*]Program in Criminal Justice Policy and Management, John F. Kennedy School of Government, Harvard University. This research was supported by funds from a number of sources, including the National Research Council, the National Institute of Justice, Forensic Technology WAI, Inc., and the Bureau of Alcohol, Tobacco, Firearms, and Explosives (ATF). The author would like to thank the members of the committee for their helpful comments and suggestions on this work. Thanks are also due to Special Agent Terrence Austin (retired), former director of the ATF National Tracing Center; Marianne Hinkle, former Assistant U.S. Attorney, District of Massachusetts; Assistant District Attorney Raffi Yessarian of the Suffolk County (MA) District Attorney's Office; and Commissioner Kathleen O'Toole, Superintendent Paul Joyce, Deputy Superintendent Paul Fitzgerald, Deputy Superintendent William Casey, Sergeant James O'Shea, Sergeant Kathy Doherty, Sergeant Mark Vickers, Sergeant John Daley, Detective Earl Perkins, and Carl Walter of the Boston Police Department.

two ways: (1) the firearms examiner may have recognized some unique markings on a cartridge casing as very similar to markings on a cartridge casing recovered at another crime scene; (2) a detective would develop an investigative lead from a confidential informant that a recovered crime gun had been used previously in another gun crime and request the firearms examiner to make comparisons of evidence across the crime scenes (Braga and Pierce, 2004).

Since adopting the IBIS technology, it has become BPD policy to test fire all recovered crime guns, and the expended bullets and cartridge casings are imaged and entered into the IBIS database (Braga and Pierce, 2004). Importantly, the BPD makes an aggressive effort to collect, image, and enter ballistics evidence from all incidents involving firearms—ranging from homicides to illegal possession cases to suicides—into the IBIS database. Only noncrime guns that are held by the BPD for safekeeping are not imaged. The BPD refers to this process as comprehensive imaging of all crime-related ballistics evidence. In sharp contrast, in the pre-IBIS period, cartridges or bullets from different crimes scenes were cross-examined by firearms examiners only in extreme circumstances or when there was a suspicion two criminal events were connected. As of December 31, 2003, the BPD ballistics unit had entered some 2,400 bullets and 12,700 cartridge casings into its imaging database and had recorded 412 confirmed IBIS-related matches.[1]

THE USE OF IBIS MATCHES IN GUN VIOLENCE PREVENTION STRATEGIES

Confirmed IBIS matches are a key part of the BPD's gun violence reduction strategy, the Street Violence Suppression Project (SVSP).[2] Every 2 weeks, the Boston Police convene an interagency working group comprised of BPD officers and detectives, ATF agents, assistant U.S. attorneys, assistant Suffolk County district attorneys, Massachusetts State Police, Massachusetts probation officers, Department of Youth Services (juvenile corrections) case workers, and other criminal justice practitioners as

[1]The original study reported 396 matches made through the first week of December 2003 (Braga and Pierce, 2004). The BPD ballistics unit has been imaging ballistics evidence for other local police departments that share gun crime problems with Boston (Braga and Pierce, 2004). For example, there are strong street gang connections between Boston and the communities of Brockton (MA), New Bedford (MA), and Providence (RI) and gang-involved gun criminals tend to travel between the cities.

[2]The SVSP was the latest incarnation of the Boston Police Department's evolving strategic response to gun violence among serious offenders. Earlier versions of BPD strategic violence prevention initiatives include Operation Ceasefire (Kennedy et al., 1996; Braga et al., 2001), which was in place between 1996 and 2000, and the Unsolved Shootings and Impact Player Assessment Project, which was in place between 2001 and 2004 (Braga and Pierce, 2004). As of January 2007, the same process is now part of the BPD Compstat process.

needed. This meeting serves as a scanning and analysis forum for ongoing conflicts among violent gangs and other gun incidents with high potential for retaliation. After specific violence problems are identified, BPD officers and detectives are assigned responsibility for devising and implementing appropriate violence prevention plans to halt outbreaks of violence. Strategies are developed at a separate response development meeting; however, implemented plans and progress updates are presented at the bi-weekly meetings to disseminate knowledge on what works (and what doesn't) and to hold officers responsible for keeping targeted groups and individuals from shooting at each other.

At the SVSP scanning and analysis meetings, BPD crime analysts and intelligence officers present information on gun incidents over the previous 2 weeks. Recent IBIS matches are highlighted at the beginning of each meeting. Members of the working group discuss the circumstances associated with the linked incidents; information developed through interviews with arrested offenders, victims, and witnesses; available intelligence on current "beefs" between gangs or the activities of serious violent offenders in the linked areas and analyses of other physical evidence collected at the crime scenes, such as DNA and fingerprints. If guns are recovered and successfully traced by ATF, information on the first retail purchaser and licensed dealer are presented. In essence, an "information chain" is constructed around the events linked by ballistics evidence. The amount and types of information associated with linked gun crime events can vary tremendously across matches; see Figure A-1.

All matches provide investigators with the caliber, crime types, dates, times, and locations of shots fired from a particular gun or from a recovered gun that is subsequently test fired by BPD firearms examiners. However, other key information that may be critical to solving a particular violent crime may or may not be available to investigators, depending on the nature of the incidents linked by ballistics evidence. To understand what happened at a crime scene, investigators have to rely on information provided by witnesses, victims, and arrested offenders. Whether these individuals are present varies across crime scenes. When they are present, the information provided may or may not be very helpful to an investigator for a wide variety of reasons. Witnesses and victims may not know the identity of the assailant(s). Witnesses may not want to share information with law enforcement agents because they fear reprisals. Victims may be active criminals who prefer street justice for their assailant(s) to the slow justice of the legal system. To avoid self-incrimination, arrested offenders may not provide investigators with any useful information. The presence of other physical evidence, such as DNA and fingerprints, and law enforcement intelligence on violent criminals feuding in the affected areas will also vary across crime scenes.

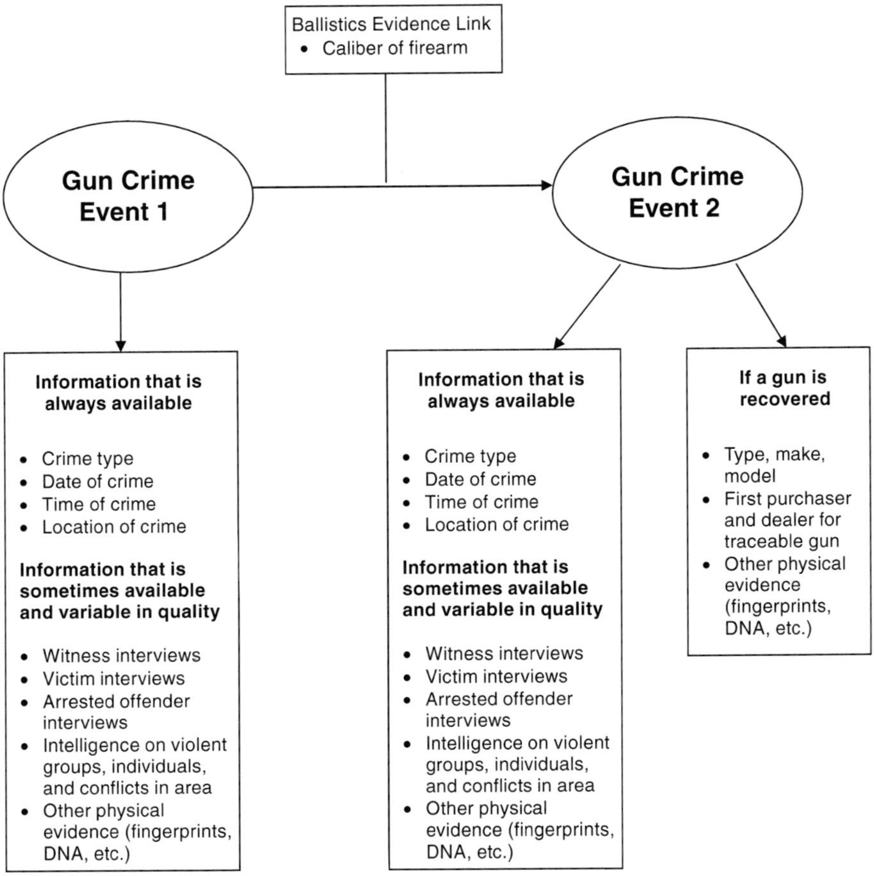

FIGURE A-1 Types of investigative information linked by IBIS-suggested matches.

While ballistic imaging makes an important investigative link between two gun crime events, the availability of key information that may be critical to resolving crimes depends on random situational characteristics of the linked events. An IBIS-suggested match that links cartridge casings from shots fired from two locations with no witnesses, victims, or suspects to interview and no other physical evidence left at the scenes has low immediate potential for making arrests. An IBIS-suggested match that links a gun assault with victims and witnesses willing to talk, to a gun possession case, in which a gun is recovered and an offender is arrested, is much more likely to generate an arrest for the first gun crime. However, while more evidence is available to investigators, arrests and successful prosecutions are not guaranteed. Leads from ballistic imaging link guns—not individuals—to crime scenes. In linked guns, a different person could have committed the first crime. For example, the first actual shooter may have subsequently sold the gun to an unidentifiable street drug dealer who then sold it to the illegal possessor apprehended in the second crime.

The resulting information chains that are constructed around gun events have value to law enforcement officials in two ways: (1) holding offenders accountable for their crimes and (2) guiding violence prevention efforts on risky groups and individuals. Obviously, law enforcement agents want to arrest violent gun offenders; making links across events can generate important leads that may result in the apprehension and prosecution of gun criminals. However, IBIS-suggested matches also provide important opportunities for Boston law enforcement agencies to better understand and respond to street violence. The links help guide violence prevention efforts by establishing patterns of violence in particular areas and among specific individuals.

Even matches that have little immediate potential for generating an arrest can have strategic value in understanding and responding to violent crime problems. For example, a match between two "shots fired" incidents with no victims, arrested offenders, and witnesses can be coupled with intelligence on active conflicts among groups in the places linked by shell casings fired by the same gun. The link serves as an early warning sign that repeat shots are being fired in a particular gang turf area. Based on this pattern, the interagency working group focuses resources on gathering additional intelligence on conflicts in the area and immediately increases their presence in the area to prevent additional violence.

ASSESSING THE VALUE ADDED TO BOSTON GUN LAW ENFORCEMENT OPERATIONS BY BALLISTIC IMAGING TECHNOLOGY

Assessment of Changes in the Productivity of the BPD Ballistics Unit

To measure the effect of ballistic imaging technology on the productivity of the BPD ballistics unit, it is important to consider the nature of the technological innovation and its potential impact on BPD operations. IBIS is able to cross-examine large volumes of evidence and suggests a small number of candidate cases that may match the evidence in question. The firearms examiner then carefully looks at the candidate cases using standard procedures to determine whether a match actually exists. The nature of a confirmed match and its utility to a criminal investigation does not change as a result of the IBIS technology (Braga and Pierce, 2004). As mentioned above, forensic evidence, such as ballistics matches, is one part of an information chain (such as eyewitness testimony, circumstantial evidence, etc.)

that leads to the ultimate arrest and prosecution of gun criminals. Arrest and prosecution is influenced by many factors beyond the forensic link of a particular gun to ballistics evidence collected at separate crime scenes. Since the value of a ballistics match to the resolution of a crime is not meaningfully different before and after the adoption of the IBIS technology, the outcome of interest is the number of matches made by the ballistics unit, not the ultimate disposition of the resulting cases. As such, Braga and Pierce (2004) examined whether IBIS changed the ability of the BPD ballistics unit to link gun crimes.

To determine whether the adoption of the ballistic imaging technology was associated with a change in productivity, the annual and monthly number of cold hits made by the BPD ballistics unit was computed for the 14-year time period between 1990 and 2003.[3] Figure A-2 presents the yearly number of cold hit ballistics matches made by the BPD ballistics unit during the study period. During the pre-IBIS period of 1990–1994, the ballistics unit made an average of 8.8 cold hits per year. After the adoption of IBIS, the productivity of the BPD ballistics unit rose dramatically to 60 cold hits in 1995 as the unit immediately entered a large backlog of ballistics evidence into the system. The yearly number of hits decreased during the 1996–1998 period; then, as the inventory of casings in the system grew, it increased again between 1999 and 2003. The ballistics unit moved to new BPD headquarters in 1998; the move limited the use of the IBIS equipment for about 2 months and was associated with the low number of matches (25) in 1998. Nonetheless, the BPD ballistics unit averaged 45.7 cold hits per year between 1995 and 2003.

The Braga and Pierce (2004) analysis of the impact on the monthly number of cold hits made by the BPD ballistics unit associated with the adoption of the IBIS technology followed a basic one-group interrupted time-series design. Of course, it would have been ideal to have a control group that did not receive the IBIS technology to make comparisons. However, given the ATF's National Integrated Ballistic Information Network (NIBIN) program, there is no major city comparable to Boston that has a ballistics unit without ballistic imaging technology. In addition, among major cities, Boston showed some of the most dramatic declines in firearms crime (Braga et al., 2001); see Figure A-3.[4] Consequently, it was also difficult to find an appropriate control city or group. In absence of a separate control group, the key to a compelling one-group interrupted time-series

[3]The findings reported here simply add an additional year of data to the original Braga and Pierce (2004) study that examined ballistics matches between 1990 and 2002.

[4]The adoption of IBIS was not associated with the drop in gun violence in Boston. Rather, a focused deterrence strategy designed to keep gangs from continuing their cycles of ongoing violence was found to be associated with the significant decrease in Boston youth gun violence (Braga et al., 2001).

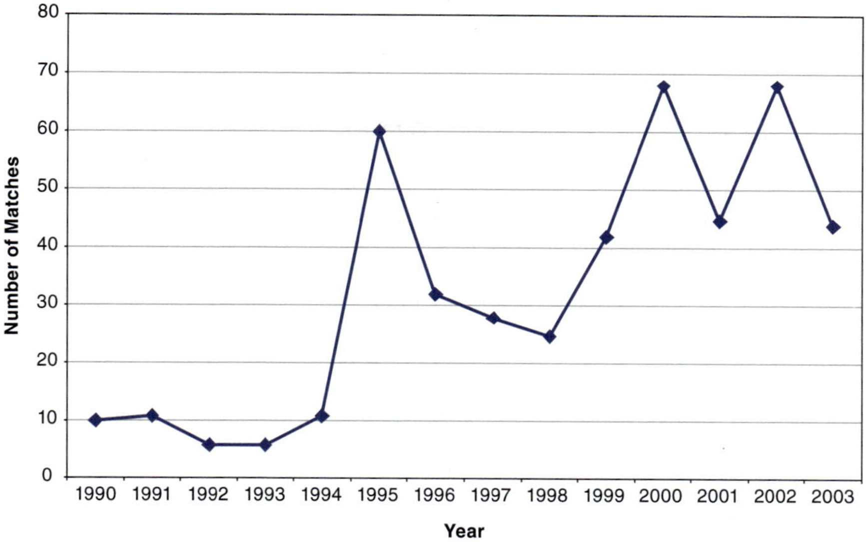

FIGURE A-2 Boston Police Department ballistics matches, 1990–2003.

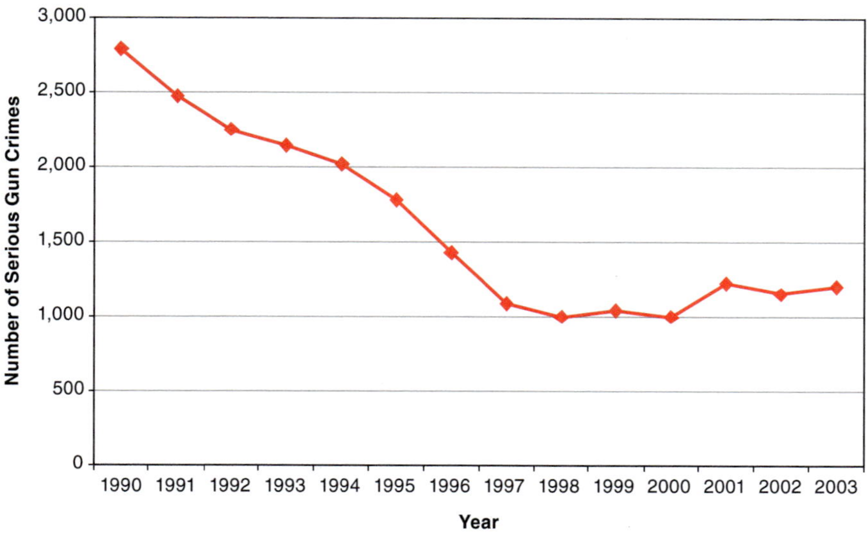

FIGURE A-3 Serious gun crime incidents in Boston, 1990–2003.
NOTE: Serious gun crime incidents are defined as gun-related homicides, aggravated assaults, and robberies.

design is the degree to which other forces not related to the intervention influence the outcome variable. If at the time the IBIS technology was introduced in Boston the staff of the ballistics unit also changed, this could pose a problem of a change in "instrumentation" (Campbell and Stanley, 1966; Cook and Campbell, 1979). However, this was not the case in Boston. As Table A-1 shows, the ballistics unit staffing level of BPD firearms examiners remained the same before and after the IBIS technology was adopted; see the period from 1993 to 1997. For the entire 10-year period, the unit had, on average, 6 firearms examiners and 10 total personnel on staff. There was a slight decrease in the number of firearms examiners and a corresponding increase in support staff, but the only substantive change in the dynamics of the ballistics unit was the addition of the IBIS technology (Braga and Pierce, 2004).

For an empirical analysis of trends in BPD ballistics matches, July 1995, the month of the first IBIS cold hit match, was selected as the date the IBIS technology was fully implemented (Braga and Pierce, 2004). The pre-IBIS time series was comprised of the monthly counts between January 1990 and June 1995; the post-IBIS time series was comprised of monthly counts between July 1995 and December 2003. A binary dummy variable indicating whether the IBIS technology was present or not was constructed to estimate the effects of the intervention on the monthly counts of cold hits. Negative binomial regression models, controlling for the monthly count of gun crimes, seasonal variations as measured by monthly dummy variables, and simple linear and nonlinear trends, revealed that the adoption

TABLE A-1 Staffing Levels of the Boston Police Department Ballistics Unit, 1993–2003

Year	Supervisors	Firearms Examiners	Support Staff	Total
1993	1	7	1	9
1994	1	7	1	9
1995	1	7	1	9
1996	2	7	1	10
1997	2	6	2	10
1998	2	5	3	10
1999	2	6	3	11
2000	2	5	3	10
2001	2	5	3	10
2002	1	4	4	9
2003	1	5	5	11

of IBIS was associated with a statistically significant six-fold increase in the monthly number of hits generated by the BPD ballistics unit.[5]

Some observers suggest that ability of IBIS technology to make links across crime scenes can be easily undermined by criminal offenders. These critics suggest that ballistic imaging technology is limited because determined criminals can alter markings on or replace barrels, slides, extractors, and firing pins. These modifications would alter the telltale markings on ballistics evidence and prevent matches from being made (see, e.g., Kopel and Burnett, 2003). Unfortunately, data are not available to determine whether criminals are modifying their firearms to avoid detection. However, if criminals are seeking to avoid detection, they can simply switch from semiautomatic pistols to revolvers because the latter are less likely to leave cartridge casings at a scene when fired. The available evidence suggests that Boston gun criminals are not switching guns to avoid detection: As Figure A-4 shows, there was no substantive change in the proportions of semiautomatic pistols and revolvers in handguns recovered by the Boston Police after the adoption of IBIS in 1995.

Extended Analyses of Boston IBIS Matches

The Boston Police Department's Unsolved Shootings Project and Impact Player Assessment meetings held between October 2001 and July 2004 generated detailed data on gun crime incidents and gun criminals involved in IBIS matches. A total of 104 sets of ballistics matches involving 244 distinct gun crimes were made over the course of this initiative.[6] The number of incidents in each set of matches ranged from 2 gun crimes to 6 gun crimes with a mean of 2.3 gun crimes per set. The amount of time between the first incident and the last incident in a set of ballistics matches ranged from a few hours to 34 months, with a mean of 6 months. Five calibers, all of which are commonly used in semiautomatic pistols, accounted for 93 percent of the crime guns used in these 104 sets of IBIS matches. The five most frequently matched calibers were 9mm (39 percent), .38 (21 percent), .40 (12 percent), .45 (11 percent), and .25 (10 percent). The 244 gun crime incidents included in the 104 sets of matches mostly involved gun assaults

---

[5]In this updated analysis, the findings are essentially unchanged from the original (see Braga and Pierce, 2004) study. The key coefficients in the updated negative binomial regression model were IRR = 6.0988, Robust SE = 2.4723, $Z = 4.46$, $P>|Z| = 0.000$, and log likelihood = –314.0913.

[6]The term "set of matches" is used to distinguish the matches discussed here from those discussed above: A set of matches involves all hits (or matches) generated by the same gun across multiple crime scenes; a match, as used above, simply is a hit based on new evidence entered into IBIS.

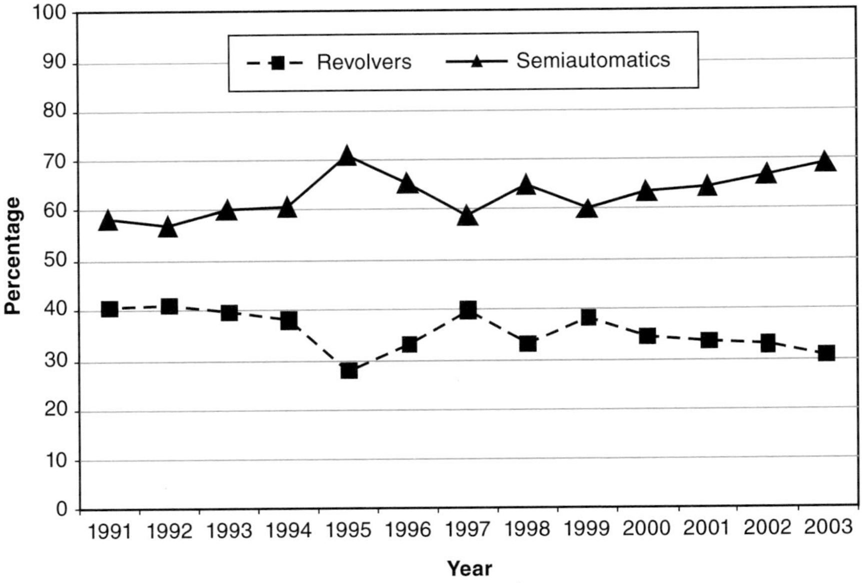

FIGURE A-4 Recovered handguns in Boston, 1991–2003.

(43 percent), shots fired (30 percent), and illegal gun possession (13.5 percent) cases; see Table A-2.

An arrest was associated with 51 percent of the match sets (53 of 104) resulting in 87 individuals arrested. An analysis of the timing of the arrests suggests a complex investigative process. In 52.8 percent of the match sets, the arrest and the last incident coincided. In these cases, the arrest of the gun offender(s) seemed to end the chain of violent events that was associated with a particular crime gun. In 32.1 percent of the match sets, an arrest was made after the last incident. This time lag suggests that additional investigative work led to the identification and eventual apprehension of the gun criminal(s) involved in a string of incidents using the same gun. At least one additional gun crime was committed with the same gun after an offender was arrested in 15.1 percent of the sets of matches. This situation suggests that, although an offender was apprehended, the crime gun was still on the street and being used in subsequent crimes.

As described above, IBIS matches do not change the inherent value of ballistics evidence in an investigation because many other factors help determine whether an arrest is eventually made. An IBIS match does not guarantee an immediate arrest. For instance, the linked incidents may not involve victims or witnesses that can or are willing to make a positive iden-

TABLE A-2 Crime Types in 104 Sets of Boston IBIS-Suggested Matches

Crime Type	Number	Percent
Gun assault	104	42.6
Shots fired	72	29.5
Illegal gun possession	33	13.5
Gun homicide	17	7.0
Warrant (search/arrest)	13	7.0
Found gun	4	1.6
Gun robbery	1	0.4

tification. Rather, matches better position law enforcement agents to identify gun criminals through strategic analyses of information and intelligence sharing. The Boston Police and their criminal justice partners use the IBIS information as a tool to shed light on the dynamics at play in violent street social networks and further their ability to apprehend violent gun criminals. IBIS provides Boston investigators with more opportunities to make links among individuals and locations through a particular gun.

The IBIS matches were associated with the arrest of very serious gun offenders that were well known to the criminal justice system. Of the 87 arrested gun offenders associated with the IBIS matches, 93 percent were male, and they ranged in age from 13 to 51 years, with a mean of 22 years of age. When the names and birth dates of these arrest individuals were run through Massachusetts state criminal history systems, 92 percent had been arraigned at least once in Massachusetts courts prior to their current arrest. Of these known offenders, 59 percent were previously convicted felons and, after their personal information was run through the BPD intelligence database system, 42 percent were known gang members. Of the known offenders, they had a mean of 10 prior arraignments for a wide variety of criminal offenses: 63 percent had at least one prior armed violent crime arraignment, 51 percent had at least one prior unarmed violent arraignment, 36 percent had at least one prior nonviolent gun crime arraignment, 60 percent had at least one prior drug crime arraignment, 75 percent had at least one prior property crime arraignment, and 75 percent had at least one prior disorder crime arraignment. These gun offenders were also extensively involved with the criminal justice system before their immediate arrest. Of the previously known offenders, 48 percent were on active probation when they were arrested, 83 percent were on probation prior to their arrest, 64 percent had been committed to a secure adult or juvenile correctional facility prior to their arrest, and 15 percent had been subjected to a restraining order before their arrest.

High conviction rates for fully adjudicated gun offenders were also associated with the IBIS matches. It is important to note again that IBIS matches do not guarantee or necessarily generate a conviction. Rather, in Boston, IBIS data are one part of an aggressive investigative process that is highly focused on sharing information and analyzing data to apprehend violent gun offenders. As such, the higher conviction rates should be credited to the overall law enforcement initiative rather than simply being credited to IBIS matches. In November 2004, 58.6 percent of the arrested offenders were fully adjudicated, 34.5 percent were still engaged in the trial process, and 6.9 percent were not charged for their crimes. Of the fully adjudicated offenders, 76.5 percent were convicted of their current gun crime. These convicted offenders were usually sentenced to incarceration (87.2 percent), with sentences ranging from 6 to 120 months (mean, 32 months; median, 18 months; mode, 12 months).

The arrested offenders associated with the IBIS matches were more serious offenders than 514 adults arrested for homicide, gun assault, gun robbery, and illegal gun possession in Boston in 1995.[7] Of these offenders, 76 percent had been arraigned in Massachusetts courts at least once before their current gun crime arrest; 37 percent of these known offenders had prior felony convictions. The IBIS offenders were also more likely to be convicted of their gun crimes than the 1995 cohort of Boston gun offenders who had a 37 percent conviction rate for past armed violent felonies and gun possession offenses.

The Use of IBIS Matches in Gun Enforcement Operations

To further document the use of IBIS matches in Boston's interagency gun violence prevention efforts, available official data associated with 44 IBIS matches made by the BPD ballistics unit in 2003 (incident reports, arrest reports, intelligence reports, ATF trace data) were collected and analyzed. These data were presented to the Boston Police investigators and Suffolk County assistant district attorneys who participated in the interagency working group meetings during 2003. The use of the 44 matches in their gun violence prevention activities was discussed in a series of interviews and focus group sessions.

The 44 matches linked 108 incidents (mean of 2.5 incidents per match, range 2–8 incidents). Collectively, 59 victims and 28 arrested individuals were involved in the 108 incidents. The presence of offenders, victims, and witnesses to interview about the gun crime varied across the events:

[7]These data were collected as part of an unpublished study of gun offender criminal histories in Boston and other cities and are available on request from Anthony Braga (see also Braga, 2003).

75 percent of the matches (33) had victims associated with at least one of the linked incidents; 59.1 percent of the matches (26) had arrested offenders associated with at least one of the linked incidents; 18.2 percent of the matches (8) did not have witnesses for any of the linked crime scenes. Crime scenes that did not have any witnesses were linked to crime scenes that did have witnesses in 47.7 percent of the matches (21). In 34.1 percent of the matches (15), witnesses were available at all linked crime scenes. Guns were recovered in 25 of the 44 matches (58.8 percent): 13 of the 25 guns (52.0 percent) were traced by ATF to the first retail purchaser; 11 (25 percent) matches involved a link to a homicide incident (one linked two homicides).

The investigators and prosecutors strongly believe that all IBIS matches added general investigative and intelligence value to their operations. However, not all matches linked information that resulted in significant additional investigative activity. Matches involving homicide incidents were more likely to generate significant investigative leads when separated from the pool of 44 matches. Homicides are more vigorously investigated than shots fired and gun assaults incidents and, generally, have more evidence that can be linked to other events (such as a victim with a known criminal history). IBIS matches did not generate any direct enforcement actions in 61.4 percent of the 44 matches and 27.3 percent of the 11 homicide matches; see Table A-3. Offenders were charged with the current offense only and not charged with a linked prior gun crime in 34.1 percent of the 44 matches. In the two matches linking homicides, the offenders were

TABLE A-3 Results of Information Linked by IBIS-Suggested Matches on Investigations by Boston Law Enforcement Agencies, 2003

Direct Enforcement Actions	All Matches (N = 44)	Homicide Matches (N = 11)
No direct enforcement action; IBIS-suggested match only had general investigative and intelligence value	27	3
Arrest based on current offense, no potential for additional charges in linked crimes	15	2
No arrests and no potential for immediate charges based on linked information	12	1
Significant investigative lead generated by IBIS match	17	8
Arrest made or arrest warrant issued as a result of linked information	8	4
Suspects identified; however, charges not filed because linked evidence was not strong enough	8	3
Case resolved as homicide victim had gun used in prior homicide	1	1

interviewed about a prior linked gun crime, but only charged in the subsequent homicide incident. Of the matches, 27.3 percent did not have arrests for current offenses or any immediate potential for charges based on linked information. In the one homicide match included in this category, the unsolved homicide was linked to a shots fired incident with no arrests, victims, or witnesses to interview.

IBIS matches generated significant investigative leads in 38.6 percent of the 44 matches and 72.7 percent of the 11 homicide matches. The linked information resulted in an arrest or an arrest warrant in 18.2 percent of the 44 matches and 36.4 percent of the 11 homicide matches. Unfortunately, linked information across crime scenes can be highly suggestive of the identity of a violent gun offender but not sufficient enough to support formal charges. In 18.2 percent of the 44 matches and 27.3 percent of the homicide incidents, likely suspects were identified and interviewed but not charged because the information chain connecting the events was not strong enough to justify an arrest. In one case, a homicide investigation was resolved but an arrest was not made because the ballistics link was made from a test fire of the gun recovered from a homicide victim who was a suspect in a prior homicide incident.

While all matches were regarded as valuable by the interviewed law enforcement agents, the matches that led to an arrest clearly added the most value to gun violence prevention strategies. The 2003 investigation and arrest of a homicide suspect—for anonymity, referred to as *A*—provides a good example of the usefulness of links between crime scenes made by IBIS matches. The Boston Police were conducting a surveillance of a known crack-cocaine drug market location in the city. The police witnessed an apparent drug transaction and, after interviewing the suspected customer, they attempted to interview *A* and *B*, the suspected sellers. *A* immediately fled and fired at least one shot at the pursuing officers. After a standoff, *A* surrendered and was arrested on assault, firearm, and drug charges; a Glock semiautomatic pistol was recovered. During booking, Boston Police officers recovered receipts from *A* documenting the purchase of the Glock pistol by another person from an out-of-state federal firearms licensee. The Glock was test fired, and the resulting cartridge casing was entered into IBIS. After the automated correlation and a microscopic comparison by a firearms examiner, the casing was matched to a cartridge casing recovered at the scene of a homicide in 2002. Witnesses were present at the time of the homicide but were not able to provide a detailed description of the assailant. Further investigation revealed an ongoing personal feud between *A* and the homicide victim. As a direct result of the IBIS match, *A* was charged with murder; *A* was subsequently convicted and is serving a life sentence for murder in the first degree.

Estimating the Costs and Benefits of IBIS

Braga and Pierce (2004) estimated the cost-effectiveness of the IBIS technology in making ballistics matches in two ways: the cost of making a match and the cost of comparing a piece of ballistics evidence to the existing inventory of evidence. In 1995, the IBIS equipment used by the BPD was purchased by ATF at a cost of $540,000. Reflecting general trends in decreasing technology costs, the same equipment cost $295,000 in December 2003. As of December 31, 2003, the BPD ballistics unit had made a total of 404 cold hit matches involving cartridge casings using the IBIS technology. Using 2003 prices, the equipment costs amount to $730.20 per cartridge casing match.[8]

There are two reasons to believe that this cost estimate will continue to decrease markedly as time progresses: (1) as more evidence is entered into IBIS, the probability of making a hit will increase and the absolute number of hits will continue to increase; (2) as with the costs of other computer-related technologies, the cost of the IBIS technology will also decline over time. As Table A-1 (above) documents, the addition of the IBIS equipment did not result in new hires by the BPD to staff the ballistics unit. Except for some time invested in training staff to properly operate the IBIS equipment, the direct annual cost to the BPD is zero. The ATF costs can be amortized on an annual basis over the course of the lifetime of the equipment.

Importantly, IBIS can routinely scan vast inventories of ballistics evidence in a manner that was for most practical purposes impossible prior to the availability of this technology. IBIS technology allows each newly entered piece of ballistics evidence to be compared against existing inventories that can easily reach thousands in a matter of minutes. Before IBIS, making cold hits was an ad hoc process that was limited by the ability of firearms examiners to compare selected cartridge casings to the larger inventory of crime scene casings in the property of the ballistics unit. For example, in September 1993, Detective John Mulligan was shot, execution style, five times in the head with a .25 caliber firearm as he sat in his car while working as a private security detail at a Walgreens pharmacy in the Roslindale neighborhood of Boston (Braga and Pierce, 2004). In an attempt to develop more information on the case, the BPD selected 50 .25 cartridge casings from recent violent crimes in the surrounding neighborhood. Five

[8]This represents an update over Braga and Pierce (2004), who reported a cost of $744 per match based on 396 matches made through early December 2003. However, either estimate is far lower than the cost estimates of $12,000 per cartridge case hit suggested by Kopel and Burnett (2003). The difference in estimates is the result of comparing IBIS in one jurisdiction (Boston) that has been operating comprehensively for a number of years to an aggregate of 222 systems across the United States, some of which received the technology only a few months before the Kopel and Burnett report and were not yet fully operational.

firearms examiners spent 10 8-hour days comparing the selected casings to the recovered crime scene evidence (Braga and Pierce, 2004). Unfortunately, this intensive effort did not result in a match.[9]

Braga and Pierce (2004) used this anecdote as an opportunity to estimate the cost of comparing one cartridge casing to the BPD's inventory of cartridge casings. In December 2003, the average BPD firearms examiner earned $50,000 per year. As such, the BPD would pay one firearms examiner $2,083.33 to work 10 days. Five firearms examiners would cost $10,416.67 for the same time period. As the story describes, the five examiners compared 50 casings to one piece of evidence during this time period. Therefore, it cost the BPD $208.33 to compare two cartridge casings. Assuming the BPD had unlimited resources and firearms examiners, it would cost more than $2.6 million to compare one cartridge casing to every one of the more than 12,700 cartridge casings in the BPD's inventory as of December 2003. Braga and Pierce (2004) observe that these figures were not meant to be precise estimates; rather, they simply illustrate that the cost of human examiners routinely scanning existing ballistics evidence inventories for likely matches is prohibitive, and even this assumes that human resources are available to make such comparisons. In contrast, the cost of routinely scanning existing ballistics evidence inventories to find potential matches, using IBIS equipment is modest.

It is important to note, however, that these cost-effectiveness estimates were calculated on basis of the performance of IBIS in matching cartridge casings. IBIS technology is not as cost-effective in making ballistics matches with recovered bullet evidence. Between 1995 and 2003, the Boston Police only made eight cold hit bullet matches. Using 2003 prices, the equipment costs amounts to $36,875 per bullet match.[10]

The benefits of IBIS to gun enforcement operations can also be assessed by estimating the number of arrests resulting from IBIS matches to the number of arrests that would have been made from traditional methods of making cold hits if the IBIS technology had not been available. In 2003, 18.2 percent of IBIS matches resulted in an arrest or the issuance of an arrest warrant for a linked gun crime. Since IBIS was adopted in 1995, 412 matches were made by the end of 2003. Using 2003 figures as a reasonable basis to estimate the role of IBIS in making arrests, 75 (18.2 percent of 412) matches would have generated an arrest. If IBIS had not been available, traditional ballistics methods would have yielded about 81 total matches between 1995 and 2003 (8.8 per year multiplied by 9 years) and about

[9]The two suspected killers were arrested after the .25 handgun was found in a vacant lot some 100 yards from the home of one of the suspects in the Dorchester section of Boston.

[10]This figure is still much lower than the $195,000 per bullet hit estimate suggested by Kopel and Burnett (2003).

15 would have yielded arrests for linked gun crimes (18.2 percent of 81). Therefore, IBIS can be associated with making arrests in an additional 60 linked gun crimes—4.4 times as many arrests for linked gun crimes—when compared with the performance of traditional ballistics methods.

CONCLUSION

The capabilities and cost advantages provided by IBIS technology can significantly increase the use of ballistics evidence by law enforcement. Ballistics matches made by IBIS are an important part of Boston's interagency efforts to prevent gun violence. According to Boston law enforcement agencies, all matches have strategic value in understanding ongoing violent conflicts among gangs and criminally active groups that are major parts of the city's violence problem. The IBIS matches, and the information chains that result from the linked gun crimes, are used to mount investigations of suspected violent gun criminals and to develop and implement violence reduction strategies to prevent additional gun crimes from happening. The BPD further asserts that the ability of IBIS to make quick comparisons to a large inventory of ballistics evidence has yielded a number of high-profile investigations that would not otherwise have been possible. For example, in 2000, a 9mm handgun was matched to 15 other gun crimes in Boston, Brockton (MA), Randolph (MA), and Providence (RI) (NIBIN Program, 2001). Boston IBIS matches, coupled with an interagency focus on apprehending and prosecuting violent criminals by all available law enforcement means, were also associated with the arrest of very serious gun offenders and high conviction rates for their immediate gun offenses.

The results of this research study suggest that the IBIS technology significantly increased the productivity of the BPD ballistics unit in linking guns crimes. The analysis found that the adoption of the IBIS technology was associated with a more than six-fold increase in the number of cold hit matches per month. Clearly, the IBIS technology significantly increases the ability of law enforcement agencies to make ballistics matches across crime scenes. The cost-effectiveness estimates and qualitative evidence also suggests that the IBIS technology allows law enforcement agencies to make hits that would have otherwise not been possible. Before IBIS was adopted by the BPD, ballistics matching across gun crime scenes was an ad hoc and tedious process. Now, the BPD can systematically compare recovered gun crime evidence to its entire inventory of evidence with little effort. The unfortunate 1993 Boston police officer execution-style slaying and the well-known 2000 investigation involving one firearm used in 15 separate incidents provide stark contrasts in the ability of the BPD to link the use of firearms across gun crime scenes.

The experience of the BPD indicates that the use of IBIS technology should be accompanied by a department-wide commitment to comprehensively image all ballistics evidence collected by a law enforcement agency. Without such a commitment, one of the major advantages of IBIS, the ability to routinely scan large inventories of evidence for potential links, is obviously reduced. Using the Boston experience as a model, the U.S. Attorney's Office in the District of Massachusetts has collaborated with the Massachusetts State Police to set up a process for collecting and analyzing ballistics evidence to aid gun law enforcement operations in 11 target cities for the U.S. Department of Justice Project Safe Neighborhood initiative. The Massachusetts U.S. Attorney's Office provides the state police with $35,000 per year to support the overtime that is necessary to ensure timely ballistic imaging at the state crime laboratory. The steps of this process are as follows:

- Local evidence collection: Participating police agencies must collect all evidence at gun crime scenes, which includes the collection of crime gun evidence at shots fired scenes where no injuries or fatalities are reported.
- Transfer to evidence officer: Once the crime scene ballistics evidence is collected, it must be immediately transferred to the department's evidence officer.
- Transfer to Massachusetts State Police: The evidence officer must immediately submit the ballistics evidence to the state police crime laboratory.
- Timely ballistics examination: The state police must immediately image the crime scene evidence and determine whether a match exists within its inventory of ballistic image evidence.
- Report to investigators: The results of ballistics examination are to be communicated by state police firearms examiners to investigators from the submitting agency as soon as available.
- Report to gang unit: The results of the ballistics examination are to be shared with relevant units within the police department, such as the gang unit, to see if additional information can be developed on the locations, individuals, and crime gun involved in the match.
- Report to prosecutors: The information must be shared with federal and local prosecutors to coordinate priority prosecutions.
- Regional or statewide analysis: Because violent criminals sometimes cross jurisdictional boundaries, ballistics evidence is to be analyzed at larger levels of aggregation beyond the city where the immediate offense occurred.

In contrast to state-level systems that image guns not involved in crime (for a critique, see Kopel and Burnett, 2003), ballistic imaging systems that are built on comprehensive imaging of all recovered gun crime evidence and supplemented by strategic data analyses and intelligence gathering seem to show great promise in apprehending violent gun criminals. The Boston experience with ballistic imaging technology suggest that ATF's NIBIN program, with appropriate support, can ensure that participating jurisdictions are well trained in the practices of comprehensive ballistic imaging.

Appendix B

Biographical Sketches of Committee Members and Staff

John E. Rolph *(Chair)* is professor of statistics at the Marshall School of Business of the University of Southern California, where he also holds appointments in the mathematics department and the law school. Previously, he spent 24 years as a statistician at the RAND Corporation, 12 of them as head of the statistical research and consulting group. His areas of expertise include statistics and public policy and empirical Bayes estimation. He served as a member of the National Research Council's (NRC) Committee on National Statistics (CNSTAT) and as chair of the committee from 1998 to 2004; he has also served on the NRC Committee on Law and Justice. He has served on several NRC panels, on topics including statistical and operational test design in defense systems, methods for assessing discrimination, and decennial census methodology. He is an elected member of the International Statistical Institute, a fellow of the American Statistical Association, a fellow of the Institute of Mathematical Statistics, and a lifetime national associate of the National Academies. He is a past editor of *CHANCE* magazine and has served in many other editorial capacities. He has a Ph.D. in statistics from the University of California, Berkeley.

Eugene S. Meieran *(Vice-Chair)* is a fellow at the Intel Corporation, currently working on knowledge management and collaboration applications to help improve manufacturing performance and help individuals and teams make better, faster, and more cost-effective decisions. A member of the National Academy of Engineering, he has taught technical courses at Stanford University and the University of California, Berkeley, and has given seminars and invited talks at many universities throughout the world.

He has published extensively in the fields of statistical process control, materials analysis and characterization technology, process and product reliability, and advanced technology applications for manufacturing. He has received three awards for best paper at international conferences based on his work in semiconductor device reliability, with particular emphasis on the phenomena of electromigration in thin films, soft error upsets in dynamic random-access memory devices, and material analysis technology. He has served on several government and industry panels dealing with manufacturing technology and policy issues, such as the Coalition for Intelligent Manufacturing Systems and the Next Generation Manufacturing Systems Advanced Manufacturing Systems Board, and the NRC Board of Assessment for the National Institute of Standards and Technology. He received his B.S. degree from Purdue University and his M.S. and Sc.D. degrees from the Massachusetts Institute of Technology in materials science.

Alfred Blumstein is J. Erik Jonsson professor of urban systems and operations research and former dean of the H. John Heinz III School of Public Policy and Management, Carnegie Mellon University. He is the director of the National Consortium on Violence Research, supported by a grant from the National Science Foundation. He has had extensive experience in both research and policy with the criminal justice system, serving on the President's Commission on Law Enforcement and Administration of Justice in 1966–1967 as director of its Task Force on Science and Technology. At the NRC he was a member of the Committee on Research on Law Enforcement and the Administration of Justice (now the Committee on Law and Justice) from its founding in 1976 until 1986, and is currently a member of the committee. He has also served on the Commission (now Division) of Behavioral and Social Sciences and Education. A member of the National Academy of Engineering, he holds a bachelor's degree in engineering and a Ph.D. in operations research from Cornell University.

Alicia Carriquiry is professor of statistics at Iowa State University, where she has also served as associate provost of the university. Her research has included applications in forensic statistics, including assessment of the elemental composition of bullet lead. She has spoken at the International Conference on Forensic Statistics and provided expert guidance and analysis to the NRC Committee on Scientific Assessment of Bullet Lead Elemental Composition Comparison. She specializes in linear models, Bayesian statistics, and general methods. Her recent research focuses on nutrition and dietary assessment. She is on the editorial board of *Bayesian Statistics* and an editor for *Statistical Science*. She is a fellow of the American Statistical Association and is an elected member of the International Statistical Institute. She received a Ph.D. in statistics and animal science from Iowa State University

Scott Chumbley is professor of materials science and engineering at Iowa State University, where he holds a joint appointment with Ames Laboratory, the Department of Energy laboratory at the university. His undergraduate and graduate degrees are in metallurgy and his field of expertise is materials characterization using optical and electron microscopy and x-ray diffraction. He has been the principal investigator on an FBI-funded proposal to study the effects of blast damage on the grain structure of iron and aluminum alloys and is currently working on a project funded by the Department of Justice to quantify and statistically analyze tool markings using three-dimensional profilometry. He is an active participant in the Midwest Forensic Research Center (MFRC), an educational and research center of Iowa State University whose goal is to provide resources and training assistance to law enforcement agencies in the Midwest. He holds a Ph.D. in metallurgical engineering from the University of Illinois.

Philip J. Cook is ITT/Terry Sanford professor of public policy studies and professor of economics and sociology at Duke University, where he is a former director of the Sanford Institute of Public Policy. His research covers a broad range of policy analysis, focusing on the regulation of unhealthy and unsafe behavior, including lotteries; sources of socioeconomic inequality, including the disparity in salaries between the elites in certain professions and the rest of the population; the administration of criminal justice, including the costs of the death penalty; and the prevention of alcohol-related problems through restrictions on alcohol availability. A member of the Institute of Medicine, he has written extensively on research on guns and violence, including studies on the costs and consequences of increased gun availability and the use of firearms tracing data in studying gun markets. He has a Ph.D. in economics from the University of California, Berkeley.

Daniel L. Cork is a senior program officer for the Committee on National Statistics, currently serving as study director of the Panel to Review the Programs of the Bureau of Justice Statistics and as co-study director for the Panel on the Design of the 2010 Census Program of Evaluations and Experiments (CPEX). He previously served as study director of the Panel on Residence Rules in the Decennial Census, co-study director of the Panel on Research on Future Census Methods, and program officer for the Panel to Review the 2000 Census. His research interests include quantitative criminology, particularly space-time dynamics in homicide; Bayesian statistics; and statistics in sports. He holds a B.S. degree in statistics from George Washington University and an M.S. in statistics and a joint Ph.D. in statistics and public policy from Carnegie Mellon University.

Marc De Graef is professor of materials science and engineering at Carnegie Mellon University. He has carried out extensive research using conventional and advanced techniques, including a fundamental study of the use of energy-filtered transmission electron microscopy. He is currently studying magnetostrictive materials using state-of-the-art chemical probes and magnetic domain analysis. He has also written textbooks on conventional transmission electron microscopy for imaging and on crystallography, symmetry and diffraction for image analysis. He won the Carnegie Mellon George T. Ladd Research Award in 1996. He has authored or co-authored over 100 publications in the open literature and is an active member of the Minerals, Metals, and Materials Society (TMS) and the Mineralogical Society of America. Dr. De Graef received his M.S. in physics from the University of Antwerp and a Ph.D. in physics from the Catholic University of Leuven, both in Belgium.

David L. Donoho is professor of statistics and Anne T. and Robert M. Bass professor of humanities and science at Stanford University. Winner of a MacArthur Fellowship, his ground-breaking research in data analysis and reconstruction is widely used and cited. This work finds application in a number of different areas ranging from medical imaging to seismology and astronomy. His earliest work deals with the problem of "blind signal processing," recovering a signal that has been blurred in an unknown fashion, a topic of interest today in cellular phone communication. More recently, he has considered approaches for the rigorous use of facial and retinal recognition scans for use in airline and other security applications. A large body of his recent research concerns the theoretical properties of wavelets (useful for pattern recognition and decomposing digital images), and he has developed a suite of interactive computer models for exploring their properties. He is a former Presidential Young Investigator and a member of the American Academy of Arts and Sciences. A member of the National Academy of Sciences and honored fellow of the Institute of Mathematical Statistics, he is a recipient of the Presidents' Award of the Committee of Presidents of Statistical Societies and the John von Neumann Prize from the Society for Industrial and Applied Mathematics. He holds a B.S. from Princeton University and a Ph.D. from Harvard University.

William F. Eddy is professor of statistics at Carnegie Mellon University. A long-time researcher in statistical computing and graphics, he is co-creator of the Functional Image Analysis Software-Computational Olio (FIASCO), a collection of tools for processing very large multidimensional arrays of data originally developed for processing functional magnetic resonance imaging (MRI) data. It has expanded to include analysis and interpretation of digital image data, including positron emission tomography (PET) scanning, genetic microarrays, and optical image data. His research concentrates on the computational and graphical aspects of statistics; the analysis has included data sources including 5 billion floating point numbers. His applications of large datasets have also included applications in disease mapping, grocery store scanner data, and airline traffic. The current chair of the Committee on National Statistics, he is also a past chair of the NRC Committee on Applied and Theoretical Statistics. He is a fellow of the American Association for the Advancement of Science, the American Statistical Association, the Institute of Mathematical Statistics, and the Royal Statistical Society, and is an elected member of the International Statistical Institute. He is affiliated with Carnegie Mellon's Center for Automated Learning and Discovery and Center for Cognitive Brain Imaging as well as the Brain Imaging Research Center (joint with the University of Pittsburgh). He was the founding co-editor of *CHANCE* magazine and is the founding editor of the *Journal of Computational and Graphical Statistics*. He has an A.B. degree from Princeton University, and M.A., M.Phil., and Ph.D. degrees from Yale University.

Gary Fischman is director of the National Materials Advisory Board and the Board on Manufacturing and Engineering Design at the National Academies. Prior to joining the Academies staff, he was a full-time consultant working for the biomedical implant industry. He was director of biomaterials and technology at the University of Illinois at Chicago, where he also served on the faculty of the College of Dentistry with joint appointments in orthopaedic surgery and bioengineering. He was founding director of the Bioceramics Institute and director of the National Science Foundation Industry University for Biosurfaces' Alfred Satellite during his time as a faculty member at the New York State College of Ceramics. He has also worked for the U.S. Food and Drug Administration. He holds B.S., M.S., and Ph.D. degrees in ceramics engineering.

George (Rusty) Gray is leader of the dynamic properties and constitutive modeling team in the materials science division, Los Alamos National Laboratories. He conducts fundamental, applied, and focused programmatic research on materials and structures. He researches and constructs constitutive, damage, and fracture models directly and contributes to process modeling through the quantification of constitutive property data. The models are utilized in integrated verification and validation codes and also to support large-scale finite element modeling simulations of structures ranging from national defense, industry, foreign object damage, and manufacturing. The models are utilized by the U.S. Navy, Air Force, and Army for both platform and munitions simulations related to performance and for manufacturing simulations. He is the project leader for a large Department of Defense Office of Munitions program on materials modeling and validation. He is an elected fellow of Los Alamos National Laboratory and has been awarded several professional titles. He has authored or co-authored over 195 publications. He has a B.S. with honors and an M.S. in metallurgical engineering from the South Dakota School of Mines and Technology and a Ph.D. in metallurgical engineering from Carnegie Mellon University.

Eric Grimson is professor of computer science and engineering and holds the Bernard Gordon Chair of Medical Engineering at the Massachusetts Institute of Technology (MIT). He also holds a joint appointment as a lecturer on radiology at Harvard Medical School and at Brigham and Women's Hospital. He currently heads the computer vision group of MIT's Computer Science and Artificial Intelligence Laboratory, which has pioneered state-of-the-art systems for activity and behavior recognition, object and person recognition, image database indexing, image guided surgery, site modeling, and many other areas of computer vision. He is a fellow of the American Association for Artificial Intelligence and was awarded the Bose Award for Excellence in Teaching in the School of Engineering at MIT. He received a B.Sc. (High Honors) in mathematics and physics from the University of Regina in 1975 and a Ph.D. in mathematics and physics from MIT in 1980.

Daniel Huttenlocher is John P. and Rilla Neafsay professor of computing, information science, and business and Stephen H. Weiss Fellow at Cornell University. He also holds an appointment in the computer science department and is Corning Director of Technology management at the Johnson Graduate School of Management at Cornell. His research interests are in computer vision, computational geometry, interactive document systems, electronic trading systems, and software development methodologies. His research in computer vision ranges from theoretical algorithms (using techniques from computational geometry and graph algorithms) to the development of end-to-end systems that apply visual matching and recognition techniques. His work in computational geometry includes efficient algorithms for computing Hausdorff distances and related distance transforms, as well as techniques for comparing three-dimensional protein structures. His work on interactive document systems has often incorporated computer vision techniques. His interest in software development methodologies stems from his involvement in the creation of large, complex software systems at Xerox Corporation and Intelligent Markets. For 11 years, he worked with Xerox PARC on electronic document image processing. More recently, he has been working with Intelligent Markets on electronic trading systems.

Michael M. Meyer works for Google, Inc., and is based in Seattle, Washington. Previously, he was co-founder and chief scientist at Intelligent Results, Inc., a Seattle-based software company specializing in collecting raw data from interviews and developing software to analyze large databases for the purpose of predicting behavior with regard to debt collection and the financing industry. He has held mathematics and engineering analyst positions at the Boeing Company and at Amazon.com. He has also served as senior research scientist in the department of statistics at Carnegie Mellon University, where he was director of special projects in computing services and director of the applications software group in computing services. From 1991–1992, on a part-time basis, he was study director for the NRC Panel to Review Evaluation Studies of Bilingual Education. He is a fellow of the American Statistical Association, in part for his role in the development and maintenance of the Statlib archive of statistical software and data resources. He received a B.A. (with honors) in mathematics from the University of Western Australia and a Ph.D. in statistics from the University of Minnesota.

Vijay Nair is Donald A. Darling professor of statistics and professor of industrial and operations engineering at the University of Michigan, and is currently chair of the department of statistics. He is a world-renowned expert in experimental design and system development, particularly in industrial applications. He has done extensive consulting work with the automotive and telecommunications industries, which has required the development, testing, and analysis of large databases for quality control. For example, he developed a structured design and data analysis strategy for robust design experiments with dynamic characteristics. Such experiments are being increasingly used to design systems that are robust to uncontrollable variation over a range of signal factors. Previously, he was a research scientist at Bell Laboratories in New Jersey for 15 years. He is a fellow of the American Association for the Advancement of Science, American Statistical Association, and the Institute of Mathematical Statistics, an elected member of the International Statistical Institute, and a senior member of the American Society for Quality. He served as editor of *Technometrics* and as joint editor of *International Statistical Review*. He is currently a member of the Committee on National Statistics and has served on NRC panels on statistics and testing in defense acquisition. Dr. Nair received his bachelor's degree in economics from the University of Malaya, Malaysia, and his Ph.D. in statistics from the University of California, Berkeley.

Angelo Ninivaggi is vice president, general counsel, and secretary of Plexus Corp., based in Neenah, Wisconsin. He is an expert on manufacturing enterprise practices in the United States and has both broad and specific familiarity with business and management practices, including the legal issues surrounding product liability, audit responsibility, and supply chain management. He was executive vice president, general counsel, and corporate secretary for MCMS, another contract manufacturing firm, until MCMS was acquired by Plexus Corp. From March 1996 until joining MCMS in February 1998, he served as corporate counsel with Micron Electronics, Inc. Prior to his employment with Micron Electronics, Inc., he worked as an associate with the law firm of Weil, Gotshal & Manges in New York. Mr. Ninivaggi holds a B.A. in economics from Columbia University, an M.B.A. in finance from Fordham University, and a J.D. from Fordham University.

Carol V. Petrie is director of the Committee on Law and Justice at the National Academies. She also served as the director of planning and management at the National Institute of Justice, U.S. Department of Justice, responsible for policy and administration. In 1994, she served as the acting director of the National Institute of Justice. She has conducted research on violence and public policy, and managed numerous research projects on the development of criminal behavior, domestic violence, child abuse and neglect, and improving the operations of the criminal justice system.

David W. Pisenti is a law enforcement consultant with an extensive background in firearms, SWAT tactics, and armor protection. From 1973–1994, he served as the supervisory special agent, Firearms Training Unit at the FBI Academy at Quantico, Virginia. He was president of Progressive Technologies of America, Inc. (1994–1996) and executive vice president of Point Blank Body Armor, Inc. (1996–2000). He has developed and implemented presentations and demonstrations on critical issues involving firearms training, technological advances in law enforcement equipment, and tactical techniques at a wide range of law enforcement and criminal justice professional conferences. Throughout his career, he has advised federal agencies and Congress on matters related to firearms and protective body armor, serving as chairman of the National Institute of Justice National Armor Advisory Board, as an advisor to the Congressional Office of Technology Assessment on body armor legislation, and as chairman of the Weapons and Protective Systems Committee, Technology Assessment Program Advisory Council, which advises the National Institute of Justice on the development of standards for police equipment.

Daryl Pregibon works for Google, Inc., and is based in New York City. He joined Google after serving as division manager of the statistics research department at AT&T Laboratories. His research interests include real-time monitoring of large networks, analysis of very large datasets, and tree-based and generalized linear models. He is a world leader in data mining, which he defines as an interdisciplinary field combining statistics, artificial intelligence, and database research. He is widely recognized as a leading expert in the manipulation and analysis of massive datasets. He has nurtured successful interactions in fiber and microelectronics manufacturing, network reliability, customer satisfaction, fraud detection, targeted marketing, and regulatory statistics. His research contributions have changed from mathematical statistics to computational statistics and include such topics as expert systems for data analysis, data visualization, application-specific data structures for statistics, and large-scale data analysis. A past member of the Committee on National Statistics, he serves on the NRC Committee on the Technical and Privacy Dimensions of Information for Terrorism Prevention and Other National Goals. A fellow of the American Statistical Association, he received his masters degree in statistics from the University of Waterloo and a Ph.D. in statistics from the University of Toronto.

Herman M. Reininga is senior vice president of operations at Rockwell Collins, Cedar Rapids, Iowa. He is responsible for overall management of Rockwell Collins' global production and material operations, including manufacturing, material, quality, and facilities and manufacturing activities. He has served on the Defense Science Board (DSB) and testified in front of the Senate Armed Services Committee on Defense Technology, Acquisition and Industrial Base. He chaired DSB's Production Technology Subgroup for Weapons Development Production Technology Summer Studies program that developed a manufacturing technology strategy for the U.S. Department of Defense. He is also called upon regularly to provide perspective for future manufacturing strategies. In 1999, he received the prestigious Meritorious Public Service Citation by the Chief of Naval Research, Department of the U.S. Navy, and in 1998 was awarded the Defense Manufacturing Excellence award endorsed by nine national trade associations and professional societies. He holds a B.S. degree in industrial engineering from the University of Iowa and a master of industrial engineering degree from Iowa State University.

James K. (Chips) Stewart is senior fellow for law enforcement domestic safety at the CNA Corporation. He previously held positions as a principle with Booz, Allen, Hamilton where he directed teams of MBAs and organization analysts in measuring, assessing, and implementing performance enhancements for large complex police organizations. His work there included a project, Validation of Neural Network Ballistic Identification Reliability in Large Data Sets, for the Federal Bureau of Investiation and state and local police performance. From 1982–1990, Mr. Stewart served as director of the National Institute of Justice, where, among many other accomplishments, he initiated a study of the feasibility of a national ballistics identification system. He has served as a White House Fellow, as executive assistant to Attorney General William French Smith, and as a Justice Department representative to the Board of Directors of the International Association of Chiefs of Police. From 1966–1981, Mr. Stewart served as the commander of the Criminal Investigations Division of the Oakland Police Department, where he was responsible for all criminal investigations carried out by the department, for the development and implementation of performance standards for detectives, and for the testing of applications of new technology in criminal investigations.

Michael Stonebraker is professor of computer science at the Massachusetts Institute of Technology specializing in database research and development. He was professor of computer science at the University of California, Berkeley from 1982–1994 and professor of the graduate school there from 1994–1999. A member of the National Academy of Engineering, he pioneered database research and technology, in particular developing the basis for the existing relational database market. He was the main architect of the INGRES relational database management system and the object-relational POSTGRES system. He is also an editor for the book *Readings in Database Systems*. He is now working on stream-based data management.

Harry Wechsler (served on the committee until May 2004) is professor of computer science at George Mason University. Since 1995, he has also been the director of the University's Distributed and Intelligent Computation Center. He has done extensive research in the field of intelligent systems, including computer vision, automatic target recognition, signal and image processing, pattern recognition, statistical learning theory, neural networks, and data mining and knowledge discovery. He has also researched face and gesture recognition, biometrics, and forensics. He has been a consultant for both government and private industry and has lectured extensively in both the United States and abroad. He has authored over 200 scientific papers and has published one book. He is a fellow of the Institute of Electrical and Electronics Engineers and the International Association of Pattern Recognition. He holds a Ph.D. in computer science from the University of California, Irvine.

Julia Weertman is Walter P. Murphy professor emerita of engineering at Northwestern University. She has conducted research on the mechanical behavior of metals and alloys and the underlying phenomena that give rise to the observed behavior. Her research currently is focused on determining the mechanical properties of a variety of nanocrystalline materials, characterizing their structure, and studying deformation mechanisms in this small grain size regime. She also continues interest in the high temperature behavior of metals. Her research has demonstrated the value of small angle neutron scattering for detection and quantification of such features as voids and pores, and for following nucleation and growth kinetics of second phase particles. She is a member of the National Academy of Engineering and a member of the American Academy of Arts and Sciences. She is past member of the NRC National Materials Advisory Board, the Committee on Women in Science and Engineering, and the Committee on Human Rights. She has served on advisory panels for the U.S. Department of Energy and the National Science Foundation, and for several national laboratories. She is on the Board of Review Editors for *Science*. She is a fellow of the Minerals, Metals and Materials Society and ASM International, received Special Creativity Awards for Research from the National Science Foundation in 1981 and 1986, a Guggenheim Fellowship in 1986–1987, the Achievement Award from the Society of Women Engineers in 1991, and the Leadership Award from TMS in 1997. She holds a B.A., M.S., and D.Sci in physics from the Carnegie Institute of Technology (now Carnegie Mellon University).